QUEST FOR THE PRESIDENCY

QUEST FOR THE PRESIDENCY

★ ★ ★ ★ ★ ★ ★ ★ ★ ★ ★ ★

The **STORIED** and **SURPRISING**
HISTORY of **PRESIDENTIAL**
CAMPAIGNS in **AMERICA**

★ ★ ★ ★ ★ ★ ★ ★ ★ ★ ★ ★

BOB RIEL

Potomac Books
An imprint of the University of Nebraska Press

All rights reserved. Potomac Books is an imprint of the
University of Nebraska Press.
Manufactured in the United States of America.

Library of Congress Cataloging-in-Publication Data
Names: Riel, Bob, author.
Title: Quest for the presidency: the storied and surprising
history of presidential campaigns in America / Bob Riel.
Description: Lincoln: Potomac Books, an imprint of
the University of Nebraska Press, [2022] | Includes
bibliographical references and index.
Identifiers: LCCN 2021037005
ISBN 9781640122307 (hardback)
ISBN 9781640125285 (epub)
ISBN 9781640125292 (pdf)
Subjects: LCSH: Presidents—United States—Election—
History. | United States—Politics and government. | BISAC:
POLITICAL SCIENCE / History & Theory | HISTORY /
United States / General
Classification: LCC JK524 .R54 2022 |
DDC 324.973—dc23/eng/20211122
LC record available at https://lccn.loc.gov/2021037005

Set in Whitman by Laura Buis.

For Brady and Jake
While I was writing about the past,
you kept me focused on the present and the future.

There is no ceremony more splendid than the inauguration of an American president. Yet inauguration is a ceremony of state. . . . Even more spectacular and novel in the sight of history is the method of transfer of those powers—the free choice by a free people, one by one, in secrecy, of a single national leader.

—THEODORE H. WHITE, *The Making of the President 1960*

The past is never dead. It's not even past.

—WILLIAM FAULKNER, *Requiem for a Nun*

Contents

Acknowledgments

This book was both an enormous project and a labor of love. I have been captivated by presidential elections for decades and so was thrilled to be able to write the book I'd always wanted to read. It would never have been possible, however, without the generations of scholars, historians, and journalists who chronicled previous presidential elections in the United States, whether by digging into old primary sources or writing about events as they were happening. I am beholden to all of them.

I am particularly indebted to my agent, Michael Palgon, who not only saw potential in this topic and encouraged me along the way but also pushed me to make this a much better book than it ever would have been without his suggestions. Likewise Tom Swanson, my editor at Potomac Books/University of Nebraska Press, who gave me the opportunity to turn my ideas into a published book. I'm thankful to everyone at University of Nebraska Press who worked on getting this manuscript out into the world: Tish Fobben, Tayler Lord, Taylor Rothgeb, Rosemary Sekora, Annie Shahan, Sara Springsteen, and many others behind the scenes with whom I never had the chance to communicate. Additionally, Judith Hoover made numerous invaluable copyediting suggestions, and Jessica Freeman did a superb job on the indexing.

I appreciate those who graciously agreed to read advance copies of this book for one reason or another: Bill Schneider, Tom Zoellner, Tom Costello, Mark Stein, Barbara O'Rourke, and Liz Callahan. Many thanks to all of you.

Neither of my parents, Bob and Ellen, lived to see this book published. But I'd like to think they still exist in some form and somehow know about it. My mom always believed her children could accomplish anything, and my dad was an inveterate reader and the first person who sparked my interest in history and politics.

Last, but certainly not least, my wife and sons. This project involved many nights and weekends of research and writing, and it was further complicated by the need to manage remote learning for two children for more than a year during a global pandemic. Lisa, I'm ever grateful for your love and support. Brady and Jake, I'm thrilled to be your dad, and you know I love you more than anything in the whole wide world.

QUEST FOR THE PRESIDENCY

Introduction

Presidential History over Coffee

Americans are enthralled by presidential elections. Every four years, the nation is held spellbound by the latest campaign, from the opening bell of the nomination contest in the snows of Iowa and New Hampshire through the counting of the last ballot in the fall. Impassioned voters are gripped by emotion, convinced the future of the country hinges on the outcome, while the media treats the contenders like gladiators on a debate stage and breathlessly covers every twist and turn of the contest. As one observer noted, "A presidential election in the United States may be looked upon as a time of national crisis. . . . A fever grips the entire nation."[1]

It was Alexis de Tocqueville who wrote that line about presidential contests, in 1835, nearly two centuries ago. Which goes to show that Americans have been riveted and riled up by these campaigns for as long as there have been elections. That's why the 1800 battle between Thomas Jefferson and John Adams is still known as one of the most bitter in history, why Americans almost went to war over the 1876 election, and why protesters fought police on the streets of Chicago during the 1968 Democratic convention. It's also why the enthusiasm that swept Andrew Jackson into office in 1828 is not dissimilar from the excitement that fueled Ronald Reagan's victory in 1980 or Barack Obama's historic win in 2008.

This book is about the thrill of all these elections. But it's about something more as well. Because as exciting as these battles may be, presidential fever can obscure something important, which is that all campaigns are linked by threads of politics and culture across the centuries. Each election is best appreciated not as a discrete event that captures our attention every four years but rather as another chapter in the continually evolving story of American democracy.

For instance, we all know about the political party that campaigned on a nativist platform, wanted to limit immigration from certain countries, and hoped to restore American culture to a previous age of greatness, don't we? Yes, the 2016 Trump Republicans, but also the 1856 American Party, popularly called the Know Nothings, which turned in one of the best third-party performances ever by campaigning against undesirable immigrants from Catholic countries, many of whom were then fleeing famine and poverty in Ireland.

Abraham Lincoln said about the party, "As a nation, we began by declaring that 'All men are created equal.' . . . When the Know Nothings get control, it will read 'All men are created equal, except negroes and foreigners and Catholics.'"[2] The fact that the Know Nothings promoted nativist ideas akin to those of the Trump Republicans shows that angst over immigration is a recurrent flash point in U.S. history and is one of those threads that link elections from different eras.

Other contests, even the less historic ones, can provide us with similarly intriguing perspectives. Take 1840, which was most notable for producing William Henry Harrison, the first Whig president. Harrison turned out to be a presidential cipher, as he died one month into his term after catching pneumonia, possibly from giving the longest inaugural speech on record in freezing weather. Today that election is perhaps most remembered for "Tippecanoe and Tyler Too," the alliterative slogan that defined the campaign.

But when we dig a bit deeper, we see that "Tippecanoe and Tyler Too" was part of a strategy to portray Harrison as a common man and military hero who supposedly lived in a log cabin and swilled hard cider. Harrison's victory marked the first time a president was promoted with such a carefully crafted marketing campaign. This set the stage for the branding of presidents to become commonplace, giving us everything from "Abe Lincoln the Rail Splitter" and "I Like Ike" to "Make America Great Again." Nowadays we can't even imagine a candidate who doesn't have an image-making strategy. And it all harkens back to the campaign strategists of 1840.

Or consider 1964, when Republican Barry Goldwater suffered a landslide loss to Democrat Lyndon Johnson. In the aftermath of that election, only a brave soul would have predicted the imminent demise of the New Deal coalition and a coming conservative revival. But that's what happened, as even in defeat Goldwater highlighted a cluster of issues that became a staple of conservative politics for decades, from limiting the size of government and lowering taxes to slashing welfare programs and restoring power to the states.

Political parties don't change overnight. But they do change in time as they adapt to changes in society, shifting demographics, and new ideas. The parties, in fact, seem to reinvent themselves every few generations. Understanding this helps us to appreciate that the political changes we're seeing in the twenty-first century echo similar transformations in the 1960s, the 1930s, the 1890s, and before.

The point is that none of these campaigns exist in isolation. Rather, all the elections together tell the story of the United States. In this sense, observing presidential history is like exploring America's DNA.

So, yes, this book is about presidential elections, and it contains a trove of entertaining campaign stories, but it's also about a new way of viewing this history. I wanted to go beyond the obvious query of "What happened?" to answer what to me is a more interesting question: "What can past battles tell us about present-day politics?" Accordingly, elections are presented not just chronologically but are also grouped into thematic chapters. And each section ends with a piece that delves into links between campaigns and considers how these connections can provide us with a deeper understanding of our democracy, both past and present.

Additionally, I wanted to tell this story in a particular way. That is, to provide depth and meaning, but also to be conversational and accessible, as if I were explaining it over a cup of coffee. Thus, the book is divided into seven political eras, and the opening piece for each period is set in a historic coffeehouse relevant to the time but which could also serve as a place to meet for coffee even now. It's a way to engage in our own coffee-fueled trek into the history and meaning of presidential elections.

In the end, this book is for everyone who catches presidential fever every four years. For anyone who agonizes over campaign battles or scrolls incessantly through political news but wishes they could put the current election into historical context. So let's begin exploring the extraordinary story of American presidential elections. Let's have some fun with it. And, yes, let's do it over coffee.

1

★ ★ ★

1789-1820

The Founding Generation

Coffee at Fraunces Tavern in New York

In the summer of 1774, a traveling lawyer from Boston wrote a letter to his wife, telling her how he'd been refused tea at a public inn and so had begun weaning himself off the beverage in favor of an afternoon coffee.

"When I first came to this House," he wrote, "it was late in the Afternoon, and I had ridden 35 miles at least. 'Madam' said I to Mrs. Huston, 'is it lawfull for a weary Traveller to refresh himself with a Dish of Tea provided it has been honestly smuggled, or paid no Duties?' 'No sir,' said she, 'we have renounced all Tea in this Place. I cant make Tea, but He make you Coffee.' Accordingly I have drank Coffee every Afternoon since, and borne it very well. Tea must be universally renounced. I must be weaned, and the sooner, the better."[1]

A lot of people that year, it seems, were giving up tea, which was a popular drink in the colonies. But this was the height of the dispute over whether Parliament had the right to tax colonists without their consent, which led to the 1773 Boston Tea Party, and no self-respecting patriot could be caught savoring a cup of tea. Coffee became the hot beverage of choice for many Americans.

The lawyer who wrote that letter was John Adams. A few months later, he was one of four delegates from his state to the First Continental Congress. In 1776 he was a driving force in the movement to declare American independence. And in 1796 he became the second president of the United States, a country that hadn't existed when he was refused tea at that inn.

It's safe to surmise that, during his political career, Adams enjoyed a few cups of coffee in public taverns. In the eighteenth century, it was common for Americans to hang out in taverns, to drink coffee, eat a meal, or perhaps imbibe a beer or whiskey. It was a place where locals socialized, held meetings, or discussed the news of the day. They were the Starbucks of their time.

One of the most well-known of these establishments was Fraunces Tavern in New York City. Located at the corner of Pearl and Broad streets in lower Manhattan, it opened in 1762 and was a popular meeting place for a who's who of the Founding Fathers.

During the revolutionary era, the tavern hosted meetings of the Sons of Liberty, a secret organization that resisted British rule. At the end of the Revolutionary War, in December 1783, Gen. George Washington held a farewell dinner there for officers of the Continental Army. In 1789 Washington's first presidential inauguration was held at Federal Hall, a few blocks away, and it's easy to imagine some of the country's early leaders making the short walk to Fraunces Tavern for a celebratory meal or drink. Fifteen years after this, on July 4, 1804, Alexander Hamilton and Aaron Burr attended a gathering of Revolutionary War veterans in the tavern, just one week before the infamous duel in which Burr killed Hamilton.

As it happens, Fraunces Tavern is still around. The building was reconstructed several times after fires and was saved from demolition in the early twentieth century by citizens who wanted to preserve it for historic purposes. It was later added to the National Register of Historic Places. Today you can enjoy a coffee or other drink there, dine on a contemporary or colonial-style meal, or walk upstairs to a museum that focuses on the history of the American Revolution. It's a perfect setting, in other words, from which to contemplate the founding generation of American politics and the county's first presidential elections.

This was a fascinating era, and not just because it gave us names like Washington, Adams, Jefferson, Madison, and Monroe. It's easy today to overlook how stirring and momentous these years were, since in the popular imagination they seem to proceed in a hop, skip, and a jump from the writing of the Constitution and the election of George Washington to the propagation of a democracy that has endured for more than two centuries.

The reality, though, is even more entertaining. In part, this is because—after launching a revolution and forging the world's biggest experiment in self-government—the Founders were somehow caught by surprise by the emergence of political parties. The Constitution was written without much thought to this possibility, but ideological factions materialized during Washington's first term.

The advent of parties made politics more impassioned and rancorous, not only because politicians and voters had different visions for government and were suddenly engaged in campaigns to defeat their opponents but also because a lot of people assumed that parties were temporary vehicles that would disappear after one faction prevailed. The early Federalists and Democratic-Republicans believed they were engaged in a zero-sum battle to save their vision of American democracy. This led to some heated contests, particularly the 1796 and 1800 campaigns between Adams and Jefferson. So intense were the political conflicts that the 1790s have been characterized as "one of America's most passionate decades."[2]

After this, the belief that the party system would fade away did seem to come true for a while, as the Federalists waned as a political force in the 1810s and the United States became a one-party country. But this lasted only a few years, and factions were again on the rise by the end of the founding generation's time in power.

During these years of political ferment, Americans also doubled the size of their nation with the Louisiana Purchase and fought the War of 1812 against the British, among other events. It was a consequential and colorful period. And it all began with the first presidential election in the winter and spring of 1789.

1789, 1792, 1796, and 1800: The First Elections—
Washington, Adams, and Jefferson

1789

On April 30, 1789, standing on the balcony of New York's Federal Hall, George Washington took the first presidential oath of office. When it was over, thirteen cannons boomed and the crowds watching from nearby streets and rooftops erupted in applause. Robert Livingston, chancellor of New York, the man who'd administered the oath, shouted, "Long live George Washington, President of the United States!"[3]

It was the culmination of a lengthy outpouring of emotion for Washington. During the seven days it took the president-elect to travel from his home in Virginia to New York, the nation's capital until 1790, he was feted at every stop. There were welcoming receptions, triumphal arches, and celebratory speeches. At Philadelphia, where twenty thousand people greeted him, he was given a white horse to mount before crossing the Schuylkill River. At Elizabethtown, New Jersey, a barge manned by thirteen oarsmen rowed him across the Hudson River to New York and a choir sang a version of "God Save the King" written for the occasion.[4]

What's surprising about these celebrations is not that people turned out to honor Washington, who was the most famous and revered American of his era, but that the United States had elected a president in the first place. Just two years earlier, when James Wilson of Pennsylvania rose at the 1787 Constitutional Convention to move that the head of the new government be a single person, it was said that a long silence descended on the room.[5] The thought of a powerful executive was anathema to many Americans, who'd just fought a war to rid themselves of a king. Edmund Randolph of Virginia spoke for many when he suggested the presidency would be a "fetus of monarchy."[6]

Moreover, the country's first constitution, the Articles of Confederation, had invested all powers in the legislature, so the United States for most of the 1780s had a government without an executive branch. Due to the fear that a president might amass too much power, a fair number of delegates to the Constitutional Convention wanted executive authority to be shared by a council.[7] Despite this, the framers of the Constitution persisted in creating the presidency, in part because they believed a single executive was needed to speak for the nation and move it beyond the interstate squabbles that defined politics under the Articles of Confederation.

They didn't know how their decision would play out in history, but they agreed that Washington was the best choice to serve as the first president.[8] The general had a reputation for an unimpeachable moral character, a status that was cemented when he gave up his post as commander in chief after the Revolutionary War and retired to his Virginia farm, even though it is conceivable he could have become king.[9] He's been described as the country's "only truly classical hero."[10]

Washington agreed to serve as president after being convinced no one else was as capable of unifying the disparate states. But he was reluctant about the prospect. "I have no wish," he said, "which aspires beyond the humble and happy lot of living and dying a private citizen on my own farm."[11]

In this first national election, there wasn't much of a campaign in advance of the electoral vote, as there was no opposition to Washington. The actual vote was held in 1789, but this was in essence the election of 1788. The Constitution had been ratified only the previous summer, so presidential electors weren't chosen until December and January. The electors then cast their ballots the first week of February 1789, and the votes were counted in Congress on April 6. Only ten of the thirteen states participated in this inaugural election, as North Carolina and Rhode Island hadn't yet ratified the Constitution, while New York's legislators couldn't agree on their electors. Nevertheless Washington was elected unanimously, with the backing of all sixty-nine Electoral College voters.

The historian Joseph Ellis has described Washington's election as "a plebiscite on who most embodied the values of the American Revolution. . . . There had been no campaign platform providing voters with his position on the contested issues, because there had been no campaign. He was not chosen for what he thought, but for who he was."[12]

The only real suspense was over the identity of the first vice president. Since Washington was a Virginian, most people agreed that a Northerner should be vice president. John Adams of Massachusetts emerged as the leading contender. Adams was known to be cantankerous at times and wasn't necessarily the most popular candidate, but he had considerable government experience. He'd been a leader in the Continental Congress and had spent much of the previous decade serving as a minister to France and the Netherlands and as the country's first ambassador to Great Britain. The attitude of many was summed up by Alexander Hamilton, who said he would "support Adams, but not without apprehensions."[13]

There was, however, a bit of strategic plotting that took place before Adams won the vice presidency. Some of the Anti-Federalists, who had opposed ratifying the Constitution, favored Governor George Clinton of New York for the job. But when New York couldn't put together a slate of electors, Clinton lost any slight chance he might have had of outpolling Adams. Then Hamilton had a bit of a panic attack over the possibility that Adams might accidentally win more votes than Washington, because the Constitution then decreed that electors should cast *two* ballots for president, with the runner-up becoming vice president.

"Everybody is aware of that defect in the constitution which renders it possible that the man intended for vice president may in fact turn up president," wrote Hamilton, who convinced some electors to throw away their second vote on other candidates to prevent such an outcome.[14] In the end, eleven men received support, but Adams easily placed second to Washington with thirty-four votes.

After Washington's victory was confirmed, a congressional emissary was sent to inform him of his election. It took a week for that messenger, who traveled on horseback, to reach Washington's Mount Vernon estate. Two days later the soon-to-be-president set out for New York and the first presidential inauguration.

1792

There are indications that Washington intended, or at least hoped, to retire after one term in office. He went so far as to ask James Madison for help in drafting a retirement announcement. But Madison and others prevailed on him to stand for reelection because no other individual could command the respect necessary to hold a still fragile government in place. "North and South will hang together, if they have you to hang on," Jefferson told him.[15]

Once again there wasn't much of a presidential contest in 1792, as there was no challenge to Washington's leadership. If there had been a campaign, it's easy to imagine its being premised on Washington's success in laying a foundation for the presidency and for his work in binding Americans together as one nation.

When he took office in 1789 there was uncertainty over the president's duties and responsibilities, as the new Constitution was more specific about legislative than executive powers. Members of Congress were even flummoxed over how to address Washington. Vice President Adams suggested he be addressed as "His Highness, the President of the United States of America, and Protector of their Liberties," which Jefferson called "the most superlatively ridiculous thing I ever heard of." The House of Representatives settled on the more democratic-sounding title of "Mr. President."[16]

But regardless of title, it was Washington who launched the American presidency, served as a role model for his successors, and established such traditions as presidential control over foreign policy. And he was keenly aware of the importance of his actions. "I walk on untrodden ground," he remarked. "There is scarcely any part of my conduct that may not heretofore be drawn into precedent."[17]

He also helped Americans forge a belief that they were "citizens of a powerful new republic" rather than just residents of a state.[18] He undertook practical steps toward this goal, such as encouraging roads to connect the nation, but he also recognized the power of imagery and undertook a tour of all thirteen states during his first term, which was no small task in that era. He visited the New England states in 1789, made a separate trip to Rhode Island in 1790 after that state ratified the Constitution, and completed a journey of several months through the Southern states in 1791, traveling thousands of miles on bumpy, dusty roads so people could see and meet the president.

Much to his chagrin, though, Washington found that his efforts to unify a country didn't have quite the same effect on a cabinet and a Congress that were increasingly divided over policy issues. This gave rise to the political factions that would play a key role in future elections. One side, the Federalists, favored a strong central government that took an assertive economic role in support of industrialists. This coalition had a base of support in the North and was led by Treasury Secretary Alexander Hamilton.

The Hamiltonian program was opposed by a Republican faction, later known as the Democratic-Republicans, led by Jefferson and Madison. This bloc, largely supported by Southern agrarian interests, was opposed to excessive concentration of executive authority and preferred to keep power in the hands of the states. More than two centuries later, though the players and the parties have changed, these remain some of the fundamental disagreements in American politics.

Washington was not officially aligned with any faction—in fact, he criticized factions as being harmful to the nation—but his actions often came down on the side of the Federalists, such as when he approved Hamilton's proposal to create a national bank over the objections of Jefferson and Madison. He also, in his farewell address, called for a larger government footprint in the form of a standing navy, a national military academy, a national university, and federal support for manufacturing enterprises.[19] Depending on one's point of view, these proposals would either connect and strengthen the nation (as the Federalists believed) or centralize too much power at the national level (in the opinion of the Democratic-Republicans).

These disagreements over policy seeped into the presidential campaign, even if Washington's reelection was never in doubt. In 1792 the thirteen original states were joined by Vermont and Kentucky, so there were now 132 electoral votes at stake. Washington was again supported by every elector and remains the only president elected unanimously by the Electoral College.

But the emergence of political factions did result in scheming over the vice-presidency. Those who supported the views of the Democratic-Republicans put up a challenger to Vice President Adams in Governor Clinton. Adams, who was favored by the Federalists, defeated Clinton in the Electoral College 77–50, but the stage was set for future partisan battles.

1796

After two relatively drama-free presidential campaigns, 1796 was the year American politics turned interesting. President Washington decided to retire after two terms in office, which not only set an important precedent but also triggered the first contested election between the country's nascent political parties, the Federalists and Democratic-Republicans.

The country's increasing partisanship may even have encouraged Washington to step back from the burdens of public life. He had long desired to return to the relative simplicity of his life at Mount Vernon, but the decision was perhaps made easier by the ideological battles that were then erupting. There were intense debates in the 1790s over the role of government in America, and once people began choosing sides, no one, not even Washington, was immune to the political sniping that followed.

What was unique about these debates is how they were intertwined with partisan disagreements about the French Revolution, particularly during the Reign of Terror, when thousands of people in France lost their heads to the guillotine. It may seem odd that violence in France influenced political disputes in the United States, but the link between the two issues is in fact helpful to understanding the early divide between America's first parties.

The violence and apparent anarchy in France horrified many

Americans, but above all the Federalists, who were afraid that populist chaos might spread to the United States. This was a scary thought for a party that feared disorder and was trying to strengthen federal authority and forge a national economy. The Democratic-Republicans, on the other hand, were more tolerant of the turmoil in France because they believed the uprising was linked to the earlier American Revolution in heralding a new age of liberty and the demise of aristocracy.[20] This fit nicely with their vision of an agrarian republic and their preference for limited government. Jefferson even remarked, "I like a little rebellion now and then. It is like a storm in the atmosphere."[21]

Americans were further divided when France went to war with Britain during the same decade. The Federalists wanted to forge commercial and trading ties with the British to grow the U.S. economy, while the Democratic-Republicans detested Britain's aristocratic culture and favored the French, who'd helped America in its own war against England. So when Washington signed the Jay Treaty in 1794 establishing a new trading relationship with Britain—despite the fact that the British Navy was then harassing U.S. merchant ships on the Atlantic—the Democratic-Republicans were outraged. They claimed the president had sided with Britain against republican France, essentially turning his back on the American Revolution.

In the aftermath of this controversy, Washington was denounced as a tyrant by some political opponents. One newspaper pronounced, "If ever a nation was debauched by a man, the American nation was debauched by Washington."[22] So the general who was glorified for defeating the British on the battlefield became the president who was pilloried for capitulating to the British, proving that not even the Father of His Country was above being pummeled by the press.

These events all formed the backdrop to the upcoming presidential race between the vice president, John Adams, and the former secretary of state, Thomas Jefferson, two men who'd been friends as fellow revolutionaries in the 1770s and as diplomats in

France in the 1780s, but who became political rivals because of disagreements over the proper function of government.

An election in 1796, unsurprisingly, was quite unlike the campaigns we're familiar with today. Political parties were still amorphous and disordered; it was considered bad form for a candidate to actively pursue the presidency; and in an age when information traveled by horseback and carriage, most people learned about the contest through newspapers and pamphlets. This doesn't mean it was a passive contest, however; something modern voters *would* recognize was the emergence of negative campaigning, which eighteenth-century politicos took to with gusto.

Adams, for instance, in a nod to his girth, was mocked as "His Rotundity" and was accused of being a monarchist who wanted to establish a royal family.[23] Jefferson was derided as a "soft and weak intellectual" who was better "suited to be a college professor" than president.[24] He was faulted too for being antagonistic to Christianity and of having an unseemly fondness for France. You might say that Jefferson was the first candidate to be accused of being an antireligious, pseudo-French, liberal elitist, a cluster of attacks that has been a staple of American politics ever since.

Since there was no popular vote in 1796, the campaigns fought a state-by-state battle to win a favorable slate of presidential electors. This process was complicated by the fact that each elector then cast two votes. The parties had their preferred candidates—Adams and Thomas Pinckney of South Carolina for the Federalists, and Jefferson and Aaron Burr of New York for the Democratic-Republicans—but electors were still free to vote for anyone they wished on one or both of their ballots.

This was an acknowledged weakness in the Constitution, which arose because the framers had expected elections to be nonpartisan. The flaw presented an opening for Hamilton, who tried to manipulate the process to deny Adams the presidency. For whatever reason, Hamilton settled on Pinckney as his choice for president, so he hatched a plan to have every Federalist elector in the North cast ballots for both Adams and Pinckney, under the assumption that Pinckney's greater popularity in the South would cause some electors there to leave Adams off their ballot and doom him to defeat. When New England electors caught wind of the plan, however, some of them cast their second vote for alternative candidates to prevent Pinckney from overtaking Adams.[25]

In the end, Adams won the presidency by three votes, 71–68. But because of the votes Pinckney lost in the North, Jefferson vaulted into second place and was elected vice president, unintentionally forming an administration led by two political rivals.

On March 4, 1797, Adams took the oath of office alongside the outgoing president and the new vice president. Three legends of the American Revolution standing shoulder-to-shoulder at the first transfer of power. Well, perhaps not quite shoulder-to-shoulder. Washington and Jefferson, who each stood at least 6'2" and still rank among the country's tallest presidents, towered over the portly 5'7" Adams, which no doubt made for an interesting tableau.

When the new administration took office, some professed hope that Adams and Jefferson could transcend the debates that were splitting the nation and bring the two factions together.[26] But it was not to be. Instead, the stage was set for an even more dramatic battle four years later.

1800

When the year 1800 dawned, it was impossible to escape the sense that a new political era was being inaugurated as another century began. Washington had died in 1799; the individual who had done more than any other to bring the nation into being was gone. Meanwhile Adams and Jefferson were preparing to face off yet again, in a campaign that marked the only time in history in which a vice president challenged an incumbent president. That sounds awfully uncomfortable from today's perspective, but political traditions at the time were still forming. And this rematch was, if anything, a natural culmination of the ideological battles of the 1790s.

Adding to the drama, the Federalists and Democratic-Republicans both saw this election as a contest to save their vision of America from what they believed was the ideological wrong-headedness of the opposition. Their dispute cut deep into the heart of how the parties viewed government and democracy. The Federalists believed a strong central government would prevent the nation from descending into anarchy, while the Democratic-Republicans just as fervently believed in limited government to avoid reverting to monarchy.[27] Or, as Jefferson aptly put it, "[One party] fears the people most, the other the government."[28]

It was a clear philosophical divide, with little middle ground. And as in the previous election, these arguments remained inter-twined with sentiments about the ongoing conflict between France and Britain. The Federalists were still trying to forge a trading rela-tionship with Britain, while the Democratic-Republicans main-tained their preference for French republicanism over British aristocracy. So when France joined England in seizing U.S. mer-chant ships in the 1790s (because each country wanted to stop the Americans from trading with their rival), and when the United States and France engaged in the Quasi-War at sea from 1798 to 1800, it is not surprising that the Federalists wanted to declare war on the French, while Democratic-Republicans resisted the idea.

As this debate churned, the Federalists and their support-ers seemed, if anything, even more fearful of French-style chaos spreading to America. By the spring of 1798, the country was awash in rumors that France was about to land an army in the United States or lead a conspiracy to overthrow the government or even burn down the capital. Philadelphia (the nation's capi-tal from 1790 to 1800) had a sizable population of French res-idents, and many Americans believed these immigrants might lead an uprising, perhaps in coordination with the "wild Irish."[29] So great was the panic that one historian compared it to the fear of Japanese Americans after the 1941 attack on Pearl Harbor.[30] It's similar, as well, to the terrorism-induced anxiety over Mus-lim immigrants in the early twenty-first century.

As anxiety increased, tensions began to bubble over. Federal-ists wore black ribbons on their hats to distinguish them from the tricolor cockades of the Democratic-Republicans. It was said that men "who have been intimate all their lives cross the streets to avoid meeting."[31] Fights even broke out between rival political activists. The worst moment was one night in May 1798, when thousands of people from both factions paraded in Philadelphia and a riot erupted. Newspaper offices were vandalized, and an anti-Federalist crowd seemed to threaten an attack on the President's House, which Adams resolved to defend "at the expense of [his] life."[32] Quiet times these were not.

Amid this hysteria, the governing Federalists overplayed their hand. In a supposed effort to prevent French sympathizers from destabilizing the government, Congress passed the Alien and Sedition Acts of 1798. The Alien Act allowed the president to deport foreigners who were deemed dangerous, while also making it harder for newcomers to become citizens, conveniently reducing the number of new immigrants who could vote. Even more contentious was the Sedition Act, a barely concealed effort to silence the opposition, which made it illegal to publish anything about the government that was seen as false, malicious, or scandalous.[33]

It sounds, perhaps, like legislation that even a few twenty-first-century politicians might want to see enacted, although it would have put a few generations of op-ed writers, satirists, and *Saturday Night Live* comedians into jail. But in 1798 the Constitution was less than two decades old and the ideal of freedom of speech was less entrenched. After the law's passage, fourteen writers and editors were indicted for sedition, and some went to prison.

For the next two years, the Democratic-Republicans used these new laws to batter the Federalists in immigrant communities and to raise a ruckus about suppression of speech. They presented the laws as proof that Federalists were indeed British-style monarchists who couldn't be trusted to preserve the hard-won freedoms of the American Revolution.

Oddly enough, even though President Adams was painted as a monarchy-loving Federalist by his rivals, and even though he'd signed the Alien and Sedition Acts, some so-called High Federalists complained he was still too restrained. Their doubts were reinforced when Adams sent an envoy to discuss peace with France, a policy in line with what the Democratic-Republicans favored. This breach between Adams and the High Federalists became so pronounced that Hamilton published a blistering critique of the president during the 1800 campaign. "There are great and intrinsic defects in his character," Hamilton wrote, "which unfit him for the office of Chief Magistrate."[34]

Still, this criticism from his own party was mild compared to the incoming fire from the opposition. In one attack, Adams was denounced as a "hideous hermaphroditical character which has neither the force and firmness of a man, nor the gentleness and sensibility of a woman."[35]

Ouch. But Jefferson didn't sail unscathed through the campaign either. Federalists attacked him as an atheist who would so sully the nation that "murder, robbery, rape, adultery and incest will all be openly taught and practiced."[36]

Just in case you thought political mudslinging has never been as bad as it is today.

In the end, the real star of the election may have been Aaron Burr, the Democratic-Republican nominee for vice president, whose efforts helped swing New York's electoral vote. Burr managed volunteers who knocked on doors and took voters to the polls in New York City's springtime legislative elections, a groundbreaking innovation in an era when parties were only just emerging. The Democratic-Republicans swept that election, largely on the strength of votes from working-class and immigrant neighborhoods. This gave the party control of the state legislature, and thereby of the twelve electors who would switch New York's electoral vote from Adams in 1796 to Jefferson in 1800.[37] This was a big deal in a close contest and helped Jefferson to a 73–65 victory that fall.

This is where the story should end, with Jefferson's election. However, an unintended constitutional problem cropped up. Since the 1796 results produced a president and vice president who were political rivals, the Democratic-Republican electors in 1800 decided not to waste their second votes on fringe candidates. It seemed like a good idea, but evidently someone should have thought to waste at least one vote, because the electors ended up casting seventy-three ballots each for Jefferson and Burr, causing the election to end in a tie.

Everyone knew Jefferson was the intended presidential candidate, but the only way to resolve the tie was through a vote of the House of Representatives, where the Federalists had just enough votes to deny Jefferson a victory. There were sixteen states, each with one ballot, so nine votes were needed to win the presidency. The Democratic-Republicans controlled eight states, the Federalists six, and two were evenly divided. And most Federalists were so ardently opposed to Jefferson they were intent on doing anything to keep him from the presidency, whether that meant keeping the election deadlocked until after the inauguration date and letting someone else take office, or electing Burr in hopes that he'd be more in their debt.

Burr never agreed to a deal with the Federalists, but neither did he disavow interest in the presidency, which might have put the matter to rest. So when the House began voting on February 11, Jefferson won eight votes from Democratic-Republican states and Burr six votes from Federalist states. The two states with split delegations were unable to cast ballots, leaving Jefferson one vote short of a majority. One week later, after thirty-five ballots, not a single vote had budged. Stories began to swirl about the potential for civil war. Virginia and other states were said to be ready to call up their militias if the Federalists prevented Jefferson from becoming president.[38]

It was actually his political rival Hamilton who helped swing the vote in Jefferson's favor. "If there be a man in the world I ought to hate, it is Jefferson. But the public good must be paramount to every private consideration," Hamilton said in pressing Jefferson's case over that of Burr, whom he considered lacking in character.[39]

The door cracked open for Jefferson on the thirty-sixth ballot when James Bayard, Delaware's lone congressman, ended the standoff. He claimed to have received assurances that Jefferson would continue certain Federalist policies, such as maintaining the nation's fiscal system, although Jefferson always denied he had made any deals.[40] In any case, Bayard and other Federalists abstained from voting, allowing additional states to swing to Jefferson's side and give him the victory.

Two weeks later, on March 4, Jefferson ate breakfast at a common table with other guests at Conrad and McMunn's boardinghouse. Then, accompanied by members of the Virginia militia and some congressmen, he walked to his inauguration along the muddy, unpaved streets of Washington, which had become the new capital just a few months earlier. Jefferson was dressed, in the words of one reporter, as "a plain citizen, without any distinctive badge of office" when he took the oath and became the third president of the United States.[41]

Presidential Democracy and the Electoral College

It's worth taking a moment to reflect on these first four elections, which inaugurated a presidential democracy that has endured for more than two centuries while establishing norms and precedents that became part of the fabric of American elections.

The most famous precedent was the decision by Washington to retire after two terms. At the time, it was popularly believed that Washington, or any president, might be reelected for life if he chose to keep running. But Washington affirmed that no leader should govern indefinitely, which led even King George III to remark that the president's willingness to give up power "placed him in a light the most distinguished of any man living."[42] No one broke this precedent until Franklin Roosevelt in 1940, and he did so only with the country on the brink of entering World War II. Even then, his action was controversial enough to prompt passage of the Twenty-Second Amendment limiting future presidents to two terms.

An equally important standard was established after the election of 1800 with the first peaceful transfer of power from one political party to another. Adams is sometimes skewered for not attending Jefferson's inauguration in 1801 and instead choosing to depart Washington DC at 4:00 a.m. that day on a public stagecoach. From one perspective, that's quite rude, to skip town in the dark just before your successor is inaugurated. But traditions were still developing, and the important point is that Adams did get out of the way. After an electoral loss to his rival, he allowed a transition to the Jefferson administration to proceed peacefully.

The act of transferring power is the lifeblood of democracy. One of the more egregious American betrayals of this tradition was when Southern Democrats after the Civil War maintained power in their states for nearly a century by using violence, intimidation, and Jim Crow laws to keep Blacks from voting. But the precedent was never challenged in a national election. At least until 2020, that is, when President Donald Trump tried to overturn the results of an election he lost. The strategy failed, and the ritual of a peaceful transfer of power held strong. But democracy was tested.

Lastly, these first elections also inaugurated the Electoral College system of electing a president. Given the intrigues of 1796 and 1800—with Hamilton trying to get Pinckney elected over Adams, and with Jefferson and Burr finishing in a tie—it may be helpful to consider why the framers created this electoral system in the first place. The question seems particularly relevant today, since two of the first three presidents of the twenty-first century were elected after losing the popular vote.

The truth is, for much of the Constitutional Convention, it was assumed the president would be chosen by Congress. But delegates feared a president elected by the legislature might not be independent and would blur the separation of powers.[43] An obvious alternative would be to have voters elect the president directly. "If the President is to be the guardian of the people," said Gouverneur Morris of Pennsylvania, "let him be appointed by the people."[44] But there was limited support for this idea, as most delegates feared an "excess of democracy" and wanted a buffer between the masses and the selection of a president.[45] Moreover, the implementation of a popular vote would have been challenging. In a country where it took a week just to travel from New York to Boston, and several weeks for news to reach the entire nation, most Americans wouldn't know enough about candidates from distant states to choose one to vote for.[46]

The delegates, frankly, were flummoxed. These days there is a widespread belief that the Founders created the Electoral College to deliberately balance the interests of large and small states. But in reality, as Madison later noted, the system created by the framers was stitched together at the last minute and was mostly a compromise born of "fatigue and impatience."[47] Since a congressional vote and a popular vote were both seemingly off the table, the decision to empower electors from each state seemed like a reasonable solution.

And if we consider what the framers actually created, the first Electoral College looks sort of like a turbocharged nominating convention. In the absence of political parties, the Electoral College during the first elections had the dual role of both nominating and electing a president. It was widely believed that most candidates after Washington would fail to win a majority, so the expectation was that the electoral vote would winnow the field to a few leading contenders, and Congress would then make the final decision.[48]

Within a few years weaknesses in the system became apparent, notably when the rise of political parties shattered the concept of independent electors. Also disconcerting were the problems that stemmed from electors having to cast two votes for president. The idea was for voters to look beyond favorite sons by requiring them to vote for two candidates from different states. But no one foresaw the machinations that would lead to the Hamilton-Adams-Pinckney and Jefferson-Burr controversies. So the Twelfth Amendment was passed after the 1800 election, establishing separate votes for president and vice president.

Since this time there have been numerous suggestions for reforming the Electoral College, including proposals to abolish it entirely and implement a national popular vote. But none has ever been enacted because there is always a powerful constituency that benefits from the existing system.

Before the Civil War, the Southern slave states were a roadblock to change due to the three-fifths clause of the Constitution. This infamous compromise, which counted three-fifths of slaves as part of a state's population for census purposes, was meant to give the South more representation in Congress than was merited based on its white population. By extension, though, it also gave the South more electoral votes because of these extra congressional seats. The upshot was that later Southerners had no incentive to give up the Electoral College.

Today, of course, there are small states that have more electoral power than they otherwise would have based on their population, as well as swing states that get inordinate amounts of attention from candidates and the media. These states likewise have little reason to change anything. And so the Electoral College lives on and remains the ultimate arbiter in the election of an American president.

1804, 1808, 1812, 1816, and 1820: The Virginia Dynasty

1804

After the tumult of the 1796 and 1800 contests, American politics settled down a bit. If there were any political junkies around in 1804, they were likely disappointed by that year's subdued campaign, which didn't come close to measuring up to the fireworks of 1800. Mostly this is because Jefferson was a popular and successful president and the Federalists couldn't muster much of an argument for ousting him.

Stylistically, Jefferson's presidency was a departure from the Washington and Adams administrations: he dressed in plain clothes, rode about town on horseback rather than in a carriage, and sometimes answered the door himself at the President's House. It was part of his attempt to model "republican simplicity."[49] Politically, Jefferson steered more of a middle course: he kept in place some of the Federalists' fiscal system, such as the Bank of the United States, while pursuing his vision of a smaller and less intrusive government.

For starters, this meant overseeing the end of the despised Alien and Sedition Acts. Jefferson also managed to both cut taxes and slash the federal deficit by shrinking the size of government.

Much of this spending reduction came from slicing the military budget in half, which Jefferson did both for fiscal reasons and because he believed a large standing army strengthened the power of government unnecessarily. Although the Jeffersonian vision diverged from the Federalist desire for a robust state, it was difficult for his opponents to find much else to complain about. This was especially true after the 1803 Louisiana Purchase, when the president bought from France an immense tract of land west of the Mississippi River—828,000 acres that now encompass parts of fifteen states from Louisiana to Montana.

The Louisiana Purchase has been described as a case of "extraordinary presidential leadership, matched with even more extraordinary good fortune."[50] France had taken the Louisiana territory from Spain and was poised to become a North American power with control over a wide swath of the continent. American history, needless to say, would have been vastly different had France held onto this region. Not only would American trade be smothered by the potential loss of access to the Mississippi River, but the nation would never have expanded westward.

"Nothing since the Revolutionary War has produced such uneasy sensations through the body of the nation," wrote Jefferson of France's inroads into North America.[51] Almost out of desperation, the president sent James Monroe to Paris to offer to buy New Orleans so the United States would at least retain access to that city's vital shipping lanes. In a stroke of luck for the Americans, Napoleon was just then realizing that his military and financial resources were precipitously low, so he decided to sell the entirety of France's North American territories. Jefferson agreed to buy the land for $15 million.

Jefferson wasn't sure he even had the constitutional authority to complete the purchase, and he was aware of the irony involved—that he, an opponent of undue executive power, was now using the presidency in a way he would otherwise have resisted. But he was more concerned about removing France from North America and protecting U.S. access to New Orleans. So he "threw overboard the ideas of strict construction" of the Constitution and asked Congress to approve the sale, which it quickly did.[52] With the stroke of a pen, the size of the nation doubled.

As Americans celebrated their growth and prosperity, the Federalists knew in their hearts they had no chance against Jefferson in the upcoming election. There was grumbling that the president was devastating the military, or that he'd spent too much money on land the country didn't need, but John Randolph expressed the more widely held opinion of Jefferson's presidency: "Taxes repealed; the public debt amply provided for . . . Louisiana acquired; public confidence unbounded."[53]

In the face of this challenge, the Federalists never met to nominate a presidential candidate and only informally supported Charles Cotesworth Pinckney of South Carolina, former minister to France and the brother of Thomas, the party's 1796 vice presidential nominee. One of the more interesting aspects of the election is that it was held amid the aftershocks of the July 11 duel in which Burr killed Hamilton. Duels weren't uncommon in the early days of the Republic, but then, most duels didn't involve a sitting vice president and a former secretary of the treasury. The Democratic-Republicans had already decided to replace Burr as their vice-presidential nominee, partly because his relationship with Jefferson had wilted after the intrigues of the 1800 Electoral College tie, but the killing of Hamilton drove a final stake into Burr's career. Jefferson's new running mate was another New Yorker, Governor George Clinton.

In the voting that fall, Jefferson won in a landslide and consolidated Democratic-Republican control of the government in a way few could have foreseen just a few years earlier. He took 162 Electoral College votes to 14 for Pinckney, who won only Connecticut and Delaware.

1808

In 1808 Jefferson followed Washington's precedent and, after eight years in office, retired to his Monticello estate in Virginia. In doing so, he helped cement the two-term tradition that held until 1940. Jefferson seemed delighted at the prospect of retirement. "Within a few days I retire to my family, my books and farms," he wrote near the end of his term. "Never did a prisoner, released from his chains, feel such relief as I shall on shaking off the shackles of power."[54]

Part of Jefferson's cheerfulness over leaving office may have come from turning the presidency over to his longtime political partner, Secretary of State James Madison, who became the third president from Virginia. But Jefferson was also no doubt gratified at finally being rid of a controversy that dented his second-term popularity.

This controversy, like many others in the early republic, originated with the seemingly never-ending battle between Britain and France. There'd been a brief lull in the conflict during Jefferson's first term, but a resumption of war between the two European powers once more ensnared the United States. Both countries were again commandeering merchant ships bound for European ports, and Britain was seizing sailors from those vessels and forcing them into service with the Royal Navy. American anger at these actions came to a head after a confrontation off the Virginia coast between a British warship and a U.S. naval frigate, the *Chesapeake*, which resulted in three American deaths and the capture of four crewmen.

The incident enraged Americans, and a demand for war swept the nation. Jefferson was disinclined to go to war with Britain, so he instead persuaded Congress to pass the Embargo Act of 1807, cutting off all trade with Europe. By keeping needed goods away from England and France, the thinking went, the United States could inflict enough suffering to convince them to stop interfering with free trade and to respect the rights of American ships.

It was a novel thought for the times, to replace military conflict with economic warfare. But the embargo collapsed the American export market. Cargo ships sat idle in ports, merchants saw their businesses wither, and farmers were unable to export crops. The U.S. economy "almost choked to death."[55] And Americans turned their scorn on Jefferson.

Jefferson's declining popularity naturally tarnished Madison, the 1808 nominee of the Democratic-Republicans. A rather unimposing figure at just 5'4" and about 100 pounds, Madison was perhaps the leading political theorist of the founding generation, having played a vital role in drafting the Constitution and coauthoring the Federalist Papers. One person commented that he'd never seen "so much mind in so little matter."[56] Yet despite his top-notch intellect and glittering résumé, Madison was often seen as more of a legislator than an executive, and he sometimes suffered in comparison with Jefferson in the political arena. So in a year when the Democratic-Republicans were being scorned for the Embargo Act, the Federalists hoped the political winds might blow them to victory. To lead them there, they went back to Charles Cotesworth Pinckney of South Carolina, their 1804 nominee.

There was again little in the way of a traditional campaign. After the 1800 contest, in fact, there wouldn't be another similarly intense battle until 1828. But the Federalists tried to batter Madison over the Embargo Act, which was condemned as the "dambargo" or, when read backward, mocked as the "o grab me" act.[57] The *New York Herald* declared that the embargo had "brought the nation into the most unexampled state of distress and debasement."[58]

In the end, the Federalists simply didn't have enough political strength outside of New England. They outperformed their 1804 vote but still fell short of victory. Madison defeated Pinckney 122–47 in the Electoral College, giving the Federalists their third successive presidential loss.

1812

Just days before Madison's presidential inauguration in 1809, Jefferson and Congress finally repealed the Embargo Act. Nevertheless the controversies over trade remained a thorn in relations between America and Britain. This was the spark for the War of 1812, a conflict that defined the next election and nearly ousted President Madison from office.

The United States declared war on Britain in June 1812, only a few months before an election that Madison and the Democratic-Republicans initially had every reason to believe they would again win easily. The official reasons for war were that Britain was restricting U.S. trade, seizing sailors and impressing them into naval service, and supporting Indians in the Northwest Territory in clashes with Americans. These were familiar complaints that stretched back years, but the Americans essentially decided they were fed up and weren't going to take it anymore. It was, in the words of one writer, a "howl of wounded pride."[59]

There was also a contingent of "war hawks" in Congress, mostly from the South and the West, who had their eyes on British Canada and Spanish Florida. They were happy to add fuel to the cries for war because they saw war as a way to acquire new territory while reducing the threat of frontier clashes with Indian tribes. It's likely as well that President Madison believed the declaration of war in itself might bring the British to the bargaining table, since England was already battling Napoleon's forces in Europe and would presumably be reluctant to commit additional forces to North America.[60]

It was a case, perhaps, where the sum of the reasons to declare war was more persuasive than any provocation on its own. But to begin a war without having first been attacked by an enemy—and to do so during an election year—was, to say the least, bound to spark debate. The decision to fight was unpopular with many Americans, notably those in the northeastern states where there was a greater reliance on trade with Britain. The vote to declare war was only 79–49 in the House of Representatives and 19–13 in the Senate. Opponents included every Federalist and a fair number of Northern Democratic-Republicans.

Ironically, unbeknownst to Americans at the time, England had already agreed to normalize trade relations with the United States. Parliament did so on June 16, 1812. News traveled slowly in those days, however. The Senate approved its declaration of war on June 17 and Madison signed the bill the next day. The announcement of Britain's change of heart washed up on American shores only some weeks later, after war had been declared.

The right to trade with Europe was just one American grievance, and the British still weren't giving up their right to seize sailors, so perhaps this concession wouldn't have forestalled the conflict. But it was a concession nonetheless, and the war's opponents were even more beside themselves when they heard the news. They derisively referred to the conflict as "Mr. Madison's war."[61]

As antiwar sentiment grew, Madison's supporters became equally aroused in support of the president. That summer, for instance, a mob attacked the offices of the *Federal Republican* in Baltimore, a paper known for its antiwar views. The Federalist staff was taken into custody by local authorities "for their own protection," but the mob stormed the jail and tortured the offenders, dripping candle grease in their eyes and killing one of them.[62]

Amid this political storm, Madison ran for a second term. However, he did so without the full support of his own party, as a dissident faction of Northern Democratic-Republicans broke away from the president. Many of them were aghast at the rush to war and, like the Federalists, preferred to pursue a peace deal and free trade. Some of them also professed a weariness with Virginian presidents, who'd governed for twenty out of twenty-four years. These insurgent Democratic-Republicans threw their support to DeWitt Clinton, the mayor of New York City and a former senator (and the nephew of Madison's vice president, George Clinton, who had died of a heart attack in April).

In a surprise maneuver, the Federalists decided to also get in Clinton's corner, but not with an official endorsement. They informally agreed to support him as a way to defeat Madison, whom they disdained. Clinton thus became a "fusion candidate" meant to appeal both to Democratic-Republicans and Federalists who were opposed to the war and who were tired of the South's domination of the presidency.[63]

The strategy nearly worked. The election of 1812 was the only one of five contests between 1804 and 1820 in which the Democratic-Republican candidate was in some danger of losing. Madison prevailed, with 128 electoral votes to 89 for Clinton, in a victory that is sometimes attributed to national elation over the surprise naval victory of the uss *Constitution* ("Old Ironsides") over the British frigate *Guerriere*.[64]

The vote reflected the country's divide, however, as Madison was strongest in the South and West, while Clinton won much of the North. The result hinged on Pennsylvania. Had the Keystone State voted for Clinton, he would have prevailed in the Electoral College by 114–103.

1816

The War of 1812 lasted less than three years and essentially resulted in a stalemate, with neither America nor Britain gaining or losing territory. The two sides finally agreed to a peace treaty that was ratified in early 1815. But while the conflict produced little in the way of strategic consequence, it did impact politics in the United States. Americans exulted in military victories near the end of the war, and the resulting upsurge in national pride transformed the electoral landscape by inflicting a fatal wound on what was left of the Federalist Party.

This wasn't a result that seemed likely at the start of hostilities. Aside from a few naval victories, the Americans stumbled in early clashes with the battle-hardened British and faced moments of despair during the first two years of fighting. The emotional nadir no doubt came in August 1814, when the British overpowered American militias and marched on Washington, sending Madison and other officials into flight. Dolley Madison famously saved a Gilbert Stuart painting of George Washington by tearing the canvas from its frame before escaping the White House, while President Madison avoided capture by moving about on horseback and taking refuge in private homes. So hasty was the retreat that British troops entered the White House to find a warm meal on the table that had been prepared for Madison. After helping themselves to the food, they set fire to the mansion and later torched the Capitol building and the buildings housing the State, War, and Treasury Departments. One resident described the city as "brilliantly lighted" that night by the many fires.[65]

After British troops withdrew from the city, which they'd occupied mostly to humiliate Americans, Madison returned to the burned-out ruins of the nation's capital. The White House was uninhabitable. Government and congressional offices, papers and books had been destroyed. Meanwhile the Treasury had little revenue, the economy was shattered, and the New England states were seething over the government's inability or unwillingness to prevent a British blockade of their ports. So maligned was Madison at the time that his wife was refused entrance to a local tavern as she fled the British attack. Later, while she was sheltering in a friend's home, the cook even refused to make her coffee.[66] The possibility of another presidential victory two years hence by the Democratic-Republicans must have seemed almost unimaginable.

But six months later, somehow, the tide had turned.

The first good news came shortly after the debacle in Washington when American troops inside a Baltimore fort withstood a brutal barrage by the British. During that battle, the lawyer Francis Scott Key spent the night on a nearby ship watching bombs burst in the sky. At dawn he was overjoyed to see the American flag still flying over the fort and wrote some words on the back of an envelope. Those words later became "The Star-Spangled Banner."[67]

A more significant event occurred in early 1815, when the British sent a large force to New Orleans with the intent of capturing its port and taking control of the Mississippi River Valley. Britain could then have laid claim to much of the Louisiana Purchase territory, which they'd never recognized as being under U.S. control.[68] Gen. Andrew Jackson set out to meet the British troops with a somewhat motley collection of soldiers, state militias, and pirates. Fighting from behind a series of barricades they'd constructed, the Americans on January 8 routed the British, who suffered more than two thousand men killed, wounded, or captured. The Battle of New Orleans was such an unexpectedly decisive victory over one of the world's strongest armies that its anniversary was celebrated for years afterward, and it catapulted General Jackson to the status of national hero. Even in the middle of the twentieth century, the echo of that victory made its way into a chart-topping 1959 single called "Battle of New Orleans."

Shortly afterward, the United States received the news that peace with Britain was at hand. American diplomats had been struggling to negotiate with the British at Ghent, Belgium, for months, when the government of Great Britain suddenly decided peace was a more desirable outcome than the battles that were draining its treasury and military. This decision was actually made prior to the Battle of New Orleans, but once again it took time for news to make its way across the ocean.

These twin headlines, which were reported within days of each other in early February, had a remarkable effect on the American consciousness. Parades and celebrations broke out across the country. The United States had challenged a stronger military and at least stood its ground. Some even called it a second war for independence, as Britain was compelled to recognize its former colonies as a legitimate nation at last.

When 1816 rolled around and President Madison confirmed his impending retirement after two terms, Secretary of State James Monroe was the presumed heir apparent. He had exemplary credentials as a politician, diplomat, and solider, but as a national leader he didn't stir great enthusiasm. It was said he "had the zealous support of nobody, and he was exempt from the hostility of everybody."[69] Consequently, there was a groundswell of support for Secretary of War William Crawford of Georgia. Monroe, though, prevailed narrowly in a vote of the congressional caucus, 66–54, and became his party's nominee.

By this point, the Federalists couldn't do much to oppose Monroe, as they were down to their last breaths in political terms. The party's electoral fortunes had been in decline since 1800, but an accident of history helped close the book on the party for good. After suffering for more than two years under the weight of a war they'd opposed from the start, New England Federalists in late 1814 called the Hartford Convention amid widespread rumors they were considering secession. What they eventually proposed was not a breakup of the nation but several constitutional changes, such as making it more difficult to institute an embargo, limiting consecutive presidents from the same state, and repealing the three-fifths clause for counting slaves.[70] Essentially, they were asking for a greater voice in the nation, given their sense that Southern presidents were pursuing policies anathema to the North but weren't paying a political price because of the extra Electoral College votes allotted to states with slave populations.

The Federalists completed their report on January 3, 1815, and appointed a three-man commission to take the suggestions to Washington DC. On their journey south, they heard the news of both Jackson's victory in New Orleans and the Treaty of Ghent ending the war. For the Federalists, the timing could not have been worse. As the nation celebrated, Democratic-Republicans condemned the Hartford Convention as treasonous. Madison refused to meet with the commissioners, and his allies were all too happy to harp on rumors of secession rather than the more temperate proposals that had emerged from the meeting.[71]

In the public mind, the Federalists had been disgraced. They never recovered. The following year, Federalist electors in a few northeastern states agreed to support Senator Rufus King of New York for president, but the party didn't otherwise mount a campaign. With only token opposition, Monroe and the Democratic-Republicans rolled to an easy victory, winning sixteen of nineteen states and piling up 183 electoral votes to 34 for King. Massachusetts, Connecticut, and Delaware were the only states to support the Federalist candidate.

1820

President Monroe was the last person who was politically active during the founding generation to serve in the White House. He had fought under General Washington at Valley Forge, studied law under Jefferson, and made his first run for Congress in 1789 (against Madison, believe it or not). Now, as president, he was both a throwback to the early days of the republic and a representative of a changing nation.

The throwback aspect was easy to spot, as Monroe was the last president "to wear a powdered wig, knee breeches and cocked hat."[72] Most other political leaders had moved on to trousers and given up the powdered hair. But in other ways, Monroe epitomized a maturing country. Albert Gallatin, the minister to France and former secretary of the treasury, remarked that the War of 1812 had "renewed and reinstated the national feeling" and that Americans were acting "more as a nation."[73]

In 1819 this nation-building involved purchasing the Florida territory from Spain for $5 million, further expanding the geographic reach of the country. The Adams-Onis Treaty finalizing the purchase also defined a border with Mexico at the Oregon territory, which gave America official access to the Pacific for the first time.[74] And Monroe oversaw a renovation of the White House and the Capitol building to erase signs of the burning of Washington, while also promoting infrastructure improvements and a stronger military.

With these latter policies, Monroe was "incorporating the remnants of Federalism" into Democratic-Republican governance.[75] After the war, there was a sense the nation needed to be stronger and more bound together to forestall future threats, which in turn necessitated moving beyond the Jeffersonian vision of minimalist government and adopting some of the old Hamiltonian platform. With partisan battles declining in favor of what seemed to be a new national consensus, this period was soon dubbed the Era of Good Feelings.

It didn't take long, however, for that sentiment to be tested. Two years into Monroe's presidency, there were challenges on both the economic and political fronts. Most immediately, the nation was overwhelmed by the Panic of 1819. The country's first economic depression caused a wave of bankruptcies and a rise in unemployment, which lasted into the 1820s. At the same time, the country was drawn into a fateful debate over whether slavery should be permitted in the western states being carved out of the Louisiana Purchase territory, with the budding state of Missouri as the first flash point.

At the time, there was an equilibrium in the nation and in the

Senate between free states and slave-owning states. But the proposed admission of Missouri, where slavery was legal, threatened to upset that balance. As the first state to emerge from the Louisiana territory, the terms of its admission into the Union would also set a precedent for the future of the West. Monroe, who was preparing to run for reelection, took the position that states should be able to set their own rules. The debate tied the nation in knots, with most Northerners preferring to limit slavery to the states where it already existed, while Southerners argued that Congress didn't have the constitutional authority to prevent the expansion of slavery. John Quincy Adams, son of the former president, spoke for many in the North when he said slavery was a "foul stain upon the North American Union."[76] In the South, conversely, where slaves accounted for roughly one-third of the region's wealth, the effort to restrict slavery was considered an example of "federal tyranny."[77]

With both sides dug into their positions, Henry Clay of Kentucky helped negotiate a compromise by which Maine (previously part of Massachusetts) would be admitted to the union as a free state and Missouri as a slave state. Additionally, the 36°30' parallel was set as a boundary so that slavery would be prohibited in future states north of that line but allowed in states to the south. On March 6 Monroe signed the Missouri Compromise of 1820. The bill doused the controversy for the moment, but the slavery debate was clearly not over by a long shot.

Despite all this, Monroe remained popular, and with the demise of the Federalists he didn't have an opponent in his run for reelection. It's pretty difficult from a twenty-first-century vantage point to imagine a president being elected without opposition, but that's where the country found itself in 1820. Monroe received 231 votes in the Electoral College to 1 for John Quincy Adams of Massachusetts. It's unclear if that one elector voted for Adams because he preferred him to Monroe or because he wanted to ensure that Washington remained the only president elected unanimously. It hardly mattered in the end, however, as Monroe sailed to a second term.

The United States as a One-Party Nation

There's little question that this era, and particularly the years 1816 to 1824, were atypical in presidential history. The collapse of the Federalists had rendered the United States a one-party democracy, a situation that would be inconceivable today. With more than two centuries of history behind us and the opportunity to study the experiences of other democracies, we now know that one-party systems almost inevitably lead to "corruption and governmental inefficiency."[78] And political parties have become so fundamental to American politics that their development has been called an "extraconstitutional reform."[79]

But there was no history with any of this in the early nineteenth century. So when the Federalists went the way of the dinosaurs, most national leaders believed they were seeing the manifestation of their belief that political parties were a short-term instrument that would fade away in a postpartisan future. After all, back in 1787 Madison had warned about the "mischiefs of faction" in the *Federalist Papers* when he wrote that parties were "more disposed to vex and oppress each other than to cooperate for their common good."[80] Three decades later, Monroe likewise contended that "the existence of parties is not necessary to free governments."[81]

From this perspective, the benefit to ending partisan sniping was that presidents would be free to make decisions in the national interest, as Monroe did when he adopted neo-Federalist positions on infrastructure and military spending. Few people gave much thought to diminished accountability for those in power because the assumption was that enlightened leaders should always govern with the common good in mind.

Another danger in a one-party system, however, is the temptation to maintain control within a tight circle. At the time, this seemed to pose more of a danger to a still young American government, especially when Monroe became the third consecutive president reelected to a second term. This feat has been repeated only one other time in presidential history—in 2012, when Barack Obama followed Bill Clinton and George W. Bush in winning back-to-back elections. But whereas Obama, Bush, and Clinton represented opposing political parties and different regions of the country when they were elected, Jefferson, Madison, and Monroe were from the same party, had been political partners for more than four decades, and were even neighbors in Virginia, living within thirty or so miles of each other.

So even if these three Virginians were governing solely in the national interest, the exclusivity of presidential succession was still unseemly, and perhaps even hazardous, for a nascent democracy. As one historian noted, the Democratic-Republicans had "accused Federalists of yearning for monarchy, but they had established the elective equivalent."[82]

By the end of this run, then, it's understandable why other leaders were declaring themselves ready to move on from the Virginia Dynasty. There was pent-up political energy ready to burst forth from other regions of the country, and this would play a key role in the next presidential campaigns.

2

★ ★ ★

1824-56

The Rise of the Democratic, Whig, and Republican Parties

Coffee at Gadsby's Tavern in Alexandria, Virginia

After two decades of relative sedateness in presidential elections, American politics became more turbulent and thrilling starting in the 1820s. No event better symbolizes this than the presidential inauguration of Andrew Jackson on March 4, 1829. It was the first inauguration held on the portico of the Capitol building, and up to twenty thousand people attended. Senator Daniel Webster of Massachusetts expressed wonder at the spectacle. "Persons have come 500 miles to see General Jackson and they really seem to think the country has been rescued from some general disaster," he wrote.[1]

There weren't enough hotel rooms to handle this crush of visitors, so people slept on floors and in fields. One person remarked that "it seemed as if half the nation had rushed at once into the capital. It was like the inundation of the northern barbarians into Rome."[2] After watching Jackson take the oath of office, many of these exultant onlookers followed the new president as he rode a horse to the White House. "Country men, farmers, gentlemen, mounted and dismounted, boys, women and children, black and white. Carriages, wagons and carts all pursuing him," said an observer.[3]

Later, as many people as could fit crammed into the White House for a public reception. This famously descended into a mob scene of guests who, in their efforts to get close to Jackson, broke pieces of china and scuffed up the presidential home. Some reports suggested that people had to be lured out with barrels of liquor on the front lawn. So great was the chaos that President Jackson sneaked away to escape the bedlam, crossing the Potomac River to nearby Alexandria, Virginia. There, on his first night as president, he slept at Gadsby's Tavern and Hotel.

Gadsby's was then a popular tavern near the nation's capital and had hosted events for multiple presidents, including Birthnight Balls to honor Washington (a precursor of the later Washington's birthday and President's Day holidays) and an inaugural dinner for Jefferson. No doubt coffee was served. Jefferson, in particular, was an inveterate coffee drinker, once estimating that a pound of coffee was consumed each day at Monticello. As luck would have it, Gadsby's is still standing today. It was designated a National Historic Landmark in 1963 and now includes both a restaurant and a museum that celebrates the establishment's place in history.

The tavern's connection to the nation's early presidents—and to Jackson's inauguration—makes Gadsby's an ideal place from which to ponder the next era of elections. This period saw a shift in the political culture, notably the expansion of popular democracy. Voters were feeling more invested in their leaders as more states implemented a popular vote for president and abolished the requirement that voters be property holders. All voters were still male and most were white, but they were now more economically diverse. While it would take more than another century before the full breadth of the adult population could legally vote, this is when the expansion of suffrage first took root.

At the same time, new states were arising on the western frontier and asserting themselves into the national conversation. The fracturing of the Democratic-Republicans into two new political parties, the Democrats and the Whigs, also ended forever the concept of a one-party nation. Ever since this time, American democracy has had competition between two major parties.

It's perhaps not a coincidence that all of this came together during the rise of Jackson, who seemed to embody this dawning new age of politics. Jackson was the first winner of a nationwide vote, the first leader of the new Democratic Party, the first president from the American frontier, and the first one who consciously represented the common man. Indeed, one famous story reports how astonished one woman was at Jackson's first nomination for president, given that she'd known him when he was a child in the Carolinas. "What! Jackson up for President? . . . The Jackson that used to live in Salisbury? . . . Well if Andrew Jackson can be President, anybody can!"[4]

Many people were thrilled by all this, believing a "great revolution" in the country was being driven by the rising voice of the average voter. Others, though, were dismayed by "the howl of raving Democracy."[5] Or, as one newspaper later put it, "The Republic has degenerated into a Democracy."[6] But regardless of one's perspective, one thing was certain. Presidential politics would never be the same.

1824, 1828, 1832, and 1836: The Jacksonian Age

1824

The election of 1824 is a lesson in how quickly things can change in politics. When Monroe was elected without opposition in 1820, many people believed that competition between parties was a thing of the past. Turns out, it was merely the calm before the storm.

It's not that there weren't ideological differences during the Era of Good Feelings. The aging Jefferson remarked, for instance, "The same parties exist now as ever did."[7] But all the factions were contained within the governing coalition, so the tensions simmered below the surface and few people perceived it as partisan conflict. That's why no one foresaw the tempest that was about to fracture the Democratic-Republican Party.

The first issue that strained the political system was fatigue with the Virginia Dynasty. The country had now been led by presidents from Virginia for all but four years since 1789, and many people were ready to look for leaders from other states. This was especially true in light of the continued growth of the trans-Appalachian territory, which meant the country was now trying to serve the divergent interests of people in the North, South, and West. Regional opinions differed on a variety of issues, from slavery and tariffs to the role of the government in funding infrastructure projects.

Moreover, it appeared the only path to becoming president was to be selected as the nominee by fellow party members during a congressional caucus. The "King Caucus" system had vetted candidates for two decades now, but a restless nation was beginning to see it as too elitist for "the increasingly democratic spirit of the age."[8] Congressmen from ten states thus chose to boycott the 1824 nominating caucus because they felt it unfairly "dictated the result of the popular election."[9]

Still, sixty-six Democratic-Republican congressmen insisted on caucusing in 1824, and they voted to back Secretary of the Treasury William Crawford of Georgia for president. Crawford, who'd been the runner-up to Monroe for the party's 1816 nomination, was long considered a leading contender, but he'd been incapacitated by a stroke in late 1823 that left him partially paralyzed. Supporters of other candidates rejected Crawford's claim to the nomination, an act that effectively killed the congressional caucus and launched a new era in presidential elections. With no other system yet in place for filtering candidates, the 1824 presidential race soon turned into a free-for-all.

Three other contenders emerged: Secretary of State John Quincy Adams of Massachusetts, son of the former president; Gen. Andrew Jackson of Tennessee; and Speaker of the House Henry Clay of Kentucky. Another potential candidate, Secretary of War John Calhoun of South Carolina, opted to run instead for vice president. Since all these men were nominally members of the Democratic-Republican Party, there wasn't much in the way of an organized campaign between opposing factions, but arguments for and against each candidate did make their way into newspapers, pamphlets, and speeches.

Crawford was supported by Old Republicans in the South who wanted to limit the power of government. He was respected for his work in Monroe's cabinet but was disregarded by many because of his stroke-related physical limitations. Adams was the most experienced contender and had the backing of New Englanders; he was praised for his knowledge and abilities but was simultaneously criticized for aloofness and lack of charisma. Clay hailed from the West and pushed a nationalist vision known as the "American System," which included more federal spending on infrastructure; he was known as a legislative master in Congress, but also for his drinking and gambling. Jackson, with support in the South and West, was a popular military hero who was promoted as a "second George Washington and a reformist leader."[10] Widely admired for his military prowess and common man persona, he was also disparaged for a lack of government experience and a history of violence.

The 1824 election marked the first time a nationwide vote was compiled, although six states didn't participate. In this tally of three-fourths of the states, Jackson led the way with 41 percent of the vote to 31 percent for Adams, 13 percent for Clay, and 11 percent for Crawford. It's unclear if Jackson would have prevailed if every state had participated, since Adams was popular in New York, one of the states that didn't schedule a popular vote.[11] Still, Jackson became the first candidate to win a national vote, a milestone in American democracy.

Ironically, Jackson also became the first popular vote winner to lose a presidential election. In the Electoral College, he finished with 99 votes, Adams with 84, Crawford with 41, and Clay with 37. Since 131 electoral votes were needed to win the presidency, this meant the final decision would be made by the House of Representatives.

The House had to choose from the top three finishers in the electoral count, pushing Clay out of the running, though he was eliminated by an excruciating twist of fate that may have prevented him from being elected president. In Louisiana, whose electors were chosen by the state legislature, Clay was favored to win that state's five electoral votes. But just prior to the balloting, two men who supported Clay were injured in a carriage accident and two others missed the vote for other reasons. In their absence, Clay narrowly lost, 30–28, to a coalition of Jackson-Adams supporters and was shut out of the state's electoral allotment.[12] If he'd won those five votes in Louisiana, he would have finished third in the Electoral College. In which case, Clay's popularity among House colleagues might have vaulted him to victory.[13] So, except for a carriage accident in Louisiana, Henry Clay may well have become the country's sixth president.

Clay was left instead to use his influence in the House to help determine the winner. Crawford retained Southern support but wasn't otherwise considered a serious candidate because he hadn't fully recovered his health. Jackson seemed an obvious choice to some because he'd won a plurality of electoral and popular votes, but his main claim to fame was as a military leader and there were "fears that he would become an American Napoleon."[14] Many also believed he lacked the requisite experience for the presidency. Clay himself was quoted as saying, "I cannot believe that killing 2,500 Englishmen at New Orleans qualifies for the various, difficult, and complicated duties of the Chief Magistracy."[15]

Then there was Adams, who'd served as a diplomat, senator, and secretary of state, and who shared some of Clay's desires for an active government. So Clay threw his support to Adams, whom he considered the only plausible president of the three contenders. Whether or not Clay's backing was crucial to the outcome is unclear, but Adams did win on the first ballot with the support of thirteen states, to seven for Jackson and four for Crawford.

After this, Jackson became incensed when Adams named Clay his secretary of state, which was considered a stepping-stone to the presidency. Rumors swirled that Clay had supported Adams in exchange for the job. No evidence ever emerged of such a deal, but talk of a "corrupt bargain" soon became a rallying cry for Jackson's supporters. Clay was reportedly burned in effigy 153 times in different states.[16] Plans for another campaign quickly surfaced, and so the election of 1824 became the first act in a two-part battle between Adams and Jackson.

1828

Almost as soon as the 1824 election ended, the 1828 campaign began. Jackson's supporters remained furious over how Adams became president, and there was never much doubt the two men would reprise their battle from four years earlier, but this time in a mano-a-mano contest with no other candidate in the race.

It's interesting how fate brought these two men together at a pivotal time for presidential elections. Adams and Jackson were the same age and were equally devoted to their country but were otherwise about as different as two individuals can be. This stark difference was evident even in their childhoods. They were born in 1767, so they were still boys when the American Revolution began. Even so, they each had extraordinary experiences during that period that provide a striking glimpse into the presidential candidates they became a half century later.

Adams was just ten in the winter of 1778 when he journeyed across the stormy Atlantic with his father, who'd been named a commissioner to France. The young man would spend much of the next eight years abroad, living with his father in France and the Netherlands, going to Russia as a fourteen-year-old to serve as secretary to the American minister, and spending months traveling through Germany, Spain, and the Nordic countries. By the time he returned home to start college, he was one of the most well-traveled Americans of his time and had enjoyed a front-row seat to political maneuverings in Europe.[17] As an adult, Adams was a writer and scholar who was conversant in several languages and had a long career in government.

Jackson, on the other hand, was born to Scots-Irish immigrants on a small farm in the Carolinas, and his father died before Jackson's birth. In 1781, when the young Adams was in Russia, the fourteen-year-old Jackson joined the Continental Army. After a skirmish, the teenager was captured and boldly refused to clean the boots of a British officer. Enraged, the officer swung at Jackson with his sword, gashing the boy's arm and head. Following a spell as a prisoner of war, Jackson saw both his mother and brother die shortly after his release, leaving him alone in the world as a teenager.

Jackson then forged a life in the frontier territory of Tennessee. It was a harsh world, where settlers clashed with Native Americans and disputes between men were resolved violently. Jackson himself was fiercely combative, killing one man in a duel and carrying bullets in his body from various fights. But despite having little education, he became a lawyer and later gained fame from his military endeavors.

Given all this, it shouldn't be a surprise to learn that a slogan about these men compared them as "Adams who can write / Jackson who can fight."[18] This catchphrase dated to 1824, when some promoted Jackson as a potential vice president for Adams, and it was meant to capture the strengths of each man. But it also caricatured them in a way that reinforced the refrains of the Jacksonians, who liked to portray "Jackson as a man of action and Adams as a bookish scholar."[19]

These contrasts were magnified because Adams and Jackson also seemed to embody all the competing strands of this era. The frontier states of the West were a rising force. The Era of Good Feelings was giving way to new factionalism. And the republicanism of the Founders, which granted most power to elites and property holders, had been upended by a mass democracy that now gave greater voice to the common man. In these collisions, Adams epitomized the East and classical republicanism, while Jackson was a symbol of the West and mass democracy. As one of Jackson's supporters suggested, and as many voters seemed to believe, the election was "a great contest between the aristocracy and democracy of America."[20]

The 1828 campaign was the hardest fought and most acrimonious contest the country had seen in twenty-eight years, since 1800. Adams barely had time to settle into office before the Tennessee legislature in 1825 nominated Jackson as a candidate for the next election. The Adams presidency also got off to a difficult start when, in his first message to Congress, he proposed a number of government initiatives, including new roads and canals, a naval academy, and a national observatory. These ideas may seem prescient from a twenty-first-century perspective, but at the time Adams was criticized for amassing government power and threatening states' rights.[21]

To add to Adams's difficulties, he was soon opposed by his vice president. Although John Calhoun was elected vice president on his own in 1824 and didn't owe his job to Adams, he'd started his career as a "staunch American nationalist" before evolving into a states' rights advocate more in line with the politics of his South Carolina home.[22] After determining that his political future would be more viable if he switched sides, Calhoun threw his support to Jackson and became that campaign's choice for vice president in 1828.

These maneuverings were indicative of how the façade of nonpartisanship was giving way again to the political factions that had battled for supremacy a few decades earlier. Jackson's supporters joined with the Jeffersonian "Old Republicans" and formed the new Democratic Party. They saw themselves as protectors of the common man against privileged interests and believed the best way to achieve this was by restraining government. Those who backed Adams were linked with the old Federalists and became known as National Republicans (and later as Whigs). They believed a strong government was needed to support industrial and financial interests and encourage economic growth.

While this revival of the party system seems inevitable in retrospect, it was helped along in 1828 by the Jacksonians, particularly Senator Martin Van Buren of New York. Van Buren, who even wrote a book on the topic, thought parties could invigorate a democracy by energizing voters—or, as he later put it, "rouse the sluggish to exertion."[23]

As the Jacksonians organized themselves, they rewrote the rules of political combat. It's been suggested the 1828 campaign was responsible for many developments that would transform

American politics, from coordinated media to organized rallies.[24] The Democrats put together a network of committees to manage volunteers, raise funds, promote events, track voters, distribute campaign materials, and feed stories to supportive newspapers.[25] Campaign workers also deftly played off Jackson's nickname, Old Hickory, which was given to him because hickory trees were known for their strength. At parades and rallies, hickory poles were raised and "hickory canes, hickory sticks, hickory brooms were everywhere."[26]

Many of these tactics were new to presidential elections, and the Adams team barely knew what hit them. One reason they were caught somewhat flat-footed by the organizational onslaught of the Jacksonians was that President Adams still idealistically maintained that rival parties weren't conducive to good government. As president, he turned down numerous speaking invitations and derided political campaigns as mere "electioneering."[27]

The personal side of the contest, meanwhile, has been called one of the "bitterest, ugliest" campaigns in history.[28] With the first real partisan contest in nearly three decades, the two sides took to negative campaigning with renewed gusto.

President Adams was hounded for his alleged corruption in the previous election and for being an intellectual elitist, but he was also falsely accused of pimping out a young woman to Czar Alexander I while serving as minister to Russia. He was criticized, as well, for putting gambling furniture in the White House. This was more accurate, though wildly exaggerated, as Adams had merely spent his own money on a billiards table. But since the game of billiards wasn't widely known, especially in the West, this was said to have hurt Adams by playing into his image as an aristocrat.[29]

It wasn't as easy for Adams to suggest his opponent was out of touch, so Jackson was politically tarred and feathered in a different manner, accused of being a murderer, an adulterer, and the mulatto son of a prostitute. Not quite your run-of-the-mill disparagement of a presidential candidate.

Jackson had killed a man in a duel and as an officer had approved the executions of numerous men for desertion or disobeying military orders. These incidents became grist for the Coffin Handbill, a pamphlet that listed the names of these men alongside pictures of coffins, under a heading that deemed the events the "Bloody Deeds of General Jackson." The handbill was first distributed as a supplement to Philadelphia's *Democratic Press* newspaper.[30]

It was also true that Jackson and his wife, Rachel, had married before her divorce to her first husband was finalized, a detail they may not have been aware of at the time. Supporters of Adams attacked Jackson for immorality and suggested he wasn't fit to be the leader of a Christian nation.[31] Then there was a rather outlandish attack against the general's late mother, which asserted she "was a common prostitute, brought to this country by British soldiers," and that she later "married a mulatto man, by whom she had several children," including Jackson.[32]

In the end, the Jacksonians were not to be denied. They swept the West and the South, defeating Adams 56 to 44 percent in the popular vote and 178–83 in the Electoral College, making Andrew Jackson the seventh president of the United States.

1832

The Jacksonian era was unlike anything the country had yet experienced. As a candidate, Jackson thrilled voters as the first representative of the common man who'd competed for the nation's highest office. As president, he governed in the style of the brash frontiersman he was, with a stubborn determination to assert control. He vetoed more bills than all his predecessors combined, for instance, which raised howls among congressional leaders, but the president maintained he was an agent of the people as the only official elected by the entire nation. He was the first executive to make this claim, perhaps because he was also the first one to win a popular vote.

Depending on one's perspective, the president was either a champion of popular democracy or a monarch in democratic clothing, and the 1832 campaign was driven almost entirely by these opposing assessments. Jackson ran for reelection as the candidate of the new Democratic Party and was opposed by Kentucky senator Henry Clay of the National Republicans. Since Clay was the former Speaker of the House who'd steered the 1824 election to Adams, he and Jackson weren't exactly members of each other's fan club. Jackson once called Clay "the basest, meanest scoundrel that ever disgraced the image of his god."[33]

Aside from Jackson's temperament, the central issue in the election turned out to be a fight over renewing the charter of the Second Bank of the United States. That doesn't sound very enthralling as a campaign topic, but Jackson seized on it as an opportunity to portray himself as an ongoing defender of the people.

The bank was a public-private enterprise that managed government revenues and payments, issued paper currency, and served as a commercial bank.[34] It was championed by National Republicans, who saw it as an instrument for maintaining a stable currency and promoting economic growth. Support for the bank was one of three pillars of the party's economic policy, known as the American System, along with funding infrastructure projects and maintaining a manufacturing tariff.

Jackson, however, opposed the bank. For starters, he had a philosophical problem with all banks because he favored gold and silver rather than paper money for financial transactions. He also thought the bank usurped the authority of the states and was representative of power held by elites. So when the House and Senate passed a bill in 1832 renewing the bank's charter, Jackson vetoed it.

His opponents were outraged over his refusal to accept a vote of Congress. They mocked him as "King Andrew" and muttered that he was "the most absolute despot now at the head of any representative government on earth."[35] But Jackson was hardly one to be cowed. "The bank is trying to kill me," he said, "*but I will kill it.*"[36] In his veto message, he said the bank would "make the rich richer and the potent more powerful," with no thought for "the humble members of society—the farmers, mechanics, and laborers—who have neither the time nor the means of securing like favors to themselves."[37] The bank's charter wasn't renewed.

Another issue that impacted the presidential race was the Nullification Crisis. Nullification is the idea that individual states can invalidate federal laws, and it seems to reappear whenever controversial legislation is passed, from the Alien and Sedition Acts of 1798 to the Affordable Care Act of 2010. The concept has never been upheld by the Supreme Court, but South Carolina pushed this idea during Jackson's presidency because of opposition to the tariffs of 1828 and 1832, which it saw as protecting the industrial North at the expense of the agrarian South. The state declared the tariffs invalid and threatened to secede. Jackson was outraged by even the thought of secession and declared nullification "incompatible with the existence of the Union."[38] The president prepared to use federal troops to rein in South Carolina.

The issue was finally finessed with the Compromise Tariff of 1833, after the next election. First, though, it shook up presidential politics by triggering a vice-presidential resignation and the rise of a new heir apparent to Jackson. That's because the politician most identified with nullification was Vice President John Calhoun, which helped convince Jackson to jettison Calhoun and make Martin Van Buren his new running mate. Calhoun resigned the vice presidency before the end of his term and was reappointed to the Senate from South Carolina. So, somewhat astonishingly, Calhoun served as vice president to both Adams and Jackson, and he was removed from the ticket in both reelection campaigns.

The 1832 election is notable as well because it was the first time that political parties used a nominating convention to select presidential candidates. The first convention wasn't convened by the Democrats or National Republicans, but by the Anti-Masonic Party, which was the country's first third-party movement. Founded in 1828 by those who feared that Masons (including President Jackson) were a secret society that held too much power in government, the party pushed for more openness and for "social and economic equality."[39] They managed to elect governors in Pennsylvania and Vermont, and in 1832 had the idea to stage a convention, enabling party loyalists from all states to gather in one place, nominate a candidate, and approve a platform.

The Anti-Masonics met in Baltimore and nominated former

attorney general William Wirt of Maryland for president. The meeting was such a success that the National Republicans and Democrats each copied it and held their own conventions, also in Baltimore.

Wirt sounds like he would have been a fringe candidate, but he received nearly 8 percent of the vote, as well as seven electoral votes from Vermont. Another eleven electoral votes went to someone who wasn't even an official candidate. South Carolina still allowed the state legislature to choose its electors and, well, there was that whole issue of nullification. So the state thumbed its nose at the presidential race and gave its votes to John Floyd, governor of Virginia and a member of the Nullifier Party, a new party that had been formed to support states' rights.

There went 18 of the 286 electoral votes, but it hardly mattered. Jackson rode his own popularity and the Democrats' superior organization to an overwhelming reelection victory. He won the popular vote 54 to 37 percent and the electoral vote 219–49.

1836

By 1836 President Jackson was aging and in poor health, so it was an easy decision to follow precedent and decline to run for a third term. He hadn't lost his strength of will, however, as demonstrated by his response in January 1835 to the first attempted presidential assassination. When Jackson walked out of Congress one day, a man jumped out from behind a pillar and fired two pistols at the president from near point-blank range. Shockingly, neither pistol discharged a bullet, possibly because the powder was damp. As soon as Jackson realized what was happening, his frontier instincts kicked in and he attacked the man with his cane. After others restrained the would-be killer (who was later deemed mentally unstable), Jackson remarked that he "was not born to be shot by an assassin."[40]

A less dramatic but more politically vital demonstration of Jackson's willpower took place that May, when the president pressured Democrats into holding their convention a full year ahead of time because he wanted to ensure no candidate could overtake his chosen successor, Vice President Van Buren. The son of a tavern owner, Van Buren had risen from humble beginnings, as had Jackson. But he was otherwise a stark contrast to the incumbent president. Van Buren stood only 5'6", was somewhat paunchy, and his most prominent feature was the pair of muttonchop sideburns that lined his face. He'd spent his career as an inside political player, which led to his nickname, "The Little Magician." Regardless, he had Jackson's full backing, and the Democrats dutifully selected him as their next nominee.

Support from Jackson was Van Buren's greatest strength and his most formidable challenge. The president was still popular with voters and the Democrats did what they could to transfer that approval to Van Buren. Hickory Clubs around the country were converted into Kinderhook Clubs, in honor of Van Buren's home in Kinderhook, New York. They also relied on the party structure built during the past two elections. Local committees hosted rallies and barbecues, distributed campaign paraphernalia, and ensured positive media coverage.[41]

But there was an energized opposition intent on taking down the Jacksonian Democrats, and Van Buren became the new target of their wrath. This opposition was led by the new Whig Party, made up mostly of National Republicans who'd undergone a makeover. The party name was chosen in homage to the British Whigs, who fought monarchism, and was aimed at reminding voters of Jackson's autocratic style.

The Whigs were joined in 1836 by former members of the Anti-Masonic and Nullifier parties, who came together in a somewhat eclectic anti-Jacksonian movement. The party couldn't agree on a presidential nominee, though, and instead backed several favorite-son candidates in hopes of denying Van Buren an electoral majority and forcing the election into the House. One Whig described the strategy this way: "The disease (Democratic rule) is to be treated as a local disorder—apply local remedies."[42]

The main Whig candidates were Senators Daniel Webster of Massachusetts and Hugh Lawson White of Tennessee, and William Henry Harrison of Ohio, a former senator and a military hero. Webster was the most prominent of the contenders, but Harrison is the one who had a breakout campaign. He was the first candidate to go on the trail, visiting old battlefields, meeting voters, and giving speeches. The Democrats complained that such campaigning was inappropriate; one newspaper lamented, "For the first time in the history of this country, we find a candidate for the Presidency traversing the land as an openmouthed electioneer for that high and dignified station."[43] But the tactic was an innovative one, and it helped Harrison become Van Buren's leading challenger.

Together, the Whigs unloaded a series of attacks on the Democratic nominee. One of the most biting criticisms came from the pen of Davy Crockett, the homespun congressman and frontier hero who later died at the Alamo. Crockett published a book-length attack on Van Buren in which he wrote that the vice president was "laced up in corsets, such as women in a town wear, and if possible tighter than the best of them. It would be difficult to say from his personal appearance whether he was a man or a woman, but for his large red and gray whiskers."[44]

In the end, though, the contest was as much a referendum on the incumbent Jackson as it was a vote for or against Van Buren. One political cartoon made light of this by showing Van Buren in a boxing ring with Harrison. Jackson is standing nearby, and Van Buren calls out to him, "Stand by me Old Hickory or I'm a gone chicken."[45]

Jackson's popularity turned out to be enough to carry Van Buren across the finish line, even against a trio of candidates. Van Buren won 50.8 percent of the popular vote, good for 170 votes in the Electoral College to 124 for his competitors. Harrison was the official runner-up, with 73 electoral votes, while White and Webster combined for another 40. Senator Willie Person Magnum of North Carolina received 11 votes from South Carolina, which again went its own way.

Van Buren's election was distinctive for several reasons. For one, this was the last time for the next 152 years that an incumbent vice president was elected to the presidency; it didn't happen again until George H. W. Bush succeeded Ronald Reagan in 1988. Van Buren was also the first president who'd been born an American, since his predecessors came into the world as British subjects before the Revolutionary War. Paradoxically, Van Buren was also the first president for whom English wasn't his first language, as he grew up in a Dutch-speaking family in New York's Hudson River Valley.

An even greater curiosity stems from that year's vice-presidential contest. Richard Mentor Johnson of Kentucky was the Democratic candidate, a hero of the War of 1812 who'd supposedly killed the Indian chieftain Tecumseh in battle, leading to a popular campaign refrain: "Rumpsey Dumpsey, Rumpsey Dumpsey, Colonel Johnson killed Tecumseh."[46]

Southerners, however, were maddened by Johnson's candidacy because he'd lived with a mulatto slave named Julia Chinn as his common-law wife and had two daughters with her. Julia died in 1833, and Johnson later took up with another slave. This was common knowledge, one reporter even writing that Johnson's wife was "a jet-black, thick-lipped, odiferous negro wench."[47] As a result, twenty-three Virginians refused to vote for him in the Electoral College, leaving him one vote short of a majority. So the decision went to the Senate for the only time in history, and the senators voted along party lines to elect Johnson vice president.

It seems surprising today that Johnson's candidacy didn't cause even more of an uproar, but perhaps it's because no president had yet died in office and the vice presidency was seen as rather inconsequential. Still, it's almost unfathomable to consider the reaction if Johnson had become president during the next four years. If Van Buren had died, the United States in the 1830s would have had a president who lived openly with slaves and acknowledged fathering mulatto children.

Popular Democracy and the Rise of New Political Parties

This era of presidential elections marked the ascent not only of a new style of politics but also of a new generation of national leaders, as the founders passed from the scene. James Monroe, the last president with a working connection to the creation of the republic, left office in 1825. John Adams and Thomas Jefferson were living out their last years in retirement and were destined soon to die on the same day: July 4, 1826. In an extraordinary cosmic coincidence, Adams and Jefferson both passed away on the fiftieth anniversary of the signing of the Declaration of Independence. Monroe too died on Independence Day, five years later, in 1831. James Madison, who passed away in 1836 (in June), was the last surviving Founding Father.

The end of the founding era happened to intersect with a new stage in American democracy, one that would be unfamiliar to the men who had drafted the Constitution four decades earlier. That's because the Founders had established a government with deliberate filters between the people and the nation's leaders. Voters were directly involved in electing only members of the House of Representatives, while senators were chosen by state legislatures, and the president by members of the Electoral College.

Moreover, as we saw, voting was restricted to white males who owned property. It was widely believed that an excess of democracy would produce disorder and that voters without a property-owning stake in society would be more susceptible to the charms of a demagogue. Even John Adams once suggested, "Very few men who have no property, have any judgement of their own."[48]

But the times had rendered this view obsolete. By 1825, twenty-one of the twenty-four states had ended the property-holding requirement and established universal suffrage for white males.[49] Women still couldn't vote, and African Americans could do so in only a few states, but that still signified the country's first expansion of voting rights. More states were also conducting a popular vote for president. In 1828, twenty-two states tallied a presidential vote. The combination of these two changes—the abolition of the property requirement and the advent of a nationwide vote—transformed presidential elections.[50] Across the country, there was a new sense "that politics and administration must be taken from the hands of a social elite . . . and opened to mass participation."[51]

Into this new world of politics stepped Andrew Jackson, whose presidency marks somewhat of a dividing line in American history. Beforehand, politics was driven by elites; afterward, "power was more diffuse, and government, for better and for worse, was more attuned to the popular will."[52] This drive was underway before Jackson came along, but he proved to be an ideal vehicle for advancing it. In 1829 he even suggested abolishing the Electoral College. "To the people belong the right of electing their Chief Magistrate," he asserted.[53] The suggestion was obviously not adopted, but it was a sign, at least, of the country's move toward greater popular democracy. As one historian suggested about the period, it was "the beginnings of the invasion of American history by 'the people,' not as rebels but as voters."[54]

The Jacksonian era was also instrumental in solidifying a two-party system in American politics. Both the Jacksonian Democrats and the anti-Jackson Whigs built a permanent party apparatus during the 1830s, and partisan competition has been entrenched ever since. Much of the credit for the return of parties during this period goes to Van Buren. Although his presidential legacy pales in comparison to Jackson's, he is as responsible as anyone for kickstarting the idea of party contests. In a book he wrote about political parties, he suggested that coalitions would promote consensus across factions, as well as reduce the risk of demagoguery by individual candidates. Van Buren also built the first national party organization to manage elections, which at the time was a groundbreaking idea.[55]

The party system was strengthened by other innovations of the era as well, including the advent of conventions. Previously, candidates were nominated by congressional caucuses or state legislatures, but conventions had the advantage of uniting party supporters behind a candidate and a platform. It also brought more citizens into the process and so was yet another step in the expansion of democracy.

The Democrats and Whigs, meanwhile, organized themselves around principles similar to those that animated the country's first political factions near the turn of the century. It's not a precise comparison because the Whigs, in contrast to the old Federalists, opposed a strong executive. They also advocated for temperance and other moral concerns.[56] But on economic issues the Whigs bore a close resemblance to the Federalists, including in their advocacy of federal funding for infrastructure. It was an idea that stretched back to Hamilton and was invigorated during the John Quincy Adams presidency, but it was the Whigs who made it part of a larger agenda to "foster national integration."[57]

The Democrats, on the other hand, criticized using federal funds for these purposes, partly because they felt such decisions should be made by the states. Equally important, for a party that saw itself as standing up for the common man, the Democrats believed federal involvement in the economy benefited only the wealthy.

For the next two decades, the Democrats and Whigs battled each other over these issues, until the parties realigned in the 1850s and 1860s. Partisan policies and voter coalitions would shift in the future, but popular democracy and the two-party system were here to stay.

1840 and 1844: Tippecanoe, Tyler, and Texas

1840

The election of 1840 may not be widely famous today, but it was the most lively and raucous contest in history to this point and it changed presidential politics in ways almost no one would have dared predict when the campaign began. By the time it was over, John Quincy Adams was calling it "a revolution in the habits and manners of the people."[58] And a half century later, one author was still defining it as "the most remarkable political contest ever known."[59]

At the start of the year, though, the only question on anyone's mind was which Whig candidate would challenge a weakened President Van Buren's bid for reelection. The president's popularity had crumpled after the Panic of 1837, an economic collapse that detonated only weeks after his inauguration and left him with the unfortunate nickname "Martin Van Ruin."

As Van Buren staggered into the 1840 campaign at the helm of a country that was still trying to shake off its economic doldrums, the leading Whig candidates to oppose him were Senator Henry Clay of Kentucky, the party's putative leader, and William Henry Harrison of Ohio, the war hero and former senator who was presidential runner-up in 1836. Clay led on the first ballots at the convention but wasn't able to garner a majority of delegates, so the Whigs turned to Harrison. Clay bemoaned his lost opportunity. "I am the most unfortunate man in the history of parties," he said, "always run by my friends when sure to be defeated, and now betrayed for a nomination when I, or anyone, would be sure of an election."[60]

The Whigs then paired Harrison with John Tyler, former senator and governor of Virginia. Since Harrison was renowned for winning the 1811 Battle of Tippecanoe (against American Indian tribes who were trying to form a Native American confederacy), this ticket led to one of the more inspired and memorable campaign slogans ever created: "Tippecanoe and Tyler Too!"

The Democrats were thrilled at first by the Whigs' nominee, since Van Buren had defeated Harrison four years earlier. While Harrison had stature from his military career, Democrats mocked the sixty-seven-year-old as "Granny Harrison." The *Baltimore Republican* newspaper reported that one opponent disparaged him this way: "Give him a barrel of hard cider, and settle a pension of two thousand a year on him, and . . . he will sit the remainder of his days in his log cabin, by the side of a 'sea-coal' fire and study moral philosophy."[61]

That seemingly innocuous piece of reporting, believe it or not, was the kindling for a political inferno that forever changed presidential campaigns.

It started when the Whigs brilliantly turned the insult on its head. Instead of defending Harrison against the slur, they transformed him into Old Tip, a soldier and frontier farmer who indeed lived in a log cabin, swilled hard cider, and wanted to return government to the people. This was in comparison to

Van Buren, whom they portrayed as an elitist, ensconced in a palatial White House and unconcerned with the problems of the common man.

It was a superb tactic, even if it was also rather misleading. The truth was, Harrison came from a wealthy family, and his father had signed the Declaration of Independence. Family friends George Washington and John Adams had given him his first military commission and his earlier job as governor of the Indiana Territory. Moreover, Harrison in 1840 lived in an impressive twenty-two-room home with a six-acre lawn overlooking the Ohio River.[62] Van Buren, in contrast, was the son of a tavern owner who had worked his way from nothing up to the presidency.

But the strategy succeeded in framing images of the two candidates. Voters either didn't know the truth or chose to believe in the image as more important than the reality, which is certainly not the only time such an approach worked in a political campaign. Simply put, the log cabin became the embodiment of the average person agitating for change.

And agitate they did. Log cabins were built as campaign offices, and log cabin floats were constructed for parades. Campaign rallies attracted tens of thousands of people, who would spend a day eating, dancing, drinking hard cider, and chanting, "Martin Van Buren, you won't do. The people's choice is Tippecanoe."[63] The Whigs also made huge campaign balls, ten or more feet in diameter, and rolled them in parades or in between towns (prompting the saying "Keep the ball rolling"). All the while, they sang:

> What has caused this great commotion, motion, motion,
> Our country through?
> It is the ball-a-rolling on,
> For Tippecanoe and Tyler too.[64]

While enjoying the rallies and parades, people could also buy such campaign paraphernalia as Tippecanoe shaving cream, Harrison and Tyler neckties, log cabin jewelry, songbooks, coffee cups, and even whiskey bottles in the shape of log cabins.[65] The genius of all this was that it helped launch the idea of presidential campaigns as vehicles for entertainment and brand marketing.

The Democrats, who prided themselves on the organization they'd built, were stunned by the deluge of activity for Harrison. It smacked of the earlier campaigns for Jackson, but on a larger scale and with more branding of the candidate. "We have taught them how to conquer us!" lamented one writer.[66]

Another novel twist in 1840 was the presence of Harrison on the campaign trail. He'd made some appearances in 1836, but this time he gave a couple dozen talks, partly to refute Democratic attacks on him as a feeble old man. Though he rarely discussed issues, Harrison was the first presidential candidate to make his own campaign speeches.[67]

The Whigs paired these tactics with merciless takedowns of Van Buren. "Whenever you find a bitter, blasphemous Atheist and enemy of Marriage, Morality, and Social Order, there you may be certain of one vote for Van Buren," hollered the Log Cabin newspaper.[68] Then there was a speech by Congressman Charles Ogle of Pennsylvania, who spent three days on the House floor excoriating Van Buren for spending taxpayer money for renovations of his "presidential palace." He taunted the president for dining on French food with gold spoons, for his "womanish but costly whim" of replacing wallpaper, and even for landscaping the White House lawn with mounds "designed to resemble and assume the form of an Amazon's bosom, with a miniature knoll on its apex to denote the nipple."[69]

Hearing all of this makes it easy to see why so many voters rebelled against Van Buren's presidency. Except that most of it wasn't true. Even some Whigs admitted that many of the claims were false.[70] Regardless, Ogle's "Gold Spoons" speech was distributed across the country, furthering the claim that Van Buren was a pampered, out-of-touch aristocrat.

The Democrats struggled to fight back. They defended Van Buren as "the pilot that weathered the storm" of the economic collapse, but the argument fell on deaf ears.[71] They even tried to turn the hard cider symbol back against Harrison with this song, to the tune of "Rock-a-Bye Baby":

Hush-a-bye baby, Daddy's a Whig
When he comes home, hard cider he'll swig
When he has swug, He'll fall in a stu
And down will come Tyler and Tippecanoe.[72]

None of it worked. The Whigs' personality-driven campaign, combined with the aftermath of the Panic of 1837, propelled Harrison to an easy victory. He won the popular vote by 53 to 47 percent and the electoral tally 234–60.

But there was an unexpected postscript to the election.

Harrison was sixty-eight when he was inaugurated, the oldest president before Ronald Reagan, Donald Trump, and Joe Biden, and gave the longest inaugural speech on record (1 hour 45 minutes) in freezing weather. These facts may or may not be relevant to what happened next, but Harrison soon caught a cold, which turned into pneumonia. And then he died, after being president for one month.

He was the first president to die in office. This provoked a constitutional dilemma because it was unclear whether the vice president was meant to become president for the rest of the term or only acting president until new elections could be held. Tyler insisted there was no question: he was the president. After some debate, Congress agreed. This was no small decision, as it set a precedent for all future presidential successions before being codified by the Twenty-Fifth Amendment in 1967.

After all the ferment of the Harrison campaign, the first Whig president lasted one month in office. And then John Tyler stepped onto the stage.

1844

The Whigs never intended for Tyler to be president. He was added to the 1840 ticket merely to balance Harrison with a Southerner who'd supported Clay. Daniel Webster, the Massachusetts senator and a Whig icon, had turned down a chance to be Harrison's vice president, proclaiming he didn't want "to be buried until [he was] really dead."[73] Tyler at least was willing to accept the job and brought electoral strengths as a Virginian.

Unfortunately for the Whigs, Tyler was also a former Democrat who changed parties because of disenchantment with the Jackson administration but who had never shed his beliefs about states' rights or strict construction of the Constitution. Consequently, he soon vetoed Whig legislation to restore a national bank. After this, the relationship between Tyler and the Whigs deteriorated so quickly that in September 1841 most of his cabinet resigned. Then the Whigs formally expelled him from their party. And it's not as if Tyler could look to Democrats for support, since he'd earlier spurned their party too. He was truly a president without a political base. And soon to be a president without a first lady, as his wife, Letitia, died in 1842 from the aftereffects of a stroke she'd suffered a few years earlier.

After a period of mourning, Tyler picked himself up and soon concocted a plan to mount a third-party run for president. His strategy centered on annexing Texas, which had been an independent republic since 1836. Mexico didn't recognize Texan independence, so there was a risk of provoking military conflict, but the issue had enough support in the South that Tyler imagined it might propel him to a second term. He instructed Secretary of State Abel Upshur to begin secret negotiations with Texas president Sam Houston. By early 1844 a treaty appeared imminent, with plans for Texas to become a U.S. territory, thereby putting off debate over admission of another slave state.[74] But then fate intervened again, scrambling both the annexation issue and the upcoming election.

On February 28 much of official Washington enjoyed a Potomac River cruise on the USS *Princeton*, a steam-powered warship with a powerful new cannon dubbed the "Peacemaker." Among the four hundred guests were the president, cabinet members, senators, and representatives. There were demonstration firings of the Peacemaker, and on the third try it exploded, killing Secretary Upshur and several others.[75]

Upshur's death upended the politics of Texas. He was replaced as secretary of state by Senator John Calhoun, who duly submitted the annexation treaty to the Senate in April. However, the South Carolinian Calhoun included a letter he'd written to the British minister in which he praised slavery and said it would be protected in Texas. The letter caused a firestorm by essentially declaring Texas would be a slave state, which roused the opposition of Northerners. It also forced presidential hopefuls to weigh in on the issue just as the election was heating up.[76]

The leading contenders at that point were Clay of the Whigs and former president Van Buren of the Democrats, who were still the dominant figures in their parties. Both came out against the annexation of Texas in letters coincidentally published on the same day, arguing it would lead to war with Mexico. This stance didn't much harm Clay's status among Whigs, and he was nominated easily at his party's convention. But it proved fatal to Van Buren's hopes by costing him the support of Southern Democrats, including Andrew Jackson. The former president said he'd "shed tears of regret" over Van Buren's position but now understood it was "impossible to elect him."[77]

When neither Van Buren nor his leading rival, Senator Lewis Cass of Michigan, could accumulate enough support for their nomination at the party convention in Baltimore, the Democrats on the ninth ballot turned to the lesser known James Polk of Tennessee, a former Speaker of the House and governor. More important, Polk supported annexing Texas and was a Jackson protégé.

Still, the Whigs seemed confident of victory. "Are our Democratic friends serious in the nomination which they have made?" asked Clay when he heard about Polk's candidacy.[78]

But Clay underestimated the Tennessean. Polk soon came out in favor not only of annexing Texas but also of absorbing the entire Oregon Territory, which was jointly held with Great Britain. "All of Texas, all of Oregon," cried the Democrats, cleverly proposing to satisfy both Northern and Southern expansionists.[79]

In the meantime, Tyler wouldn't go away. He formed a new Democratic-Republican Party and launched a presidential campaign under the banner "Tyler and Texas."[80] He also got remarried, to Julia Gardiner, a twenty-four-year-old woman who was thirty years his junior, making him the first president to marry while in office. The age difference caused tongues to wag, but Julia settled into life as first lady, and the couple had seven children together after Tyler's presidency.

Despite his hopes of forging a new political coalition, Tyler eventually gave in to reality. He knew he could only spoil Polk's chances in the contest, helping to defeat the party that supported his signature issue of annexing Texas. So he withdrew from the race in August.

However, a different third-party candidate remained in the race: James Birney of the abolitionist Liberty Party. Birney wasn't a major factor in the contest, except for the fact that much of his slim support came from Northern antislavery voters who might otherwise have backed Clay. Thus Tyler's withdrawal and Birney's candidacy *both* benefited Polk.

After the hullabaloo of 1840, the 1844 campaign was less raucous. Which is not to say that partisans were quiet. The Democrats widely attacked Clay, who was known to be a drinker and gambler, for his morals. One handbill accused him of being "a notorious Sabbath-breaker, Profane Swearer, Gambler, Common Drunkard, Perjurer, Dueler, Thief, Robber, Adulterer, Man-stealer, Slave-holder, and Murderer."[81]

The Whigs, meanwhile, mostly focused on Polk's supposed lack of qualifications. As one campaign song put it, "Ha, ha, ha, what a nominee / Is Jimmy Polk of Tennessee."[82]

In the end, Polk narrowly defeated Clay. He won the popular vote 49.5 to 48.1 percent, with 2.3 percent going to Birney, and he prevailed 170–105 in the electoral vote. Although the Liberty Party's vote was minimal, it may have been decisive. In New York, Birney received 15,812 votes in a contest that Polk won by 5,106. Without Birney in the race there's a good chance Clay would have won New York and, with it, the Electoral College.[83] Abraham Lincoln, then a young Illinois Whig, believed that to be true. "If the Whig abolitionists of New York had voted with us . . . Clay would now be President, Whig principles in the ascendant and Texas not annexed," he said.[84]

Manifest Destiny and the Impact of Elections on History

Just 5,106 votes in New York. That was the difference between James Polk and Henry Clay in the race for president in 1844. But the difference in American history, and in the geography of the country, is perhaps incalculable. Would Texas today be part of the United States, or an independent nation? Would California have remained in Mexico? What would have been the fate of the Southwest and the Pacific Northwest? Many outcomes were within the realm of possibility.

As it turned out, after the 1844 election President Tyler claimed Polk's victory was a mandate for the annexation of Texas, and on his last day in office he submitted an annexation offer. Texas later ratified the agreement and joined the United States in 1846. The Texas border, however, remained in question. Was it the Nueces River or the Rio Grande further west? When Mexico refused to sell the disputed area to the United States, Polk sent troops under Gen. Zachary Taylor to the region. Inevitably there was a skirmish on territory claimed by both nations, which led Polk, somewhat controversially, to ask Congress to declare war.

The Mexican-American War lasted two years and generated considerable debate. It was favored by expansionists during this era of "manifest destiny," a term coined in an 1845 article that suggested it was America's "manifest destiny to overspread the continent."[85] The war had many opponents as well, including Congressman Lincoln and Henry David Thoreau, who spent a night in jail for refusing to pay taxes that might support the war. Many believed it was a naked grab for territory and feared the addition of more slave states to the Union. Some Northerners derisively referred to it as "Mr. Polk's war," just as they'd scorned "Mr. Madison's War" in 1812.[86]

On the battlefield, the United States conquered land as far south as Mexico City and forced the Mexicans into peace negotiations. With the 1848 Treaty of Guadalupe Hidalgo, Mexico not only accepted the loss of Texas but also ceded to the United States what is now California and the Southwest. During these same years, Polk signed a treaty with Great Britain that split the Oregon Territory between the two nations at the 49th parallel. This gave the United States control of what is now Washington, Oregon, and Idaho, while the British held on to British Columbia.

It's safe to say that Polk's was a consequential presidency, but how might history have been different if Clay had won in 1844? Or if the Whigs had nominated Clay in 1840 and Tyler never became president? Texas might still have joined the Union eventually, although there was also support for it to remain independent. Clay himself espoused this position, saying, "Texas is destined to be settled by our race, who will carry there, undoubtedly, our laws, our language, and our institutions, and that view of her destiny reconciles me much more to her independence. . . . We may live as good neighbors, cultivating peace, commerce and friendship."[87]

Of course, with no Texas dispute and no war, California, Arizona, New Mexico, Utah, and Nevada could today still be part of Mexico. Or California may have gone the way of Texas. Immigrant Americans would almost surely still have moved there with the Gold Rush, and some historians think this would have led California to choose independence from Mexico.[88] In which case, the United States, Canada, California, and Texas might now all be independent English-speaking democracies in North America. Finally, without new U.S. territories in the West, there would have been no heated debate over the expansion of slavery and, possibly, no Civil War.

It's all speculative, obviously, but it does go to show the impact that presidential elections can have on history. Even those decided by 5,106 votes in one state.

1848, 1852, and 1856: North-South Tensions Upend U.S. Politics

1848

President Polk may well have been reelected in 1848 had he chosen to run, but he declined to stand for a second term. He was exhausted by the job and had pledged to serve just four years, so he set sail for retirement.

There was initially no clear favorite to replace Polk, although it was obvious that a prominent issue would be the debate over slavery in the West. This dispute had been on the verge of exploding ever since the authors of the 1846 Wilmot Proviso had proposed banning slavery in lands acquired from Mexico. The bill never passed Congress, but it persisted as a symbol, outraging Southerners while emerging as a core principle for antislavery Northerners.[89]

With this issue smoldering in the background, the Democrats met in May to nominate Polk's successor. They settled on Senator Lewis Cass of Michigan, a former secretary of war and governor of the Michigan Territory. Cass, however, believed in popular sovereignty, the idea that settlers in new territories should decide for themselves whether or not to accept slavery. This didn't go over well with antislavery New Yorkers, known as Barnburners, who staged a convention walkout.[90] Just like that, slavery leaped to the forefront of the presidential campaign.

The Whigs then met in June and considered nominating Clay yet again. But party members thought he was unlikely to win after three previous losses, so they cast their eyes on an unorthodox candidate, Gen. Zachary Taylor, a Kentucky native and Louisiana resident. A career soldier who'd never run for office, Taylor wasn't a typical presidential contender, but he'd become a national hero during the Mexican-American War and the Whigs sensed "Old Rough and Ready" might be the "fresh face with wide appeal" they needed.[91] He also happened to be a slaveholder, which would presumably appeal to "Cotton Whigs" in the South.

Taylor's lack of political experience was of some concern, as he'd be the first president to go directly from the military to the presidency with no background in government. In fact, when one Whig politician first proposed that he run for president, Taylor himself responded, "Stop your nonsense and drink your whiskey!"[92] Moreover, he didn't belong to a political party and admitted that he was "a Whig but not an ultra Whig."[93] Despite these concerns, the party still nominated him, presuming he'd be a popular candidate but a complacent executive who would go along with congressional initiatives.

Not everyone lined up behind the nominee, however. Daniel Webster disparaged Taylor as "an illiterate frontier colonel" and declined a chance to be his vice president, just as he'd turned down Harrison in 1840.[94] Instead, former New York congressman Millard Fillmore became Taylor's running mate. Meanwhile, the antislavery "Conscience Whigs," who were livid that their party nominated a slaveholder, staged their own convention walkout.

These walkouts by the Conscience Whigs and Barnburners turned out to be more than mere protests. That August, joined by former Liberty Party members, all the antislavery factions merged to form the Free Soil Party. They nominated former Democratic president Martin Van Buren to head a national ticket, with Whig Charles Francis Adams (son of John Quincy) as the vice-presidential nominee. The party adopted the slogan of "Free Soil, Free Speech, Free Labor and Free Men." Notably, the Free Soilers didn't call for abolishing slavery, as had the Liberty Party in 1840 and 1844. Instead they called for the more moderate goal of stopping slavery's expansion.[95]

Even with a former president at the head of the Free Soil ticket, however, the primary electoral battle was fought between Taylor and Cass. During the campaign, Taylor was purposefully vague on the issues. The Whigs portrayed this as a willingness to rise above partisanship, while the Democrats condemned it as lacking principle. One political cartoon showed Taylor telling questioners, "[You'll] find out what I think when I'm president."[96] The Democrats also attacked Taylor for supposedly being "semi-illiterate" and a "cruel slavemaster," while the Whigs suggested Cass was a corrupt politician, a windbag, and, most amusingly, a "pot-bellied, mutton-headed cucumber."[97]

In the end, Taylor's reputation as a war hero and his ability to appeal to Northern Whigs while tempering the fears of Southern slaveholders helped him prevail. He defeated Cass and Van

Buren 47 to 43 to 10 percent in the popular vote and 163–127–0 in the Electoral College, to become the second Whig president.

Polk, the outgoing president, noted that his replacement was "a well-meaning old man" but "uneducated, exceedingly ignorant of public affairs, and . . . of very ordinary capacity." But he would never see how Taylor's presidency turned out. The fifty-three-year-old Polk died three months after leaving office, likely from cholera contracted in New Orleans during a post-presidential tour of the South.

1852

By 1850 the Whig Party must have thought it was cursed. In 1840 the party elected William Henry Harrison, only to see him die and be replaced by John Tyler. In 1848 they elected Zachary Taylor, and then he too died.

President Taylor lasted longer than Harrison had, serving for sixteen months, but passed away in July 1850. Taylor was apparently felled by gastroenteritis after eating contaminated food during July 4 celebrations, since Washington then had a notoriously unsanitary water and sewer system. There were, however, conspiracy theorists who believed Taylor was murdered by arsenic poisoning. His remains were even exhumed and tested in 1991, though lab results showed only natural levels of arsenic, not enough to kill him.[98] Leaving aside the peculiarity of a president being disinterred for such testing 141 years after his death, the real intrigue for our purposes is *why* anyone thinks Taylor might have been quietly assassinated.

The answer: slavery. Everything in this era was linked in some way to this controversy, and Taylor's presidency happened to coincide with a fraught debate over slavery and the status of the new California and New Mexico territories.

California at the time was struggling to deal with the chaos caused by Gold Rush settlers and wanted to form a government. And New Mexico had a boundary dispute with Texas, which claimed land as far west as Santa Fe and was threatening to take it by force. Taylor recommended that Congress accept these territories as states, thus giving California the government it needed and New Mexico the ability to adjudicate its boundary dispute in the courts.

It seemed like a simple enough solution, except it left the decision about slavery to each state. This pleased those who were amenable to popular sovereignty, and it even satisfied antislavery Northerners who assumed neither state would be hospitable to slavery. But it enraged Southern slaveholders, who insisted on a constitutional right to take their property to any new territory. Some began advocating for secession.

In early 1850 Clay proposed a compromise: admitting California as a free state, creating two territories of New Mexico and Utah under popular sovereignty, and compensating Texas for relinquishing its territorial claims. He also proposed abolishing the slave trade in Washington, while writing a Fugitive Slave Law to require the return of escaped slaves. The proposal had a little something for everyone, but President Taylor opposed it, partly because he disagreed with imposing a Fugitive Slave Law on the nation.

While this debate meandered along, however, New Mexico went ahead and wrote its own free-state constitution, Texas threatened to use force against New Mexico, and Taylor vowed to resist Texas with federal troops. Instead of a compromise, it appeared conflict was brewing—between the federal government and Texas over borders, and between the U.S. government and the South over slavery in the West.

And then Taylor died.

Vice President Millard Fillmore succeeded Taylor and, although he was a New Yorker and opposed to slavery, he was more concerned with avoiding a conflict that might threaten the Union. So Fillmore disavowed Taylor's recommendations and supported Clay's Compromise of 1850, which soon became law. Hence the conspiracy theories over Taylor's death.

Historians have tried to imagine how history might have been different had Taylor lived. Most agree he likely wouldn't have signed the Compromise of 1850, but beyond that it's pure conjecture. Some believe that, given his reputation as a military hero and slaveholder, he could have forced a settlement on his terms, built a new political coalition, and averted the Civil War. Others think the Civil War may have just started a decade earlier.[99]

As it was, Fillmore was left to navigate the choppy waters of the slavery debate. Unhappily for him, his role in approving the Fugitive Slave Law incensed his fellow Northerners, who were furious at being asked to help return escaped slaves. This doomed his chances for a second term. Paradoxically, the renomination of the New Yorker Fillmore was supported by Southern Whigs, whereas Northerners preferred Gen. Winfield Scott of Virginia. Scott eventually prevailed on the fifty-third ballot, but his nomination spurred some Southerners to abandon the Whig Party.[100]

The Democrats faced their own regional divisions while choosing a candidate. Through forty-eight ballots, the leading contenders were Senator Cass of Michigan, the 1848 nominee, who drew support from Northern states, and former secretary of state James Buchanan of Pennsylvania, who was favored by Southerners. When no one could break the deadlock, the convention compromised on Franklin Pierce of New Hampshire. A former senator and a brigadier general in the Mexican-American War, Pierce was a forty-eight-year-old Northerner with an engaging personality and enough sympathy for Southern positions to make him acceptable to both regions. He was considered a "doughface," a Northerner with Southern principles.[101] But he hadn't held elective office for a decade and, after his nomination, reportedly said, "You are looking at the most surprised man that ever lived!"[102]

The Free Soil Party returned in 1852 and nominated Senator John Hale of New Hampshire. The party gained 5 percent of the vote, but most everyone else lined up behind Pierce or Scott in a battle that turned on character traits and the enthusiasm of each party's voters.

Pierce was known to have had a drinking problem, so the Whigs taunted him as the "hero of many a well-fought bottle." They also mocked him as a coward for having apparently fainted during combat. The truth was that Pierce passed out from an injury after his

THE RISE OF THE PARTIES

horse fell over some rocks, but that didn't stop Whigs from having fun with the story.[103] Pierce had a secret weapon, however, in a laudatory campaign biography written by his college friend Nathaniel Hawthorne, who'd recently gained acclaim for *The Scarlett Letter* and *The House of Seven Gables*.

Scott, on the other hand, had an accomplished military career stretching back decades, but his less-than-ideal nickname was "Fuss 'n Feathers," bestowed because of his apparent vanity. The Democrats gleefully battered him over the label. They also delighted in a slogan that played off their victory of eight years earlier: "We Polked 'em in '44, we'll Pierce 'em in '52."[104]

The pivotal factor in the campaign turned out to be the desertion of Southerners from the Whig coalition. This helped Pierce defeat Scott by 51 to 44 percent in the popular vote and 254–42 in the Electoral College. Scott won only four states, in an ominous sign of the decline of the Whig Party.

1856

When Franklin Pierce took office in 1853, it wasn't with the burst of hopefulness one might expect but rather on the heels of a tragedy that would soon seem like an omen for his next four years. Two months before the inauguration, Pierce's family was in a train accident, and he and his wife saw their eleven-year-old son, Benjamin, die in front of them. He was their last surviving child, and the death sent them into despair. Jane Pierce had never been happy with her husband's political career, and she blamed her son's death on retribution for Franklin's pursuit of office. The heartbreak cast a shadow over Pierce's presidency.

Once in office, two of Pierce's goals were to add more territory to the United States and move the country past its divisions over slavery. On both counts, his successes and failures were, curiously, linked to the country's desire for a transcontinental railroad. But what no one could have foreseen was how these efforts would exacerbate North-South tensions and remake American politics.

Pierce's expansionist impulse first led his administration to consider annexing Cuba and to look longingly at Central America, which would have added new slave territory to the Union. These plans weren't successful, but Pierce did add territory to the southwestern United States via the 1854 Gadsden Purchase, which came about because there was no easy route for a southern railroad except through a strip of Mexican desert. His administration tried to remedy this by offering to buy all of northwestern Mexico and Baja California. When Mexico refused, Pierce settled for thirty thousand square miles of what is now southern Arizona and New Mexico, enough for a railroad route. It was the last territorial addition to the contiguous United States.

The effort to procure a northern route for a railroad, meanwhile, turned into something altogether different. It became the biggest crisis of Pierce's presidency, crushed his hopes for a second term, and generated what some have called "the first bloodshed of the Civil War."[105]

It started when Senator Stephen Douglas of Illinois, hoping to pave the way for a railroad from Chicago to San Francisco, shepherded the Kansas-Nebraska Act of 1854 through Congress, with Pierce's support. The legislation created two new territories and wrote the concept of popular sovereignty into law, allowing settlers to decide about slavery for themselves. The Kansas and Nebraska territories were above the 36°30[] parallel, however, so Douglas's bill also repealed the Missouri Compromise that had previously barred slavery in that region. This was a key to gaining Southern support, but it incensed Northerners, who regarded the 36°30[] line as a "sacred compact."[106]

The Kansas-Nebraska Act turned out to be the match that lit a fuse of social and political upheaval. It began with an influx of settlers into Kansas who were intent on ensuring the state would pass either a pro- or antislavery constitution. At one point, the territory had two competing governments. The battle descended into violence, and there were so many attacks and reprisals that the struggle became known as "Bleeding Kansas." The agitation seemed to erupt all at once in the late spring of 1856. On May 21 a mob ransacked and burned the town of Lawrence, which was founded by antislavery settlers from New England, killing five people. Three days later the abolitionist John Brown retaliated against a proslavery settlement by dragging five men from their homes and butchering them.

The same week, Congressman Preston Brooks of South Carolina walked into the Senate and beat the antislavery senator Charles Sumner of Massachusetts unconscious with his cane because of a speech Sumner had given. The *New York Post* asked, "Has it come to this? Are we to be chastised as they chastise their slaves?"[107] The country reeled from the growing hostility. "We are treading upon a volcano," said former senator Thomas Hart Benton of Missouri.

It was against this background that the country's politics were transformed, beginning with the fracture and collapse of the Whig Party. Whigs who identified as states' rights Southerners began drifting to the Democratic Party, while some Northern Whigs joined the Free Soilers in forming an "anti-Nebraska" faction that was opposed to the expansion of slavery. A small meeting of this anti-Nebraska group in Ripon, Wisconsin, in 1854 led to a larger gathering in Jackson, Michigan, and out of these assemblies the new Republican Party was born.

Not all Whigs became Republicans or Democrats, however, as some of them moved instead to the new, nativist American Party. A wave of immigrants had recently flooded into the country, many of them Irish and German Catholics fleeing famine and poverty. This sparked a backlash from people who feared their jobs, religion, and culture might be swamped by the new immigrants. Nativist gangs attacked Catholic communities, killing residents and burning homes and churches. Secret societies dedicated to anti-Catholicism also arose, with members instructed to say "I know nothing" if questioned about their existence. The term stuck and, when nativism grew into a political movement, members of the American Party were called Know Nothings. They advocated barring foreign-born immigrants and Catholics from office and increasing from five to twenty-one years the naturalization period for becoming a citizen.

For a while, the Know Nothings seemed more likely than the Republicans to become a major party. The Republicans had no chance of gaining Southern support by virtue of their antislavery views, whereas the Know Nothings were primed to become the party of American nationalism. The movement was soon the "rage of the day," so much so that vendors slapped the Know Nothing name on products, from candy to stagecoaches.[108] The party won several dozen seats in Congress and a slew of statewide offices. The *New York Herald* even predicted a Know Nothing would win the next presidential election.[109] That forecast didn't sound so outlandish when the party convinced former Whig president Millard Fillmore to be its nominee in 1856, under the slogan "Americans to rule America."[110]

Among Democrats, meanwhile, President Pierce wanted a second term, but he faced opposition because of his support for the Kansas-Nebraska Act. Senator Douglas was opposed for the same reason. So Democrats on the seventeenth ballot of their convention compromised on former secretary of state James Buchanan, another Northern doughface. Buchanan was said to be the "most available and unobjectionable" option.[111]

A third presidential candidate joined the race when the Republican Party made former California senator John Frémont its first nominee. Frémont, who'd become nationally famous after leading expeditions to explore the West, was known as "the Pathfinder." He had a nominal record in politics but had strong antislavery views, and he was embraced as a "romantic figure" to lead the new party.[112] The Republicans ran on the slogan "Free Soil, Free Men and Frémont."

The nominations of Buchanan, Frémont, and Fillmore set the stage for a turbulent three-way campaign, and each candidate faced his own unique attacks.

The Democrat Buchanan was accused of favoring an oligarchy built on slavery.[113] A bachelor who'd never married, he was also derided as a "fussy old man."[114] Interestingly, with the emergence of gay marriage and LGBTQ rights in the early twenty-first century, there has been renewed speculation over whether Buchanan might have been the country's first gay president.[115] He was very close to Alabama senator William King, and Andrew Jackson mocked the two as "Aunt Nancy and Miss Fancy."[116] But no conclusive evidence has emerged one way or another, and there's little indication his being a bachelor played a role in the 1856 campaign aside from snide remarks about Buchanan's personality.

The Know Nothing Fillmore, not surprisingly, was attacked for leading a nativist movement. Ironically, Fillmore didn't have strong nativist beliefs himself, but he saw the Know Nothings as the best vehicle for endorsing nationalism and preserving the Union.[117] This sentiment was no doubt shared by others, as many Know Nothings were torn between backing Fillmore and risking a Republican win, or else deserting their nominee for Buchanan as a surer way to keep the country together.

Finally, the Republican Frémont was denounced as a closet Catholic and a "black Republican" who would force racial equality on the nation. In a particularly staggering example of these fears, one parade showcased young girls in white dresses who held banners that read "Fathers, save us from n—— husbands."[118]

Frémont did have the benefit of his wife, Jessie, however, who became a celebrity while helping manage his campaign. She might have actually been a better candidate than her husband. While he was a taciturn hero, she attracted female fans who copied her hairstyle and her favorite color, violet. People gathered outside the family's New York home and cried, "Give us Jessie!" Newspaper headlines and campaign banners promoted "Fremont and His Jessie." But Jessie couldn't run, of course, and women couldn't vote. And Republicans were still a regional party with not quite enough strength in the Electoral College. Northern voters, it was said, "feared disunion more than they hated slavery."[119]

So the 1856 contest was a tale of two elections. In the South, Buchanan outdistanced Fillmore with 56 percent of the vote and carried fourteen of the fifteen slave states. Frémont garnered a microscopic total of 0.1 percent in the region. In the North, conversely, Frémont defeated Buchanan with 45 percent of the vote and carried eleven of the sixteen non-slave states. Overall, Buchanan amassed 45 percent of the national vote to 33 percent for Frémont and 22 percent for Fillmore, and he prevailed in the

Electoral College by 174–114–8. The difference in the election was Buchanan's strength in states such as Pennsylvania and Illinois, which Republicans took note of for 1860.

A Changing Nation, a Changing Political Landscape

The United States in the 1840s and 1850s was a nation in transition. The country now stretched from the Atlantic to the Pacific, and the railroad and telegraph were dramatically shortening the sense of distance between states. Women were making their presence felt, as symbolized by the 1848 Seneca Falls Convention launching the women's rights movement. Even American literature was reaching new heights, with Hawthorne's *Scarlet Letter*, Herman Melville's *Moby-Dick*, Thoreau's *Walden*, and Walt Whitman's *Leaves of Grass*, all published between 1850 and 1855. In a sign of the times, though, the best-selling book of the era was Harriet Beecher Stowe's *Uncle Tom's Cabin*, a provocative novel that fueled the debate over slavery.[120]

Perhaps not surprisingly, various new political parties also sprang into existence during this period. In 1848 an Ohio newspaper noted that people seemed "to be cutting loose en masse from the old party organizations."[121] The Liberty, Free Soil, Know Nothing, and Republican parties were all born between 1840 and 1854.

The Liberty and Free Soil parties demonstrated the scope of the antislavery vote and paved a path for Republicans, while the Know Nothings highlighted a nativist strain of politics that was potent at the time and recurs at certain points in U.S. history. It's not hard to find links between the 1856 Know Nothings and political factions of other eras, including the 2016 Trump Republicans. In both cases there were voters who believed immigrants were taking American jobs and driving up the crime rate and who desired to return the nation to a previous age of perceived purity or greatness.

Ultimately, all this ferment led to a political realignment, as the Democrats splintered, the Whigs collapsed, and a new Republican Party arose. The extent of this realignment wouldn't be clear until after 1860, but the signs of change were evident.

The Democrats remained the party of the common man, limited government, and states' rights, but the party's strength in the South caused it to become increasingly proslavery. Even Northern Democrats defended slavery, whether or not they supported the practice, through such compromises as popular sovereignty.

The Republicans, on the other hand, wanted to stop the expansion of slavery. They were also successors to the Whigs and Federalists in believing that government should play an active role in economic development. This was the later impetus for the Homestead Act to provide land to settlers, and the Agricultural College Act to assist states in establishing institutes of higher education. As Lincoln would remark, the goal was "to allow the humblest man an equal chance to get rich with everybody else."[122]

And yes, some of these policies seem topsy-turvy compared to the present-day stances of the parties, as Democrats are now more activist and Republicans favor limited government. We'll explore this more in another chapter, but it was the changes wrought by industrialization that eventually moved the parties closer to the positions we recognize today.

In any case, the nation's politics were clearly morphing into something new. As Buchanan took office, the only certainty was that the Whigs had fragmented. Beyond that, there was an antislavery Republican Party that drew strength from the North, a Democratic Party trying to hold together its sectional factions, and a nativist Know Nothing movement that was most passionate about American nationalism. How it would all shake out was anyone's guess.

3

★ ★ ★

1860-92

The Civil War and Its Aftermath

Coffee at Café du Monde in New Orleans, Louisiana

The Civil War frames the next era of presidential history. The conflict left physical and emotional scars on the nation, killed more than six hundred thousand people, incited the first presidential assassination, and shaped national politics for decades.

The bloodiest single day of the war was September 17, 1862, at Antietam Battlefield in Maryland, with more than 22,000 casualties, including 3,650 dead. It was a critical battle because Confederate troops were thwarted in an attempt to invade Union territory, and the outcome persuaded President Lincoln to issue the Emancipation Proclamation, freeing Confederate slaves. It's a lot of history for one battle, and yet a prominent monument at Antietam is dedicated, interestingly, to none of the above but rather to a nineteen-year-old Ohio soldier who was praised for serving hot coffee and warm food to his troops.

Coffee was a big deal for soldiers in the Civil War. They often brewed it themselves over fires, and it's been said that coffee "was often the last comfort troops enjoyed before entering battle, and the first sign of safety for those who survived."[1] That afternoon at Antietam, a young commissary sergeant behind the front lines knew that his troops had been engaged in fierce battle since early morning without food or water. So he loaded food and gallons of coffee onto wagons, then steered the horse-drawn carriages toward the fighting, ignoring two orders to turn back. He pressed forward through a field bursting with artillery fire and survived a cannonball hitting his wagon before reaching the Twenty-Third Ohio regiment. There, he served coffee and meat to the exhausted troops, prompting cheers from his fellow soldiers.[2]

After the war, the story of his bravery was repeated often as he ran for office, won election to Congress, and became governor of Ohio. In 1896, thirty-four years after the Battle of Antietam, former commissary sergeant William McKinley was elected president of the United States. He was the last Civil War veteran to be president.

It's an intriguing tale at the intersection of presidential politics, the Civil War, and coffee. Understandably, though, there aren't any historic cafés near the McKinley Monument. But the very same year as the Battle of Antietam a notable coffee shop did open in Confederate territory, in New Orleans, and has been in business ever since. That makes Café du Monde an appropriate setting in which to consider the next political era.

The coffee shop in the New Orleans French Market is a well-known tourist haunt these days, but it originally catered to workers who passed their days at gritty wharves along the Mississippi River. The early 1860s was an unusual time to launch such a venture because a Union blockade of New Orleans meant coffee was scarce. To stretch supplies, residents would mix coffee with roasted chicory root. As fate would have it, locals took a liking to the brew and it became a tradition. And today Café du Monde is not only still around, but still sells chicory coffee with its beignets.

The café has had a front-row seat to much history, starting with the Civil War. For the first few years of Café du Monde's existence, New Orleans was under Union occupation, while northern Louisiana remained Confederate. Then, during Reconstruction, New Orleans and other Louisiana towns experienced their fair share of postwar violence. In 1866 the New Orleans Massacre happened just minutes from Café du Monde. It left as many as 48 people dead, mostly Blacks who were attending a constitutional convention to promote voting rights. Seven years later, in 1873, African Americans defending the Colfax courthouse were attacked by a mob, and up to 150 were killed.

These tensions spilled into the political arena, most prominently during the 1876 presidential election, when Louisiana was one of three Southern states to submit dueling electoral results. This blocked any candidate from claiming victory and threw the contest into chaos for months before Republican Rutherford B. Hayes was declared the winner.

The Civil War, Reconstruction, and a divisive 1876 election. These are three of the seminal events of the 1860–92 era, and Café du Monde was surely the backdrop for many an impassioned conversation during this era of raw feelings, which makes it a suitable setting from which to consider our next political era.

1860 and 1864: Abraham Lincoln and the Civil War

1860

If we were to make a list of the most momentous presidential campaigns in history, it would be hard to lead off with anything other than the election of 1860. This is the year that American politics finally fractured after decades of disagreements and discord over slavery.

When James Buchanan entered the White House in 1857, he believed he might go down in history as the leader who ended the nation's bitter divide. Instead he limped out of town four years later with the country on the verge of civil war. Perhaps no president could have managed the schisms of the era, but Buchanan's tenure spiraled out of control almost immediately. As he prepared to take office, he knew a Supreme Court ruling was imminent in the *Dred Scott* case, in which a slave was suing for freedom because his owner had taken him to free states in the North, so Buchanan predicted in his inaugural address that the justices would soon settle the country's "long agitation" over slavery.[3]

But when the court's decision was announced two days later, it settled nothing. In fact, it inflamed tensions because the justices not only ruled against Scott, but they also asserted that Blacks weren't citizens and that Congress couldn't ban slavery in new territories. The ruling even declared, somewhat astonishingly, that Blacks were "so far inferior that they had no rights which the white man was bound to respect." The decision infuriated Northerners, intensified the slavery debate in the territories, and had a fateful impact on presidential politics.

In part, this was because the "Bleeding Kansas" controversy was still raging, and settlers there had formed dueling antislavery and proslavery governments in anticipation of statehood. Buchanan endorsed the proslavery government, leaning on the court's ruling that slavery couldn't be prohibited in the West. But Illinois senator Stephen Douglas, an advocate for popular sovereignty, dissented after thousands of Missourians crossed the border to illegally vote in favor of the proslavery Kansas constitution.[4] Douglas was instrumental in convincing Congress to reject the proslavery government, a move that would soon prove costly to his presidential hopes.

This dispute lingered into the 1860 election. When the Democratic convention opened in Charleston, South Carolina, in April, Douglas had support from a majority of delegates but had to contend with Southerners who were incensed at him because of the Kansas dispute. So when Douglas refused to accept a proslavery platform, scores of Southerners walked out, depriving him of the two-thirds majority he needed to win the nomination. After fifty-seven ballots, the delegates gave up and adjourned. The convention reconvened in June in Baltimore, but Southerners again left in protest. This time, the exasperated remaining delegates nominated Douglas. The Southerners then staged a third Democratic convention, also in Baltimore, and nominated Vice President John Breckenridge of Kentucky, leaving the party split between Northern and Southern factions.[5]

With Democrats in disarray, the Republicans convened in Chicago in May. In this case, Senator William Seward of New York was the favorite, but some party members feared his extreme anti-slavery reputation would hurt him in swing states, which left the door cracked open for another candidate to emerge.

Abraham Lincoln wasn't the most prominent contender, but he'd gained renown during the 1858 Lincoln-Douglas debates and had electrified a New York audience earlier in 1860 with a speech at Cooper Union in which he famously declared, "Let us have faith that right makes might." Reprints of that speech sent his reputation soaring. Still, Lincoln's only national experience consisted of a single term in Congress, and he'd lost his last Senate race, so he didn't have the stature of more experienced candidates.

Lincoln's campaign team thus labored mightily to keep Seward from winning on the first ballot and to make Lincoln everyone's favorite second choice. They even forged thousands of convention tickets so Lincoln supporters could crowd the hall. One observer said the shouting for Lincoln was so loud that "a thousand steam whistles, ten acres of hotel gongs, and a tribe of Comanches might have mingled in the scene unnoticed."[6]

Seward led the early voting, but when he failed to garner a majority the convention turned to Lincoln on the third ballot. Delegates thought Lincoln's geographic base would give him a better chance of winning the crucial swing states of Illinois, Indiana, and Pennsylvania, where Frémont had faltered four years earlier. Still, it's hard to imagine today how much of a surprise Lincoln's nomination was to many observers at the time. The *New York Herald* complained that Republicans had passed over a statesman for a "fourth-rate lecturer."[7] And when word reached Washington, politicians reacted with "incredulity." The House was in "such a state of confusion" at the news that it adjourned for the day.[8]

In the meantime, another party also emerged. The Constitutional Union Party was founded by former Know Nothings and Whigs who were neutral on slavery and dedicated to preserving the Union above all else. It's not that other parties *didn't* want to keep the country intact, but what set the Unionists apart was their reluctance to take any position on slavery, seeing it as a distraction. The party nominated former senator John Bell of Tennessee for president. The Unionists thought they could force the election into the House, where Bell would emerge as the most acceptable candidate.[9]

So the 1860 campaign kicked into gear with four contenders. Soon thereafter, Douglas became the first candidate to embark on a national speaking tour. Harrison had delivered some talks two decades earlier, but it was far from a nationwide endeavor. Douglas, on the other hand, who was known as the Little Giant because he was only 5'4", made speechmaking a feature of his campaign. The strategy was still considered demeaning for a potential president, but Douglas saw it as his only chance of winning, given the factures in his party.

To his credit, when Douglas heard in October of Republican success in state elections in Pennsylvania and Indiana, he saw the writing on the wall and set a new goal of trying to head off the threat of Southern secession. "Mr. Lincoln is the next president," Douglas said to advisors. "We must try to save the Union." He remained in the race but turned his speaking tour to the South and, in the face of hostile crowds and death threats, tried to convince voters to abide by the democratic process no matter who won the presidency. Lincoln's election, he said, would not be "justification for breaking up this government."[10]

Others weren't so gracious about Lincoln's candidacy. Although he won the nomination partly because his rhetoric on slavery was less extreme than Seward's, this helped him only in swing states. Southerners, on the other hand, whipped up fears about "black Republicans" who would force white girls to marry Black men or encourage slaves to murder their owners.[11] Lincoln was compared to a monkey and lampooned as "Old Ape."[12] One writer said the South would "never submit to such humiliation and degradation as the inauguration of Abraham Lincoln."[13]

One political cartoon showed Lincoln being carried into a lunatic asylum, followed by supporters asking him to give more rights to Blacks and women at the expense of white men and to provide aid to poor people even if they didn't want to work.[14] The attacks are uncannily familiar, except that today similar charges are leveled against Democrats, showing that while the parties have changed, certain issues and tactics have withstood the test of time.

The Republicans, meanwhile, strived to make the election about more than slavery. They targeted key constituent groups with support for a transcontinental railroad, the Homestead Act, and a tariff. They also fostered an image of "Honest Abe," a president who would reform government. But the real flair of the Republican campaign was in branding Lincoln as "the Rail Splitter," playing up his identity as a self-made man of the West who'd built many a split-rail fence in his day.

Republicans were also bolstered by the emergence of the Wide Awakes, groups of young men who helped with campaign activities and organized torchlit parades for Lincoln. They wore black capes, carried banners, and sang songs. There were more than four hundred thousand members nationwide, one of the first instances of youthful energy being harnessed for a presidential election. It was such a phenomenon that other contenders formed copycat groups, like the Little Giants and Bell Ringers, but with less success.[15]

Lincoln also received an unexpected boost in 1860 from a simple photograph. The craft of photography was still relatively new, but when he was in New York for his Cooper Union speech he posed for Mathew Brady, the country's most prominent photographer, who was famous for his portraits of public figures and later for battlefield photos of the Civil War. The photo showed him in a dignified pose, belying the stereotype of him as an unsophisticated westerner, and it later appeared on campaign pins, on prints sold by Currier & Ives, and as an engraving for a campaign biography. Lincoln later remarked, "Brady and the Cooper Union speech made me president."[16]

Despite these bursts of enthusiasm for Lincoln, the race went down to the wire. As expected, Lincoln was strongest in the North, Breckenridge in the South, and Bell and Douglas in the border states. Lincoln won 40 percent of the national vote to 29 percent for Douglas, 18 percent for Breckenridge, and 13 percent for Bell. In the Electoral College, Lincoln prevailed with 180 votes to 72 for Breckenridge and 51 combined for Bell and Douglas. A narrow victory in New York put Lincoln over the top, otherwise the election would have gone to the House and history might well have turned out differently.

So Lincoln became president, with Hannibal Hamlin of Maine as vice president. In response, the South followed through on its secession threat. By February 1 seven states had formed the Confederate States of America. Buchanan, who was still president, denied the South had a constitutional right to secede. Paradoxically, he also concluded that he couldn't stop a state from seceding since presidents were empowered only to execute laws. This muddled response brought scorn from all sides. "Oh, for one hour of Jackson!" pleaded an Illinois newspaper, alluding to the former president's show of resolve against South Carolina's secession threat in 1832. Various compromises were floated, but none gained traction, and Buchanan limped through the end of his term. On some days the mental strain left him unable to get out of bed.[17]

As the country splintered, Lincoln prepared to take office in the face of numerous threats on his life. For his March 4 inauguration, soldiers lined the streets and sharpshooters were positioned on nearby rooftops. Amid this tense atmosphere, with the nation on edge and the future uncertain, Lincoln took the oath of office as the sixteenth president.

1864

In Lincoln's 1861 inaugural address, he assured the South he had no plans, or even the constitutional power, to interfere with slavery where it existed. "In your hands," he told Southerners, "is the momentous issue of civil war. . . . You can have no conflict without being yourselves the aggressors."[18] One month later, on April 12, Confederate troops fired the first shots of the Civil War on Fort Sumter in South Carolina.

At the start, few Americans imagined the conflict would last as long and be as destructive as it turned out. Soon enough, though, reality set in. The Union and Confederate armies settled into a bloody stand-off, and casualties mounted on an unprecedented scale. Lincoln claimed new powers as a wartime executive, expanding the military and blockading Southern ports without congressional approval. More controversially, he arrested suspected Confederate sympathizers and suspended habeas corpus, partly to prevent Maryland from seceding, which would have left the capital trapped in Confederate territory.

In 1862 Lincoln issued the Emancipation Proclamation. On September 22, acting with emergency powers as commander in chief, he declared slaves in Confederate territory free as of January 1, 1863. The act was so momentous that some believed Lincoln wouldn't follow through. When the new year dawned, people gathered by the thousands to await word at telegraph offices. After Lincoln's signing of the Proclamation was announced, celebrations erupted across the North. "Slavery from this hour ceases to be a political power in the country," shouted the *Boston Daily Evening Transcript*.[19]

Later that year, on November 19, Lincoln delivered the Gettysburg Address while consecrating a wartime cemetery. His brief, 272-word speech suggested a meaning for the Civil War beyond a desire to preserve the Union. Calling for a "new birth of freedom," Lincoln portrayed the conflict as a battle to defend the very idea of popular government and to ensure the nation lived up to its own Declaration of Independence.[20]

Looking back from today, these achievements seem to raise Lincoln's presidency to great heights. Not only the Emancipation Proclamation and Gettysburg Address but also legislation for the transcontinental railroad, the Homestead Act, land-grant universities, and more, a record that's been compared to the Washington and FDR presidencies.[21] At the time, however, Lincoln was criticized from every side. There were Peace Democrats who wanted him to negotiate with the South even if it meant preserving slavery or letting go of the Confederacy, as well as Radical Republicans within his own party who fumed that he was too timid in trying to end slavery. As one historian noted, "Conservatives thought him a radical and liberals thought him a failure."[22]

By early 1864, with war fatigue blanketing the nation, even

moderate Republicans were in despair over the president's prospects for reelection. "Mr. Lincoln is already beaten," wrote Horace Greeley, editor of the *New York Tribune*. "He cannot be elected. And we must have another ticket to save us from utter overthrow."[23] Some Republicans called for a stronger nominee, perhaps Treasury Secretary Salmon Chase or Gen. Ulysses S. Grant. Incredibly, the man who today is lionized as possibly our greatest president was opposed in 1864 by members of his own party who thought he was a weak candidate for reelection.

In the end, Lincoln rounded up enough support to secure the nomination. Republicans then rebranded themselves as the National Union Party and replaced Vice President Hamlin with Andrew Johnson, a Southern Democratic senator who'd stayed loyal to the Union and was now military governor of Tennessee. These moves were meant to bolster Lincoln's message of resolve and attract War Democrats, those who opposed many of Lincoln's policies and were content to let slavery continue but who were concerned with keeping the Union together. Even while trying to attract some Democrats, however, the GOP struggled to maintain intraparty unity, as the Radical Republican faction called a separate convention to nominate John Frémont, the party's 1856 candidate and a favorite of abolitionists.

The Democrats then put forth Gen. George McClellan, a popular military leader who'd been fired by Lincoln. Just as the Republicans were divided, though, so were the Democrats, torn between their war and peace wings. McClellan was a War Democrat, but the party platform, curiously, had been written for Peace Democrats. The *New York Herald* compared the party to "a stork by a frog pond" that didn't know what leg "to rest upon."[24] What held most Democrats together was an aversion to Lincoln, a preference for limited government, and a distaste for fighting a war to emancipate slaves.

In the campaign, Republicans mocked McClellan's military record and warned that a vote for the Democrat would undo all the sacrifice of the war. The Peace Democrats were especially scorned. They were dubbed "copperheads," after the snake, described by one newspaper as "venomous enemies of our government."[25]

THE CIVIL WAR AND ITS AFTERMATH

From the other side, President Lincoln was attacked for incompetence. One writer characterized the Republican ticket as "two ignorant, boorish, third-rate backwoods lawyers." Lincoln was disparaged as "Abraham Africanus," who had issued the commandment "Thou shalt have no other God but the negro."[26]

The contest was also enlivened by a pamphlet titled *Miscegenation*. This was a new word coined to mean "race-mixing," and the booklet declared that the white and Black races should be deliberately blended. It was widely publicized, and Democrats were soon conjuring fears about the race-mixing that would inevitably follow a Republican victory. It turned out, though, that the pamphlet was a hoax invented by journalists for a partisan newspaper to scare voters away from Lincoln.[27]

For much of the summer, many observers expected Democrats to win the presidency.[28] The Republican operative Thurlow Weed told Lincoln his reelection was "an impossibility" because voters were "wild for peace."[29] In the Confederacy, the *Richmond Examiner* gloated, "The obscene ape of Illinois is about to be deposed."[30] Lincoln himself believed he'd lose to McClellan, but he disregarded those who suggested postponing the vote because of the war. The election, he later said, was "a necessity" because the country could not "have free government without elections."[31] In August, in fact, he wrote and sealed a letter in which he pledged that after his defeat he would cooperate with the incoming president and continue working to "save the Union between the election and the inauguration."[32]

But as summer turned to fall, Lincoln's fortunes improved. On September 2 Gen. William Tecumseh Sherman's capture of Atlanta split the Confederacy at a strategic point, while General Grant was aggressively attacking the Confederate Army in Virginia. With Union forces in sight of victory, Frémont withdrew from the race on September 22, unwilling to risk splitting the Republican vote and electing a Democrat who might preserve slavery.

The stars aligned for Lincoln just in time for election day and he rolled to another victory, winning 55 percent of the vote and 221 of 233 electoral votes in the Union states that participated.

Between his election and inauguration, Lincoln worked assiduously to collect votes for the Thirteenth Amendment, abolishing slavery. It passed Congress, barely, when five Democrats voted with Republicans, and was later ratified by the states. Lincoln was delighted; now no future president could restore slavery or reverse the Emancipation Proclamation.

President Lincoln gave what is widely considered his greatest speech, the Second Inaugural Address, on March 4, 1865. He suggested the Civil War was, in a sense, punishment for the nation's shared sin of slavery. He pleaded with the country to come together in the aftermath of the conflict, "with malice for none; with charity for all . . . to bind up the nation's wounds."[33]

On April 9 Gen. Robert E. Lee surrendered the Confederate Army to General Grant at Appomattox Court House in Virginia. The war was over. It had begun one month after Lincoln's first inauguration, and it ended one month after his second.

Then, on April 14, five days after Lee's surrender, Lincoln went to see the play *Our American Cousin* at Ford's Theatre in Washington. During the performance, the actor John Wilkes Booth, a Southern sympathizer, walked into the presidential box and shot Lincoln in the back of the head. The president died the next morning, the country's first victim of an assassination. As the nation reeled from the shock, the newly elected vice president, Andrew Johnson, was thrust into the presidency.

Northerners and Southerners, Republicans and Democrats

The Civil War era reshaped American politics. Out of this fragmented political landscape, the Republicans and Democrats emerged as the country's leading parties, a status they still hold today. Each party was dominant in one region, with Republicans initially controlling the North and Democrats the South. The adversaries thus continued to face off against each other, but in presidential campaigns rather than war. It's not that North and South had ever seen eye-to-eye, of course. They'd split over many issues, from the War of 1812 to the annexation of Texas, but the sectional divide had intensified over slavery and the Civil War.

When the Confederacy was founded, Vice President Alexander Stephens declared that the new government was based on "the great truth that the negro is not equal to the white man; that slavery—subordination to the superior race—is his natural and normal condition."[34]

Northerners, however, had a different take. It's not that they saw Blacks as socially equal to whites, but they believed African Americans were at least equally entitled to freedom. That's why they often reacted with anguish when confronted with slavery, such as when William Seward and his wife cut short a trip to the South because of what they saw there. One day, they came across ten young Black boys tied together and being lashed as they walked. The boys, who were between six and twelve years of age, were sobbing. They'd been purchased that day from various plantations and had just been ripped from their families and were on their way to be sold at auction.[35]

"If the negro is a man," asked Lincoln, "is it not . . . a total destruction of self-government, to say that he too shall not govern himself?"[36] This was the crux of the debate: Were slaves mere property, or were they human beings with natural rights?

The dueling perspectives were unbridgeable, which is why Southerners advocated for the regions to separate. Instead, war broke out. What's sometimes overlooked is that the conflict wasn't fought specifically over slavery, even though slaves were later emancipated. And it wasn't about states' rights either, at least not in the way it's described nowadays. Rather, it was about whether the United States was an indissoluble nation or a league of states. The South took the latter view, which made secession acceptable, while Republicans in the North insisted on the permanence of the Union. The outcome of the war, it's been said, is what finally made the United States a nation.[37]

What the war didn't do, however, was resolve political and cultural differences between North and South. The party loyalties that were cemented during this era persisted for decades. As one writer later recalled about his youth in Ohio, "The Republican Party was not a faction, not a group, not a wing, it was an institution. . . . It was inconceivable that any self-respecting person should be a Democrat." Southerners felt the same way, with the identities reversed.[38] The parties swapped geographic bases after the civil rights struggles of the 1960s, but in many ways this North-South divide remains a prominent feature of American politics.

1868, 1872, and 1876: Ulysses S. Grant and Reconstruction

1868

In the aftermath of the Civil War, Americans were bitterly divided over postwar Reconstruction. The economy and infrastructure of the South had been destroyed, federal troops remained in the region, millions of former slaves had to try establishing a livelihood while living among their former masters, and Congress was debating how to reintegrate the Confederacy into the Union.

Lincoln had recommended that former Confederate states be treated leniently. "We must extinguish our resentment if we expect harmony and union," he said.[39] He also voiced the belief that at least some Blacks should have the right to vote because "the ballot will be their only protection after the bayonet is gone."[40] But after Lincoln's death the job of governing postwar America fell to Andrew Johnson, and while the new president agreed the Confederacy should be treated mercifully, he didn't concur with Lincoln's belief in giving new rights to former slaves. That's because Johnson was, at heart, a white supremacist who saw Blacks as inferior.

"White men alone must manage the South," Johnson declared, arguing that Blacks had "less capacity for government than any other race of people. . . . Left to their own devices they have shown a constant tendency to relapse into barbarism."[41]

The new president soon vetoed a Civil Rights Act, rescinded an effort to provide former slaves with farmland, and opposed the Fourteenth Amendment providing equal protection rights. Johnson maintained the federal government couldn't dictate such policies to the states. The Republicans still managed to pass legislation by overriding Johnson's vetoes, but the president's situation began resembling that of John Tyler's in the 1840s. Johnson had been a Southern Democrat before running on a unity ticket with Lincoln, and now he found himself, quite by accident, leading the Republican Party and at loggerheads with its leaders.

The debate over Reconstruction intensified when Southern states passed a series of Black Codes that kept former slaves as close to bondage as possible without actually being enslaved. African Americans were forced to sign contracts to work on plantations or in mills, were subject to arrest if they couldn't prove employment, and could be whipped if they exhibited signs of defiance. This is also when the Ku Klux Klan was founded, resulting in a wave of terrorist attacks to frighten, intimidate, or murder Blacks.

Congressional Republicans responded by dividing the South into military districts under federal control. They also passed the Tenure of Office Act, which was designed almost solely to prevent Johnson from firing cabinet members who favored congressional policies. So when Johnson fired Secretary of War Edwin Stanton anyway, Republicans began impeachment proceedings. They'd been eager to find a reason to remove the president, who infuriated many with his vetoes, his confrontational style, and his bias in favor of white Southerners.

The House voted to impeach Johnson in February 1868, after which a trial was held in the Senate. With fifty-four senators, thirty-six votes were needed to convict the president. There were forty-two Republicans, but seven of them voted with all twelve Democrats for acquittal because they feared that impeachment for partisan reasons would weaken and degrade the presidency itself.[42] So Congress fell one vote short of the two-thirds majority needed to remove Johnson from office.

When it was time to choose a presidential candidate for 1868, the Republicans, to the surprise of no one, passed over Johnson for Gen. Ulysses S. Grant, the Union hero of the Civil War. Grant exhibited little interest in the job but was nominated by acclamation at the Republican convention. "I have been forced into it in spite of myself," he told General Sherman. If he didn't accept the nomination and a Democrat won the presidency, Grant said, the nation would lose "the results of the costly war which we have gone through."[43]

Grant had no experience in government, aside from a five-month stint as acting secretary of war. Although his Civil War feats brought him national fame, he had actually risen quite dramatically from near obscurity. He had a solid reputation as a young officer during the Mexican-American War but left the army in 1854, bored by military life during peacetime. Grant's life floundered afterward. He struggled to make a living and went to work in his father's leather goods shop. When the Civil War broke out, he returned to the military with the Illinois militia. With his talent as a battlefield tactician and strengths as a leader, he quickly rose through the ranks.[44] In three years he went from working as a store clerk to being commanding general of the U.S. Army. Four years after that, he was the Republican nominee for president.

The Democrats had thought about making Johnson their own nominee in 1868, but he never rose above second place over twenty-three ballots at the party convention. Delegates instead nominated New York governor Horatio Seymour. Amazingly, Seymour didn't want to run for president either. "Pity me!" he said to a friend after failing to convince delegates to remove his name from consideration. Seymour finally accepted the nomination, while gaining the nickname "The Great Decliner."[45]

It would be unimaginable today for a political party to nominate a candidate who wasn't eager for the office, but nineteenth-century elections were different affairs. In most cases, candidates and their supporters did maneuver to win the nomination, but there were no active campaigns, no party primaries, no speechmaking. Decisions were left to delegates at each convention, and occasionally they turned to someone who hadn't angled for the job. Although neither Grant nor Seymour had a burning desire to be president, each felt duty-bound to run for the office once nominated.

During the fall campaign, there was the usual politicking and sniping on both sides. Democrats attacked General Grant for allegedly being a drunk and the father of an illegitimate child with an Indian woman.[46] Republicans also started a long practice of blaming Democrats for the Civil War. "Scratch a Democrat and you'll find a rebel under his skin," observed the *New York Tribune*.[47]

The most important words of the campaign, however, were written by Grant in his letter accepting the Republican nomination: "Let us have peace."[48] For a nation that was exhausted from war, Reconstruction battles, a presidential assassination, and an impeachment trial, peace sounded like a pretty fine goal to most voters. Grant prevailed easily, 53 to 47 percent in the popular vote and 214–80 in the Electoral College, winning twenty-six of thirty-four states.

1872

Peace may have been what the nation longed for, but it's not entirely what they got during President's Grant's first term. Wounds from the Civil War were still raw, and the debate over Reconstruction remained acrimonious.

In response to continued violence against Blacks in the South, Grant convinced Congress to pass the Enforcement Acts and the Ku Klux Klan Act, giving the government the authority to protect elections and civil rights. The president then acted to protect former slaves by arresting hundreds of Klansmen, which Southerners condemned as a violation of states' rights. What was more surprising was that Grant's policies were also opposed by some Northern Liberal Republicans. But after nearly a decade of conflict, these Republicans were exhausted by war issues and were eager to move on to new concerns.

One of these concerns was a desire to reform civil service laws after an array of scandals erupted during the Grant administration. The president himself was considered honest, but political patronage was an issue, and some of Grant's appointees were implicated for profiting from their positions in scandals dubbed the Whiskey Ring and the New York Custom House Ring. The term "Grantism" was coined to describe corruption and cronyism in government.

The movement to reform government was so important to Liberal Republicans that they opposed Grant's reelection in 1872. The president was supported by most of his party and was easily nominated for a second term, but Liberal Republicans convened their own convention to select a different nominee. Unexpectedly, they settled on Horace Greeley, editor of the *New York Tribune*. Greeley was well known nationally for his writings on politics, but his entire political experience involved a three-month interim term in Congress. He also had a quirky personality and eclectic interests, encompassing spiritualism, temperance, socialism, vegetarianism, and utopian communities. He would have been an unusual nominee even today, never mind in the nineteenth century.

This intraparty dispute among Republicans became a bigger threat to Grant when Democrats, lacking any obvious candidate of their own, also latched onto Greeley as their nominee. This was similar to how Federalists joined with a breakaway group of Democratic-Republicans in 1812 to oppose James Madison over the war with Britain. Still, this was an odd marriage of convenience because the abolitionist Greeley had for many years criticized Democrats for their policies, especially regarding slavery. The two factions shared little except a desire to defeat Grant and to implement more lenient Reconstruction programs.

The election was also notable for another distinctive nominee, as the Equal Rights Party put forth Victoria Woodhull for president. Women didn't have the right to vote yet, of course, but the party comprised an eclectic group of activists who were eager to shake up the system. They also nominated the African American Frederick Douglass for vice president. Douglass, a Grant supporter, never accepted the nomination, but it's striking that any political party during this era would even contemplate a ticket led by a woman and an African American. The party was ahead of its time in other ways as well, with a platform that called for labor laws, a graduated tax system, and an end to capital punishment.[49]

Woodhull herself was a fascinating personality. A thirty-four-year-old activist for women's rights, she was the country's first female stockbroker, a newspaper publisher, a spiritualist, and an outspoken advocate for free love, or experimentation with non-monogamous relationships.[50] It's too bad there were no candidate debates back then, because Woodhull and Greeley would have made for a tantalizing show.

The Equal Rights Party, unsurprisingly given the times, had

no impact on the election. Woodhull even spent Election Day in prison after publishing an article about adulterous affairs allegedly committed by the preacher Henry Ward Beecher. She approved of the affairs because of her belief in free love but condemned Beecher for hypocrisy. The article, however, led to her arrest for sending supposedly obscene publications through the mail. She was acquitted but spent several weeks in jail awaiting trial. The woman's suffragist Susan B. Anthony was also arrested that year, though in her case it was for voting illegally.

In the campaign between the major party candidates, President Grant was accused of being dictatorial and corrupt, and he faced a recycled charge from 1868 for supposedly being a drunk. But by this point Grant was a known entity, whether or not people agreed with his politics, and it was Greeley who faced the brunt of the attacks. Despite the editor's evident intelligence, he was portrayed by Republicans as a "scatter-brained incompetent."[51] He was also pilloried for his comment that North and South should "clasp their hands across the bloody chasm." It was meant as a postwar gesture of reconciliation, but the cartoonist Thomas Nast contorted the meaning and produced a series of images ridiculing Greeley for his words, such as one that showed the candidate reaching out to John Wilkes Booth across Lincoln's grave.[52]

Greeley probably never had a chance against the still popular Grant, but the attacks took their toll. Grant trounced Greeley 56 to 44 percent in the popular vote and 286–66 in the Electoral College. By the time the campaign was over, Greeley was exhausted from the strain, humiliated over how he'd been portrayed, and devastated by the death of his wife just before the election. He collapsed and died three weeks later. As a result, most of his electoral votes were later cast for other candidates.

1876

The 1876 election coincided with the centennial year celebration of the nation's independence. It seemed a perfect time to salute American democracy, but the country instead became embroiled in the biggest electoral controversy in its history, one that's been called "the last battle of the Civil War."[53]

When the campaign began, voters were still reeling from continued fights over Reconstruction, were weary of the government scandals of the past eight years, and were distressed by the Panic of 1873, a depression that bankrupted thousands of businesses and sent the unemployment rate soaring. The governing Republicans were understandably held responsible for all three issues, so the time appeared ripe for Democrats to prevail in a presidential race for the first time in twenty years.

The Democrats chose Governor Samuel Tilden of New York as their nominee. A political reformer who'd made his name breaking up the corrupt Tweed Ring and Canal Ring in New York, Tilden was an easy choice for Democrats who wanted to present the image of a party that could cleanse government.

On the Republican side, the favorite was a former Speaker of the House and now senator James G. Blaine of Maine, a popular candidate who was hailed as a "plumed knight."[54] But Blaine's involvement in a scandal over special treatment for railroad companies hurt him in a year when government corruption was a key issue. Despite leading on the first ballot at the convention, Blaine couldn't muster a majority. So on the seventh ballot, Republicans turned to Governor Rutherford B. Hayes of Ohio. Hayes was a less exciting choice, but he was respected, intelligent, and, most important, free of any whiff of scandal.

The Democrats campaigned hard on the issues of economic hard times and government scandals. "Tilden and Reform!" they shouted.[55] And they sang:

> Sam Tilden is a gentleman,
> A true and honest man, sir;
> And when we call for honest work
> He's just the chap to answer.[56]

It was difficult for Democrats to portray the upstanding Hayes as corrupt, so they tried to tie him to Grant-era scandals or flung other mud at him, such as a wild accusation that he'd stolen money from dead soldiers during the Civil War.

The Republicans, meanwhile, continued to harp on Democratic links to the Confederacy, which was a potent tool for the party during this era. As a popular slogan of the time put it: "Not every Democrat was a Rebel, but every Rebel was a Democrat."[57] Republicans reminded veterans to "vote as they shot."[58] They also claimed Tilden was not a genuine reformer. They called him "Slippery Sammy" and suggested he was guilty of tax evasion and of working as a lawyer for robber baron businessmen.[59]

When the campaign ended, a record 81.8 percent of voters had cast ballots, still the highest rate for any presidential election. Initially it seemed that voters' desire for change had won the day. Tilden prevailed in the popular vote by 51 to 48 percent and had a seemingly insurmountable lead in the Electoral College.

Before the election was officially called for Tilden, however, some GOP officials suggested that three Southern states with nineteen electoral votes had ambiguous results. If they could win these states, it would be just enough to put Hayes over the top, so on election night they telegrammed state officials: "Hayes is elected if we have carried South Carolina, Florida and Louisiana. Can you hold your state?"[60]

The next morning, to the surprise even of Hayes, who'd already accepted his loss, the headline in the *New York Times* announced "A Doubtful Election," with Tilden up 184–181 and Florida still uncalled. The Republican Party's national chairman went further, announcing to the press, "Hayes has 185 votes and is elected."[61]

The country was soon awash in controversy, with the vote count now being disputed in three states. Republicans controlled these state governments and used their power over election boards to invalidate thousands of Tilden votes. Their reasoning was that Southern Democrats had used violence and intimidation to prevent Blacks from voting. Democrats then pointed to separate reports of ballot box stuffing in favor of Republicans.[62]

With so many reports of voter suppression and fraud, the actual count was nearly impossible to unravel. Consequently both parties claimed victory and submitted dueling electoral results. There was also disagreement over the eligibility of one Hayes elector from Oregon. Thus, with twenty ballots in limbo, Tilden held an electoral lead of 184–165—excruciatingly, just one vote short of the 185 he needed for victory.

The one Oregon vote appeared to belong to Hayes, as the dispute was merely over whether an elector had submitted his resignation from a federal job in time. Many Democrats also conceded that Hayes had likely carried South Carolina.[63] But in Florida and Louisiana, apparent Tilden wins had been overturned. The election was in uncharted territory and appeared headed to Congress for a resolution. But disagreement reigned there, as well, because Democrats controlled the House and Republicans were in charge of the Senate. Constitutionally, the House was empowered to decide the winner if no candidate had an electoral majority, so Democrats asserted that body's right to conduct a presidential vote. On the other hand, since the Senate president had to first open electoral certificates for counting, Republicans claimed the power to determine the legitimacy of each state's ballot.

With seemingly no way out of this dilemma, a fifteen-member electoral commission was formed, five members each from the Senate, House, and Supreme Court. The congressional commissioners were divided 5–5 between Democrats and Republicans, but the justices were split 3–2 in favor of Republicans. The commission originally had one Supreme Court justice, David Davis, who was considered an independent. If everyone else voted along party lines, he would be the deciding vote. Davis, though, was soon thereafter elected to the Senate from Illinois and resigned his commission seat. He was replaced by a Republican, Joseph Bradley.

After studying the evidence, the commission ruled 8–7 along party lines in favor of Hayes in every state dispute, giving him a 185–184 win in the Electoral College. This triggered an eruption of rage among Democrats, which only grew when reports circulated that Justice Bradley had been planning to side with Democrats over the Florida vote but was convinced to change his mind at the last minute. Democrats were beside themselves, even though no evidence surfaced to prove this one way or another. Some talked of armed conflict, shouting, "Tilden or Blood!"[64] President Grant alerted troops to be prepared to move to Washington.[65] But Tilden refused to sanction further action. "I will never be a party to any course which will array my countrymen in civil war," he asserted.[66]

So Democrats gave up the fight. The decision was made easier for some by the Compromise of 1877, as Republicans reportedly agreed to withdraw troops from the South and effectively end Reconstruction. Southern Democrats were more willing to acquiesce in Hayes's election if it meant regaining control of their states. And Northern Democratic businessmen, it was said, were "more anxious for quiet than for Tilden."[67]

So Congress finally certified the electoral vote and declared Hayes the winner on March 2, three days before the inauguration. Even when it was over, Democrats remained convinced Hayes had been elected illegitimately. "A cheat is to sit in the seat of George Washington," cried the *New York Sun*.[68] The *Cincinnati Enquirer* called it the "fraud of the century."[69] And Tilden went into the history books as the only candidate to win more than 50 percent of the popular vote and still not be elected president.

The Legacy of Reconstruction

It's been said that the North remembers the Civil War, even today, as a series of battles that culminated in freeing the slaves and preserving the Union. In the South, though, the cultural memory is different. There the war is recalled as a sorrowful defeat, compounded by the sufferings of Reconstruction.[70] Part of the suffering, at the time, was rooted in being forced to accept freedom for former slaves, who were seen as "unfit for the usages of citizenship."[71]

Given these feelings, it's not surprising there was a backlash in the South to Reconstruction, or that this is when the Ku Klux Klan grew dramatically. Sadly the backlash took the form of random and brutal violence directed at African Americans, many of whom were lynched, shot, or burned to death. One official who went South to investigate reported seeing numerous Black corpses left hanging from trees or decomposing in ditches and on roadways.[72]

There were also mass murders of Blacks for various reasons. In New Orleans, up to forty-eight were massacred for meeting to discuss voting rights. In Memphis, fifty-one were killed and dozens of homes burned in a one-night frenzy of violence. And in Pine Bluff, Arkansas, a Black community was burned and twenty-four men, women, and children were lynched.[73] One man wrote to President Grant, pleading for help: "We are hunted and shot down as if we were wild beasts."[74]

White Southerners were dismayed to see Blacks being elected to office. By the early 1870s there were a half dozen Blacks in the House, and Hiram Rhodes Revels of Mississippi was the country's first African American senator. In response to this perceived take-over of their states, Southerners formed White Leagues to drive Republicans from office and to intimidate Blacks. Armed whites would disrupt political meetings and campaign events and force Black voters away from polling places, sometimes even chasing and killing them.[75] The intimidation succeeded, as the African American voting rate plummeted. "We've made up our minds," said one former slave, "to let politics alone till the time comes—if it ever does—when we can vote just as we please without risking our lives every time we go to the ballot box."[76]

Meanwhile, Northern voters had only perfunctory concern for Black civil rights, and by 1876 even those who truly cared were drained of willpower after years of violence and conflict. President Grant continued to push for action, but as one Republican remarked, "The truth is, our people are tired out with this worn-out cry of Southern outrages!"[77]

Although President Hayes was assured that the civil and voting rights of former slaves would be protected when he removed the last federal troops from the South, things didn't quite turn out that way. Southern states instead implemented Jim Crow laws that segregated the races and shut most Blacks out of American democracy for nearly another century. These actions were aided by Supreme Court decisions. Under the theory of strict constructionism, the court ruled that the Fifteenth Amendment didn't guarantee an absolute right to vote, that voting regulations were controlled by each state, and that the duty of protecting citizens from violence or terror could be enforced only by states. Most infamously, in *Plessy v. Ferguson* the court upheld racial segregation under the "separate but equal" doctrine, essentially sanctioning an "American apartheid."[78] "If one race be inferior to the other socially, the constitution of the United States cannot put them on the same plane," declared the court.[79]

Republicans did occasionally try to pass legislation to counter the effect of Jim Crow laws, such as the Lodge Bill of 1890, giving the government authority to oversee elections. But the bills inevitably failed or were filibustered by Southern Democrats, so Republicans just stopped trying. It wasn't until the 1950s that the "separate but equal" doctrine was overturned, and not until the 1960s before the Voting Rights Act guaranteed suffrage to all Blacks. Even then, as we'll see, there was yet another backlash, just as there was to the 2008 election of the first African American president.

That, in fact, may be the real legacy of how Reconstruction played out: as a series of backlashes that have, in different ways, washed up on the shores of American politics ever since.

1880, 1884, 1888, and 1892: Presidential Standoffs during the Gilded Age

1880

After the controversial election of 1876, President Hayes was hounded for the next four years by taunts of "Rutherfraud" and "His Fraudulency."[80] But by most accounts, Hayes ran a dignified, scandal-free administration. His actions in ending Reconstruction haven't fared well in the history books, though he may not have had a choice given the compromise that helped resolve his electoral victory. It's unknown whether he could have won a second term, as he'd promised not to run for reelection and he stuck to that pledge in 1880.

Hayes's biggest contribution to the politics of his time was an effort to enact civil service reform, in response to concerns about corruption. The issue, however, provoked heated divisions even within his own party. And, through a circuitous turn of events, these divisions ended up impacting the 1880 Republican nominating contest and led, indirectly and bizarrely, to the assassination of the next president.

The cause of all this was the patronage system that then dominated American politics. The winners of national elections gained control of tens of thousands of government jobs to hand out to party supporters, a benefit known as the spoils system, after the phrase "To the victor belong the spoils." The quote dates to the Jacksonian period, but the practice reached its zenith in the post–Civil War years.

By the 1880s, though, with the Gilded Age in full bloom, many were becoming convinced that civil service jobs should be awarded not through patronage but via a merit-based system. Hayes supported the idea, even if this didn't endear him to certain leaders in his own party, who were already perturbed over his appointments to some important patronage positions.[81] Most significant was when Hayes replaced the collector of the New York Customs House, a man named Chester Arthur. This infuriated New York senator Roscoe Conkling, leader of the Republican Stalwarts, who were known for their "stalwart" defense of party traditions, including the patronage system.[82]

In 1880, with Hayes not running for reelection, the Stalwarts endorsed Ulysses Grant for an unprecedented third term as president. Grant had recently returned home to renewed popularity after a two-year trip around the world, during which he was feted by kings, queens, and emperors from London to Cairo and Tokyo. The Stalwarts saw Grant as a strong leader able to deal with a still recalcitrant South, but also as someone who wouldn't interfere with the party's patronage inclinations.[83]

This caused a Republican rift, as not everyone favored another term for Grant and some feared being tarred with old corruption scandals from his time in office. This faction was known as the Half-Breeds because they were said to be half-loyal to Grant and half-loyal to the idea of government reform.[84] They preferred the popular senator James Blaine, who'd just missed the nomination in 1876.

The party was still divided when the Republican convention opened in June in Chicago. On the first ballot, Grant garnered 304 votes to 284 for Blaine, with 379 needed for nomination. When the vote count barely budged for the next thirty-three ballots, it became obvious that neither Grant nor Blaine would ever gain a majority. On the thirty-fourth ballot, in an attempt to break the deadlock, the Wisconsin delegation surprised the convention by shifting 16 votes to Representative James Garfield of Ohio.

Garfield was a nine-term House member and had been a major general during the Civil War, so he was a plausible candidate. But he'd already given a nominating speech for Treasury Secretary John Sherman, a fellow Ohioan, who himself hoped to be a compromise candidate. So Garfield protested, "No man has a right, without the consent of the person voted for, to announce that person's name, and vote for him, in this convention. Such consent I have not given."[85]

On the next ballot, however, Garfield's total grew to 50 as delegates saw a possible way out of their deadlock. Garfield refused to sanction the movement, but Blaine, who'd been following the vote via telegram from Washington, freed his delegates to support Garfield if it would block Grant and the Stalwarts from winning. Sherman similarly urged the Ohio delegation to vote for Garfield. After this, "the stampede came."[86] Garfield was nominated on the thirty-sixth ballot. This set off a raucous celebration, while the nominee sat stunned on the convention floor. "Won't you telegraph my wife?" Garfield asked a friend. "She ought to know of this."[87]

When the vote ended, the Grant supporters were distraught over their candidate's defeat. Knowing this, the convention agreed to nominate a Stalwart for vice president. When Congressman Levi Morton of New York turned down the opportunity, the delegates surprisingly turned to Chester Arthur, the former collector of the New York Customs House. The Customs House job was hardly typical preparation for national office, but since Arthur was the preferred choice of New York Stalwarts, whose support would be crucial in the fall election, the delegates gave him the nomination.[88]

The Democrats, meanwhile, had little drama at their convention. Many wanted Tilden to run again for the office they believed should have been his four years earlier. When he demurred, the party instead united behind Gen. Winfield Scott Hancock, a career soldier and a Union hero for his exploits at Gettysburg.

In the general election campaign, Hancock was predictably praised for his military service, but Republicans disparaged him for a supposed lack of knowledge about government. They published a pamphlet about his political achievements that consisted entirely of blank pages.

On the other hand, Republicans highlighted Garfield's rise from humble beginnings. He'd been born in a log cabin and once worked driving mules along Ohio Canal towpaths, so they formed Towpath Clubs and heralded the candidate as "Boatman Jim." Horatio Alger wrote a campaign biography titled "From Canal Boy to President."[89]

Democrats countered by accusing Garfield of corruption for allegedly receiving stock in exchange for votes favorable to the Union Pacific Railroad during the Grant years, a charge he denied. A more interesting attack on Garfield came in the form of a forged letter in which the candidate seemed to advocate for using Chinese immigrants as cheap labor. This was a big issue at the time, as tens of thousands of Chinese workers came to the United States to build the railroads and later settled in the West. Their presence generated resentment over their alleged stealing of American jobs, similar to the 1850s furor over Irish immigrants, and anti-Chinese riots broke out in various cities during the 1870s and 1880s. The Garfield letter was shown to be a fake, but it appeared late in the campaign and may have cost him a victory in California, which he narrowly lost.

In the end, Garfield won the election, but it was one of the closest popular votes in history. Of more than 9 million ballots cast, fewer than ten thousand votes separated the contenders, with Garfield winning 48.3 to 48.2 percent. The Electoral College margin was wider, with Garfield prevailing 214–155 due to his strength in the North.

Then, less than four months after his inauguration, President Garfield was shot by an assassin. The shooting was linked, astonishingly, to the drama between Stalwarts and Half-Breeds that had marked the Republican convention the previous summer. That's because, during Garfield's first months in office, he was engaged in a "titanic struggle over patronage" with Senator Conkling, the Stalwart leader who'd also battled with Hayes.[90] A conflict over the collector of the New York Customs House grew so bitter that, when Garfield refused to yield to Stalwart demands, Conkling resigned his Senate seat. As it happened, Vice President Arthur supported Conkling and his old Stalwart colleagues over the president, a choice that would haunt him.

Garfield was shot on July 2, 1881, while walking through the Baltimore and Potomac Railroad Station in Washington. The assassin, Charles Guiteau, was a deranged man acting on his own, but he was also a Stalwart supporter who believed he'd been unfairly passed over for a diplomatic appointment. After the shooting, Guiteau declared, "I am a Stalwart and Arthur will be president."[91]

The news rocked the nation. People had always assumed that Lincoln's assassination was an outlier, a tragic consequence of the Civil War. But now another president had been shot. And for what? A dispute over political patronage.[92] By coincidence, Arthur and Conkling were together in New York when the news came over the wires. As people realized the attack was motivated by anger over the spoils system and was an effort to install Arthur in the presidency, fingers were pointed accusingly at the two men, who received death threats.

Garfield survived the initial shooting and was moved to the

White House, where he lingered in serious condition for the rest of the summer. The bullet in his body turned out to be the least of his problems. The president also suffered a series of infections caused by doctors probing his wound with hands and instruments that hadn't been sterilized, which wasn't yet a common medical practice. Today it's assumed the president would have survived if he'd received better medical care.[93] As his condition deteriorated, Garfield was moved to a seaside home near Long Branch, New Jersey, in hopes the ocean air would revive him. He died there on September 19.

Soon thereafter a messenger appeared at Arthur's door in New York City, informing him of Garfield's death. The vice president broke down, "sobbing like a child, with his head on his desk and his face buried in his hands," according to a report.[94] He'd never aspired to the presidency and had spent the past few months in a stupor, distraught over reports of the Stalwarts' unintended complicity in the assassination. And now Garfield was gone. That night at 2:15 a.m., in the front parlor of his home, Chester Arthur took the oath of office as the twenty-first president.

1884

The country reeled from the twist of fate that elevated Arthur to the presidency. Although three previous presidents had died in office, no one imagined it happening to Garfield, who was a healthy forty-nine-year-old. And now the inexperienced Arthur was the new chief executive. One person spoke for many when he exclaimed, "Chet Arthur? President of the United States? Good God!"[95]

Moreover, Garfield's death seemed to have achieved his assassin's goal of preventing civil service reform, since Arthur was a Stalwart who owed his career to patronage. But the assassination spurred President Arthur to a change of heart and gave new impetus to the reform movement. In 1883 Arthur signed into law the Pendleton Act, which created the Civil Service Commission and ensured that federal employees would thereafter be hired on merit rather than by their ties to a politician.

The civil service grew into the federal bureaucracy that so many people bemoan these days. The upside is that it ended a system that treated elections as patronage contests, in which political bosses were in control of most federal jobs. The reforms started small, covering less than one-fifth of the workforce, but protections grew over time and eventually helped to professionalize government and reduce the potential for corruption.[96]

By most accounts, Chester Arthur had a modest yet successful presidency. His biggest achievement was the passage of civil service reform, but he also took steps to modernize the navy. Along the way, though, he found himself in somewhat of a political no-man's land. The Stalwarts forsook him when he went down the path of civil service reform, while the reformers never fully embraced him.[97]

Arthur attempted to win the Republican nomination in his own right in 1884 but lacked a base in the party. His effort may have been half-hearted, in any case, as his health was faltering. He'd been diagnosed with Bright's disease, a kidney disorder, which proved fatal two years after he left the White House. At the party convention in June in Chicago, Arthur finished second in the first round of balloting. He couldn't overcome James Blaine, whose supporters, known as Blainiacs, were determined to get him the nomination after losses in 1876 and 1880.

Not all Republicans cheered the choice of Blaine, however. Before the convention there was an effort to draft Gen. William Tecumseh Sherman, who famously responded, "If nominated, I will not run. If elected, I will not serve," a statement described thereafter as Shermanesque.[98] And even after Blaine's nomination, liberal reformers expressed dismay over the candidate's record, including the 1876 revelation that he was apparently paid for influencing railroad legislation.

When Democrats met for their convention in July, also in Chicago, the party lacked a compelling national figure, and so delegates turned to Governor Grover Cleveland of New York, who had a reputation for forthrightness and honesty. Almost entirely on that basis, he'd made a rather stunning political rise in just three years, from mayor of Buffalo to governor of New York and now presidential nominee. Cleveland wasn't particularly charismatic, and he'd never even set foot in Washington, but he was "honest, selfless and dedicated" at a time when people were hungry for integrity in government.[99] Cleveland's slogan was, simply, "Public Office is a Public Trust."[100]

Cleveland's nomination prompted the reform-minded Republicans to abandon Blaine for the Democratic nominee. This drew the ire of other Republicans, who scornfully referred to them as Mugwumps, a term derived from an Algonquin Indian word that was meant to accuse them of being self-righteous. It was popularly said that a Mugwump had his "mug" on one side of the fence and his "wump" on the other.[101] The Mugwump uprising was akin to the 1872 revolt by the Liberal Republicans who supported Horace Greeley. In both cases, the dissenters were disenchanted with a political system built on patronage and corruption.[102]

Just when it seemed the contours of the battle were set, however, an eruption of scandals turned the race upside down. The contest morphed into what observers of the time said was "the vilest" presidential campaign yet waged.[103]

The first shoe to drop was a surprising story about Cleveland. The *Buffalo Evening Telegraph* on July 21 revealed the Democratic nominee had seduced a widow, fathered a child out of wedlock, and then abandoned mother and son. In an instant, the entire rationale for Cleveland's candidacy seemed to collapse. He was transformed from "Grover the Good" into a "a moral leper."[104]

Cleveland didn't deny the affair, but the reality of the situation was more nuanced than first reported. There was some doubt about the actual father of the child, who'd been named Oscar Folsom Cleveland. Oscar Folsom was the name of Cleveland's best friend in Buffalo—and he was married, whereas Cleveland was a bachelor. So, not knowing if the boy was even his, Cleveland accepted paternity and provided financial support for the woman and baby, who was later adopted by another family when the mother turned out to have drinking problems.[105]

All the same, it was the first real sex scandal of any presidential campaign, and Republicans had a field day with the allegations. For the rest of the contest, they relentlessly tormented Cleveland, pushing baby carriages in parades while chanting, "Ma, Ma, Where's my Pa?"[106] Mark Twain was bemused by the reaction. He mocked the "grown men apparently in their right minds seriously arguing against a bachelor's fitness for president because he has had private intercourse with a consenting widow."[107]

Blaine, meanwhile, had his own scandals to confront. First, there was a report that he was forced into a shotgun wedding and that his wife gave birth just three months after their marriage. Blaine denied it, claiming he was married privately one year before holding a public ceremony.[108] Whether or not that claim was plausible soon became irrelevant, as the allegations were swamped by an even bigger scandal.

In September new information was unearthed about the railroad corruption affair that torpedoed Blaine's 1876 candidacy. The *Boston Journal* published a letter Blaine wrote eight years earlier, with instructions for how a railroad attorney should exonerate him. Most damaging was the last line: "Burn this letter." Democrats were soon merrily chanting:

> Blaine! Blaine! James G. Blaine!
> The continental liar from the state of Maine.
> Burn this letter![109]

As his conduct came under fire, Blaine was depicted in a political cartoon as the "tattooed man," implicitly comparing him to a Barnum and Bailey attraction of the time. In this case, Blaine's body was printed with the names of his various scandals.[110] In response to this avalanche of mud, the Democrats cleverly suggested the campaign was about "public integrity, not private misconduct," in which case Cleveland should be the obvious choice as the candidate with the unblemished public record.[111]

Amid this pileup of scandals, there was still an election to be held. The race went down to the wire, with New York appearing to be the key swing state. Blaine was seen as a narrow favorite until his momentum crashed to a halt on October 29.

On that day, Blaine appeared at a meeting of Protestant ministers in New York, where the Rev. Samuel Burchard made news in his opening address by suggesting Democrats were the party of "Rum, Romanism and Rebellion." The "rum" and "rebellion" references were long-standing Republican attacks against Democrats over temperance and the Civil War, but the allusion to "Romanism" was an anti-Catholic insult, echoing the Know Nothing smears of three decades earlier. It caused consternation in the Irish Catholic community, where Blaine was pushing for votes, and Democrats gleefully plastered the remark in newspapers and campaign flyers.[112]

Later that same day, Blaine attended a fundraising dinner in New York with two hundred of the richest men in the country, a political slipup for a candidate trying to appeal to workers and immigrants. The *New York World* published a story titled "The Royal Feast of Belshazzar Blaine and the Money Kings," with a cartoon showing Blaine and his millionaire friends gorging themselves on "patronage" and "monopoly soup" while a starving family begged for help.[113]

The twin debacles of October 29, along with the Mugwump rebellion, appear to have cost Blaine thousands of votes in New York, and very possibly the presidency.[114] Cleveland won the popular vote by 48.5 to 48.2 percent and the electoral vote 219–182. In New York, Cleveland's victory was minuscule, just 1,149 out of 1.1 million ballots. If that state, with thirty-six electoral votes, had gone the other way, Blaine would have won the election.

Instead Cleveland became the first elected Democrat in twenty-eight years. And Democrats happily added a rejoinder to the Republicans' famous refrain about Cleveland:

Ma, Ma, Where's my Pa?
Gone to the White House, Ha, Ha, Ha.[115]

1888

Cleveland's election represented not just the return of Democrats from the political wilderness but the reappearance of a governing philosophy that had been absent from Washington for more than two decades, as the new president was a conservative Democrat. That species of politician may now be nearly extinct, but in the late nineteenth century the Democrats were still a Southern-dominated party that believed in small government.

To underscore these beliefs, Cleveland vetoed a whopping 414 bills in his first term, more than his twenty-one predecessors combined. One veto that symbolized his philosophy was the rejection of an effort to help Texas farmers who'd been devastated by a drought. He insisted it wasn't the government's job to relieve individual suffering. "Though the people support the government," he wrote, "the government should not support the people."[116]

In addition to his conservative politics, two other storylines defined Cleveland's presidency and the next election. First, there was a surprising turn in his personal life, as the bachelor president got married on June 2, 1886, to twenty-one-year-old Frances Folsom. Cleveland was the first president married in a White House ceremony, and the new Mrs. Cleveland became the youngest first lady in the country's history. Curiously, she was the daughter of Cleveland's old Buffalo friend, Oscar Folsom, who died a decade earlier in a carriage accident. Cleveland was executor of his friend's estate and became Frances's virtual guardian. She even called him Uncle Cleve. But when Frances became an adult, their relationship grew into a romantic one.[117]

It's an unusual story, for sure, one that twenty-first-century media would have a field day with, but the couple had six children together and remained married until Cleveland's death in 1908. Frances Cleveland became a beloved first lady and a political asset. Her picture adorned campaign posters and buttons in 1888, and Frankie Cleveland Clubs sprang up across the country.[118]

An even bigger factor in the next election, however, was Cleveland's effort to lower tariff rates. The tariff debate is another issue that reappears periodically in U.S. elections, in connection with disputes over protectionism and free trade. In the 1880s tariffs were the government's primary revenue source, accounting for more than 60 percent of income. Cleveland contended that lower tariffs would reduce consumer prices and that high tariffs hurt exporters by encouraging other nations to also erect trade barriers. Since the government was running a surplus, the Democrats also saw the tariff as unnecessary taxation. Not to mention that it hit hardest the farmers and laborers who comprised the party's base.

But Republicans, who controlled the Senate, were long-standing protectionists, like the Whigs and Federalists before them. They believed tariffs protected U.S. industries and that tariff revenue was vital to funding government programs, such as infrastructure. The manufacturers who benefited from the tariff also tended to be the party's major donors.[119] So when a new tariff bill stalled in Congress because of divided government, the debate spilled into the next campaign.

President Cleveland was unanimously nominated by Democrats in 1888 to run for a second term, while Republicans took a few more ballots to settle on a candidate. At the Republican convention in Chicago, Senator John Sherman of Ohio wasn't able to sew up the nomination despite leading the early vote. There was an effort to draft Blaine, who still retained considerable support after his narrow defeat in 1884, but he declared himself uninterested. So, on the eighth ballot, the convention turned to the well-respected but not so charismatic Benjamin Harrison, a former Indiana senator and the grandson of President William Henry Harrison.

The Republican and Democratic candidates took different approaches to the fall election. Harrison did some stump speaking in the form of a front-porch campaign. He gave ninety or so speeches from his front lawn or in a park near his home, the transcripts later printed in newspapers and campaign pamphlets.[120] Cleveland didn't campaign at all, preferring to stand on his record.

The contest had minimal drama compared to 1884, although there was the usual back-and-forth flinging of mud. The Republicans called Cleveland the "Beast of Buffalo," accusing him of drinking too much and beating his wife. Frances Cleveland was forced to respond to what she called a "foolish campaign story" and said her husband was "kind, considerate and affectionate."[121]

The Democrats tried to mock Harrison with unkind comparisons to his president grandfather. One slogan was "His grandfather's hat—It's too big for Ben." The Harrison campaign responded with their own slogan, linking the two Harrison campaigns in a more favorable light: "Tippecanoe and Tariff, Too" not only evoked the winning campaign of 1840 but also played up the main policy issue in the 1888 contest.[122]

Manufacturers who supported protectionism warned that a Cleveland victory would lead to layoffs, while Republicans contended that low tariffs would "destroy American freedom" and that Cleveland was a "stooge of British free traders."[123] The message that Cleveland was somehow anti-American was amplified by what became known as the Murchison affair. A California Republican, using the assumed name of Charles Murchison, wrote a letter to the British minister in Washington, asking for advice on how to vote. The minister responded that Cleveland's election would be best for U.S.-British relations. When the Republicans released the letter to the media, the publication caused an uproar, particularly among Irish voters in New York who were stridently anti-British.

The incident may well have damaged Cleveland's reelection hopes, as the result was again exceedingly close. Cleveland won the popular vote by 48.6 to 47.8 percent, but Harrison prevailed in the Electoral College by 233–168. Cleveland thus became the second person in twelve years to win the popular vote and lose the electoral balloting. The only difference between 1884 and 1888 was that New York and Indiana flipped from the Democrats to the Republicans by narrow margins. As with Blaine in 1884, if Cleveland had won New York he would have won the election.

When Cleveland departed the presidency after this narrow loss, however, he seemed to have his sights already set on a return. On his last day in office, his wife told the staff, "We are coming back just four years from today."[124]

1892

The 1892 election was unique in history. Not only was it a rematch of 1888, with Benjamin Harrison again facing Grover Cleveland, but it also featured two presidents running for a second term.

Both candidates won their party's nomination on the first ballot, though neither was unopposed. Some Republicans who weren't ardent fans of Harrison unsuccessfully put up Blaine and Ohio governor William McKinley as challengers. On the Democratic side, Cleveland was still considered formidable after two successive popular vote wins, and at the convention in Chicago he dispatched a challenge from New York senator David Hill.

Curiously, for what would seem to be a momentous battle between two presidents, the general election was rather devoid of fireworks. One historian remarked, "Honest bearded Benjamin Harrison confronting honest mustached Grover Cleveland in a tariff debate was a repeat performance that did not inspire parades with torches or the chanting of campaign ditties."[125]

The candidates themselves avoided the fray. Cleveland retreated to a Cape Cod vacation home, while Harrison remained in the White House and cared for his sick wife, Caroline. When she passed away two weeks before the election, her death cast a sense of melancholy over the contest.

Despite the lack of campaign fireworks, the parties did have considerable differences on some key issues. Just as in 1888, tariffs dominated. Republicans had recently passed the McKinley Act, significantly raising tariffs to further protect domestic manufacturing industries. But when the cost of imported goods increased, the country was awash in complaints that Republicans had taken the side of wealthy manufacturers over consumers. Democrats denounced the policy as "robbery . . . of the American people for the benefit of the few."[126]

A related concern surfaced over labor rights. In 1892 workers at the Carnegie Steel Company in Homestead, Pennsylvania, went on strike to protest a pay cut, which seemed to refute the Republican argument that higher tariffs led to higher wages. Even worse, when Pinkerton detectives were hired to help break the strike it sparked an armed battle that left at least ten people dead.[127]

These issues dented Harrison's popularity, while also giving rise to a third-party movement. The People's Party was a populist group with a base of support among farmers in the West and

South and a belief that the major parties were dominated by financial elites. At a convention in Omaha, Nebraska, the party nominated former Iowa congressman James Weaver, who declared that an "aggressive plutocracy ha[d] usurped the government."[128] The platform endorsed the free coinage of silver (an issue that would grow in potency in 1896), a graduated income tax, popular election of senators, and the nationalization of the railroad, telegraph, and telephone industries.

By Election Day there were too many challenges for Harrison to overcome. Cleveland again prevailed in the popular vote, this time by 46 to 43 percent, and easily won the Electoral College, 277–145. The People's Party won 8 percent of the vote and 22 electoral votes in four states in the best third-party showing since before the Civil War.

In regaining the presidency, Cleveland became the only president elected to nonconsecutive terms. He's also one of three presidents, along with Franklin Roosevelt and Andrew Jackson, to win the popular vote three times.

Political Ferment in the Gilded Age

Thomas Wolfe in 1934 wrote a short story, "The Four Lost Men," in which he depicts, through a father's memories, the four Republican presidents from 1876 to 1892. He describes "the proud, vacant, time-strange and bewhiskered faces of Garfield, Arthur, Harrison and Hayes. . . . For me they were the lost Americans."[129]

Even then, less than a half century removed from the Gilded Age, these presidents were relics of a different time. Looking back from today, the era is even more remote and enigmatic, a seemingly mislaid slice of history between the Civil War and the twentieth century. But there was actually considerable ferment stirring in the country during this period, and the stage was being set for another political transformation.

The Gilded Age itself was a time of contrasts and contradictions. It was when the Rockefellers, Vanderbilts, and Carnegies grew rich; when Americans invented the electric light and the telephone and built the Brooklyn Bridge; but also when work-

ers labored in sweatshops, poor families crowded into dirty tenements, and corrupt politicians took bribes from industrialists. As
in the Twain novel that gave the age its name, the gilded veneer
of wealth didn't match the reality for most people.

A different dichotomy was reshaping the nation's politics. On
the surface, it was a time of competitive balance between the
major parties. There were four presidential elections from 1876
to 1888 in which the results could have been reversed. In two
elections, the candidate who won the popular vote lost the Electoral College. In three contests, the contenders were separated
by less than 1 percent in the popular vote.

These elections were powered by some of the highest participation rates in history, often near 80 percent of voters. The country
was far from being fully democratic, as Black participation was
suppressed in the South, and women didn't yet have the right to
vote, but it was an era, as one historian said, when "politics had
never roared louder."[130] There were parades that attracted tens of
thousands of people, and party rallies with speeches that went
on for hours.[131]

Beneath this façade of popular politics, however, upheaval was
simmering. New issues were galvanizing people to action. Women's
rights, labor strife, tariff and trade disputes, corruption in government, currency concerns, and poverty among urban workers and
rural farmers: these topics eclipsed the old Civil War and Reconstruction debates that had framed politics for decades. The best-
selling book of the era was *Progress and Poverty* by Henry George,
in which the author noted "an increased bitterness among the
working classes" and suggested taxing landownership to help
ameliorate disparities in wealth.[132]

With these new issues came new political movements, and a
proliferation of third parties sprang to life. There was the Equal
Rights Party, which in 1872 nominated Victoria Woodhull for
president, and the National Equal Rights Party, which put forth
Belva Lockwood in 1884 and 1888, and Woodhull again in 1892,
with new ideas about "humanitarian government," food safety,
and better housing.[133] The Prohibition Party, which opposed the

sale and consumption of alcohol, topped 2 percent of the national vote in 1888 and 1892.

There were also various parties dedicated to economic concerns. Most prominent was the Greenback Party, which endorsed expanding the money supply to help struggling farmers and workers. Other groups formed around labor rights, farm issues, and government reform. These factions all laid the foundation for the People's Party, the populist movement that won four states in the 1892 election.

So while Republicans and Democrats fought through some razor-thin presidential elections, greater changes were afoot in the nation, changes that were a harbinger of the next era of American politics.

4

★ ★ ★

1896-1928

A New Politics for a New Century

Coffee at the Wilder House in Plymouth, Vermont

On August 2, 1923, Vice President Calvin Coolidge was visiting his seventy-eight-year-old father at their farmhouse in Plymouth Notch, Vermont. Coolidge spent part of the day working in the yard, blissfully unaware of how his life was about to change. Late that night, Coolidge's father was awakened by an insistent rapping on his front door. The home didn't have a phone, so a messenger had come from a nearby telegraph office with an urgent dispatch. After reading the note, John Coolidge climbed the stairs and called out to his son in a trembling voice.

"I knew that something of the gravest nature had occurred," Calvin later recalled. Indeed, President Warren Harding had died a few hours earlier of a heart attack. Father and son looked at each other in the quiet of a dark Vermont night and tried to absorb the news. Within the hour Plymouth Notch was alive with activity. Reporters who were staying a few miles away in Ludlow rushed to the Coolidge home. Neighbors heard the commotion and came out of their houses. Then, at 2:47 a.m., by the light of a kerosene lamp in the parlor, John Coolidge, a notary public, administered the oath of office to his son, the new president of the United States.[1]

It was an evocative moment in the annals of American democracy. Fortunately, that Coolidge farmhouse is still standing today. As is the Wilder House down the road, the childhood home of the president's mother, which was later turned into a coffee shop and a restaurant. Both buildings are part of a historic district that has kept the bucolic village of Plymouth Notch looking much as it did a century ago. That makes the Wilder House a picture-perfect location at which to grab a coffee and contemplate the changes that swept through presidential politics during this era, above all the emergence of a new debate between progressivism and conservatism.

Coolidge, for his part, was a progenitor of modern conservativism. Ronald Reagan hung Coolidge's portrait in the White House to honor their shared belief in limited government. "Human nature cannot be changed by an act of the legislature," Coolidge said, in summing up his philosophy. "It is too much assumed that because an abuse exists it is the business of the national government to remedy it."[2]

On the other side of the spectrum was progressivism, a political movement that emerged early in the twentieth century and first blossomed during the presidencies of Theodore Roosevelt and Woodrow Wilson. Roosevelt, in particular, was a forceful advocate for progressivism, asserting that "the object of government is the welfare of the people."[3]

These political ideologies could hardly be more different, and yet they both flourished during this era, which kicked off with William McKinley's election in 1896. At the time, a rising populist movement was forcing the country to confront the inequities of industrialization. This led, in turn, to the Progressive reforms of the 1900s and 1910s. A decade later, after World War I, the country moved back to a more conservative era of governance under Republican presidents.

The swinging of the pendulum between progressivism and conservatism marked not only this era but also the next century of American politics. For that reason, it would be fascinating to survey these next elections from coffee shops linked to *both* Coolidge and Roosevelt, especially since Roosevelt loved coffee, reportedly drinking up to a gallon each day, and because some of his children opened their own café in New York in 1919, the Double R Coffee House. Unfortunately the Roosevelts' café is no longer around, so in the Green Mountains of Vermont we'll ponder an era that transformed presidential campaigns and unleashed a debate between progressives and conservatives that continues to animate politics today.

1896, 1900, 1904, 1908, and 1912: Roosevelt, Wilson, and the Progressive Era

1896

When Grover Cleveland won the popular vote for the third straight time in 1892, Democrats were in the ascendant and it seemed the Republicans' post–Civil War coalition had run out of gas.[4] During the next four years, however, the political landscape shifted dramatically. By 1896 Cleveland's popularity was in tatters and American politics was on the verge of another shakeup.

This transformation was precipitated by an economic crash that lasted from 1893 to 1897. Railroads went bankrupt, banks and factories closed, and millions of workers lost their jobs in the biggest economic disaster the nation has faced outside the Great Depression. Cleveland was unlucky enough to take office just as the economy was cratering, much like Martin Van Buren had in 1837.

If this weren't problematic enough, the president in 1893 was also diagnosed with a cancerous tumor in his mouth. Fearful of alarming the public during an economic crisis, he convinced his doctors to perform the necessary surgery secretly. So, in a makeshift operating room on a yacht off Long Island Sound, doctors anesthetized Cleveland and cut out the tumor and part of his upper jaw. The media was told the president was on a fishing trip and, later, as he recuperated from what could have been a life-threatening health scare, that he was vacationing on Cape Cod. It was an audacious deception, which only came to light two decades later, when one of Cleveland's doctors set the record straight for the sake of history.[5]

Cleveland recovered his health within a few months; the economy wasn't as fortunate. By 1894 there were "thousands of homeless and starving men in the streets," in the words of one reporter. Some of the unemployed organized a march on Washington. This was followed by a Pullman strike, a massive walkout of railway workers that immobilized railroad traffic in the West.[6] Everywhere the president looked, unrest was boiling over.[7]

Amid this turmoil, Republicans were increasingly confident of their chances in the next election. However, while the economy was indeed a pivotal issue in 1896, the topic that stirred the most angst and passion was the gold standard, which had become a popular scapegoat for the country's troubles.

The backdrop, in brief, is that advocates of the gold standard believed a currency tied to gold was vital to keeping inflation and spending in check, since the money supply couldn't expand unless the country's gold reserves were increased. The downside to this policy, though, became evident when gold production declined, reserves diminished, and the money supply tightened, leading to deflation.

Falling prices meant farmers, for one, made less money, which in turn made their debts more onerous. This gave rise to the agrarian populist movement that made noise in the 1892 election as the People's Party. Populists promoted a return to "bimetallism," a currency linked to both gold and silver, which was U.S. policy before 1873. There was an abundance of silver in mines in the West, and it was believed the free (or unlimited) coinage of silver would increase the money supply, inflate the economy, and provide struggling workers with access to more cash. This proposal was anathema to bankers, who would see the value of their financial holdings decline with inflation. One editorial complained it would "whack the stuffing out of creditors" for the benefit of "the lazy, greasy fizzle, who can't pay his debts."[8]

With the economy in dire straits and voters desperate for a remedy, this debate riveted the nation in a way no other issue had for years. Supporters on either side became known as "silverites" and "goldbugs." A pro-silver pamphlet titled Coin's Finan-

cial School sold an astonishing 1 million copies. So thoroughly did the topic penetrate society that it's even thought to be a source for *The Wizard of Oz*, which was published in 1900.[9]

That may seem hard to believe, but the story acquires a surprising new slant if we overlay the politics of the 1890s. Dorothy's Kansas, for instance, was a hotbed of the pro-silver populist movement. And her house is picked up by a twister and deposited in Oz, where it lands on and kills the Wicked Witch of the East. Oz is an abbreviation for "ounce," and the Wicked Witch hails from the same region as the despised bankers who owned the farmers' debts.

Dorothy then acquires the witch's slippers, sets off on the yellow brick road to Emerald City to see the wizard, and meets the Scarecrow, Tin Man, and Cowardly Lion. In this view, the yellow brick road would symbolize the gold standard, Emerald City is Washington DC, and the wizard who isn't so powerful once you pull back the curtain is the president. The Scarecrow and Tin Man are the farmers and factory workers who've been victimized by powerful interests. And at the end, of course, Dorothy discovers that her slippers have the power to send her home. Fascinatingly, those slippers, which are red in the movie, are silver in the book. So it's silver that has the power to return her to safety, away from the yellow brick road, just as silver was meant to rescue the nation from the gold standard.

To be fair, the author, L. Frank Baum, never admitted any link between his story and the decade's politics, but the evidence is so overwhelming that some historians now accept the story as a satire of the era. A children's book with an inside joke, you might say. In any case, this is one example of how gold and silver were very much on the minds of Americans as they turned their attention to the next presidential election.

The Republican convention came first, in St. Louis in June. The party nominated Governor William McKinley of Ohio, who'd been a prominent congressman before moving to the state house. McKinley managed to win the nomination without groveling to party bosses who wanted promises from him about cabinet and patronage positions. Instead, he and his campaign manager, Mark Hanna, organized a state-by-state campaign that bypassed the bosses and won them their own slates of delegates. Their slogan was "The People against the Bosses."[10]

This was a notable change in tactics for a nomination battle, and it signaled the rise of more candidate-centered campaigns. When McKinley won more than 70 percent of votes on the first ballot the *Chicago Tribune* called it a win for the "rank and file of the party over its self-centered and presumptuous leaders."[11]

The convention wasn't all smooth sailing, though, as delegates battled over the contentious issue of gold and silver. When the Republican platform added a plank in support of the gold standard, twenty-three delegates from pro-silver western states walked out in protest.

But this was mild compared to the storm at the Democratic convention in July in Chicago. There a rising populist faction endorsed a pro-silver platform and even denounced Cleveland, their own president, as a "tool of Wall Street."[12] The pro-silver populists prevailed in the nomination battle, making former congressman William Jennings Bryan of Nebraska the party's candidate, a decision that disheartened pro-gold Democrats.

Bryan, who was only thirty-six and had served just two terms in Congress, was a long shot when the convention began. But he won over delegates with his "Cross of Gold" address, still one of the most famous speeches in political history. One of Bryan's main themes was that there were "two ideas of government." Republicans, he said, believed "if you just legislate to make the well-to-do prosperous, that their prosperity will leak through on those below." Democrats, on the other hand, felt that "if you legislate to make the masses prosperous their prosperity will find its way up and through every class that rests upon it."[13]

This sentiment resonated well into the twenty-first century, with obvious echoes in the debate over trickle-down economics, but at the time it was a stunning statement for a Democrat, whose party had preached limited government since the days of Jefferson and Jackson. Now, with urban laborers battling to survive and farmers crushed by debt, Bryan and the populists were suggesting that government could protect individuals from the excesses of industrialism.[14] He essentially detonated the blast that pushed Democrats toward progressivism, although it would take a few more decades before the new politics fully sorted itself out.

Throughout the speech, said one writer, Bryan "reached out a mighty vocal hand and clutched his listeners by the throat and heart."[15] At the end, while arguing passionately for free silver, he brought the audience to its feet with this final line: "You shall not press down upon the brow of labor this crown of thorns; you shall not crucify mankind upon a cross of gold!" The delegates erupted in a boisterous and spontaneous demonstration. They waved flags, stomped their feet, and threw hats in the air. Some men put Bryan on their shoulders and carried him around the convention floor. A conga line formed. People cried. "Everyone seemed to go mad at once," wrote a reporter.[16]

After Bryan's nomination, the New York World observed, "Political power has passed from the strong certain hands of the East to the feverish, headstrong mob of the West and South." The pro-gold delegates from the East responded to this defeat by breaking away to form the new National Democratic Party. They did so with the support of President Cleveland, who said, "I cannot write or speak favorably of Bryanism."[17] The National Democrats nominated seventy-nine-year-old Senator John Palmer of Illinois for president. They didn't expect to win in November, but decided a third-party candidate who drained Democratic votes and elected McKinley was more acceptable than seeing Bryan take permanent control of their party.

After this, the fall campaign was an exceptional battle, and it ushered presidential politics into a new era.

First of all, Bryan embarked on perhaps the most legendary speaking tour in presidential history. It was still rare for candidates to campaign for themselves, and Bryan went far beyond what any previous contender had attempted, traveling eighteen thousand miles by train and giving more than five hundred speeches to several million voters. He was considered the most enthralling orator of his time and could make "rugged, ragged men of the soil weep like children," said the novelist Willa Cather.[18]

The Democratic nominee spoke anytime and anywhere a crowd would gather, whether for seventy thousand people in Boston or a handful of farmers in the middle of the night at a lonely railway station in rural America. He sometimes talked for twenty hours a day, catching quick naps between speeches. Bryan booked his own tickets, carried his own luggage, grabbed meals at train depots, and changed trains like every other traveler. He wore out the journalists who covered him. The campaign was "almost too intense for life," said one reporter. It wasn't until October that the Democrats finally got their candidate his own train car with a private compartment.

Bryan also gained the endorsement of the Populists, who'd won four states in 1892 as the People's Party, as he strived to build a coalition that connected farmers and factory workers. His campaign unnerved Republicans, some of whom urged McKinley to go on the trail himself. But McKinley wouldn't hear of it. "I might just as well put a trapeze on my front lawn and compete with some professional athlete as go out speaking against Bryan," he remarked.[19]

So the Republicans came up with their own McKinley-friendly innovation, the Front Porch Campaign, building on a strategy used by Harrison in 1888. McKinley stayed home and let people come to him. In all, 750,000 people from thirty states journeyed to Canton, Ohio, many of them on reduced fares subsidized by the railroads. McKinley talked to hundreds of delegations, each one of which was met at the train station by local volunteers and escorted to the candidate's home. Sandwiches and drinks were provided, and McKinley spoke from prepared remarks, which were distributed to the press.[20] So the candidate met voters and got media coverage, all while sleeping in his own bed.

Another departure from previous campaigns was in the money that flowed into the race. The Republicans amassed a record war chest of $3.5 million, almost ten times what Democrats raised, much of it from Wall Street financiers and wealthy industrialists who opposed Bryan. With these funds, the party mailed an unprecedented amount of campaign literature to voters and hired hundreds of speakers to spread their message, which promised economic recovery by way of "a full dinner pail" for workers.[21]

Republicans also revved up a fearmongering campaign against Bryan, with an assist from the business community. Some workers received a note with their paychecks warning, "If Bryan is elected, do not come back to work. The plant will be closed."[22] Some companies placed orders with manufacturers that were contingent on a McKinley victory. Creditors warned that overdue mortgages would be foreclosed on. Some companies even transferred workers to new locations so they'd be in the wrong place to vote on Election Day.[23]

Democrats benefited from their own version of coercion, because Southern states still disenfranchised Black voters. Nevertheless, the fear of losing manufacturing jobs did contribute significantly to McKinley's victory. Factory workers largely voted Republican, preventing Bryan from uniting farmers and laborers and making it nearly impossible for him to win the crucial midwestern swing states.

McKinley won the popular vote by 51 to 47 percent and the Electoral College 271–176. He built a coalition based in cities and small towns across New England and the Upper Midwest that would help the GOP dominate national politics for a few decades. The Bryan Democrats, meanwhile, remained strong in the Deep South and gained ground in the West, particularly in Plains states where the populist movement had been strongest.[24]

1900

When President McKinley took office in 1897 he benefited from an economy on the verge of recovery, a fortuitous contrast to the economic freefall that had greeted Cleveland in 1893. Not only that, but gold reserves were growing again with the discovery of new mines in South Africa, Australia, and the Yukon. This expanded the money supply, which is what Bryan and the pro-silver faction had been clamoring for all along, via different means. In any case, the country in the late 1890s enjoyed a period of exceptional prosperity.[25]

This put Republicans in a strong position going into 1900, although they had to contend with an issue that wasn't on anyone's radar four year earlier: imperialism and America's role in the world, which was a new subject for presidential campaigns.

The debate was triggered when the United States acquired international possessions after the 1898 Spanish-American War, a conflict that began as a Cuban struggle for independence from Spain. There were calls for American intervention in Cuba, both because of distress over Spain's harshness in quelling the revolt and because American commercial interests were at risk, but the event that convinced McKinley to get involved was the sinking of the uss *Maine* in Havana harbor.

On February 15, 1898, an explosion ripped apart the *Maine* and killed 266 sailors. Almost overnight, war fever gripped the country, most everyone assuming Spain was to blame. When a naval investigation determined an external explosion had indeed sunk the ship, the slogan "Remember the Maine" swept the nation. McKinley couldn't resist demands for action, so on April 25 he asked for a declaration of war.[26] Not everyone was convinced Spain was the culprit, however, and to this day there is doubt as to whether the sinking was actually due to a mine. A naval review of the evidence in the 1970s, in fact, concluded that a coal bunker fire aboard the ship, a common occurrence at the time, likely triggered the fatal blast. If so, it means the precipitating factor for war was an accident.[27]

Regardless, the United States and Spain were soon engaged in battle. The war lasted only a few months and ended when Americans defeated the Spanish in naval clashes in Cuba and the Philippines. The Treaty of Paris then granted independence to Cuba and gave America possession of Spanish colonies in Puerto Rico, Guam, and the Philippines.

This turn of events sparked intense debate and gave rise to an anti-imperialist movement, headlined by such luminaries as Mark Twain, Andrew Carnegie, and former president Cleveland. They claimed the acquisition of foreign territories went against American ideals of democracy and self-government. President McKinley, conversely, saw new territories as a way to expand trade. It was also during this period, in 1898, that the United States formally annexed Hawaii. In the blink of an eye the nation became a rising power, with territories stretching from the Caribbean to the Pacific.

With the economy humming and McKinley's popularity at its height, the president was a prodigious favorite to win reelection in 1900, and Republicans nominated him by acclamation. The biggest intrigue at the convention in Philadelphia was over who should be McKinley's running mate, as Vice President Garret Hobart had died of a heart attack the previous year.

There was a groundswell of support among delegates for Governor Theodore Roosevelt of New York, a captivating new political figure who became famous after leading his Rough Riders on a celebrated charge against Spanish troops during the Battle of San Juan Hill in Cuba. Roosevelt had previously been assistant secretary of the navy, and his status as a war hero catapulted him into the governor's office, where he set out to reform state politics. Ironically his reformist crusade became such a thorn in the side of New York Republicans that party leaders practically begged McKinley to take Roosevelt off their hands.

It was a solution that worked for everyone, because McKinley could then add a popular governor and war hero to his ticket. But Senator Mark Hanna of Ohio, chairman of the Republican National Committee, opposed the idea. "Don't any of you realize," complained Hanna, "that there is only one life between that madman and the White House?"[28] There was no way to quell the passion of delegates, however, who chanted "Teddy, Teddy, Teddy" on the convention floor. Hanna bowed to the inevitable, while fatefully telling the president, "Now it is up to you to live."[29]

The Democrats, meanwhile, nominated Bryan again at their convention in Kansas City in July, making the contest a rematch of the 1896 election. Since the gold-versus-silver issue had been silenced by the improved economy, the biggest campaign debate was over "the burning issue of imperialism."[30] More troops had been needed to pacify Cuba and put down an insurrection in the Philippines, a turn of events that horrified those Americans who didn't want to govern a colonial empire. Bryan declared that colonialism "nullifies every principle set forth in the Declaration of Independence."[31]

Another topic that struck a chord with voters was the issue of monopolistic corporate trusts, which Democrats complained were destroying competition and unfairly concentrating wealth. Bryan even tried to link the issues of imperialism, trusts, and the gold standard as three aspects of the same battle "between plutocracy and democracy."[32] But none of it was enough to sway voters during good times. When Republicans campaigned on the slogan "Four more years of the full dinner pail," it was difficult for Democrats to counterattack.[33]

Bryan embarked on another speaking tour, but this time Roosevelt went blow-for-blow with him, giving hundreds of speeches in twenty-four states. He warned audiences of Bryan's "populistic and communistic doctrines" and countered the imperialism argument by declaring America to be "a nation of men, not a nation of weaklings."[34]

McKinley rolled to an easy victory, taking the popular vote by 52 to 46 percent and the electoral tally 292–155. He was the first president since Grant, nearly three decades earlier, to win a second consecutive election.

Then, six months into McKinley's second term, the president was assassinated.

On September 6, 1901, he was shot by the anarchist Leon Czolgosz at the Pan-American Exposition in Buffalo. Anarchists of the era, who rejected authority, had previously murdered several European royals. Czolgosz admitted he shot McKinley because he didn't "believe we should have any rulers."[35] Initially it appeared the assassination attempt had failed, as McKinley survived the shooting and showed improved health for the next few days. But he became critically ill from gangrene and blood poisoning and died on September 14.[36]

A NEW POLITICS FOR A NEW CENTURY

Roosevelt, told McKinley was recovering, was on a camping trip in the Adirondacks at the time. When the president's health plummeted suddenly, a park ranger was sent to track down Roosevelt near the summit of Mount Marcy. The vice president raced back to Buffalo, a journey that began with a hair-raising carriage ride along a twisting precipice in the middle of the night. A *New York Herald* headline described the trip as "that wild ride down the mountain side."[37]

McKinley died that night. Roosevelt arrived in Buffalo by train the next day. There, surrounded by teary-eyed cabinet members, he took the oath of office in the parlor of a local home. At forty-two years old, he was the youngest president in history.

1904

Theodore Roosevelt was one of the most unique characters ever to serve as president. Born to wealth in New York and educated at Harvard, he transformed himself into a rancher in the Dakota Badlands and then into a war hero, while distinguishing himself as a politician, historian, naturalist, and author. After taking office in 1901, his exuberant style, willingness to take decisive stands, and use of the "bully pulpit" (a term he coined) helped him craft an identity that seized the public imagination.

Roosevelt was the first president to push progressive reforms, starting in 1902 when his administration launched an antitrust suit against the Northern Securities Company, a railroad monopoly. Although he wasn't philosophically opposed to big corporations, seeing them as part of the modern economy, Roosevelt believed government needed to thwart unwarranted concentrations of economic power and to protect workers. "We draw the line against misconduct, not against wealth," he said.[38]

On the international front, he set in motion the building of the Panama Canal, seeing it as key to extending American commerce and deploying naval power to the Pacific. When he couldn't get approval for the canal from Colombia, he tacitly sanctioned a revolt by Panamanian nationalists, then recognized Panama's independence from Colombia and negotiated a canal treaty with the new country.

These actions weren't universally popular, but voters still thrilled to Roosevelt's accomplishments and his swashbuckling image, making him an easy favorite to win election in 1904. While he didn't have the full support of conservatives in his party, nobody else could match his stature and popularity. At the national convention in Chicago, he was nominated unanimously.

The Democrats, in the meantime, at their convention in St. Louis, nominated Alton Parker, chief justice of the New York Court of Appeals. The choice was somewhat of a rebuke to Bryan, who'd lost two straight elections, since Parker was a conservative, pro-gold candidate. The Democrats chose him because he was considered a "safe and sane" candidate respected by both parties.[39]

The fall contest was fairly uneventful. Compared to the battles between McKinley and Bryan, one writer found it "a dullish and well-bred election."[40] Roosevelt focused his campaign on the idea of a "Square Deal," encompassing his policy initiatives of consumer protection, regulation of corporations, and conservation of natural resources. "All I ask is a square deal for every man. Give him a fair chance," he said.[41] The fact that Roosevelt was a progressive Republican and Parker a conservative Democrat meant there weren't many policy differences over which to battle. The political world did seem a bit topsy-turvy, since some progressive Democrats backed Roosevelt, while conservative Republicans countered by supporting Parker.

With no compelling reason to turn the incumbent out of office, Roosevelt's personal popularity carried the day and he won a landslide victory, 56 to 38 percent in the popular vote and 336–140 in the Electoral College. Four months later, on the night before his inauguration, Roosevelt remarked to a friend, "Tomorrow I shall come into office in my own right. Then watch out for me!"[42]

1908

Roosevelt wasn't kidding with his inauguration eve prediction. During his second term, he persuaded Congress to pass an array of consequential laws: to protect food and medicine, provide for inspections of meat plants, regulate railroad rates, and reform campaign finance.[43] His love for nature moved him to initiate far-reaching conservation programs. By the end of his presidency, with help from the 1906 Antiquities Act, he had created five new national parks and eighteen national monuments and set aside millions of acres for national forests and game preserves. On top of this, he even won the 1906 Nobel Peace Prize for negotiating an end to the Russo-Japanese War.

In 1908 Roosevelt declined to be a candidate for another term, having promised four years earlier not to run again. It was a pronouncement he regretted. "I would cut my hand off," he told a friend, "if I could recall that written statement."[44] Roosevelt was still immensely popular and likely could have been nominated again. At that year's Republican convention in Chicago, delegates erupted when a speaker mentioned the president's name. They chanted, "Four—four—four years more!" and cheered for forty-nine minutes.[45] Instead, Roosevelt backed Secretary of War William Howard Taft, who was nominated on the first ballot.

Taft, who today might be most remembered for being the country's heaviest president, topping out at 340 pounds, was well-regarded for his tenure in Roosevelt's cabinet, and before that as governor-general of the Philippines and a court of appeals judge. "I do not believe there can be found in the whole country a man so well fitted to be president," commented Roosevelt.[46]

Meanwhile the Democrats met in Denver, the first time a national convention was held in the West. But amid the new surroundings, the party nominated a familiar face in Bryan. Despite having lost the 1896 and 1900 elections, he was still the party's most compelling figure, and Democrats hoped he would mount a stronger campaign against a new opponent.

When the contest got underway, a new technology helped voters engage with the contest in a novel way, as Bryan and Taft recorded speeches for the Edison Record Company. It was the first time voters could hear the candidates' voices through a phonograph, and the recordings were played at rallies and used to stage mock debates.[47]

During the campaign Bryan declared the central question of the election to be: "Shall the people rule?"[48] He called for greater federal control of interstate commerce and the railroads, an eight-hour workday, an income tax, and direct election of senators. His candidacy, however, was undercut by the fact that Republicans under Roosevelt had promoted similar policies. "What is the real difference between the Democratic and Republican parties?" asked Joseph Pulitzer of the *New York World*.[49]

Bryan's other challenge was that Taft was running as the chosen successor of a popular president. He and Roosevelt were so closely linked that a running joke claimed that "Taft" stood for "Takes Advice From Theodore."[50] Taft was by nature a more cautious politician than the incumbent, but he promised to maintain Roosevelt's agenda. And in 1908 that was enough to ensure victory. Taft won the popular vote by 52 to 43 percent and prevailed in the Electoral College 321–162. "We have beaten them to a frazzle!" exulted Roosevelt.[51]

1912

After ensuring Taft's election, Roosevelt got as far away from presidential politics as possible. He went on safari in East Africa, where he hunted big-game animals, collected specimens for the Smithsonian, and gathered material for a book. Then he toured Europe, met world leaders, and accepted his Nobel Peace Prize. All told, Roosevelt was out of the country for more than a year. Gone, but not forgotten. When he sailed back into New York harbor there were hundreds of boats awaiting his arrival, and one hundred thousand people cheered him during a parade up Broadway, leaving little doubt that the former president was still the most imposing persona in American politics.

Back in the United States, Roosevelt promoted a new progressive agenda. In a 1910 speech at Osawatomie, Kansas, he outlined his vision for a New Nationalism, calling for "a genuine and permanent moral awakening." He proposed income and inheritance taxes, prohibition of child labor, more corporate regulations, and conservation of natural resources.[52] He later also advocated for voters to be able to recall judicial decisions, declaring it was unreasonable for courts to prevent elected legislatures from passing a workmen's compensation law, which they'd recently done.[53]

Progressives had been disappointed with Taft, believing he sided too often with party conservatives and was plagued by "weakness and indecision."[54] In time, Roosevelt also came to doubt his successor was up to the job, writing to a friend that Taft was a "commonplace leader; good natured, feebly well meaning . . . and totally unable to grasp or put into execution any really great policy."[55] Soon a chorus of people were urging Roosevelt to make another presidential run.

His first inclination was to support Taft's reelection, but Roosevelt's outlook shifted when Senator Robert La Follette of Wisconsin launched his own progressive challenge to Taft. Once again, the old Rough Rider heard the siren call of politics. By February 1912 he'd made up his mind. "My hat is in the ring!" he declared. "The fight is on and I am stripped to the buff!"[56]

It was a daring move to try wresting the presidency back from his handpicked successor, particularly since most establishment Republicans were on Taft's side and feared Roosevelt had moved too far left.[57] But this was the first presidential contest in which voters had a say in the nominating process, through primary elections in a dozen states. This innovation was pushed by progressives who wanted voters to have more influence. Roosevelt said it was a way to ensure "the absolute right of the people to rule themselves."[58] In 1912, therefore, the nation was treated to a new spectacle: presidential candidates competing openly for their party's nomination.

Roosevelt took to the campaign trail with gusto. He declared Taft was beholden to "the bosses and the great privileged interests" and suggested the president "means well. But he means well feebly."

Taft initially didn't want to go on the attack, but then realized he had no choice. "Sometimes a man in a corner fights," he said.

"I am going to fight." He claimed Roosevelt's agenda was radical and out of the mainstream, and said he wanted to stop his predecessor "from wrecking the Republican Party."[59] The attacks took their toll on Taft, as he'd been close to his former boss. After one day of speeches, a reporter found him weeping. "Roosevelt was my closest friend," he said.[60]

The two presidents battled through the spring, but no matter how hard Taft fought he couldn't overcome Roosevelt's irresistible hold on voters. In the twelve states that held primaries, Roosevelt won nine contests, including Taft's home state of Ohio. He won nearly four hundred thousand more votes and finished with 278 delegates to 48 for Taft and 36 for La Follette.

By today's standards, Roosevelt crushed the field and should have emerged as the presumptive nominee. In 1912, however, most delegates were still controlled by state parties loyal to the sitting president. So while Roosevelt held a delegate lead over Taft going into the party's June convention in Chicago, he didn't command a majority. Before the voting began, the New York Tribune reported, "No man in this city, nor any man of this hemisphere . . . knows, absolutely, who will be nominated by the convention."[61]

The result was essentially decided when the Republican National Committee assigned 235 of the 254 delegates that were still being contested to Taft, drawing howls of outrage from Roosevelt's supporters. Estimates were that Roosevelt would have been short of a majority in any case, but with his fair share of delegates he could have denied Taft a first ballot victory and taken the fight to the floor.[62] As it was, with 540 votes needed for a majority, Taft received 561 and won the nomination.

The meeting ended with the Republican Party fractured, as Roosevelt's supporters promptly organized another convention in Chicago in August. There they founded the Progressive Party and nominated their hero for president. It was, according to observers, a cross between a political convention and a religious revival, with delegates breaking into such songs as "Battle Hymn of the Republic."[63] This was also the first convention with women delegates, including the social reformer Jane Addams, who was the first woman to give a nominating speech.

The new party became known as the Bull Moose Party, after Roosevelt remarked to reporters that he felt as "strong as a bull moose."[64] The platform was a litany of early twentieth-century progressive ideals: labor laws to limit working hours, end child labor, and establish a minimum wage; social insurance programs for the elderly and unemployed; and election reforms to support women's suffrage and limit campaign contributions.

During his convention speech, Roosevelt called for a new progressive vision and accused the major parties of being "husks with no real soul."[65] He told the delegates, "Whatever fate may at the moment overtake any of us, the movement itself will not stop. . . . We stand at Armageddon, and we battle for the Lord."[66]

The Democrats watched the Republican split with satisfaction, believing it gave them a chance to win the White House for the first time since 1892. Even so, after losing three of the past four elections with the progressive Bryan as their nominee, and one with the conservative Parker, the party needed a new leader. The early favorite was Speaker of the House Champ Clark of Missouri, who had won the most primary delegates. But Clark's performance in the primaries wasn't as dominant as Roosevelt's had been, and there was a sense among many that he might not be the strongest candidate. As the New York World put it, "He is a dear old boy, but his leadership is not the sort of leadership the Democratic Party requires in the year 1912 if it is to win the election."[67]

Clark's competition was Woodrow Wilson, a newcomer to national politics who'd served two years as governor of New Jersey. Before that he was president of Princeton University. Wilson was a fresh face who'd been a reformist governor, and he'd won the second most primary delegates.

At the party's Baltimore convention, Clark led Wilson on the first ballot by 440½ to 324. He then seemed to gain control of the nomination on the tenth ballot, when the political machine Tammany Hall swung New York's vote his way, giving Clark a majority of 556 delegates. The Democratic rule, however, was that a candidate needed a two-thirds majority to prevail, so when no new rush of support emerged to push Clark over that threshold, the deadlock persisted for three dozen more ballots.

During that time a few key moments slowly moved the vote in Wilson's direction. The first break came on the fourteenth ballot, when Bryan, who was previously uncommitted, announced he wouldn't back a nominee who was supported by Tammany Hall and Wall Street and was therefore delivering his vote to Wilson. Then, on the twenty-eighth ballot, Indiana switched to Wilson with the promise of vice-presidential consideration for its governor, Thomas Marshall. Still, it was a slow climb, and it wasn't until the forty-sixth ballot that Wilson became his party's nominee.

It's interesting to speculate about how history might have been different had Clark prevailed. While it's easy to assume he would have been elected, given the Republican divisions, Clark was a moderate and a lackluster campaigner, whereas Wilson was more progressive and a more commanding speaker. With Clark as the Democratic candidate, it's just as reasonable to think Roosevelt would have gained the support of progressives from both parties and won the presidency.[68] In which case, it's probable the nation's politics would have realigned in the 1910s, with the Progressives emerging as a major party, leaving Republicans and Democrats to fight for the conservative mantle. Indeed Roosevelt seemed to have that very thought in mind, as his son Kermit remarked that his father was "praying for the nomination of Champ Clark."[69] And some Progressive Party leaders said their movement was "a protest against the entire American political alignment, and for the forcing of a new and better one."[70]

But it was Wilson, not Clark, who faced off against Roosevelt and Taft in 1912, in one of the country's more intriguing and consequential elections.

Wilson headed into the fall campaign as a reformer, but not as a populist. He didn't rail against elites but rather against the power of corporate trusts that stifled competition and distorted markets. His solution was to break up the trusts and promote more opportunities for individuals and small businesses. "What this country needs," he said, "is a body of laws which will look after men who are on the make rather than the men who are already made."[71]

Wilson sold his agenda as the New Freedom to distinguish it from Roosevelt's New Nationalism. The difference was dismissed by some, since both candidates wanted to reduce the power of trusts, but Roosevelt erred on the side of regulating corporations to reduce the exploitation of workers, whereas Wilson preferred to break up large companies to foster competition.[72] Also, Wilson didn't believe the government should regulate child labor or a minimum wage, and he derided Roosevelt's faith in a paternalistic government. "I do not want a government that will take care of me," Wilson said. "I want a government that will make other men take their hands off so that I can take care of myself."[73]

Many of these arguments, of course, still form the basis of our political debates. What's interesting, though, is that the Democrat Wilson was the moderate candidate, criticizing his opponent for trying to centralize power, while the Republican Roosevelt ran on what was then a radical program of government activism.

Also interesting is that Roosevelt was himself outflanked on the left by a serious Socialist candidate, Eugene Debs, who argued that only his party could end the abuses of an industrial economy. The Progressives may have adopted some Socialist causes, said Debs, but they still represented "the present capitalist system, aiming only to mitigate some of its most glaring evils."[74] Debs had previously run for president in 1904 and 1908, but this year he gained more support than any Socialist candidate in history, making 1912 the only election aside from 1860 in which four candidates received at least 5 percent of the vote.

With all this attention on Wilson, Roosevelt, and even Debs, the incumbent president was sometimes an afterthought in the fall campaign. Taft told friends he was "reconciled to defeat" because of Republican divisions and complained that the media paid little attention to him "except that [he] played golf."[75] Taft knew his genial, mild personality wasn't suited to the times. "I have been told that I ought to do this, ought to do that . . . that I do not keep myself in the headlines," he remarked. "I know it, but I can't do it."[76]

There was more than a little irony in the fact that Taft, who'd run four years earlier as Roosevelt's progressive heir apparent, was now left to rely almost solely on the support of Republican conservatives. But he seemed to find comfort in making the Republican Party, as he said, "solid for conservatism."[77] The government, he declared, "cannot create good times. It cannot make the rain to fall, the sun to shine, or the crops to grow."[78]

If this multicandidate race weren't enough drama for one election, there was also an assassination attempt. On October 14, while campaigning in Milwaukee, Roosevelt was shot by a man named John Schrank, who claimed McKinley's ghost told him to stop the former president from a third term. The bullet fractured a rib and lodged in Roosevelt's chest, less than an inch from his heart, after fortuitously being slowed by an eyeglass case and a fifty-page copy of his speech.

Incredibly, Roosevelt insisted on addressing the audience before going to the hospital. "I will deliver the speech or die, one or the other," he said. On stage he announced that he'd just been shot and revealed his bloody shirt, drawing gasps from the crowd. "But it takes more than that to kill a Bull Moose," he declared. He later spent a week in the hospital. Surgeons decided not to remove the bullet unless an infection developed.[79] It remained in his body for the rest of his life.

For a time, it appeared that attention and sympathy from the shooting might vault Roosevelt to victory, but the split among Republicans was too much to overcome. Wilson won 42 percent of the vote to 27 percent for Roosevelt and 23 percent for Taft and easily triumphed in the Electoral College, 435–88–8.

Taft's loss represented the worst performance ever by an incumbent president. But in 1921 he was named chief justice of the Supreme Court, a position he'd longed for even more than the presidency. He thus became the only person to serve as both president and chief justice.

The Birth of Modern Politics

It's not an exaggeration to suggest that modern American politics was born during the sixteen years between 1896 and 1912.

During this era the excesses of industrialization gave life to agrarian populists and urban reformers, and the fusion of these crusades forged what we now know as the Progressive movement.[80] There was, as we've seen, a surge of reform legislation enacted at this time, particularly labor regulations and social insurance for workers, but equally significant was the transformation of American democracy.

Among the changes to politics and presidential elections during these years were the rise of candidate-centered campaigns, the advent of primary elections, and the dawn of the progressive-versus-conservative debate. These new dynamics turned elections into contests that would be almost unrecognizable to a mid-nineteenth-century voter, and each one of these elements is still integral to campaigns today.

Let's start with candidate-centered elections. McKinley had a role in this when he shunned party leaders during his 1896 nomination battle, but the trend escalated with the performances of Bryan and Roosevelt on the campaign trail. Before the twentieth century, it was the rare candidate who dared make a personal case for himself. Soon, though, it became a staple of campaigns. Whereas candidates were once beholden to party organizations and platforms, today it's the other way around, with parties largely taking their cues from victorious candidates.

These developments were amplified by the rise of primary elections in 1912, which was the most significant change to the way nominees were chosen since the first party conventions in 1832. For the next six decades, candidates would navigate a two-tiered system, competing both for primary votes and for support from party leaders, until the 1970s when voters finally overtook political parties as the most important factor in nomination battles.

As the influence of parties declined, however, so did the voter turnout rate. In the nineteenth century, the major parties made sure politics was embraced as a community event, with rallies and torchlight parades. Voter participation was consistently in the 70 to 80 percent range. But when candidates moved to center stage and media and advertising gained in importance, the ability of parties to get out the vote began to wane. Other factors played a role, including more entertainment options for an urbanized middle class, which fragmented the electorate's attention, but voter turnout rates fell below 60 percent and have mostly stayed there ever since.[81]

Finally, this was the era that set Democrats and Republicans on their different courses as, respectively, the nation's liberal and conservative parties.

It was the societal tremors caused by industrialization that first led the parties to swap some of their nineteenth-century philosophies. The Democrats went from being the party of limited government to one that believed in activism, and Republicans dashed off in the other direction. Their core values didn't change, as Democrats still saw themselves as protectors of the individual from exploitation by more powerful interests, while Republicans were still more concerned with the needs of the corporate and financial classes. What changed was that Democrats came to believe that government needed to serve as a "counterweight to the . . . huge industrial corporations" and was the only force capable of ameliorating inequality, whereas Republicans concluded that keeping government out of the way of business interests was a better way to promote commerce.[82] These changes began in 1896, with Bryan's nomination, but they particularly took hold after 1912, when the Wilson-led Democrats moved in a progressive direction and Republicans embraced a more conservative philosophy.

The politics of all this didn't fully shake out until the 1930s, when the Democrats under Franklin Roosevelt cemented themselves as the progressive, or liberal, party. But the dominoes were set in motion during these decades. All in all, it was a rather remarkable era. Without it, present-day politics would look vastly different.

1916, 1920, 1924, and 1928: World War I
to the Roaring Twenties

1916

After his victory in 1912, Wilson embarked on a historic presidency, shepherding a considerable amount of reform legislation through Congress. This included the creation of the Federal Reserve system to manage monetary policy, laws to reduce the power of monopolies and take aim at unfair business practices, the introduction of a graduated income tax, the enactment of an eight-hour workday for railroad workers, and the formation of the National Park Service. It was a torrent of progressive legislation that had been germinating for two decades, and it transformed the government and the major political parties.[83]

Then, in 1914, Wilson's presidency took an unexpected turn when a byzantine series of events plunged Europe into what would become World War I. For two years Wilson maintained a neutral posture toward the conflict. This policy was tested when German submarines attacked neutral ships in British waters and sank the ocean liner *Lusitania* on May 7, 1915. Nearly 1,200 passengers were killed, including 128 Americans, which supercharged a national debate between those who wanted to prepare for American involvement in the war and those who wanted to avoid the fight entirely.

During this period Wilson suffered the death of his wife, Ellen, to a kidney disorder, a loss that drove the president into depression. A year later, though, he met Edith Bolling Galt, a widow and business owner, and the two were married in December 1915.

As the parties geared up for the 1916 presidential contest, Republicans were confident about defeating Wilson's bid for reelection because they believed their 1912 loss was due solely to the Roosevelt-Taft split. The challenge for Republicans was in choosing a candidate. Teddy Roosevelt hinted at his availability and was the strongest voice on the side of war preparations, but party members were still incensed over the former president's third-party run in 1912. The candidate who seemed most popular with all GOP factions was Charles Evans Hughes, a former governor of New York, although he was now a Supreme Court justice and reluctant to return to politics.

When no other major contender emerged from the primaries, the Republicans nominated Hughes anyway, on the third ballot at their June convention in Chicago. Hughes accepted the nomination, noting that while he "wished to remain on the bench" he couldn't decline his party's call.[84] He remains the only active justice ever nominated for president.

The Progressive Party, meanwhile, nominated Roosevelt for another third-party run, but he chose to support Hughes rather than risk splitting the Republican vote again. Roosevelt campaigned energetically for Hughes, despite privately complaining about the candidate's flat speaking style. He referred to him as the "bearded iceberg."[85]

Hughes campaigned largely on traditional Republican issues such as the tariff, which the GOP had long supported as a way to protect manufacturers and raise revenue for the government. He opposed the eight-hour workday for railway workers that Wilson had pushed through Congress, in a sign that Republicans were moving further toward the "small government, anti-labor union, antiregulation positions" that would eventually become the party standard.[86]

Wilson, on the other hand, happily promoted his efforts on behalf of the working class. "I am a progressive," he noted. "I do not spell it with a capital P, but I think my pace is just as fast as those who do."[87]

This was the essence of the message Wilson wanted to campaign on: his progressive achievements. But the growing menace of war in Europe added an air of unpredictability to the election. Try as he might, Wilson was unable to escape talk of the conflict, especially with the bellicose Roosevelt beating the war drum on the campaign trail. Roosevelt even suggested that with a stronger president "the Lusitania would never have been sunk."[88]

Curiously, though, the more Roosevelt battered Wilson, the more it seemed to help the president. Like him, the American public, it seemed, was not that interested in joining the war. So, in an odd twist of fate, Wilson's 1916 reelection campaign turned not on his domestic policy successes but on the slogan "He kept us out of war."[89] When Democrats sensed this was a winning message, they tied Hughes to Roosevelt and claimed a Republican win would mean certain war. Advertisements asked "Wilson and Peace with Honor? Or, Hughes with Roosevelt and War?"[90]

In the end, it was an exceedingly close contest. Wilson had a popular message, but Republicans had a stronger electoral base. When Hughes swept most of the Northeast on Election Day, several papers called the election for the Republican. The news even flashed across screens in Times Square, where one hundred thousand people awaited the results. The candidates went to bed on election night believing Hughes had won.

But the next day Wilson roared back with a better than expected showing in late balloting from the West. Numerous states had razor-thin margins, with New Hampshire decided by just 56 votes, North Dakota by 1,735, and New Mexico by 2,530. When the final results were tallied, Wilson prevailed by 49 to 46 percent in the popular vote and 277–254 in the Electoral College.

The president's success in the West was widely attributed to a peace vote driven by women, as this was the one region where most states allowed women to vote.[91] The decisive state was California, which Wilson won by just 3,773 out of 1 million ballots and where a perceived Hughes snub of the progressive governor Hiram Johnson was a factor. Had California voted Republican, Hughes would have won the electoral vote 267–264, and Wilson would have lost reelection despite winning the popular vote.

1920

As Wilson prepared for another four years in office, he was the dominant figure in American politics and had what the *New York Tribune* described as a "hold on the popular imagination."[92] But he would soon need to turn his attention away not only from the domestic affairs that marked his first term but also from his winning reelection message of keeping the nation out of war, as international concerns took hold of the headlines and altered the course of his presidency.

In January 1917 Germany announced it would resume unrestricted submarine warfare on all ships, a practice it had paused. March then brought news of an intercepted telegram from the German foreign minister, proposing a military alliance with Mexico and the possible return of Texas, New Mexico, and Arizona to the Mexicans. After this, the Germans sank three American ships. Wilson could no longer resist the inevitable. In April the United States entered World War I.

American involvement in the conflict, one of the most destructive in history to that point, helped turn the tide in favor of the Allies. The war ended in November 1918 and Wilson took a lead role in peace negotiations. He issued a Fourteen Points plan for a postwar world that called for such goals as free trade, freedom of the seas, self-determination for ethnic groups, and the formation of an association of nations to settle disputes through diplomacy. Wilson traveled to Paris for the peace conference, becoming the first sitting president to visit Europe, and was hailed by huge crowds as a hero. No one could have imagined then that Wilson's presidency would come undone within a year.

When the Treaty of Versailles was signed on June 28, 1919, it included Wilson's proposal to form what came to be known as the League of Nations. Back home, however, Wilson's signature accomplishment couldn't muster the two-thirds Senate majority needed for ratification, partly due to the president's stubbornness in refusing modifications. "I shall consent to nothing," he insisted.[93] Instead he set out in September 1919 on an extended speaking tour to present his vision to the people. But after speaking in Colorado on September 25, Wilson suffered a stroke. His physician announced he was suffering from "nervous exhaustion," and the president returned to Washington. Back in the White House, on October 2, he had a more massive stroke, which partially paralyzed him.

Astoundingly, Wilson's wife, physician, and top aides conspired to keep his condition a secret. For the rest of his term, the debilitated president was rarely seen in public. Edith Wilson served as de facto chief of staff, passing communications to her husband. Vice President Thomas Marshall should have assumed the presidency, but no one would declare Wilson incapacitated.[94]

These last years of the Wilson presidency were also a time of considerable national stress and upheaval. In 1918 Americans were ravaged by what was then known as the Spanish flu pandemic, which killed 50 million people worldwide and 675,000 in the United States.[95] The pandemic triggered mass shutdowns of businesses and schools as the country tried to control the spread of infections, and even President Wilson became severely ill with the virus.

The following year the nation had barely recovered from this trauma when it was battered by waves of racial and labor strife. The Great Migration of Blacks out of the South in the 1910s had caused increased racial tensions, and this hostility erupted in 1919. That year white mobs incited dozens of racial riots, during which at least 250 African Americans were lynched, shot, or beaten to death and thousands of homes and businesses were destroyed. It was dubbed the Red Summer for the amount of blood that was shed.[96] Meanwhile a postwar recession and rising unemployment generated labor discord, leading more than 4 million workers to go on strike.

Amid these tensions, cynicism with government gave rise to an anarchist movement. Activists unleashed a series of urban bombings, including a 1920 blast on Wall Street that killed thirty-eight people and was at the time the worst terrorist attack on American soil. This happened to coalesce with the Red Scare, the fear that a communist movement would infiltrate the United States in the wake of the 1917 Russian Revolution. In response to all this unrest, the government arrested and deported thousands of immigrants with links to left-wing movements. They were prosecuted under the Espionage and Sedition Acts, which Congress had passed during the war. These same laws also ensnared Socialist Party leader Eugene Debs, who—despite leading a party that won 6 percent of the 1912 presidential vote—was imprisoned merely for giving an antiwar speech.[97]

Needless to say, this was a lot of turmoil for a few years. It all merged in the public mind, so when the 1920 election rolled around many voters longed for nothing more than a return to simpler times. This sentiment would greatly influence that year's presidential election, which was the first contest in which women nationwide were allowed to vote, following passage of the Nineteenth Amendment.

When the contest began, neither party had a clear frontrunner. On the Democratic side, the primaries were inconclusive and the nomination battle was waged at that summer's convention in San Francisco. The top contenders were former treasury secretary William McAdoo of California, who was Wilson's son-in-law, and Ohio governor James Cox. A stalemate ensued for dozens of ballots over three days before momentum shifted to Cox, who triumphed on the forty-fourth ballot. Cox was a popular governor who'd been a newspaper publisher before entering politics, but reaction to his nomination was mixed. Newspapers called him "a fine fellow" and "a man of the people" but also a "man of mediocre ability."[98]

Among Republicans, the early favorite was Teddy Roosevelt, now back in the good graces of his party. But Roosevelt's health had been in decline, and the country was shocked when he unexpectedly died in late 1919. Absent Roosevelt, the main contenders were Gen. Leonard Wood, former army chief of staff, and Governor Frank Lowden of Illinois. But neither Wood nor Lowden could attract a majority of delegates at the party convention in Chicago, forcing Republicans to consider other candidates.

Attention turned to Senator Warren Harding of Ohio, also a former newspaper publisher. He'd been considered a fringe contender before performing dismally in the primaries. Nevertheless he was from a vital state and was a superior orator. He'd made a speech in Boston in May that seemed to capture the tenor of the times. "America's present need is not heroics, but healing," he said, "not nostrums, but normalcy; not revolution, but restoration."[99]

After party leaders settled on Harding as a compromise candidate, he won the Republican nomination on the tenth ballot. Much as with Cox, though, reaction was subdued. The *New York*

Times declared Harding "a very respectable Ohio politician of the second class."[100] Senator Frank Brandegee of Connecticut summed up how even fellow Republicans felt: "There ain't any first-raters this year. We've got a lot of second-raters and Warren Harding is the best of the second-raters."[101]

So the campaign began, curiously enough, with two Ohioans who'd been newspaper publishers before migrating to politics, Cox with the *Dayton Daily News* and Harding with the *Marion Daily Star*. Even more interesting, in terms of history, was that the vice-presidential candidates would have more of a lasting impact on the country than did the men at the top of the ticket. The Democrats chose an up-and-coming thirty-eight-year-old from New York named Franklin Roosevelt, then the assistant secretary of the navy, and Republicans went with Governor Calvin Coolidge of Massachusetts.

That fall, Cox traveled widely and gave hundreds of speeches to more than 2 million people, while Harding mostly engaged in a front-porch campaign from his home. This didn't seem to fit the new age of presidential campaigns, not after Wilson and Roosevelt, but Harding was consciously evoking a simpler time. He even imported the flagpole from McKinley's front yard as a reminder of his fellow Ohioan's 1896 effort. In a similar vein, Harding masterfully riffed off his springtime speech and promised a "return to normalcy."

In a choice between Wilsonian activism and a return to normalcy, there was little question where voters stood. The country was simply exhausted by war and upheaval. As one writer remarked, "The nation was spiritually tired. Wearied by the excitements of the war and the nervous tension of the Big Red Scare, they hoped for quiet and healing."[102] And so Harding crushed Cox. He won the popular vote 60 to 34 percent and the electoral vote 404–127 to become the twenty-ninth president.

1924

Warren Harding today sits low in historical rankings of presidents, but he was popular while in office. He received credit for an economic recovery, and his administration lowered taxes, increased tariff rates, and implemented a new system for managing the federal budget. Mostly, though, Americans liked him because he exuded a casual optimism that comforted them after the dramas of the past decade.

One of the reasons he gets dinged by the history books is because his administration was wracked by corruption, including the infamous Teapot Dome scandal that saw the interior secretary accept bribes for granting leases to oil companies to drill on federal lands. The president himself wasn't implicated in those scandals, but he fathered a daughter after an extramarital affair with a younger woman, Nan Britton, who later wrote a tell-all book about their relationship. Britton was accused by many of spinning a far-fetched tale, and it wasn't until 2015 that genetic testing proved her story.[103]

Additionally, historians don't have a full perspective on the Harding presidency because he didn't live to the end of his term. In the summer of 1923 he embarked on a western speaking tour, becoming the first president to visit Alaska. During this journey he suffered a heart attack and died on August 2 in San Francisco.

Vice President Calvin Coolidge succeeded Harding and also proved to be a popular chief executive. It didn't hurt to preside during an era of prosperity, of course, but Silent Cal, a famously taciturn New Englander, focused on lowering taxes and reducing the size of government. This prompted one supporter to remark that Coolidge "never wasted any time, never wasted any words, and never wasted any public money."[104] At the 1924 Republican convention in Cleveland, Coolidge was overwhelmingly nominated to run for his own term. The convention was so sedate, however, the humorist Will Rogers suggested opening the churches "to liven things up a bit."[105]

The Democrats, in contrast, had anything but an easy time in finding a nominee. The leading candidates were Governor Al Smith of New York and McAdoo again. Smith was a popular governor and McAdoo had created the Federal Reserve system while serving in Wilson's cabinet, but neither contender controlled enough delegates to claim the nomination at the convention in New York. To complicate matters, the party's two biggest constituencies each backed a different candidate and were bitterly divided over key issues.

For decades the party's core base was the rural, Protestant vote in the South and West. This electorate in 1924 strongly favored Prohibition, the constitutional amendment outlawing alcohol. A fair number of these delegates were also affiliated with the newly revived Ku Klux Klan, which was not only anti-Black but also anti-Catholic, anti-Semitic, and anti-immigrant. The KKK was, essentially, a nativist movement that opposed anyone who seemed to threaten the perpetuation of a white, Protestant American culture. And the organization had several million members in the 1920s, with groups in every state.

These issues of nativism and Prohibition were more interrelated than they seem on the surface, and in a way that was hugely problematic for Democrats. That's because Prohibitionists connected the problem of alcohol abuse to urban immigrants. The "immigrant and the saloon," in this view, were "inseparable evils from which Americans had to be protected."[106] Well, as fate would have it, the Democrats' other longtime base consisted of, yes, immigrants. These voters clustered in Northern cities, were loyal to urban political machines, were opposed to Prohibition, and happened to include large numbers of Catholic and Jews.

So the party's two key sources of support were in direct and visceral opposition to each other in 1924. McAdoo, a Georgia native, supported Prohibition and was backed by the rural South and West. And Smith, a native New Yorker and a Catholic, denounced Prohibition and was supported by Northerners, urban residents, and immigrants. Klan members were especially vehement in opposing Smith, calling him "that Catholic" from "Jew York."[107]

The convention thus turned into a cultural clash as much as a political battle. When Smith's supporters offered an amendment condemning the Klan, it triggered a heated debate, as even some McAdoo supporters who opposed the Klan didn't want to risk a backlash by formally condemning the group. In the end, the resolution was defeated by a single vote.[108]

On top of this the Democrats still had a convention rule that required nominees to win a two-thirds majority, which was a recipe for stalemate in a closely divided party. On the first ballot, McAdoo received 431 votes to 241 for Smith. On the fifteenth ballot, it was McAdoo 479 and Smith 305. The seventieth ballot brought McAdoo 415 and Smith 323. The delegates just kept casting the same votes, day after day, and neither faction would budge. One historian said it was as if the battle was "between the Pope and the Imperial Wizard of the KKK, so solidly did the Catholic delegates support Smith and the Klan delegates support McAdoo."[109]

New York was experiencing a record heat wave that summer, which turned Madison Square Garden into a virtual sauna and led the convention to be dubbed a "Klanbake."[110] As the proceedings dragged on for more than two weeks, tempers flared and fistfights broke out between delegates. The nation's voters, who were listening to a political convention on radio for the first time, were horrified by the intraparty brawl.

Finally, mercifully, after ninety-six ballots, McAdoo and Smith mutually withdrew their candidacies. On the 103rd ballot of the longest convention in history, the delegates compromised on John Davis of West Virginia, a former congressman and ambassador to the United Kingdom. "Is it true, or is it a dream?" asked one delegate when it was over.[111]

Davis was well-regarded by many people. The *Saturday Evening Post* called him "a great lawyer, efficient and experienced public servant, a cultivated and courteous gentleman."[112] But there was one rather significant problem: he was a conservative, the sort of candidate the Democrats hadn't nominated since Parker and Cleveland. He was "an honest and attractive conservative," said one person, "but nonetheless a conservative."[113]

Progressives in both parties were appalled, since they were now left with a choice between the conservative Davis and the even more conservative Coolidge. This sparked a third-party movement, as progressives staged a third convention that summer, also in Cleveland, and nominated the Republican La Follette for president. The move had echoes of 1912, when Teddy Roosevelt mounted a similar third-party campaign. In both cases, the Progressive Party hoped to unite liberals under one banner and spur a realignment of national politics. But this time, lacking the star power of a Roosevelt to attract support and without a cohesive party structure, the Progressives struggled to coordinate a national campaign on short notice.[114]

Despite their organizational struggles, the Progressives found themselves on the receiving end of considerable fire from Republicans. Believing that La Follette provided a sharper contrast with Coolidge than Davis did, the GOP ran as if the Progressives were their real challenger. One publication remarked that the president's habit of "coolly ignoring his Democratic opponent is the one novel feature of the contest. Nothing like it has ever been known."[115]

This led to an odd scenario where Davis actually complained that Republicans were disregarding him. The only thing Republicans talked about, he said, was the fear that "under every bedstead lurks a Bolshevik ready to destroy them."[116] The GOP framed the election as "Coolidge or Chaos," and in a line of attack that sounds uncannily familiar even today the president asserted that the question facing the country was "whether America will allow itself to be degraded into a communistic or socialistic state, or whether it will remain American."[117]

The Republicans focused on the theme of prosperity as well, and came up with one of the great campaign slogans in "Keep Cool with Coolidge." They also played up the president's rural roots, with photo ops of Coolidge in overalls, pitching hay on the Vermont farm.[118] A campaign song, "Keep Cool and Keep Coolidge," reminded voters of how the president took the oath of office at his father's farmhouse:

> In a quaint New England farmhouse on an early summer's day,
> A farmer's boy became our Chief in a homely, simple way.
> With neither pomp nor pageantry he firmly met the task.
> To keep him on that job of his is all the people ask.[119]

Davis did what he could under the circumstances, but it was difficult for him to sway voters in a booming economy. Even talk of the Harding-era scandals fell with a thud, since Coolidge hadn't been involved. And the 103-ballot debacle at the Democratic convention was fresh in voters' minds, which didn't help Davis at all. Davis later noted that he was always completely honest during his campaign, except for one thing: "I went around the country telling people I was going to be elected, and I knew I hadn't any more chance than a snowball in Hell."[120]

Coolidge breezed to victory, winning the popular vote by 54 to 29 percent over Davis, with La Follette taking 17 percent in third place. In the Electoral College, Coolidge won 382–136–13.

1928

Few people in the 1920s would have disputed that Coolidge was a successful president. He led the nation for much of the Roaring Twenties, a period of tremendous economic growth that became known as the Coolidge Prosperity.[121] There was a housing boom, a stock market surge, and a consumer spending eruption as many Americans bought cars, radios, and household appliances for the first time.

Coolidge declined to run for reelection in 1928, asserting that he lacked the desire and energy for another term. In his typically laconic manner, he gathered reporters for a press conference and handed each one a slip of paper with the words "I do not choose to run for president in 1928." He then dismissed them without answering questions.[122]

The president did explain himself further to a friend, however. Referring to the trauma of the late 1910s, he said, "The people wanted rest, and that is what I was naturally adapted to give them, and did give them. They have prospered under those conditions. . . . But a different condition now confronts us. From this time on, there must be something constructive applied to the affairs of government, and it will not be sufficient to say, 'Let business take care of itself.' . . . I do not feel I am the man to fill that sort of position."[123]

To succeed Coolidge, Republicans united behind Herbert Hoover, who was the party's most popular candidate despite never having held office. Hoover is most remembered today for presiding over the start of the Great Depression, but he'd had a remarkable career before that. Orphaned as a child, he became an engineer and a prominent businessman, then gained international renown as a humanitarian during World War I after organizing a campaign to deliver food to 10 million civilians in Belgium who were trapped between German and Allied lines. He later became food administrator under Wilson and commerce secretary under Harding and Coolidge.

There was talk about him as a presidential candidate as early as 1920. At the time, he described himself as an "independent progressive" and it was unclear which party he favored. Franklin Roosevelt, who worked with Hoover in the Wilson administration, remarked, "He is certainly a wonder and I wish we could make him President." Some floated the possibility of a Hoover-Roosevelt ticket for Democrats, which sounds astonishing now in light of later history.[124] Hoover, though, aligned himself with the Republicans. By 1928 he was so popular with the public, who admired him "as the embodiment of the American dream," that it was almost preordained he'd be the nominee.[125] He won an easy first-ballot victory at the convention in Kansas City.

The Democrats, meanwhile, were determined to put memories of their 1924 convention fiasco behind them. Despite continued resistance from some rural delegates, Al Smith won a first-ballot victory at the convention in Houston and made history as the first Roman Catholic nominated for president.

Smith was as much of a self-made man as Hoover and yet was an entirely different character. The governor was a home-grown product of New York City, with the accent to prove it. Born in a third-floor tenement on the Lower East Side, he dropped out of school in eighth grade to help support his family by getting a job in the Fulton Fish Market. He came up in politics through the Tammany Hall machine, then authored numerous labor reforms, including the country's first workmen's compensation law, before becoming a popular four-term progressive governor.[126]

This set up a fascinating general election between the business-oriented Hoover, a reserved Quaker and product of rural America, and the lifelong politician Smith, an urban Catholic known as "the Happy Warrior." The contest even had a nickname, the "Brown Derby" campaign, because of Smith's hat wear. But Hoover represented the incumbent party and had a flourishing economy on his side, whereas Smith was handicapped mightily by his religion and his background. A wide swath of rural, Protestant voters in the South and the West just couldn't bring themselves to support an Irish Catholic from New York. And so, in the fall of 1928, the same urban-rural and Catholic-Protestant divide that had ruptured the Democratic convention four years earlier was replayed on the national stage.

"A Vote for Al Smith Is a Vote for the Pope" was a common refrain.[127] The evangelist Bob Jones, an ardent Prohibitionist, said he'd "rather see a saloon on every corner than a Catholic in the White House."[128] Rumors about Smith tore through church congregations and small towns. It was said that Protestant marriages would be annulled, that Smith had secret plans to extend the Holland Tunnel under the Atlantic to the Vatican, and that the pope was planning to move to Washington DC.[129] One political cartoon merged the issues of Catholicism, Prohibition, and Smith's lack of formal education in a single image: it showed Smith driving a beer truck with the message "Make America 100% Catholic, Drunk and Illiterate."[130] As one journalist explained, "The whole Puritan civilization which has built a sturdy, orderly nation is threatened by Smith."[131]

It was truly a tale of two campaigns. Smith attracted throngs of adoring fans for speeches in major cities but was greeted by burning crosses in Indiana, Oklahoma, Montana, and other stops.[132] Hoover barely had to campaign. He was promoted as a "great engineer" for a time when "the big problems of government are engineering problems," and a president who would ensure continued prosperity.[133] Republicans promised voters a "chicken in every pot and two cars in every garage."[134]

"You can't lick this prosperity thing," said Will Rogers.[135] The economic successes of the 1920s perhaps made Hoover's victory all but inevitable in 1928, regardless of the Democratic nominee, but Smith's religious handicap no doubt contributed to the wide margin of his loss.

On Election Day, Hoover trounced Smith by a landslide margin of 58 to 41 percent in the popular vote and 444–87 in the Electoral College. Hoover won forty of forty-eight states, including in traditionally Democratic areas of the Deep South. Despite Smith's loss, his vote presaged a coming political shift, as Catholics and immigrants helped him to wins in the country's twelve largest cities, an urban vote that would soon play a key role in Franklin Roosevelt's New Deal coalition.

Cultural Change in the Jazz Age

The 1920s stand out even now, a century later, as an almost mythical period of parties and prosperity. One writer called it a "whirligig of jazz and speakeasies, Model Ts and skyscrapers."[136] It was also described as an era of "hip flasks, joy rides, and bathtub gin parties."[137]

But it wasn't all fun and frolic. The Jazz Age was also the time of the fabled "Lost Generation," a term coined by Gertrude Stein and made famous by Ernest Hemingway to describe young Americans who were disillusioned and trying to find their place in the world in the aftermath of the world war. Additionally, the country's politics were being impacted by rising inequality, cultural and demographic changes, a revived nativist movement, and an urban-rural divide—all factors that impact present-day politics as well.

One of the more vital cultural transformations of the era had to do with the role of women, who won the right to vote in every state as of 1920 and were joining the workforce in great numbers. These changes helped ignite the era of the "new woman," at least in urban areas, as "hemlines rose, young women bobbed their hair, smoked cigarettes, and sipped cocktails in speakeasies."[138]

Similarly, African Americans were becoming more visible and prominent, spurred by the Great Migration. In 1917 and 1918 alone, five hundred thousand Blacks left their lives behind in the South to take on factory jobs in Northern cities. This increased urban tensions and sparked race riots, but it also spread African American culture to more corners of the nation. Jazz music helped define the decade, and the artistic eruption of the Harlem Renaissance blossomed in the 1920s.

The other big demographic shift came from an immigration surge, as many new citizens arrived from southern and eastern Europe, including Italian and Polish Catholics, Russian Jews, and others. This spurred a nativist backlash as strong as the one that gave rise to the Know Nothings of the 1850s. It helped increase membership in the KKK and led to legislation in 1921 and 1924 that limited immigration and set quotas on newcomers from specific countries, such as Italy, while favoring new arrivals from northern Europe.

These changes all helped magnify divisions between urban and rural residents. The gulf wasn't exactly new, but these Americans were finding it harder to relate to each other. For rural citizens, in particular, the fast-growing cities were foreign cultures, with their factories, tenements, saloons and speakeasies, newly confident women, hordes of immigrants, and growing numbers of Blacks. One writer described the rural fears of a changing nation this way: "The America of our grandfathers was a land of blond men of Nordic or so-called Anglo-Saxon blood, who lived outdoors, tilled the soil, herded cattle. . . . The America of our grandsons will be a heavily populated country of short, dark-skinned men, living for the most part in the most crowded, complicated and enormous cities the world has ever seen, depending on manufacturing, trade and commerce for their living."[139]

By the end of the decade it was apparent that the Roaring Twenties and the Coolidge Prosperity were real enough, but so were the social and demographic tensions that were roiling the political waters. The frivolity of the Jazz Age, in retrospect, helped mask the reality of a country in transition.

5

★ ★ ★

1932-64

The New Deal to the Great Society

Coffee at the White Horse Tavern in Newport, Rhode Island

The age of presidential politics that runs from the 1932 to 1964 elections was marked at the start by the Great Depression, in the middle by World War II, and at the end by a postwar world that transformed American culture and politics. By the 1960s the country and the presidency looked vastly different than they had in the 1930s. As such, no single place defines these decades. Near the end of this era, though, presidential politics was unusually well-connected to a stretch of coastline in southern Rhode Island, which makes the White Horse Tavern in Newport an intriguing spot from which to reflect on this next presidential epoch.

These connections begin in 1952, when some visiting Republican businessmen at a country club in Watch Hill, Rhode Island, were chatting about the need for a good slogan for Dwight Eisenhower's presidential campaign. They contacted the adman Rosser Reeves for his thoughts. Reeves, who is purportedly an inspiration for the character of Don Draper in the *Mad Men* TV series, came back with a proposal not for a slogan but for an entire television advertising campaign, a new idea for presidential politics.[1] This led to a series of spots called "Eisenhower Answers America," which revolutionized the marketing of candidates.

One year later, on September 12, 1953, a few dozen miles down the road, a young Massachusetts senator named John Kennedy married Jacqueline Bouvier at St. Mary's Catholic Church in Newport. Kennedy wasn't yet a national figure, but the glamour of the union made the event a big story, with photos in *Life* magazine.

Then, in September 1957, President Eisenhower was vacationing in Newport when he sent federal troops to escort Black students into classes at Little Rock Central High School in Arkansas and to restore order amid protests over desegregation. Eisenhower returned to Newport in 1958 and 1960 and maintained a summer White House in the Commandant's Residence at Fort Adams, now known as the Eisenhower House.

When Kennedy succeeded Eisenhower as president in 1961, he also had a summer White House in Newport. In Kennedy's case, it was at Hammersmith Farm, his wife's childhood home. The entrance drive to Hammersmith Farm, as it happens, is less than a half mile from the entrance to Fort Adams, so that little expanse of road was quite a center of presidential power for a half dozen years.

This confluence of events is what makes Newport a fitting site for our next coffee excursion. And the White Horse Tavern is a unique setting in itself because it has links not only to this period of time but to all of presidential history, having opened in 1673.

Yes, 1673. That means the White Horse, the oldest restaurant in the country, was already almost a century old when George Washington journeyed to Newport in 1781 to meet General Rochambeau of France and plan the Revolutionary War campaign that led to the defeat of British troops at Yorktown. Washington and Rochambeau may even have met at the White Horse, though rumors are unconfirmed. The tavern is just blocks away from Touro Synagogue, the recipient of a famous letter that Washington wrote about religious liberty after a presidential visit to Rhode Island in 1790.

The White Horse was there a century later, too, during the Gilded Age, when the Vanderbilts and others built mansions in Newport—and when a vacationing President Chester Arthur in

1882 caused a stir by skipping a local clambake he'd been expected to attend (because he was in the early stages of the kidney disease that would later kill him).[2] And the tavern was there in 1942 when thousands of young naval officers, including John Kennedy and Richard Nixon, underwent training at bases near Newport during World War II.

That's just some of the presidential history that has unfurled within a few miles of the White Horse Tavern. And yet the best presidential connection may be the simplest one, because the tavern was one of Jackie Kennedy's favorite spots in her Newport hometown. She even had a preferred table there, in an alcove by an upstairs window.

The White Horse Tavern, it should be noted, is today a restaurant and not a coffee shop, much like Fraunces Tavern and Gadsby's Tavern from earlier eras. But you can enjoy a coffee with dessert or just relax with a drink at the bar. Or you can enjoy a meal and a coffee in the tavern, then point your car to Newport's Ocean Drive, cruise past the summer White Houses at Fort Adams and Hammersmith Farm, then stop at Brenton Point and gaze at the waters of Narragansett Bay, where President Kennedy used to sail. There you can muse about the presidential era that ended in the 1960s but that began in 1932 with the election of another president who enjoyed sailing, Franklin Roosevelt.

1932, 1936, 1940, and 1944: FDR, the Great Depression, and World War II

1932

When Herbert Hoover accepted the Republican nomination for president in 1928, he touted the economic successes of the previous decade: "We in America are nearer today to the final triumph over poverty than ever before in the history of any land. . . . The poorhouse is vanishing from among us."[3]

One wonders how many times President Hoover wished he could take back those words. A little more than a year later, in October 1929, the stock market crashed and the Roaring Twenties came to a screeching halt. The collapsing market wasn't the only cause of the Great Depression that followed, but, in short order, investors lost wealth, business investments declined, consumers stopped spending, trade dwindled, farmers defaulted on loans, banks collapsed, and unemployment rocketed from 3.2 percent in 1929 to 23.6 percent in 1932.[4] Soup kitchens and homeless encampments sprang up like weeds.

The Hoover administration tried to reinvigorate the economy by funding public works projects and providing loans to shore up banks in a foreshadowing of later New Deal programs. But the president was more of an engineer than a politician and didn't know how to soothe a frazzled nation. "You can't make a Teddy Roosevelt out of me," he admitted.[5]

Perhaps Hoover's biggest political error, though, was in clinging to a philosophy that disdained government assistance to individuals. Local communities and private charities simply weren't equipped to deal with such a wide-ranging calamity as the Depression. But when Congress tried to fund unemployment assistance, Hoover insisted that government shouldn't replace the "responsibility of the individual man and woman to their neighbors."[6] Senator Robert Wagner of New York asked why it was acceptable to provide aid to bankers but not to "that forlorn American . . . who has been without wages."[7]

So, rightly or wrongly, the image of Hoover that settled into the public mind was that of a coldhearted bureaucrat. Homeless camps became known as Hoovervilles. Newspapers were Hoover blankets. A person who was Hooverized had been impoverished.[8] Through all the misery, however, Hoover never lost faith that a recovery was imminent. When Republicans nominated him for a second term, he believed an improving economy would be the catalyst for his reelection.

The leading Democratic contender to oppose Hoover in 1932 was Franklin Roosevelt, the two-term governor of New York. Roosevelt won eleven of thirteen state primaries but went into the convention facing stiff challenges from former governor Al Smith, the 1928 nominee, and Speaker of the House John Nance Gar-

THE NEW DEAL TO THE GREAT SOCIETY

ner of Texas. Together they had the votes to stop Roosevelt from reaching the two-thirds threshold for the nomination. On the first ballot at the Democratic convention in Chicago, FDR built a 464-vote lead over Smith but was still 104 delegates short of victory.

When not much changed on the next two ballots, the convention seemed headed for a stalemate. Former secretary of war Newton Baker of Ohio was discussed as a compromise candidate. But the nomination battle changed course after the third ballot, when Garner realized he couldn't win and concluded that a drawn-out fight would hurt his party. The media mogul William Randolph Hearst, a Garner supporter who held sway over the California delegation, wanted to keep Baker off the ticket. So together they swung the Texas and California votes to Roosevelt on the fourth ballot, giving him the nomination. In exchange, Garner became FDR's running mate.[9]

After securing the victory, Roosevelt announced he would fly to Chicago to accept the nomination in person. This was a dramatic gesture; it not only broke a long-standing tradition of candidates waiting at home for a formal notification, but air travel was still considered risky. FDR "wanted to let people know that his approach was going to be bold and daring," an aide recalled.[10] So Roosevelt, his family, and a few assistants made what was then a noisy and jarring journey from Albany to Chicago.[11] The American Airways charter took nine hours and had two refueling stops; today you can make the same trip nonstop in a little over two hours.

It's hard to grasp today how audacious this journey was perceived to be at the time, but it was only five years after Charles Lindbergh electrified the world by flying solo across the Atlantic, and just a month after Amelia Earhart repeated the same feat. More than ten thousand people gathered at Chicago's Municipal Airport to await Roosevelt's flight. The New York Times described the excitement that greeted his landing as reminiscent of "the arrival of a transatlantic flier."[12]

Roosevelt appeared at the convention to the tune of "Happy Days Are Here Again," which became his theme song for the rest of his career. He told delegates, "Let it be from now on the task of our party to break foolish traditions. . . . This is no time for fear, for reaction or for timidity. . . . I pledge you, I pledge myself, to a new deal for the American people."[13] The next day a newspaper cartoon showed a farmer looking up at an airplane, on which was emblazoned the words "New Deal." And so, somewhere between a plane ride, a speech, and a political cartoon, FDR's New Deal was born.

Roosevelt's candidacy was historic for yet another reason, for he was the first nominee with a physical disability. He'd been stricken with polio in 1921, when he was thirty-nine, just a year after being a vice-presidential candidate. His leg muscles withered, and he had to use a wheelchair the rest of his life. He could stand with help from iron leg braces, and he gave speeches by holding onto railings or podiums. With much effort and determination, he learned to walk short distances by locking his braces, pivoting his hips, and using family members for support.[14]

It was public knowledge that Roosevelt had polio, although the magnitude of his disability was rarely discussed. Photographers avoided pictures of him in his wheelchair or being helped into or out of vehicles. Instead the public saw images of a vigorous candidate from the waist up, flashing his high-wattage smile. There were some who didn't think he was physically up to the demands of the presidency, while others believed his struggles gave him strength. Roosevelt himself remarked, "If you spent two years in bed trying to wriggle your big toe, after that anything else would seem easy!"[15]

That fall, Roosevelt presented himself as Hoover's opposite by endorsing the idea that the government should assist individuals "not as a matter of charity, but as a matter of social duty."[16] When he refused to be pinned down to a specific set of programs, Hoover called him a "chameleon on plaid."[17] FDR responded that the times demanded "bold, persistent experimentation. . . . It is common sense to take a method and try it: If it fails, admit it and try another. But above all try something."[18]

With the economy in its third year of distress, Hoover had little to offer voters other than his belief that conditions would be even worse under the Democrats. Roosevelt's philosophies, he said, would "alter the whole foundations of our national life."[19] And he suggested the country shouldn't be "changing horses in the middle of a stream." Democrats retorted, "Change horses or drown!"[20]

On Election Day, Roosevelt won in a rout. He took the popular vote 57 to 40 percent and the Electoral College 472–59, winning forty-two of forty-eight states.

Even after winning the election, however, Roosevelt's presidency almost never happened. On February 15, 1933, as he prepared to address twenty thousand people in Miami (the Twentieth Amendment moving inaugurations to January 20 took effect in 1937), an unemployed bricklayer named Giuseppe Zangara fired at the president-elect from ten yards away. Somehow the bullets missed Roosevelt, instead hitting Mayor Anton Cermak of Chicago, who died of his wounds. That's how close the country came to having John Nance Garner as the thirty-second president.

For Americans, it must have seemed like one more sign that the world was still spinning out of control. Indeed during the four months between the election and the inauguration, the economy sank deeper into misery. The unemployment rate rose to nearly 25 percent, the financial system teetered closer to the brink of collapse, and frightened bank customers tried to withdraw deposits. So dire was the situation that one FDR advisor rated the chance of imminent revolution as "about even."[21]

As the inauguration approached, someone told Roosevelt that, depending on his success in overcoming the Depression, he might be remembered as the greatest president in history, or the worst. "If I fail," said Roosevelt, "I shall be the last one."[22]

1936

After taking the oath of office in 1933, Roosevelt tried to soothe an anxious nation with the famous line in his inaugural address, "The only thing we have to fear is fear itself." He then closed the banks temporarily, called Congress into special session, and embarked on the much mythologized "first hundred days" of activism.

The deluge of legislation in those first months included bills to invest in infrastructure projects, insure bank deposits, expand business loans, create conservation jobs, restructure the farm economy, and regulate labor, wages, and prices. The president also suspended the gold standard, giving the Federal Reserve more freedom to increase the money supply and inflate the economy. It was a far-reaching program, but there was no grand plan behind the New Deal. It was all improvisational. As Roosevelt remarked, it was akin to the shifting strategies of a football game where "future plays will depend on how the next one works."[23]

When Roosevelt began his reelection campaign in 1936, the economy was on the upswing. Unemployment was still 17 percent, which would usually be considered horrific, but the situation had stabilized and relief programs were helping the poor. Despite this progress, those around FDR still had a simmering fear that American democracy and capitalism remained at risk. Fascist governments were in power in Germany and Italy, communism was entrenched in Russia, and America wasn't immune to the lure of these ideologies. During Roosevelt's first term, some Wall Street financiers approached a retired general about raising troops to overthrow the government and install a fascist dictatorship. The "Wall Street Putsch" failed because Gen. Smedley Butler instead reported the conspiracy to the FBI, but it was front-page news in 1934.[24]

There was also a threat from left-wing autocrats, notably Huey Long, a populist Louisiana senator and former governor who'd run his state as a quasi-dictatorship. Long founded a "Share Our Wealth" movement, which called for limiting personal fortunes, redistributing wealth, and providing guaranteed incomes. He had millions of followers nationwide; a poll commissioned by Democrats indicated that a third party headed by Long could imperil Roosevelt's reelection.[25] Long's effort, though, like the Wall Street Putsch, was quashed by the hand of fate when he was assassinated by a political opponent back home. But the reality is that the United States in the 1930s had to be alert for signs of rebellion from both the right and the left.

Partly in response to this electoral threat, Roosevelt in 1935 added more populist proposals to his agenda, including bills to provide jobs for the unemployed, to guarantee the right of labor unions to organize, and to create a Social Security insurance system for the elderly and disabled. This became known as the Second New Deal and arguably gave Roosevelt a longer-lasting legacy than did his flood of earlier legislation.

In 1936 the president was easily renominated at the Democratic convention in Philadelphia, where the party also abolished the two-thirds rule that had bedeviled it for decades. Roosevelt told delegates that their generation had "a rendezvous with destiny" and was fighting a war "for the survival of democracy."[26]

Governor Alfred Landon of Kansas emerged as the Republican nominee. He was a plainspoken former businessman and fiscal conservative who supported New Deal social legislation, making him attractive to both conservatives and progressives. The Republican convention in Cleveland was flooded with sunflowers, the Kansas state flower, and by the endless playing of "Oh! Susanna," Landon's favorite song.[27]

The Republicans campaigned on the slogan "Life, Liberty and Landon!"[28] They didn't oppose, at least initially, popular New Deal programs that aided the jobless or the poor, but rather suggested Roosevelt was doing it all wrong, with high taxes, overspending, and too many regulations. "I believe a man can be a liberal without being a spendthrift," declared Landon.[29]

But as the campaign went on, GOP attacks turned more scathing. The Republican National Committee distributed leaflets in factories, warning about Social Security: "You're sentenced to a weekly pay reduction for all your working life. You'll have to serve this sentence unless you help reverse it November 3." The leaflets skipped over the part about the funds going for old-age pensions, but the Republican chairman did go on the radio to spread the rumor that workers would be forced to wear dog tags stamped with their Social Security number.[30] Roosevelt hit back in a speech at Madison Square Garden in the fall. "Never before in all of our history have these forces been so united against one candidate as they stand today," he said. "They are unanimous in their hate for me—and I welcome their hatred."[31]

Democrats were confident of victory despite a downbeat *Literary Digest* poll that had accurately called the past four elections and was now forecasting a Landon triumph. The poll was embarrassingly wide of the mark, possibly because it polled car owners and people listed in phone books, while missing an entire class of voters who owned neither cars nor phones but who overwhelmingly supported Roosevelt.

In the end, Roosevelt won all but two states, Maine and Vermont, in rolling up a 61 to 37 percent popular vote victory and a crushing electoral win of 523–8. "I don't think that it would have made any difference what kind of a campaign I made," Landon later said. "That is one consolation you get out of a good licking."[32]

1940

In normal times, President Roosevelt would almost surely have retired after two terms. He'd already designed a personal retreat space at his Hyde Park estate, on a hill overlooking the Hudson River, and was planning a presidential library and thinking about his memoirs. He told one political ally, when asked about a third term, "I just can't do it. . . . I have been here a long time. I am tired. . . . I want to finish my little house on the hill. I want to write history."[33]

But these weren't normal times.[34] Nazi Germany had recently overrun a half dozen European countries, had formalized an Axis military alliance with Mussolini's fascist government in Italy, and was preparing an air assault against Britain. And Americans were in the midst of an impassioned debate between internationalists, who thought the country would inevitably be pulled into war in Europe, and isolationists, who insisted the United States should just let the European battle between fascism and democracy play itself out.[35]

The isolationist view was strongest among Republicans, some of whom framed the debate as being between Americanism and internationalism.[36] Congress a few years earlier had passed the

Neutrality Act, prohibiting the United States from selling arms to any participant in a foreign conflict, even an ally, and the famous aviator Lindbergh declared that Americans should stay out of foreign affairs and focus instead on "building and guarding our own destiny."[37] When Lindbergh later formed the America First Committee, it attracted eight hundred thousand members.

These events weighed on Roosevelt. The existence of Western democracy outside the United States seemed at risk, and if the Axis alliance conquered Europe, FDR believed Hitler would turn his attention to America.[38] Then Americans would "have to face the military might of fascism alone."[39] When Roosevelt looked at his potential successors, however, he feared that few of them were equipped to deal with a world at war. That sounds like presidential ego talking, but the reality was that many leading candidates either were isolationists or were inexperienced in world affairs.

The leading Republican candidates were District Attorney Thomas Dewey of New York and Senator Robert Taft of Ohio. Dewey, who'd gained national fame for criminal prosecutions of mob bosses, was just thirty-eight and had no experience in federal or state office. And Taft, a prominent conservative and the son of a former president, was a committed isolationist who once said there was more danger of "the infiltration of totalitarian ideas from the New Deal circles in Washington than there ever will be from activities of the communists or the Nazis."[40]

Among Democrats, the most popular candidates were Vice President Garner, Postmaster General James Farley, and Secretary of State Cordell Hull. Roosevelt didn't believe Garner or Farley could win a national election, and he feared as well that neither was committed to his New Deal reforms.[41] That left Hull. The secretary seemed to be the only candidate who Roosevelt thought could both win a national election and skillfully manage international affairs. Except that Hull was sixty-nine years old and not enthusiastic about mounting a campaign.[42]

Consequently Roosevelt kept everyone guessing about his own intentions, perhaps because he had no idea himself what he wanted to do. This is where American politics stood as the political parties prepared for their 1940 conventions.

The Republicans went first, in Philadelphia in June. Dewey and Taft each controlled about 300 delegates, with 501 needed for nomination. Dewey led the polls and had won key primaries, but his youth and lack of national experience were concerns. Taft's isolationism likewise triggered anxiety, as European nations kept falling to the Nazi blitzkrieg. Beyond this were a collection of long shots, including the "darkest horse in the stable," a non-politician named Wendell Willkie who was rising in the polls on the back of a grassroots campaign and a media blitz.[43]

Willkie was an Indiana lawyer who'd moved to Wall Street and become president of Commonwealth and Southern, a public utility company. A former Democrat, he was a charismatic speaker who gained attention as a critic of Roosevelt's domestic policies, even being featured in *Time*, *Life*, and *Fortune* magazines. Willkie believed that progressives were right to rein in the worst practices of big business, but that the New Deal went too far in fostering big government. Americans, he said, should be "as much opposed to excessive concentration of power in the hands of government as . . . in the hands of business."[44]

While he attacked Roosevelt, however, he also criticized Republicans for isolationism. He didn't believe the United States could remain neutral in the battle between fascism and capitalist democracy in Europe, because Americans had an interest "in the continuation in this world of the English, French and Norwegian way of life."[45] This was key to Willkie's appeal to the corporate world, as he was a pro-business internationalist in a way that set him apart from other contenders. But he also had a certain charm and freshness about him that sparked a grassroots campaign on his behalf, with Willkie Clubs springing to life across the country.

When Willkie traveled to Philadelphia for the convention, he attracted a crowd of onlookers and reporters who followed him on foot from the train station to his hotel, where he walked into the bar, ordered a drink, and chatted with people about politics. One writer said he was "at once a novelty, a sparkling political prism and a thrilling entertainment. He appears to say anything he really thinks."[46]

Many Republicans, though, didn't know what to think. Willkie had come out of nowhere to rise to second behind Dewey in the polls, but he was a political novice and, more worryingly, new to the Republican Party. As a former senator told Willkie when asked for his support, "Well, Wendell, you know that back home in Indiana it's all right if the town whore joins the church, but they don't let her lead the choir the first night."[47]

When balloting began, Dewey garnered 360 votes to Taft's 189 and Willkie's 105. Dewey's numbers then began slipping, and by the fourth ballot it was a battle between Taft and Willkie. Taft was supported by establishment conservatives, but the galleries were packed with Willkie supporters, who kept up a lively chant of, "We want Willkie!"[48] The delegates themselves seemed unable to avoid the growing passion for the newcomer, and on the sixth ballot the floodgates opened. Wendell Willkie became the Republican nominee for president.

"Nothing exactly like it ever happened before in American politics," announced Newsweek. "Willkie had never held public office or even sought it. Virtually a neophyte in politics, he had entered no primaries, made no deals, organized no campaign." Another writer said Willkie's nomination was fueled "by a strange combination of big-business backers . . . and zealous 'amateurs' . . . who were weary of the old-type politicians and political hacks and wanted a new face and new blood."[49] Other Republicans said it was just "the damnedest convention that ever was."[50]

Prior to this, every nominee of a major party had experience in elective office, in a cabinet post, or as a military general. Willkie was the first to come directly from the business world. It would be another seventy-six years before this happened again, with the 2016 nomination of Donald Trump.

As Willkie celebrated his success, who his opponent would be remained a mystery. When the Democratic convention opened in Chicago in July, the only announced candidates were Garner and Farley, but almost no one expected either to be the nominee.[51] Most delegates supported Roosevelt, despite the fact that the president still hadn't announced a desire to run. Behind the scenes, though, the wheels were turning. Roosevelt had apparently resolved to be a candidate because of the international situation, but thought he should be drafted by delegates rather than mount an active campaign for the nomination.

That's why, in his opening address, Senator Alben Barkley of Kentucky conveyed a message from Roosevelt, who asserted that he had no desire to remain president and wanted to "make it clear that all the delegates to this convention are free to vote for any candidate."[52] The vague remarks left it unclear whether Roosevelt was expressing openness to a draft or refusing the nomination. Before delegates could decipher the meaning further, however, a booming voice filled the room, chanting, "We want Roosevelt! The world wants Roosevelt! America needs Roosevelt!" In an instant, banners were unfurled and the band began playing "Happy Days Are Here Again." Delegates cheered and danced in the aisles.[53]

The whole thing was obviously planned. The mysterious booming voice belonged to Thomas Garry, Chicago's superintendent of sewers, who was chanting into a microphone from the basement, and it sparked a forty-five-minute demonstration, which one reporter called "premeditated pandemonium."[54] After this there was little doubt Roosevelt would be nominated. Delegates voted overwhelmingly for the president on the first ballot, 942 votes to 72 for Farley and 61 for Garner. Vice President Garner not only didn't win the nomination, but at Roosevelt's request he was replaced on the ticket by Secretary of Agriculture Henry Wallace of Iowa.

Roosevelt spoke to delegates in a radio speech, saying he couldn't refuse the nomination in light of the international situation: "Today all private plans, all private lives have been repealed by an overriding public danger. In the face of that danger all those who can be of service to the Republic have no choice but to offer themselves."[55]

Willkie made his own acceptance speech in August in his hometown of Elkwood, Indiana. It was a blisteringly hot day, with the temperature soaring past 100 degrees. Still, up to two hundred thousand people turned out to see the candidate, who played up his small-town roots. The Democrats used the spectacle to lampoon Willkie as the "simple, barefoot Wall Street lawyer."[56]

That fall Willkie barnstormed the country, traveling thirty-four thousand miles by train and giving more than five hundred speeches in thirty-four states. He railed against the New Deal, not for its ambitions but for an excess of regulations, taxes, and deficits.[57] And he criticized Roosevelt for running for a third term, warning, "Dictatorships always begin by asking people to give up some law or tradition."[58]

Initially Republicans had high hopes. Although the economy had improved from eight years earlier, the country had suffered another downturn in 1937, dubbed "the Roosevelt Recession," and Republicans believed the president was vulnerable. Everything was upended, though, by the war in Europe. When a German air attack battered Great Britain into the fall, Roosevelt pulled away in the polls. Voters seemed wary of electing a president "who would have to learn on the job."[59]

Republicans thus turned to the only weapon they had left, which was to charge FDR with leading the country into war. One radio commercial declared, "When your boy is dying on some battlefield in Europe and he's crying out 'Mother! Mother!'—don't blame Franklin D. Roosevelt because he sent your boy to war— blame yourself, because you sent Franklin D. Roosevelt back to the White House!"[60]

In the end, the country opted to stick with the hand that was already at the wheel. The New Deal coalition hung together and Roosevelt won comfortably, 55 to 45 percent in the popular vote and 449–82 in the Electoral College. For the first time in American history, a president was elected to a third term.

1944

In 1941 the war everyone feared finally came, but not before another year of debate over America's role and responsibilities in the world.

One month after the 1940 election, in response to urgent pleas for assistance from Britain, Roosevelt devised the Lend-Lease program to loan military equipment to allied nations. He promoted the idea in a December 29 "fireside chat," asserting that the United States needed to be "the great arsenal of democracy." Then, in his 1941 State of the Union address, he linked his international and domestic initiatives by advocating for a "a world founded upon four essential freedoms," which he declared were freedom of speech, freedom of religion, freedom from want, and freedom from fear.[61]

Eleven months later came the surprise attack on Pearl Harbor, on December 7, 1941. The next day Congress approved a declaration of war against Japan, and three days after that Germany and Italy declared war on the United States. For the rest of Roosevelt's third term, all attention was on the war. The tide turned in the Allies' favor by the middle of 1944, particularly after the D-Day invasion of Normandy, but the war was still ongoing when it came time for another election.

Unlike four years earlier, there was never much doubt that FDR would run for another term. It seemed unfathomable that he'd leave office in the middle of the war, though he wistfully dreamed of retirement. In a letter to the chairman of the Democratic National Committee he wrote, "All that is within me cries out to go back to my home on the Hudson River. . . . But we of this generation chance to live in a day and hour when our Nation has been attacked, and when its future existence and the future existence of our chosen method of government are at stake." He concluded, "If the people elect me, I will serve. . . . I have as little right to withdraw as the soldier has to leave his post."[62]

Almost by default, then, FDR became the Democratic nominee for the fourth time. Most people didn't know, however, that his health was rapidly declining. Publicly the president seemed tired after twelve years of facing down the stresses of the Great Depression and World War II, but what wasn't reported is that he had heart disease. A navy cardiologist in 1944 noted after a medical examination that the president had "some degree of conges-

THE NEW DEAL TO THE GREAT SOCIETY

tive heart failure," but FDR's physician, Surgeon General Ross McIntire, declined to make this report public.[63]

It's unclear if anyone else, even the president, was officially told the diagnosis. Roosevelt's aides, though, could clearly see that he'd aged, that his hands shook, and that he had occasional memory lapses. Vice President Wallace, meanwhile, was unpopular with party bosses and with Southern Democrats, whether for his liberal ideology, his promotion of racial equality, or his eccentric personality. So, although FDR still liked Wallace, the decision was made to find another running mate. This drama would ultimately be as important to the 1944 election as was the actual presidential campaign.[64]

One early contender to join the ticket was former senator and Supreme Court justice James Byrnes of South Carolina, who was known as the assistant president in his job as director of the Office of War Mobilization. Byrnes had political liabilities with labor unions and Blacks, however, so party leaders instead settled on Senator Harry Truman of Missouri, who was well liked and who'd made a name for himself as chairman of the Truman Committee to investigate waste in wartime defense spending.

But Truman didn't want the job. He enjoyed being a senator, and his wife hated the spotlight. He told one reporter, "The plain fact is, I don't want to be president."[65] Democrats persisted in wooing him anyway. A key moment came at the party convention in Chicago when Robert Hannegan, chairman of the Democratic National Committee, phoned the president while sitting with Truman.

"Have you got that fellow lined up yet?" Roosevelt asked.

"No. He is the contrariest goddamn mule from Missouri I ever dealt with," replied Hannegan, as he held out the receiver for Truman to hear.

"Well, you tell the Senator that if he wants to break up the Democratic party in the middle of the war, that's his responsibility," barked Roosevelt.

Truman was flabbergasted. "But why the hell didn't he tell me in the first place?" he asked.[66] What he didn't know was that Roosevelt and Hannegan had planned the call ahead of time.[67] Afterward the senator from Missouri finally agreed to have his name put in nomination for the vice presidency.

This still wasn't the end of the matter, as Wallace wanted to remain vice president and was popular with the liberal base. He gave a stirring nominating speech for FDR, setting off a pro-Wallace demonstration, during which "New Dealers cheered" and "conservatives squirmed," *Time* magazine reported.[68]

After Roosevelt was nominated for a fourth term and gave an acceptance speech on the radio, yet another Wallace demonstration broke out. Thousands of his supporters packed the galleries and chanted, "We want Wallace!" The organist played "Iowa, Iowa, That's Where the Tall Corn Grows" in honor of the vice president's home state. Party leaders panicked when it seemed the convention might be bulldozed into nominating Wallace. One aide was ordered to stop the organist, even it meant taking an axe to "chop every goddamn cable there is," and the mayor of Chicago agreed to declare the crowded hall a fire hazard. Democrats adjourned the convention for the night and stopped the demonstration.

The next day Wallace won the first ballot over Truman 429–319 but was short of a majority as several states strategically voted for favorite-son candidates. On the second ballot, at the instruction of party bosses, those states turned to Truman. Because of how he was nominated, Truman was derided as "the Missouri Compromise."[69] And liberals were aghast at the tactics used to derail Wallace. Even Roosevelt's daughter, Anna, complained to one party official that he was a "son of a bitch" for his role. "So's your old man," he told her.[70]

The Republicans met in Philadelphia and, with hardly any fuss, selected Governor Thomas Dewey of New York as their candidate. Dewey was initially expected to battle Wendell Willkie, the 1940 nominee, for the prize. Willkie had written a best-selling book, *One World*, about the interdependence of nations and still commanded a legion of supporters. But after Dewey won the Wisconsin primary in April, Willkie withdrew from the race. After that,

Dewey had little competition and was nominated on the first ballot at a drama-free convention.

Dewey was a curious blend of political traits. Just forty-two, he was known nationally for being a crime-fighting district attorney prior to becoming governor. Hollywood had produced films about his mafia prosecutions, with actors like Humphrey Bogart playing characters loosely based on Dewey.[71] While he was considered intelligent and efficient, though, Dewey wasn't beloved. One writer said he was "like the beautiful girl at the cocktail party who turns out to be dull and superficial."[72] A popular joke was, "You really have to know Tom Dewey well in order to dislike him."[73]

Nevertheless he was seen as the strongest candidate against Roosevelt. Dewey contrasted his youth and freshness to the incumbent administration, which he said had "grown old in office."[74] In arguments similar to the GOP campaigns of 1936 and 1940, he promised to run the New Deal more efficiently and to stop strangling free enterprise. "It's time for a change!" was his motto.[75]

Dewey might have won a different election, since it's rare for one party to win four consecutive presidential contests, but he had a difficult task in trying to unseat the popular Roosevelt during wartime. When Dewey's tactics failed to gain traction, Republicans threw harder punches. They alleged that the Democrats were beholden to communists and charged Roosevelt with wanting to turn the country into a monarchy.

After a lethargic start to his own campaign, Roosevelt came to life in the fall. In September he made a speech in Washington in which he reminded voters about the economic "mess which was dumped in our laps in 1933." He drew the biggest response for comically answering charges that he'd used taxpayer money for travel for his dog, Fala. "Well, of course, I don't resent attacks . . . but Fala does resent them," said FDR. "Being a Scottie, as soon as he learned that the Republican fiction writers . . . had concocted a story [about him], his Scotch soul was furious. He has not been the same dog since." The audience loved it, and *Time* magazine compared the president to "a veteran virtuoso . . . playing what he loves to play . . . politics."[76]

On October 21 Roosevelt toured the boroughs of New York in a motorcade, driving fifty-one miles in an open car through lashing rain and wind. Water dripped down his hat and face for five hours as he waved to a crowd of 2 million people. "How can they talk about a tired old man now?" asked one person.[77]

Whether it was Roosevelt's performance near the end of the campaign or just that people were afraid to entrust management of the war to a newcomer, Americans voted emphatically to keep the president in office. Roosevelt won the popular vote 53 to 46 percent and the electoral tally 432–99.

Then, on April 12, 1945, less than three months into his fourth term, Roosevelt died of a cerebral hemorrhage while visiting his retreat in Warm Springs, Georgia.

FDR's death suddenly and dramatically ended the longest presidency in U.S. history. Winston Churchill said the news hit him like "a physical blow."[78] Lyndon Johnson, then a Texas congressman, said he cried. The author I. F. Stone wrote, "The Romans must have felt this way when word came that Caesar Augustus was dead."[79]

For Harry Truman, it was the day "the moon, the stars, and all the planets had fallen upon me."[80] Truman was on Capitol Hill that afternoon when he got a message to come to the White House "as quickly and quietly" as possible.[81] Once there he was ushered into a room with First Lady Eleanor Roosevelt. She walked up and put her arm on Truman's shoulder. "Harry, the president is dead," she said.

"It was the only time in my life," recalled Truman, "that I ever felt like I'd had a real shock. I had hurried to the White House to see the president and when I arrived I found I *was* the president."

"Is there anything I can do for you?" asked a stunned Truman.

"Is there anything *we* can do for *you*?" Mrs. Roosevelt responded. "For you are the one in trouble now."

The Roosevelt Era and New Deal Liberalism

So much changed in the twelve years from 1933 to 1945 that it seems as if presidential politics should be divided into "before Roosevelt" and "after Roosevelt" eras.

For starters, the presidency itself was redefined. The international stature of the president grew after World War II because of the country's new role as a global superpower. Domestically, too, the scope of the presidency expanded with the advent of New Deal programs and the growth of the federal government. But the differences most relevant to this book are those that impacted presidential elections and American politics, including the realignment of the major parties and the rise of New Deal liberalism.

After the Great Depression took a sledgehammer to the existing alignments, Roosevelt assembled a new Democratic coalition. He brought together progressives, urban residents, Blacks, labor unions, farmers, immigrants, Catholics, and, of course, the white Southerners who were already longtime Democrats.[82] This coalition mostly held together for the next three decades and generated a raft of progressive legislation, from Social Security and labor reforms in the 1930s to Medicare and civil rights laws in the 1960s. Ever since Roosevelt's presidency, the Democrats have been identified as the party that believes in government activism and intervention in the economy. It was already trending this way, but after 1932 the Democrats never looked back and never again nominated a conservative, as they had in 1904 and 1924.

This isn't to say the Democrats had no internal tensions; the white Southerners, for instance, were quite a bit more conservative than other party members, and during Roosevelt's second term his agenda was frequently stymied by a conservative coalition of Republicans and Southern Democrats. The president's frustration over these divisions caused him to try purging his party of conservative Southerners during the 1938 midterm elections. When that failed, he suggested the parties should organize more strictly along liberal-conservative lines.

"I think the time has come," he said, "for the Democratic Party to get rid of its reactionary elements in the South and to attract to it the liberals in the Republican Party."[83] He went so far as to suggest to aides that he and Willkie might work together after the 1944 election. FDR was, in essence, seeing the future of American politics. Even though Willkie believed Democrats went too far in the direction of big government, his support for the aspirations of the New Deal tied him more closely to Roosevelt than many Southern Democrats were to their own president.

But history never had a chance to find out if Willkie and Roosevelt could have joined forces in the 1940s, because Willkie died of a heart attack in October 1944, at just fifty-two, and Roosevelt passed away six months later. This ideological realignment did eventually happen on its own, but only after several more decades of policy disagreements and political upheaval.

Along with the rise of this Democratic coalition, the era was also significant for the emergence of New Deal liberalism. This political philosophy was in many ways an extension of the Progressive movement that bloomed earlier in the century, but the Roosevelt-era Democrats added a new twist by passing laws to ameliorate inequality and to directly benefit the working class and the poor.[84]

The belief that government has an obligation to assist the needy was easily the most revolutionary part of the New Deal. What's often forgotten, though, is that the Roosevelt administration also resisted more radical ideas that were being pushed at the time. This is when populists like Huey Long wanted to cap personal fortunes and dramatically redistribute wealth, when some liberals wanted to nationalize the banks, and when adherents of communism and fascism believed capitalism was outdated. The *New York Times* in 1936 endorsed Roosevelt as a president who would "provide insurance against radicalism."[85]

The Roosevelt agenda is perhaps best understood in the context of its era as an effort to reform the economy by finding a "middle way between state socialism and laissez-faire capitalism."[86] The liberalism that emerged from the period encompassed social insurance programs for the elderly and the unemployed, progressive taxation, funding of public works projects, support for labor, regulation of the economy, a more expansive federal government, and a stronger presidency.[87] Other elements were added later, but New Deal liberalism remained the ideological foundation of the Democratic Party.

THE NEW DEAL TO THE GREAT SOCIETY

In response, Republicans became further identified as a party opposed to government programs and regulation, deepening a trend that began in 1912. They did accept elements of the New Deal, in practice if not in rhetoric, as every Republican president from the moderate Dwight Eisenhower to the conservative Ronald Reagan has kept Social Security and similar programs in place. But in contrast to Democrats, Republicans maintained a belief in smaller government and limited intervention in the economy. So it was the Roosevelt era that fully launched the "big government versus small government" debate between liberal Democrats and conservative Republicans that persisted into the twenty-first century.

1948, 1952, and 1956: Truman, Eisenhower, and Postwar America

1948

When Harry Truman became the thirty-third president, he'd barely spent time with Franklin Roosevelt and hadn't been briefed on any major issues. But during his first four months in office, Nazi Germany surrendered, the United States dropped atomic bombs on two Japanese cities, and the Soviet Union made its first moves toward domination of Eastern Europe. And it's not like history slowed down after that, either, with the Marshall Plan, the Berlin Airlift, the creation of the United Nations, the founding of Israel, and the desegregation of the U.S. military all landing on Truman's desk in the next few years.

These days Truman is consistently ranked by historians as a near great president for his deftness in dealing with these challenges. During his presidency, however, he was considered a failure. His job approval rating was abysmally low, and the Los Angeles Times remarked that he was "the most complete fumbler and blunderer this nation has seen in high office in a long time."[88]

What gives? It's hard to square such a disparity in perspectives, but we can start with the fact that Truman had to follow FDR and his larger-than-life charisma. The country was also frustrated by postwar economic challenges and by the start of the Cold War so soon after fighting World War II. And frankly, many voters were just ready for a change after sixteen years of Democratic presidents.

For all these reasons, Republicans believed they were on track to win back the White House in 1948. At their convention in Philadelphia, they again nominated Thomas Dewey, who'd run a respectable campaign against Roosevelt four years earlier. Dewey beat back a challenge from Senator Robert Taft of Ohio and Governor Harold Stassen of Minnesota. He consistently led Truman in the polls by about 10 points, and the journalist and former congresswoman Clare Booth Luce said the incumbent president was a "gone goose" whose "situation is hopeless."[89]

Many Democrats felt the same way. Some wanted to replace Truman with a new candidate, Gen. Dwight Eisenhower. The World War II hero was the most popular person in the country, and though he'd never articulated his political views, he was perceived as a formidable nominee. One columnist said he was "a kind of dream boy embodying all the unsatisfied wishes of all the people who are discontented with the way things are."[90] Eisenhower, however, didn't want to run for president—at least not in 1948 as a Democrat—and announced that he would refuse any nomination.

So the Democrats were stuck with Truman. When the party held its own convention in Philadelphia, one reporter described "a spirit of defeatism" among delegates who believed "President Truman seemed to have little chance of election."[91] A sign at the convention read "We're Just Mild About Harry."[92] And this was *before* the party splintered in multiple directions.

The Democrats first divided along North-South lines over a plank in the platform endorsing Truman's civil rights legislation, in which he had proposed to outlaw lynching, abolish the poll tax, prohibit discrimination on trains and buses, and organize a commission on job discrimination.[93] Delegates approved the amendment after a stirring speech by Mayor Hubert Humphrey of Minneapolis, who declared, "The time has arrived for the Democratic Party to get out of the shadow of states' rights and walk forthrightly into the bright sunshine of human rights."[94] But the policies were vehemently opposed by Southerners, prompting delegates from Alabama and Mississippi to walk out of the convention.

Some of these Southern Democrats later staged another convention in Birmingham, Alabama, where they nominated Governor Strom Thurmond of South Carolina for president under the banner of the States' Rights Democratic Party, popularly known as the Dixiecrats.

The Democrats then split again, along left-center lines, when the party's more zealous liberals broke away to form a new Progressive Party. They nominated former vice president Henry Wallace to lead a crusade for national health insurance, the nationalization of key industries, more public housing, and racial and gender equality. These differences were more a matter of degree than of philosophy, as Truman in 1949 would propose his own Fair Deal agenda of national health insurance, aid to education, and other liberal goals. But the split between Truman and the Progressives was more acrimonious on foreign policy.

Wallace believed the United States and the Soviet Union could end the budding Cold War by forming a working relationship, and he thought the Soviets' desire for a sphere of influence in Eastern Europe stemmed more from their fear of attack than from a desire to threaten the West. This was counter to the new Truman Doctrine of Soviet containment.[95] Given this agenda, it's fascinating to contemplate how history might have been altered if Wallace hadn't been booted from the 1944 ticket. The Truman policy became the foundation for U.S. foreign policy for the rest of the Cold War, so if Wallace had become president in 1945, his desire to engage with the Soviets would certainly have nudged history in a different direction, for better or for worse.

For the 1948 election, however, this Democratic rupture meant Truman would be pinched between two extremes, with Dixiecrats siphoning conservative votes in the South and Progressives taking liberal votes in the North. None of it boded well for the president's reelection hopes. Truman seemed at times to be the only person who believed he could defeat Dewey. He began his campaign to convince everyone else with his convention address, which began at the ungodly hour of 2:00 a.m. Somehow, against all odds, he electrified the previously gloomy delegates.

"I will win this election, and make these Republicans like it, don't you forget that," Truman thundered. "The reason is that the people know the Democratic Party is the people's party, and the Republican Party is the party of special interests and it always has been and always will be." Truman's confidence and his slashing style brought delegates to their feet. The *New York Times* said Truman "set the convention on fire."[96] His speech gave Democrats a sense of fight, at least, even though the president was still regarded as a hopeless underdog.

In early September the pollster Elmo Roper pegged Dewey as having a 44 to 31 percent lead nationally, which Roper pointed out was similar to Roosevelt's lead over Landon in 1936. Since a "political convulsion" was the only thing that could stop Dewey from winning, Roper said, he wouldn't poll the race any further that fall.[97]

Even so, Truman dove into battle. "I was not brought up to run from a fight," he declared.[98] Instead he embarked on his now famous whistle-stop campaign. During three trips by train, Truman traveled more than thirty thousand miles over thirty-three days in his specially outfitted *Ferdinand Magellan* car. It was the rail equivalent of today's Air Force One, encased in armor and bulletproof glass. The president gave as many as a dozen speeches a day from the train's rear platform.[99]

At every stop Truman tore into Republicans. He called them "gluttons of privilege" and "bloodsuckers with offices in Wall Street" who had "stuck a pitchfork in the farmer's back." "Give 'em hell, Harry!" people shouted.[100]

It was a fierce populist campaign, which one writer described as "sharp speeches fairly criticizing Republican policy and defending New Deal liberalism, mixed with sophistries, bunkum piled higher than haystacks, and demagoguery tooting merrily down the track."[101] But it worked. As the rail campaign wore on, Truman's crowds grew. Reporters, who still thought the president was headed for defeat, kept "pinching themselves at the size of the crowds and their cordial response."[102]

Dewey, meanwhile, ran a campaign that was the opposite of Truman's. As the prohibitive favorite, he tried to remain above the fray. "When you're leading, don't talk," he advised.[103] His addresses were so bland Kentucky's *Louisville Courier-Journal* mocked him by remarking, "Four of his major speeches can be boiled down to these historic four sentences: Agriculture is important. Our rivers are full of fish. You cannot have freedom without liberty. Our future lies ahead."[104]

Dewey also struggled with the continuing perception that he was distant and aloof. Political cartoonists lampooned him as robotic by drawing him with the body of a mechanical adding machine.[105] And Alice Roosevelt Longworth, Teddy's daughter, famously skewered him by saying he looked like "the little man on the wedding cake."[106]

Despite these challenges, no one believed Dewey would lose. The Gallup, Crossley, and Roper polls all forecast a Republican victory. *Life* magazine confidently called Dewey "the next president." And *Newsweek* asked fifty political reporters and found not a single one who thought Truman would win.[107]

Even when Truman took an early lead on Election Day, belief in Dewey's inevitability held strong. Most people went to bed assuming Dewey would overtake Truman as votes were tabulated during the night. The *Chicago Tribune* published an infamous first edition with the headline "Dewey Defeats Truman," which the reelected president gleefully held up for photographers the next morning.[108] Truman shocked everyone, winning the popular vote by 49.6 to 45.1 percent, and the Electoral College 303–189.

The electoral margin, it should be noted, was closer than it seems on the surface. Five states were decided by less than 1 percent, and in Ohio, California, and Illinois the margins were seven thousand, seventeen thousand, and thirty-three thousand votes, respectively. If two of these three states had gone to Dewey, neither candidate would have won a majority. That's because the Dixiecrats, despite winning just 2.4 percent of the popular vote, came out on top in four Southern states, with thirty-nine electoral votes. The Progressives also won 2.4 percent of the vote but didn't win any states. So Truman's narrow wins in a few states are all that prevented the election from being decided in the House of Representatives.[109]

While Truman would seemingly have won a bigger victory without these third-party challenges, many observers believe the Dixiecrats and Progressives actually helped the president by positioning him as a more centrist candidate.[110]

In the end, reporters and pollsters were left to wonder how they'd missed one of the great upsets in presidential history. "We were wrong, all of us," admitted columnist Marquis Childs, "the commentators, the political editors, the politicians—except for Harry S. Truman. And no one believed him."[111]

As Senator Arthur Vandenberg of Michigan put it, "Everybody had counted him out but he came up fighting and won the battle. That's the kind of courage the American people admire."[112]

1952

Notwithstanding his historic victory in 1948, Truman didn't get a breather from the momentous events shaking the world in the mid-twentieth century. During his next term, he dealt with the Korean War, the development of the atomic bomb by the Soviet Union, the founding of the North Atlantic Treaty Organization (NATO), the Russian occupation of Eastern Europe, a communist takeover of China, labor strikes in the railroad and steel industries, and the start of the McCarthy investigations into alleged communist influence in the U.S. government.[113]

It was a whirlwind of challenges that would have tested any president, and the mounting crises took their toll on Truman's popularity. By 1952 his approval rating was at 22 percent.[114] After being battered by the political storms for nearly eight years, the president announced in March 1952 that he would forgo another campaign and retire to his hometown of Independence, Missouri.

There was no obvious heir apparent to Truman among Democrats, however. Senator Estes Kefauver of Tennessee wanted the nomination and won the most state primaries, but he lacked support from party leaders because of his reputation as a maverick. Vice President Alben Barkley of Kentucky was popular, but at seventy-four he was thought to be too old for the job. Senator Richard Russell of Georgia was a Southern favorite but, as a segregationist, was unacceptable to Northern Democrats.

Others, including Truman, tried to lure Governor Adlai Stevenson of Illinois into the race, given that he led an important state and was known for his intelligence and eloquence. "Adlai, if a knucklehead like me can be president and not do too badly," Truman told him in one meeting, "think what a really educated smart guy like you could do in the job."[115] But Stevenson declined the overtures.

As fate would have it, though, the 1952 Democratic convention was in Chicago. And Stevenson, as that state's governor, gave a welcoming address to delegates who still lacked a clear and obvious favorite for their party's nomination.

"What counts now is not just what we are *against*, but what we are *for*," Stevenson told the convention. "*Who* leads us is less important than *what* leads us—what convictions, what courage, what faith."[116] So impressive was the speech that Stevenson again vaulted to the top of many wish lists. One columnist suggested the Illinois governor might "be dragged protesting to the presidential altar."[117]

What happened next is unclear, although pressure to join the fray apparently got to Stevenson and he finally agreed to let himself be nominated. He called Truman, who reportedly told him it was about damn time, or something to that effect.[118] On the convention's first ballot, Kefauver led with 340 votes, with Stevenson at 272 and Russell at 268. There was little movement on the second ballot, so Truman intervened. He asked several delegations with favorite sons to release their delegates to Stevenson. And so, on the third ballot, Governor Adlai Stevenson, who hadn't mounted a campaign and who'd agreed to be a candidate only a few days earlier, became the Democratic nominee for president.

Stevenson followed in the path of other hesitant nominees, such as Charles Evans Hughes in 1916 and James Garfield in 1880. In his acceptance address he told delegates, "I have not sought the honor you have done me. . . . I *would* not seek your nomination for the presidency because the burdens of that office stagger the imagination." Nevertheless, "from such dread responsibility one does not shrink with fear. . . . So 'if this cup may not pass from me, except I drink it, Thy will be done,'" he concluded, echoing Jesus's acceptance of his fate in the Garden of Gethsemane.[119]

On the Republican side, the favorite was Senator Robert Taft, who was known as "Mr. Republican" and who'd been a contender since 1940. Taft led the party's conservative wing, known as the Old Guard, which wanted to shrink government and tended toward isolationism in foreign policy. The party's moderates, conversely, weren't thrilled by the prospect of Taft's candidacy because they were internationalists who believed the United States needed to take a leading role in the world. Their preferred candidate was General Eisenhower.

But Eisenhower was still reluctant. He'd written in his journal as recently as 1950, "We are just not capable, in this country, of conceiving of a man who does not want to be president."[120] His mind seems to have been changed, however, by Taft's isolationism. Eisenhower met with Taft and offered to publicly decline interest in the presidency if the senator would support NATO and the need for collective security arrangements. When Taft declined, it pushed the general toward a run as a way to save his party from what he saw as the error of isolationism. Later, Eisenhower told reporters that he became a candidate because Taft's "election would be a disaster."[121]

Even after joining the race, however, Eisenhower's nomination was no sure thing. He was popular with the public but not with the Old Guard Republicans, who didn't want to be led by another Thomas Dewey–style moderate. At the Republican convention, Taft supporters passed out flyers that implored delegates, "End Dewey's Control of Our Party."[122] And Senator Everett Dirksen of Illinois spoke for many in the Taft faction when, during a speech, he pointed at Dewey and said, "We followed you before and you took us down the road to defeat. . . . Don't do this to us again."[123]

Taft went into the convention with the most support, but the Eisenhower team sparked an uproar over the alleged stealing of delegates, particularly in Texas, where the general won the caucus but the state committee still awarded most delegates to Taft. They flooded the convention with signs saying "Thou Shalt Not Steal," while playing up the argument that Eisenhower was a stronger general election candidate than Taft.[124]

The message worked, as the convention voted to overrule the Credentials Committee and award contested delegates to Eisenhower, leaving Taft short of a majority. Without this ruling, Taft almost certainly would have been the Republican nominee. Instead Eisenhower capitalized on this momentum to win the first ballot 595–500, just nine votes short of a majority. After this, several states switched their votes, and Eisenhower took the nomination, much to the consternation of the Old Guard conservatives. For his running mate, the general selected Senator Richard Nixon of California, a thirty-nine-year-old rising star in the party with a reputation for fierce anticommunism. This launched a national career that would see Nixon serve five times as his party's presidential or vice-presidential candidate during the next two decades.

That fall Eisenhower and Stevenson were a study in contrasts. Stevenson presented himself as informed and eloquent, while Eisenhower cultivated a down-home persona.

Stevenson's speeches were so widely praised that a published copy of them later became a bestseller, and the novelist John Steinbeck said it was the first time he'd read a political speech for "pleasure."[125] But Stevenson also often lost his audiences with grandiose concepts and a wooden delivery. He did come up with some crafty phrases, such as when he suggested that GOP stood for "Grouchy Old Pessimists," but mostly he just acquired a reputation for giving high-flown speeches.[126] One columnist complained that no one understood Stevenson's talks except other intellectuals, whom he branded "eggheads," in reference to the candidate's baldness.[127] Ever since, the term "egghead" has been used to mock intellectuals for not understanding the common man.

Eisenhower, on the other hand, sprinkled his speeches with plainspoken expressions, such as how his wife was "giving me the dickens about prices."[128] He is "no fancy orator," said one journalist who followed him on the campaign trail, but "more than one listener has remarked to me after a rally: 'That man sure is sincere.'"[129]

Eisenhower's good name and affable personality also gave rise to one of the most enduring slogans in presidential history: "I like Ike." It used the candidate's nickname to capture a sense of voter comfort with the man who was widely credited with ensuring victory in World War II. The country was flooded with "I like Ike" buttons and paraphernalia.

The Republicans also happened upon an innovative way to promote Eisenhower when they aired the first television commercials in a presidential campaign. Television use had grown rapidly between 1948 and 1952, and about 40 percent of homes now had a TV, so the campaign filmed spots called "Eisenhower Answers America."[130] They were simple in structure, with Eisenhower providing modest answers on camera to questions from everyday people. For instance, to a query about the high cost of living, he replied, "My wife, Mamie, worries about the same thing. I tell her it's our job to change that on November fourth."[131]

The ads themselves are unremarkable in comparison to what presidential advertising would later become, but at the time it was a groundbreaking tactic. Democrats complained that Republicans were marketing the presidency as if it were a consumer product, and Stevenson predicted the campaign would fail. "This isn't . . . Ivory Soap vs. Palmolive," he said.[132] Well, maybe not, but it *was* Ike vs. Adlai, and the commercials proved effective for Eisenhower.

The Republicans were also successful in making forceful attacks against Democratic governance, centering their message on "Korea, corruption, and communism." They dubbed it the "K_1C_2" campaign, claiming the Korean War was a mess, the government was corrupt, and communism was spreading everywhere.[133] Nixon called

THE NEW DEAL TO THE GREAT SOCIETY

Stevenson "Adlai the Appeaser," saying he had a degree from the "College of Cowardly Communist Containment."[134]

The smooth-running Eisenhower campaign did hit a speed bump in September, when a news story broke about a secret slush fund for Nixon, one that was bankrolled by wealthy donors and which supposedly kept him "in style far beyond his salary."[135] It turned out the fund was neither secret nor illegal, and an audit showed it was largely used for political, office, and travel expenses. Still, with Republicans running hard against supposed Democratic corruption, it became a potent political issue. Many Republicans called on Nixon to leave the ticket.

Instead, a defiant Nixon gave a live speech on television to defend himself. He denied wrongdoing, talked about his humble background, and went into detail about his own limited finances, including his mortgage payments and the value of his car. He became the first candidate to release a financial statement and called on the Democratic ticket to do the same. Nixon did admit that a supporter gave his daughters a dog, named Checkers. "And you know, the kids, like all kids, love the dog, and I just want to say this, right now, that regardless of what they say about it, we're gonna keep it."[136] He finished by asking viewers to wire the Republican National Committee with their views on whether or not he should continue as a candidate.

Reports were that Eisenhower, while watching the speech, jammed a pencil into his legal pad twice, once when Nixon called on candidates to release their financial statements and a second time when he asked viewers to contact the RNC, which meant his running mate was effectively making an end run around the general. But 2 million people did call in support of Nixon. And, for the first time, all four presidential and vice-presidential candidates released their financial statements to the public. The "Checkers speech" was a sensation and is credited with saving Nixon's spot on the ticket and possibly his political career.

Eisenhower led the 1952 race from start to finish, although it was competitive until near the end. In mid-October, amid constant criticism from Republicans over his management of the

Korean War, President Truman demanded to know what better ideas Eisenhower had to "bring the boys back home." On October 24 Eisenhower responded, declaring he would "go to Korea" as president to find a way to end the war. It wasn't a solution, exactly, only a promise to find one, and perhaps no other candidate could have gotten away with such a vague statement. But the American people trusted Eisenhower, and somehow this settled it.[137]

After the Korea speech, Eisenhower's moderate polling lead swelled to double digits. On Election Day he won the popular vote by 55 to 44 percent and the Electoral College 442–89, becoming the first Republican in twenty-four years to win the presidency.

1956

The country liked Ike, and nothing in Eisenhower's first term changed that perception. The Korean War ended, albeit in a stalemate; the country was prosperous, Americans were buying homes and moving to the suburbs, and Eisenhower's genial optimism seemed to represent the times. In 1956 few people believed Eisenhower could be defeated in a bid for reelection. The only question was whether he would run again.

Since Eisenhower had never pined for the presidency, he considered retiring after one term. This possibility gained credence on September 24, 1955, when the almost sixty-five-year-old president suffered a heart attack while vacationing in Denver. After spending a few months recovering, however, Eisenhower was cleared by his doctors and agreed to run for a second term.

The president was renominated that summer at the Republican convention in San Francisco. Eisenhower's campaign promoted his philosophy of "modern Republicanism," a middle way between the larger federal state favored by liberals and the small-government views espoused by conservatives. He accepted New Deal social programs and initiated new spending for such projects as the interstate highway system, while promoting free enterprise and individual liberty. He wanted to maintain a strong military but believed in diplomacy and didn't want defense spending to bust the budget. One writer called it "the Authentic American Center in politics."[138]

To challenge Eisenhower, Adlai Stevenson again emerged as a top Democratic contender, but there would be no draft for the Illinoisan this time around. In the primaries, Stevenson outdueled Senator Estes Kefauver of Tennessee, and then at the convention in Chicago he fought off a challenge from Governor Averill Harriman of New York, who'd been endorsed by Truman. Stevenson won the nomination on the first ballot, 905–210 over Harriman.

Stevenson then added an element of suspense to the selection of a vice-presidential nominee, giving the choice to delegates. Two top candidates emerged: Kefauver and the thirty-nine-year-old senator from Massachusetts, John Kennedy, who waged a spirited fight before faltering on the third ballot to the Tennessee senator. Despite the loss, this battle raised Kennedy's national profile and gave him a springboard to contend for his party's nomination four years later.

With Eisenhower and Stevenson again the nominees, the 1956 election was the first presidential rematch since McKinley and Bryan faced off in 1900. In the fall campaign, Stevenson traveled more than fifty thousand miles and delivered hundreds of speeches. In part this was an effort to demonstrate his vigor for office and to quietly contrast himself with Eisenhower, who'd been laid low by debilitating health issues for six months, between his heart attack and a later surgery for ileitis, an inflammation of the small intestine. But Stevenson's efforts did little to move the electoral needle.[139]

In his speeches Stevenson focused on his call for a "New America," with proposals for improving education, fighting poverty, and tackling racial issues. He charged that Republicans saw "progress as something you measure on a slide rule, and prosperity as a statistic."[140] He also called for a worldwide halt to nuclear weapons testing. Some of these ideas would return as part of the 1960s agenda of Kennedy's New Frontier and Johnson's Great Society.[141]

In 1956, however, it was clear the country didn't see a need to change direction. Stevenson liked to tell the story of a conversation he had with a farmer, which illustrated the challenge of running against the incumbent. The farmer complained about the government's farm policy, so Stevenson asked him, "But why aren't people mad at Eisenhower?" To which the farmer replied, "Oh, no one connects *him* with the administration."[142]

Even if there were any doubts about Eisenhower, world events in the week before the election caused voters to think twice about changing presidents. First, Egypt's nationalization of the Suez Canal, a vital shipping route, led to an October 31 invasion by Israel, Britain, and France that nearly sparked a wider war with the Soviet Union. A few days later, in Hungary, the Soviets sent tanks to Budapest to crush an uprising, killing up to two thousand Hungarians.[143]

Both crises were front-page news when Americans voted on November 6. The international challenges seemed to remind voters that they were soothed by having Eisenhower at the helm of state. The president rolled to an even bigger victory than he had four years earlier, winning the popular vote 57 to 42 percent and the electoral vote 457–73.

Transition between Eras

The postwar presidencies of Truman and Eisenhower stand, in retrospect, as somewhat of a transitional age between two dramatic eras.

From 1929 to 1945 Americans were engaged in a long battle to overcome the Great Depression and win World War II. And from 1963 to 1975 the country endured a turbulent period of political assassinations, a presidential resignation, and controversies over the Vietnam War and racial issues. Between these times of turmoil was the era later mythologized in sitcoms like *Leave It to Beaver* and *Happy Days*. The 1950s, in particular, are often evoked when politicians talk of returning the country to some golden age of the past. American life wasn't as serene and orderly in reality as in our imagination; this was the time of the Cold War, the Korean War, the McCarthy hearings, civil rights protests, and other upheavals. But it was still an age of relative calm and contentment compared to what came before and after.

Even leaving aside all this history, the country was clearly in transition from one *political* era to another. For starters, just consider how presidential campaigns evolved. In 1948 Truman's whistle-stop campaign was conducted entirely by rail, and most Americans that year got their news primarily from newspapers and radio broadcasts. A mere twelve years later, in 1960, the presidential campaigns of Kennedy and Nixon used jets to hop from state to state, and voters largely followed the contest on television.[144] Between 1950 and 1960 the number of families with a TV set grew from 11 percent to 88.[145] The differences between 1948 and 1960 are immense, and the intervening decade served as a bridge between old-style and modern presidential elections.

Also significant during these years were the ideological battles *within* the Democratic and Republican parties. Both coalitions would be upended in the 1960s, and early signs of this shift were evident during the Truman-Eisenhower era.

Most obvious was the Democratic rupture of 1948, when the Dixiecrats and Progressives broke off to form third parties. Of these, the rift with the Dixiecrats was the most consequential. The Progressive split was similar to other disagreements over the years between more extreme and more moderate liberals, but the Dixiecrat revolt presaged a bigger rebellion to come by Southern conservatives, one that would drastically alter the political landscape.

Southerners had always been more conservative than their Northern colleagues, but they were ardent Democrats by heritage and tradition, going back at least to Reconstruction and in many cases to the days of Jefferson and Jackson. However, the civil rights movement supported by Northern Democrats in 1948 caused some Southerners to reconsider their party allegiance. The Dixiecrat nominee, Strom Thurmond, later said that his biggest impact was "to pull four states away from the national Democratic Party and show the sky wouldn't fall."[146] While it took several more elections for the dam to fully break, the South eventually swapped its political loyalties and emerged as a Republican stronghold. It turned out that 1948 was the beginning of the end of the Solid South for the Democratic Party.

As this was happening on the Democratic side, Republican conservatives were also growing disenchanted with their own party. Every Republican nominee from 1936 to 1960 accepted the New Deal premise that government should provide people with some level of social insurance, even if they disagreed over the extent of government assistance. As Eisenhower said in 1954, "Should any political party attempt to abolish social security, unemployment insurance and eliminate labor laws and farm programs, you would not hear of that party again in our political history."[147]

But while this was the opinion of GOP presidential nominees, it wasn't shared by many party conservatives, who *did* want to overturn the New Deal. The problem for conservatives was that they lost out to moderates in six consecutive nomination contests and so were continually frustrated by an inability to promote their views in a national race.

These are the root causes that later spurred the Dixiecrat Democrats and Republican economic conservatives to move toward each other politically, under a shared belief in states' rights.[148] This movement didn't fully transform politics in the South until the 1968 and 1980 elections, but the cracks in political coalitions that appeared in the 1940s and 1950s were the first signs of what was to come.

1960 and 1964: The JFK and LBJ Campaigns

1960

In the history of presidential elections, the 1960 contest stands out as an almost mythical campaign between John Kennedy and Richard Nixon. It was the first contest to be fought largely on television, the first to feature presidential debates, and the first to elect a Catholic president.

Even before this history became apparent, though, there was a sense that 1960 would be a noteworthy election. Eisenhower was then the oldest president in history and the most visible representative of a World War II era that was slowly ebbing into the past. Now he was retiring, just as a new decade was dawning. Both parties responded by nominating a fortysomething candidate, Nixon promising voters a continuation of the Eisenhower years and Kennedy aspiring to chart a new course. Norman Mailer, in a pre-election essay for *Esquire*, remarked that voters would have to decide whether "the desire of America was for drama or stability, for adventure or monotony."[149]

Before the fall contest could unfold, however, there were nomination battles to be won. Vice President Nixon had no serious competition for the top spot on the Republican ticket and was easily nominated at the party's convention in Chicago. The only drama that arose was when conservatives protested a party platform they believed was too liberal. Senator Barry Goldwater of Arizona, foreshadowing the GOP future, said in a speech, "Let's grow up, conservatives. . . . If we want to take this party back— and I think we can someday—let's go to work."[150]

The Democratic race, on the other hand, was anything but humdrum, with several contenders plotting different paths to the nomination. Kennedy's strategy was to compete in state primary elections, along with Senator Hubert Humphrey of Minnesota, while Senator Lyndon Johnson of Texas believed he could prevail at the convention with support from party leaders. Two-time nominee Stevenson waited in the wings as someone who might unite the party in case of a deadlock.

In Kennedy's case, party elders had doubts about the forty-three-year-old senator because of his Catholicism and his youth. So Kennedy focused on primaries as a way to prove his mettle and his vote-getting ability. He'd been thinking about the race since 1956 and had spent months on the road, making contacts with local officials and putting together a campaign staff, marking the first time any new candidate had built an organization this far in advance of an election.[151] He also cultivated his brand—part "political philosopher," which is how one newspaper described him after the publication of his 1956 book, *Profiles in Courage*, and part celebrity.[152] Kennedy became the first national politician to appear on a late-night TV program when he was a guest on Jack Paar's *Tonight Show*, an early example of how the lines would later blur between politics and entertainment. It was also a sign of how the candidate would successfully use television during his campaign.[153]

The decisive Democratic primary battles took place in Wisconsin and West Virginia.[154] These were proving grounds for Kennedy, as Wisconsin bordered Humphrey's home state of Minnesota, while West Virginia was 96 percent Protestant and presumably not friendly territory for a Catholic. But Kennedy defeated Humphrey in both states, forcing Humphrey's withdrawal from the race, and went on to win the rest of the eight primaries he entered.

Kennedy was a skilled campaigner, although his victories were also powered by the campaign structure he'd built and by his greater access to money. He could fund a larger staff, buy more advertising, and even afford a private plane, as compared to Humphrey's rented bus. While the candidates campaigned during a cold Wisconsin winter, Humphrey slept on a cot on his bus between stops. Once, he recalled, he "heard a plane overhead. On my cot, bundled in layers of uncomfortable clothes, both chilled and sweaty, I yelled, 'Come down here, Jack, and play fair.'"[155]

Kennedy adeptly handled the issue of his Catholicism by cleverly tying the question to his military record. Many voters knew that, in 1943, after his PT boat was sunk by a Japanese destroyer in the Pacific, he and his crew swam three miles through open ocean to seek safety on a nearby island, and that Kennedy made the trek while towing an injured man via a life vest strap in his mouth. "Nobody asked me if I was a Catholic when I joined the United States Navy," he told voters, while reminding them that one of his brothers had died in combat in World War II. "I'm able to serve in Congress and my brother was able to give his life, but we can't be president?"[156]

Kennedy went into the Democratic convention in Los Angeles with about 600 of the 761 delegates necessary for a majority.[157] He corralled the remaining votes he needed from previously uncommitted delegates and defeated Johnson on the first ballot, 806 to 409.[158] After this, Kennedy offered Johnson the vice-presidential nomination, overruling advisors who were vehemently opposed to the Texan and who sometimes referred to him as "Colonel Cornpone."[159] In retrospect, the choice was a monumental one, not only because Johnson succeeded Kennedy as president but also because Kennedy might have lost the election without Johnson's appeal in Texas and the South.

After securing the nomination, Kennedy's team staged his acceptance speech before eighty thousand people in the Los Angeles Coliseum. It was a novel idea to move the address out of the convention hall and, like FDR's flight to Chicago in 1932, was meant to show that Kennedy would take a fresh approach to politics. It was in this address that Kennedy invoked the image of a New Frontier: "Today some would say that . . . all the horizons have been explored, that all the battles have been won, that there is no longer an American frontier. . . . But I tell you the New Frontier is here, whether we seek it or not. . . . I believe the times demand new invention, innovation, imagination, decision."[160]

After this it was off to the races for the fall campaign between Kennedy and Nixon, two men who had more in common than one might think given their current historical reputations. They were both navy men; they entered Congress together in 1946; and they were on friendly terms. Nixon had been invited to Kennedy's wedding in 1953, though he couldn't attend, and visited Kennedy in the hospital in 1954 after JFK's near-fatal back surgery.[161] They were also both moderates; conservatives merely tolerated Nixon, while liberals were suspicious of Kennedy. In 1959 Kennedy even told a friend that if he didn't win the Democratic nomination he'd vote for Nixon.[162]

Instead Kennedy faced off against Nixon, who campaigned on his experience as vice president and on inheriting the Eisenhower legacy. He pointed to his foreign policy background, including a famed 1959 "Kitchen Debate" in Moscow with Soviet Premier Nikita Khrushchev, as proof that he was more ready to deal with Cold War issues. Kennedy retorted that the Eisenhower-Nixon administration had allowed America to fall behind the Soviet Union, noting the recent launch of the first Sputnik satellite, as well as Fidel Castro's communist takeover of Cuba.

In the experience argument, Kennedy received an unanticipated assist from Eisenhower. At an August press conference, reporters asked the president about Nixon's input into major decisions. Eisenhower, who was tired and trying to end the questioning, replied, "If you give me a week, I might think of one."[163] He appeared to be flippantly suggesting that he'd answer the question at the next press conference, but the comment was widely interpreted as being dismissive of Nixon.

Aside from this typical campaign melodrama, three events in particular—pertaining to religion, civil rights, and the growing power of television—helped define the election.

First, the controversy over his Catholicism plagued Kennedy into the fall despite his best efforts to move beyond it, so he agreed to address the Greater Houston Ministerial Association in September. Speaker of the House Sam Rayburn warned Kennedy, "[Those ministers] hate your guts and they're going to tear you to pieces."[164] But Kennedy gave a well-received speech and handled some tough questions. He repeated his assertion that Catholic leaders couldn't control his politics any more than he could influence Church theology. He reminded the audience again that religion wasn't a prerequisite for serving in the military, then added a twist that resonated with Texans. At the Alamo, he said, "side by side with Bowie and Crockett died Fuentes and McCafferty. . . . But no one knows whether they were Catholics. For there was no religious test there."[165]

The Kennedy team was pleased with the address and later rebroadcast portions of it in other states. Rayburn, when it was over, expressed his admiration for Kennedy's performance: "As we say in my part of Texas, he ate 'em blood raw."[166]

A second notable event concerned Martin Luther King Jr., who had emerged as a national leader of the civil rights movement. In October 1960 King was arrested during a sit-in at Atlanta's Magnolia Room restaurant and was controversially sentenced to four months of hard labor in state prison for an old charge of driving with an out-of-state license. His wife, Coretta, who was six months pregnant, feared for King's life in jail.

THE NEW DEAL TO THE GREAT SOCIETY

Shortly thereafter Kennedy phoned Mrs. King to express his concern. And Robert Kennedy, his brother's campaign manager, who was upset over the lack of due process afforded King, intervened with the Georgia judge who'd imposed the sentence and got the civil rights leader released.[167] The Kennedy camp was divided over the wisdom of these actions, as Democrats feared the news might cost them key support from Southern whites who despised King. But when Nixon refused to comment on the case, Kennedy's action became an electoral game changer in a different and unexpected way.

King's father was also a prominent minister and had been a Nixon supporter. Kennedy's phone call changed his mind. "It took courage to call my daughter-in-law at a time like this. He has the moral courage to stand up for what is right," said King Sr.[168] After this, Kennedy's support soared in the African American community, and he went on to win 80 percent of the Black vote nationwide, enough of an increase from 1956 to impact the electoral result in up to five states.[169]

Finally, of course, one of the enduring legacies of the 1960 campaign was the airing of the first presidential debates.[170] This was a signature moment in American politics, one that revolutionized campaigns and may have decided the election. There were four debates in September and October, but it was the first broadcast that made history and is most remembered today. About 70 million people tuned in, an astounding two-thirds of the adult population.[171]

The format seems almost quaint now, as candidates had eight minutes for their opening statements and two and a half minutes to respond to questions; contemporary candidates rarely have more than one minute to churn out a statement or a response. Interestingly, writers like Theodore White, who wrote *The Making of the President 1960*, complained even then that this wasn't enough time to formulate a thoughtful answer to weighty questions. White did acknowledge, though, that the debates provided "a living portrait of two men under stress" and allowed voters to make an "emotional judgement."[172]

In this case, that seems to be exactly what happened. Radio listeners judged the candidates to be evenly matched in that first debate, while television viewers gave Kennedy the victory. Onscreen, Kennedy appeared cool, confident, and unflappable, whereas Nixon was panned for his shaky appearance, which was variously attributed to sickness, fatigue, or a decision to forgo makeup. Beads of sweat glistened on Nixon's face as he spoke into the camera. A headline the next day in the *New York Times* read "Most Viewers Call Kennedy the 'Winner'—Many Say Nixon Looked Unwell."[173] One columnist remarked that Nixon "looked like a suspect who was being questioned."[174]

Ironically, Nixon had agreed to the appearances because he'd been a champion debater and believed he could deliver a knockout blow by highlighting Kennedy's inexperience. "I can take this man," he told advisors.[175] He did better in the next three debates, having learned his lesson about being rested, wearing makeup, and even making sure the studio temperature was cooler so he wouldn't sweat. But Kennedy's success in the first debate caused voters to see him in a new way, and he began attracting larger and more enthusiastic crowds. One poll after the election suggested the debates were a deciding factor for 6 percent of voters, with 72 percent of these favoring Kennedy. If so, this accounted for more than Kennedy's final margin in the popular vote, meaning the debates might well have been decisive.[176]

In late October, Kennedy held a small polling lead. Nixon closed the gap when the popular Eisenhower hit the trail for several high-profile appearances in support of his vice president. The candidates ended in a virtual tie, and the Gallup Poll refused to predict a winner.[177] The choice seemed to rivet the nation, as voter turnout was 62.8 percent, then the highest for any election after 1908.

The Kennedys gathered at their family compound in Hyannis Port, Massachusetts, to await the results, and the Nixons did the same in Los Angeles. As Americans went to the polls, Nixon wanted to escape for a few hours, so he and some aides drove down the Pacific Coast to Tijuana for Mexican food, making him almost surely the only presidential candidate to spend part of Election Day in another country.[178]

That night millions of Americans stayed up late to watch the results. The election was so close that one critic said it was "the most suspenseful evening anyone ever spent in front of a TV set."[179] It wasn't until the next day that Kennedy emerged victorious, winning the popular vote by just 49.7 to 49.6 percent. Only 112,000 votes separated the two men out of nearly 69 million ballots cast. Kennedy won the electoral vote 303–219. Another 15 votes went to Senator Harry Byrd of Virginia. Byrd wasn't a candidate, but these electors, mostly from Mississippi and Alabama, voted for him to protest Democratic support for civil rights.

After the election there were numerous charges of voter fraud, particularly in Illinois, where Kennedy won by fewer than nine thousand votes on the strength of a huge margin in Chicago, home to a political machine controlled by Mayor Richard Daley. There was also speculation that Johnson's operation in Texas had padded the ballot boxes, although that state had a larger margin, of forty-six thousand votes. The fact that Nixon would have won the presidency if he'd carried both Texas and Illinois gave rise to countless conspiracy theories, but Nixon declined to challenge the results. It would have been a difficult legal case, and he didn't want to create a constitutional crisis. Various recounts and investigations were later conducted and failed to turn up anything conclusive that would have changed the outcome. It was, in the end, a close election that could have gone either way.[180]

As vice president, Nixon had the dubious honor of presiding over the congressional session on January 6 that certified the electoral count. He gracefully announced Kennedy's victory. "In our campaigns," Nixon said, "no matter how hard fought they may be, no matter how close the election may turn out to be, those who lose accept the verdict and support those who win."[181]

1964

Kennedy has always maintained a unique place in the pantheon of presidents: the young, charismatic leader with a glamorous family, the president who stared down the Soviet Union during the Cuban Missile Crisis, and the orator who inspired Americans to go to the moon. Yet his reelection in 1964 wasn't a certainty. He would have been favored to win a second term, but his 1960 victory was excruciatingly close and his administration had endured its share of failures, including the botched Bay of Pigs invasion of Cuba. So it's impossible to know how the next contest would have turned out with Kennedy on the ballot.

The question was made moot, though, by the bullets that tore through the air on November 22, 1963, in Dallas, Texas. The shots fired by Lee Harvey Oswald made Kennedy the fourth victim of a presidential assassination. Johnson took the oath of office as the thirty-sixth president a few hours later on Air Force One. At the swearing-in, Jackie Kennedy stood next to Johnson, her pink Chanel suit still splattered with her husband's blood.

In the weeks and months ahead, Johnson tried to pick up the torch of the Kennedy legacy and strived to pass civil rights legislation that JFK had introduced. It took seven months and required overcoming a filibuster by Southern senators, but in July 1964 Johnson signed a new Civil Rights Act, banning racial segregation in public places and prohibiting employment discrimination. It burnished the Kennedy-Johnson legacy and, more important, was a landmark achievement in the long battle for civil rights, fulfilling goals that stretched back at least to the Reconstruction era.

It was during this period that Johnson introduced his Great Society agenda. "The Great Society rests on abundance and liberty for all," he said in a speech at the University of Michigan. "It demands an end to poverty and racial injustice. . . . There are those timid souls who say this battle cannot be won; that we are condemned to a soulless wealth. I do not agree. We have the power to shape the civilization that we want."[182]

With the triumph of the Civil Rights Act behind him and the theme of a Great Society propelling his campaign forward, Johnson set out in 1964 to win the presidency in his own right. At the Democratic convention in Atlantic City he was nominated by acclamation. "All the Way with LBJ" was his slogan.[183]

In a mirror image of 1960, this time it was the Republican nomination battle that provided drama. It ended, in fact, with the party's conservative and moderate wings nearly at war with each other.

The conservative favorite was Senator Barry Goldwater, a staunch proponent of limiting government, slashing social welfare programs, lowering taxes, and restoring power to the states. In his 1960 book, *The Conscience of a Conservative*, Goldwater wrote, "I have little interest in streamlining government or in making it more efficient, for I mean to reduce its size. I do not undertake to promote welfare, for I propose to extend freedom. My aim is not to pass laws, but to repeal them."[184]

These pronouncements thrust Goldwater into the role of conservative hero. Patrick Buchanan, the columnist and politician who would later run for president himself, was in his twenties when Goldwater's book came out. "[The book] was our new testament," he said. "For those of us wandering in the arid desert of Eisenhower Republicanism it hit like a rifle shot."[185]

Even as Goldwater was hailed by the right wing of his party, however, he was dismissed as an extremist by other Republicans because his ideas weren't yet in the political mainstream. One columnist suggested Goldwater was not a conservative but "a radical reactionary who would, if we are to believe what he says, dismantle the modern state."[186]

Party leaders were dismayed by Goldwater's penchant for making drastic statements. At various times he had suggested that NATO commanders should be able to launch nuclear weapons, that Vietnam could be defoliated with nuclear bombs, and that he'd like to "lob one into the men's room of the Kremlin."[187] These comments fueled Goldwater's reputation as an extremist, even as supporters claimed his words shouldn't be taken so literally. One political cartoon showed the senator, gun holstered on his hip, walking away from reporters and saying, "Of course you're prejudiced—you print everything I say."[188]

As the nomination contest heated up, Goldwater managed to attract both devotion and revulsion from within his own party.

It didn't seem to matter at first, as many observers believed he would lose the nomination battle to New York governor Nelson Rockefeller, a moderate in the mold of recent nominees Eisenhower and Dewey. But Rockefeller's personal life intruded on his politics in 1963, when the divorced governor married Margaretta "Happy" Murphy, a woman eighteen years his junior who had divorced her husband only a month earlier and who gave up custody of her four young children to remarry.[189] Even today this would be a major news story, but in the 1960s it was downright scandalous. Rockefeller's image took a beating and his polling lead evaporated.

By 1964 the story had died down enough so that Rockefeller was again a plausible contender. By then, though, he was up against a Goldwater campaign that had proved devastatingly effective at amassing delegates via party caucuses, particularly in the West and South. Rockefeller's best hope was to defeat Goldwater in some key primaries and then convince the convention that he was a more electable candidate.

Their decisive head-to-head battle was in California in June. Rockefeller seemed to be surging, as he'd just won the Oregon primary and led Goldwater in California by 49 to 40 percent in a Harris poll.[190] Then, in a fateful coincidence of timing, his personal life intruded once more. His wife gave birth to a son just days before the California vote, and suddenly all the old doubts about the morality of Rockefeller's second marriage came hurtling back into public consciousness. Ministers preached against his candidacy, and Goldwater supporters printed signs that read "Do You Want a Leader or a Lover in the White House?"[191] On primary day Goldwater overtook Rockefeller by the slimmest of margins, just sixty-eight thousand votes out of more than 2 million, but it knocked Rockefeller out of the race.

Republican moderates were aghast to realize that Goldwater was on the verge of winning the nomination. They were even more discouraged later that month, when Goldwater was one of six Republicans to vote against the Civil Rights Act. While Goldwater had previously shown a commitment to racial equality in his own life, working to desegregate the Phoenix public schools and the Arizona Air National Guard, he now joined Southern Democrats in taking the states' rights view that it was unconstitutional for the government to make laws about public accommodations and employment practices.[192] He couldn't impose his judgment "on the people of Mississippi or South Carolina," he reasoned, because "that's their business, not mine."[193]

In a last-ditch effort by moderates to stop the Arizonan, Governor William Scranton of Pennsylvania declared himself a candidate just weeks before the convention, saying he didn't want his party to be seen as an "ultra-rightist society."[194] He was buoyed by a Gallup poll that showed him leading Goldwater among Republicans by 55 to 34 percent.[195] But Scranton was too late to the game. Goldwater won the nomination on the first ballot, with 883 votes to 214 for Scranton and 114 for Rockefeller.

Despite the ease of Goldwater's victory, the convention wasn't smooth sailing for Republicans. When Rockefeller came onstage for a speech condemning extremism, he was drowned out by a cascade of boos from Goldwater supporters. And the lasting image of the convention was of Goldwater's own acceptance speech, when he famously declared, "Extremism in the defense of liberty is no vice! And let me remind you also that moderation in the pursuit of justice is no virtue!"[196] Far from moving to the center for the fall campaign, as most nominees do, Goldwater had instead embraced his image as a political extremist. "My God, he's going to run as Barry Goldwater," exclaimed one reporter.[197]

When the fall campaign kicked off, Johnson held a gargantuan lead in the polls and never relinquished it. The president was still riding a wave of sympathy after Kennedy's death, and his opponent had been branded, fairly or not, an extremist. One historian summarized Goldwater's dilemma this way: "When the soundness of the man became the issue, rather than the soundness of his ideas, it was over."[198] One Johnson campaign advisor suggested, "The big issue of the campaign was whose finger do you trust on the button."[199] This, ultimately, is how the contest was framed in the public's mind. Goldwater's team, for example, came up with the slogan "In Your Heart You Know He's Right!" but Johnson's supporters turned it into "In Your Guts You Know He's Nuts!"[200]

This perception influenced one of the most famous political commercials ever made. The "Daisy Ad" showed a young girl picking petals off a flower just before a nuclear explosion lit up the screen. "Vote for President Johnson on November 3," intoned the announcer. "The stakes are too high for you to stay home." The ad aired only once, yet many Americans saw the spot because it was continually replayed and discussed in news broadcasts.

The media's fascination with the commercial stemmed from the fact that it was the first negative ad broadcast on television. Negative campaigning is as old as the presidency, as we've seen, going all the way back to the Adams-Jefferson battles. But political commercials on TV were first aired in 1952 and had previously been used to communicate positive messages about candidates, not to attack an opponent.[201]

Goldwater was naturally frustrated by all this. He had initially envisioned a great debate of conservatism versus liberalism but got no such engagement from Johnson. So Goldwater counterpunched, going after Johnson on issues of crime and culture. "The moral fiber of the American people is beset by rot and decay," he thundered. There was a "wave of crime in our streets" and a "breakdown of the morals of our young people."[202] It was a theme that would be repeated in Republican campaigns for decades to come, but it didn't resonate in 1964. Johnson won a record 61 percent of the popular vote to 38.5 percent for Goldwater, and he swept the Electoral College 486–52. It was the biggest landslide since FDR's victory in 1936.

Launching a Conservative Revival

In the aftermath of the 1964 election, most observers treated President Johnson as the second coming of Franklin Roosevelt and the conservative cause as lost.

"Barry Goldwater . . . has wrecked his party," wrote James Reston in the *New York Times*. The Republican defeat "was so complete that they will not have another shot at party domination for some time to come," reported *Time* magazine. "By every test we have, this is as surely a liberal epoch as the 19th century was a conservative one," said the historian James MacGregor Burns.[203]

In a few short years these assertions would prove laughable. Instead Johnson's election turned out to be "the last hurrah of New Deal liberalism."[204] This was a shocking turn of events for anyone who was there in 1964, when the most conservative Republican nominee since the 1920s suffered a crushing defeat to a liberal Democrat. Why would anyone have thought a conservative revival was just around the corner?

Not only that, but various cultural signposts had also seemed to herald the emergence of a new liberal age. In 1962 the book *Silent Spring* by Rachel Carson awakened environmental consciousness. A year later *The Feminine Mystique* by Betty Friedan helped spark a women's movement. In 1963 Martin Luther King inspired two hundred thousand people at the Lincoln Memorial with his "I Have a Dream" speech. Heck, in 1964 the Beatles even came to America, and Bob Dylan wrote "The Times They Are-a-Changin'." Clearly something new was brewing.

In national politics, though, what was brewing was a conservative counterrevolution. Goldwater lost the election, but his ideological vision forged the foundation for a long run of conservative political success. The revolution wasn't fully realized until 1980, but the elements started coming together in 1964.

It began with Goldwater's takeover of the GOP, which pushed the philosophy of limited government and states' rights to the forefront of the party's agenda. This overthrow of Republican moderates caught the attention of Southern Democrats, who'd been at odds with their own party for decades. The Republican emphasis on states' rights provided an opening for racial and economic conservatives in the two parties to find common ground. The principle of states' rights worked as a unifying philosophy because it appealed equally to Southerners who opposed racial integration and to small-government conservatives who disagreed with the New Deal. These factions had other differences, but they were all opposed to "intervention and control by a far-off government in

Washington."[205] This was the spark for a new conservative coalition that would come to dominate national politics.

To be fair, this idea of an alliance between racial and economic conservatives wasn't entirely new. As early as 1947 a book titled *Whither Solid South?* by an attorney, Charles Wallace Collins, had suggested that Southern Democrats and conservative Republicans could unite to form "the strongest party in the country, provided that the issue of Negro equality was left to the sponsorship of a new Liberal Party."[206] It wasn't until 1964, however, that political conditions grew favorable for such a realignment. And by that time even Johnson knew it. After signing the Civil Rights Act, the president looked at one of his aides and said, "I think we just delivered the South to the Republican party for a long time to come."[207]

There were other signs, too, of how political coalitions were shifting, such as when Governor George Wallace of Alabama won a significant minority of the vote in even Democratic presidential primaries in Wisconsin, Indiana, and Maryland with his own states' right message. This showed that the concept of a backlash to federal overreach and to civil rights resonated with both Southern segregationists and working-class Democrats in the North who feared a minority invasion of their neighborhoods.

These factors all existed in 1964, and yet Goldwater still suffered a historic defeat. There are various reasons for this, including the legacy of Kennedy's popularity, a reluctance to vote out Johnson less than a year after JFK's death, and apprehension over Goldwater's desire to roll back programs like Social Security. There was also Goldwater's tendency to make extremist statements. He wasn't the best messenger for a new conservative era.

Which brings us to one other component of the conservative revival that, almost by accident, also made an entrance in 1964. One of Goldwater's supporters, it seems, was a Hollywood actor who delivered some well-received speeches for the candidate. Goldwater's campaign bought TV time for one of these addresses, and on October 27 the "Time for Choosing" speech aired nationally. The speaker promoted the Goldwater cause, but in a soothing cadence and an optimistic tone. "You and I have a rendezvous with destiny," he said, echoing FDR. "We'll preserve for our children this, the last best hope of man on earth."[208] The response to the speech was startling. Viewers sent money to Goldwater and asked for the talk to be rebroadcast. One Republican operative said it had "created a new political star and a new spokesman for conservatism."[209]

The actor's name was Ronald Reagan, and that speech helped launch his political career. Two years later he was elected governor of California. Sixteen years later he became president, with a platform that echoed the Goldwater economic agenda. It became known to history as the Reagan Revolution.

6

★ ★ ★

1968-2004

Upheaval in American Politics

Coffee at Hamburg Inn No. 2 in Iowa City, Iowa

Iowa is the birthplace of President Herbert Hoover and one of the nation's great agricultural states. In presidential politics, however, the state became famous during this era for the Iowa caucuses, which began a tradition of kicking off the presidential nominating season every four years. A strong finish in Iowa, or in the subsequent New Hampshire primary, powered the campaign of many candidates who won a major party's presidential nomination.

While primaries first became a feature of presidential races in 1912, for six decades they were merely an opportunity for candidates to prove their vote-getting ability in a few states, as nominations were still mostly controlled by party leaders at the conventions. But the rules were eventually changed to encourage more primaries and public caucuses and to move nomination battles out of the smoke-filled rooms. George McGovern in 1972 was the first candidate to win a presidential nomination on the strength of support from voters over that of party leaders.

Then, in 1976, Jimmy Carter revolutionized the Iowa caucuses.[1] This wasn't yet considered a major event on the road to the White House, but Carter spent months crisscrossing the state to meet voters at a time when he barely registered in national polls. His strong showing generated a great deal of media coverage, which boosted him a few weeks later to an upset win in the New Hampshire primary. Other Democratic candidates barely knew what hit them as the previously unknown Georgia governor with a fresh face and folksy manner took the lead in the nomination battle and never looked back. Eventually this all became standard campaign strategy, but in 1976 it was an innovative tactic.

Nearly three decades after Carter propelled the Iowa caucuses to prominence, the owner of the Hamburg Inn No. 2 had an idea. In 2004 this Iowa City diner launched the Coffee Bean Caucus, giving customers the chance to vote for their favorite candidates by dropping coffee beans into labeled mason jars, with the winners announced just prior to the actual caucuses. The contest attracted international media attention and a tradition was born. A year later the TV show *The West Wing* featured a presidential candidate visiting the diner during a campaign swing.

The Hamburg Inn didn't really need the publicity, as it was already an Iowa City institution, having opened in 1948. A few blocks from the University of Iowa, it's been a longtime gathering place for locals, students, writers, and visiting politicians. The Iowa Writers' Workshop is nearby, so many authors have toiled over manuscripts in the diner, and Presidents Ronald Reagan and Bill Clinton came by in 1992 and 2003. Nevertheless the Coffee Bean Caucus put the Hamburg Inn on the map in a new way. The diner's walls grew crowded with photos and press clippings of presidents and candidates who visited.

This makes the Hamburg Inn No. 2 an intriguing place at which to ponder the next period of presidential history, for it symbolizes how campaigns became more responsive to voters and less controlled by party elites. These changes were triggered by the turbulent election of 1968. In fact, pretty much everything that happened during this era, from the expansion of presidential primaries to the rise of conservatism and a rift over social issues, has *some* connection to the events of 1968, which is where we now turn.

1968, 1972, and 1976: The Vietnam War and Watergate Era

1968

There has rarely been an election year like 1968. Aside from the pre–Civil War contest of 1860, it's hard to think of many other presidential campaigns that produced as much drama, division, and discord in the United States.

This was an astonishing about-face from four years earlier, when Lyndon Johnson's landslide triumph convinced people the country was united behind his Great Society agenda. After LBJ's inauguration, the president introduced a blizzard of new initiatives, including Medicare, Medicaid, Head Start, and other environmental, consumer, and antipoverty programs. Johnson's presidency, however, as well as his hopes for winning another term, would eventually be consumed by a trio of issues that surfaced in the summer of 1965.

On July 28 of that year, the president announced a decision to deploy 125,000 troops to Vietnam. On August 6 he signed the Voting Rights Act, outlawing racial discrimination in voting. And on August 11 the Watts riots erupted in Los Angeles. These events didn't appear at the time to be signs of a coming political earthquake, but in retrospect this two-week period was the beginning of the end of the Johnson presidency. The escalation of the Vietnam War gave rise to a vociferous protest movement that damaged the president politically. The Voting Rights Act and other Great Society programs turned conservatives and Southerners more vehemently against the Democrats. And the Watts rioting, initially provoked by an altercation between a white policeman and a young Black man, was a harbinger of dozens more urban uprisings during the next few years.

By 1968 controversies over Vietnam, racial issues, and urban unrest were roiling the nation. And by the end of that year American politics had been thrashed, battered, and transformed in ways that still reverberate today.

It began on the Democratic side, with the white-hot heat of an antiwar movement. As casualties rose into the tens of thousands,

President Johnson was hounded by protesters, who gathered outside the White House and chanted, "Hey! Hey! LBJ! How many kids did you kill today?"[2] The passions that erupted over Vietnam convinced Senator Eugene McCarthy of Minnesota to challenge Johnson for the Democratic nomination.

Most politicians and journalists saw McCarthy as a protest candidate with little chance to derail a sitting president. But college students joined McCarthy's effort and flooded into New Hampshire ahead of that state's primary. They knocked on thousands of doors and were known as the "Clean for Gene" campaign because they were clean-shaven and well-dressed when canvassing voters.[3] In the March 12 primary, New Hampshirites gave McCarthy 42 percent of the vote. Johnson won with 49 percent, but McCarthy's performance was so far above expectations that his second-place finish was the headline of the day. Just like that, the "presumed inevitability of Johnson's renomination had been punctured."[4]

Four days later, on March 16, Senator Robert Kennedy of New York, brother of the late president, also threw his hat in the ring. Then, on March 31, after addressing the nation about Vietnam, President Johnson stunned everyone by declaring "I shall not seek, and I will not accept, the nomination of my party for another term as your president."[5] In less than a month Johnson had gone from being a candidate for reelection to withdrawing from the race.

The country barely had time to process Johnson's words before it endured another shock: on April 4 a gunman outside the Lorraine Motel in Memphis, Tennessee, shot and killed the civil rights leader Martin Luther King Jr. As news of King's death spread, riots raged in Black communities across the country. During the next week twenty thousand people were arrested and thirty-nine were killed, while burned-out buildings and broken glass scarred the nation's streets.

Amid this turmoil, a wide-open presidential contest took shape. Vice President Hubert Humphrey also joined the Democratic race and chose to pursue the nomination the old-fashioned way, by corralling delegates at state caucuses and locking down the support of the party establishment. No one knew it at the time, but

Humphrey would be the last major party candidate to run for a presidential nomination without going before the voters. Kennedy and McCarthy, meanwhile, set out to demonstrate their viability in select primaries. Both wanted to end U.S. involvement in Vietnam, but Kennedy was more popular with minorities and working-class voters, while McCarthy was a hit with students and college-educated progressives. Kennedy won in Indiana and Nebraska, and McCarthy in Oregon. This led to a showdown in delegate-rich California on June 4, where Kennedy triumphed by 46 to 42 percent, essentially ending McCarthy's hopes and setting himself up as the main challenger to Humphrey.

When it was apparent around midnight that he'd won, Kennedy addressed supporters in the ballroom of the Ambassador Hotel in Los Angeles. "On to Chicago," he told the crowd, "and let's win there!"[6] He walked offstage and through the kitchen, where he shook hands with waiters and cooks. There a Palestinian immigrant named Sirhan Sirhan, angry over Kennedy's support for Israel, shot him. Kennedy died the next day. Coming just two months after King's assassination, this tragedy seemed almost too much for the country to comprehend. Humphrey compared it to a national "mental breakdown."[7]

Two months later, in a country still numb with grief, the Democratic convention convened in Chicago. It's impossible to know if Kennedy would have won the nomination had he lived. Some analysts have concluded it was unlikely, since Humphrey amassed a substantial number of delegates even before Kennedy's death.[8] However, Kennedy was a popular enough figure that he was often swarmed by crowds who rushed forward to shake his hand, "to touch him, to feel the magic."[9] When a funeral train carried Kennedy's body from New York to Washington for burial on June 8, 2 million people of all races turned out and stood along more than two hundred miles of track to salute him.

Since some Democrats thought Humphrey was a weak general election candidate, it's at least possible the party could have been persuaded that Kennedy was a stronger nominee.[10] In which case the future of Democratic politics might have played out quite differently, as Kennedy appealed to the same white voters who would later flee the Democratic Party over racial anxieties, social issues, and an aversion to identity politics. These voters supported Kennedy despite his support for civil rights for minorities, mostly because Kennedy was seen as a leader who would also protect working-class and rural white voters.[11]

In any case, it's all hypothetical. Instead of a Humphrey-Kennedy floor fight for the nomination, the country saw something entirely different at the 1968 Democratic convention. They saw a party, and a country, being ripped apart.

Antiwar activists and student groups had long planned to converge on Chicago to agitate for change and to protest the war policies of the Johnson-Humphrey administration. But Mayor Richard Daley was determined to head off any strife, so he denied permits for most demonstrations, put more than twenty thousand police and national guardsmen on alert, and had the convention site encircled with barbed wire.[12] Daley's tactics, though, only served to raise tensions between police and protesters, and on August 28 the pressure cooker erupted.

That day a demonstration that began with thousands of people in Grant Park broke up when police shot tear gas into the crowd. The protesters then spilled into the streets and marched down Michigan Avenue toward the Hilton Hotel, where Democratic leaders were staying. About one hundred yards from the hotel several thousand marchers were blocked by police lines. Most demonstrators remained nonviolent, but others threw rocks and bottles. The journalist Theodore White watched the protest unfold and made a note at 7:55 p.m. that the marchers were chanting, "Fuck you, LBJ!" At 8:05, just ten minutes later, he wrote, "The Democrats are finished."[13]

What White saw in those ten minutes was a fury of violence that stunned the nation. The sequence of events remains mysterious, but something—some projectile, some expletive, some provocation—set off the police. The next thing anyone knew the police were charging into the crowd. They chased marchers and clubbed bystanders. They attacked reporters and broke cameras.

They removed their police badges so they couldn't be identified. They set off tear gas, which filled the air and wafted up vents into hotel rooms.

A *New York Times* reporter wrote about watching police push a barrier against a crowd on the sidewalk, causing the group to crash through the plate-glass window of a restaurant, "sending screaming middle-aged woman and children backward through broken shards of glass. The police then ran into the restaurant and beat some of the victims who had fallen through the window and arrested them."[14] The streets and walkways became stained with blood, and protesters chanted, "The whole world is watching!" The scene was so astonishing that White compared it to "a movie of the Russian revolution."[15]

When delegates found out about the street clashes, anger boiled over in the convention hall, which was already tense because of conflicts between establishment Democrats who supported Humphrey and antiwar delegates who'd favored Kennedy or McCarthy. Senator Abraham Ribicoff of Connecticut veered from his speech to criticize "Gestapo tactics on the streets of Chicago." Mayor Daley, sitting in the front row, responded by unleashing a barrage of obscenities at Ribicoff in full view of the television cameras.

Reactions were coarse, intense, tempestuous. It was, as Lawrence O'Donnell has written, "the darkest, most dangerous night in the history of American political conventions."[16] That evening images of the "Battle of Michigan Avenue" were broadcast to the nation, interspersed with footage of Humphrey becoming the Democratic nominee. Humphrey won the nomination on the first ballot, but it almost didn't matter. His achievement was drowned out by the violence; his campaign nearly shattered before it began.

For Americans who were already weary of war protests and urban riots, it was one more example of a country that seemed to have become unhinged. Against this backdrop, Richard Nixon won the Republican nomination for president and presented himself as a safe harbor from the turmoil.

Nixon hadn't started out as the GOP frontrunner. After losing the 1960 election, and then a 1962 campaign for governor of California, his political career seemed over. But he rehabilitated his image and was back in the ring in 1968 with a campaign slogan that declared "Nixon's the one!"[17] Early polls showed him trailing George Romney, the popular Michigan governor (and the father of Mitt Romney, the 2012 Republican nominee), but Romney struggled as a candidate. His most infamous moment came when an interviewer asked him why he'd changed his mind about the Vietnam War. Romney said he'd been "brainwashed" by military leaders into supporting the conflict before studying the issue in more depth and reaching a new conclusion. The second half of his answer was perfectly reasonable, but the media picked up on his "brainwashed" line. It became a national story, and his candidacy collapsed.

After Romney withdrew, there were still two other potentially formidable Republican candidates, although neither one seriously threatened Nixon. The first, New York governor Nelson Rockefeller, was the nation's foremost liberal Republican, but his base was a dwindling faction of moderates in a party that was moving rightward. The second was California governor Ronald Reagan, leader of the growing conservative movement. Nixon early in the year had seen Reagan as a legitimate threat, particularly if Democrats nominated Kennedy. In that situation, he thought, the GOP might unite behind the former Hollywood actor as a way to "fight glamour with glamour."[18] But the scenario never came to pass, and Reagan didn't even enter the presidential race until very late.

When the party convention opened in Miami Beach, Nixon was just short of the 667 delegates needed for the nomination. That created an opening to stop him from winning on the first ballot, but Nixon was better organized than Rockefeller or Reagan, and his team rounded up enough support to push him over the top.

But it makes one wonder, if the political landscape had tilted just a tiny bit this way or that, how different the 1968 election might have been. If McCarthy hadn't entered the Democratic primaries, for instance, Johnson may well have remained a candidate for reelection. If RFK hadn't been shot, there might have been another Nixon-Kennedy contest. Or, as we just saw, 1968 could conceivably have given the country a Kennedy-versus-Reagan showdown. Imagine *that* one.

Those aren't the only alternate realities that might have altered the 1968 election. For much of the fall it even seemed possible that no candidate would win a majority of electoral votes and that the contest would be decided in the House of Representatives. This was because of the third-party candidacy of George Wallace, the segregationist Alabama governor who ran under the banner of the American Independent Party. Wallace appealed to Southern conservatives and working-class Northerners, as he promoted law and order, railed against civil rights laws, and raged at government bureaucrats, activist judges, communists, antiwar protesters, and the media.

With the campaign slogan "Stand up for America," Wallace attracted voters who feared "their good jobs, their modest homes, and their personal safety were under siege both from liberal authorities above and angry minorities below."[19] At his rallies he fulminated about "ivory tower folks with pointy heads who couldn't park their bicycle straight" and about liberal elitists who "have looked down their noses at the average man in the street for too long."[20]

His audiences loved it. Wallace attracted throngs of followers who cheered him with "frenzied, pulsating passion," as one reporter described it.[21] Not surprisingly, protesters were also present at his rallies, and there was often an undercurrent of anger and violence whipping through the crowd. Demonstrators burned Confederate flags, cried "Sieg Heil!" and made Nazi salutes, while Wallace's fans responded by screaming at the demonstrators and calling them "dope addicts," "Commies," and "n—— loving homosexuals." Fistfights broke out regularly. Wallace fed off the energy. He blew kisses to the protesters, told them they needed a haircut, and offered to autograph their sandals.[22]

Wallace's segregationist politics were abhorrent to many, but he found a political wave to ride. The more chaos there was in America, the higher his polls rose. In the spring, he was at 9 percent; in September, after the unrest at the Democratic convention, he was at 21 percent.[23] His popularity threatened the two major parties because his strategy was to win enough electoral votes to prevent any candidate from gaining a majority. He hoped to be a kingmaker in the Electoral College, thinking he might extract concessions in exchange for the support of Wallace electors.[24]

Nixon responded by pushing his own law-and-order agenda, but without straying into Wallace-style extremism. In his acceptance speech at the GOP convention, he talked about an America "enveloped in smoke and flame" with "sirens in the night." The real America, he said, could be found in the "quiet voice" of "the forgotten Americans—the non-shouters, the non-demonstrators. . . . They are good people, they are decent people; they work, and they save, and they pay their taxes, and they care."[25]

Nixon appealed to these "forgotten Americans" and pledged to lead the country out of the maelstrom. He launched an ad campaign that featured jarring images of war and of burning cities and bloodied protesters. Each ad ended with the tag line "This time vote like your whole world depended on it."[26]

Humphrey, meanwhile, began the fall campaign in dreadful shape. In late September he trailed Nixon in the Gallup poll by 43 to 28 percent and was barely ahead of Wallace.[27] The uproar over the Vietnam War was a greater problem for Humphrey than for Nixon because of how it splintered the Democrats. The vice president was booed and heckled perpetually by antiwar protesters. "Stop the war!" they chanted, or, "Dump the Hump." They used bullhorns to interrupt his speeches and called him a fascist and a murderer.

Finally, Humphrey could take no more. "I'm probably going to lose this election," he told his staff, "but win or lose, I'm going to speak my mind, and I'm going to fight."[28] He planned a speech in Salt Lake City on September 30 that Democrats paid to have telecast nationwide. Humphrey told the country that, as president, he would stop the bombing of North Vietnam "as an acceptable risk for peace."[29] It wasn't a huge change in direction, but it was at least a declaration of independence from the Johnson administration. The impact on Humphrey's campaign was enormous. Almost instantly the hecklers disappeared. In their place were new signs: "Humphrey, if you mean it, we're with you" and "Hecklers for Humphrey—We Came Back."[30]

After this, Humphrey campaigned with more gusto. He nicknamed Nixon "Richard the Chickenhearted" for refusing to debate and called Wallace the "apostle of the politics of fear and racism." He asked voters, "Who can you trust?"[31] Humphrey cut Nixon's polling lead in half.

Humphrey and Nixon also benefited from an unforced error by Wallace. Needing a vice-presidential nominee, he chose Gen. Curtis Lemay, a hero of World War II and former chief of staff of the air force. Lemay burnished Wallace's foreign policy credentials, but he was also, as one writer noted, "something of a nut."[32] He was the model for a crazed general in the 1964 movie *Dr. Strangelove*, a political satire about the possibility of a nuclear holocaust, and he lived up to that reputation when introduced as Wallace's running mate. "We seem to have a phobia about nuclear weapons," Lemay told reporters. "I don't believe the world will end if we explode a nuclear weapon."[33] When the comments became headline news, Wallace's poll numbers began a slow plunge.

As the campaign neared the finish line, Humphrey gained strength by the day. There was even a last-minute breakthrough in Vietnam that might have catapulted him past Nixon. On October 31 President Johnson went on national television to announce that North Vietnam had agreed to join peace talks in return for a U.S. bombing halt, a deal that might eventually end the war. But one day later America's ally, South Vietnam, disavowed support for the pact. This led people to accuse Johnson of having embellished the truth to help his vice president.[34]

In actuality, the agreement was real but had been thwarted behind the scenes. Johnson learned, courtesy of intelligence surveillance, that a Chinese American named Anna Chennault, a Nixon fundraiser, had passed word to South Vietnam that it could get a better deal from a future Nixon administration. The Nixon team, it seemed, had sabotaged the peace talks to save its campaign. Johnson kept quiet about the matter, however, because no evidence linked Nixon to the meddling until several decades later, when historians discovered the Nixon campaign was indeed involved in back-channel talks. On October 22, according to a note found in campaign documents, Nixon told aides, "Keep Anna Chennault working on SVN [South Vietnam]."[35]

There's obviously no way to know if the election would have turned out differently absent this involvement. The final Gallup poll did show that Humphrey had just about caught Nixon, who held a minuscule lead of 43 to 42 percent, with Wallace at 15 percent.[36] That's where the election carousel stopped spinning, however. On Election Day, Nixon defeated Humphrey by 43.4 to 42.7 percent, but he prevailed more comfortably in the Electoral College, 301–191. Wallace garnered 13.5 percent of the vote and won five states with 46 electoral votes.

Despite how close Humphrey came in the popular vote, he received 12 million fewer votes than Johnson had in 1964. Much of the loss came in the South, where Democrats were nearly shut out for the first time, winning only in Texas. Wallace won the Deep South states, and Nixon won the rest, in a sign of elections to come.

Wallace's strategy of blocking other candidates from an electoral majority obviously failed. But not by much. If fewer than seventy-eight thousand votes in Missouri and Illinois had flipped from Nixon to Humphrey, no candidate would have won the Electoral College. Wallace's 46 electors would then have become the bargaining chip he desired, or else the election would have gone to Congress.

Wallace's efforts to manipulate the outcome alarmed Americans, and a movement arose to replace the electoral system with a national popular vote.[37] In 1969 legislation to amend the Constitution passed the House of Representatives by the overwhelming margin of 338 to 70. It was endorsed by President Nixon and backed by 80 percent of the public. But the bill died in the Senate when it couldn't overcome a filibuster by Southern senators who weren't thrilled with the idea of putting Blacks on an equal footing with whites in one-person-one-vote elections.[38] This was the closest the country ever came to replacing the Electoral College.

1972

When Richard Nixon was sworn in as the thirty-seventh president in 1969, he acknowledged the divisions that were tearing at the country's fabric. "We are caught in a war, wanting peace. We are torn by division, wanting unity," he said in his inaugural address. "To a crisis of the spirit, we need an answer of the spirit."[39]

But answers didn't always come easily, and midway through Nixon's first term American nerves were still on edge. For starters, the Vietnam War raged on, despite a reduction in troop deployments. This kept the antiwar movement alive, and in May 1970 four students at Kent State University in Ohio were shot and killed by National Guard troops during a protest. There was an extraordinary rise in homegrown terrorist acts, as left-wing groups such as the Weather Underground exploded hundreds of bombs in U.S. cities. Most were detonated at night, so as to damage property rather than to kill, but the attacks added to the nation's stress. Inflation and unemployment were also on the rise. By mid-1971 the president's approval rating had slipped below 50 percent, and he trailed top Democrats in polling for the next election.[40]

And yet one year later Nixon won a landslide reelection victory, with one of the highest popular vote tallies in history. This was a tribute to his political skills, certainly, though other factors also played a role in the 1972 result, including the fracturing of the Democratic coalition, the use of some devious campaign tactics, and possibly even a car accident on Martha's Vineyard.

Let's begin with President Nixon, who, amid these first-term storms, still racked up notable achievements, including historic moves to establish relations with China and negotiate an arms control agreement with the Soviet Union. He also had a domestic record that was alternately conservative and liberal. He proposed cuts in housing and antipoverty programs, for example, but also created the Environmental Protection Agency, funded Amtrak, and even proposed a health care plan with an employer mandate.[41] Today it seems almost incomprehensible that such policies were proposed by a Republican president. It shows how American politics continually morphs into new shapes.

In any event, there was never any question that Republicans would nominate Nixon for a second term, which they did almost unanimously at the party convention in Miami Beach in August. The only question was which Democrat would challenge Nixon in the general election.

Senator Ted Kennedy of Massachusetts, the brother of John and Robert Kennedy, was an early frontrunner, but he declined to run, mostly because he was happy in the Senate, but also in part because his popularity took a hit in the aftermath of the Chappaquiddick incident. Kennedy, after a late-night party in July 1969, had accidentally driven his car off a small bridge on Martha's Vineyard and was unable to rescue his passenger, twenty-eight-year-old Mary Jo Kopechne, who drowned. He didn't report the accident until the next morning and received a two-month suspended sentence for leaving the scene. Many questions were raised about Kennedy's version of events, and it wounded him politically.

With Kennedy out, the mantle of frontrunner fell to Senator Edmund Muskie of Maine, who'd been Humphrey's running mate in 1968. Muskie was tied with Nixon in the polls in early 1972, but then his candidacy collapsed after an infamous meltdown in the snows of New Hampshire.

William Loeb, the conservative publisher of the *Manchester Union-Leader*, had attacked Muskie mercilessly in print, even denigrating his wife for her alleged drinking and cursing. Loeb also published the "Canuck letter," from a man in Florida who said he'd heard Muskie describe French Canadians (Canucks) as New Hampshire Blacks. This was a big deal in a state where French Canadians made up a significant bloc of voters, and Muskie plummeted in state polls. Muskie was outraged and held a press conference in front of the newspaper's offices. He called the publisher "a mudslinging, vicious and gutless liar." But "what really got me," said Muskie, "was this editorial attacking my wife." At this point Muskie choked up and his voice cracked.[42]

In that instant his candidacy was fatally wounded. David Broder of the *Washington Post* criticized Muskie for having tears on his face and for being "a grown man standing in a snowstorm and unable to speak." Muskie was derided as weak and emotionally unstable, "not the man I want to have with his finger on the nuclear button," in the words of another writer.[43] Although he hung on to narrowly win the New Hampshire primary, his campaign fell apart soon afterward. And it later came to light that the Canuck letter was a forgery; it was actually written by a Nixon staffer and was one of several instances of sabotage and espionage conducted against political opponents that year by the Committee for the Re-Election of the President.

So the two Democrats who polled best against Nixon, Kennedy and Muskie, were out of the running. The Democrats had several other candidates, including Congresswoman Shirley Chisholm of New York, who made history as an African American woman running for the nomination, but the strongest remaining contenders were former vice president Humphrey, Governor George Wallace, who ran as a Democrat this time around, and Senator George McGovern of South Dakota, a favorite of liberals and antiwar activists.

Wallace still spoke in racial code words, but he'd moderated his tone somewhat from 1968. Although many Democrats objected to Wallace, his fusion of a New Deal–style economic agenda with a states' rights, antibusing message helped him to primary wins in five states, including Florida and Michigan. But Wallace's candidacy was cut short when, on May 15, he was shot in an assassination attempt. The shooting paralyzed him from the waist down and ended his campaign.

That left Humphrey and McGovern. Humphrey's strategy was to again win establishment support from party leaders and labor unions, whereas McGovern assembled an "army of grassroots volunteers, amateur Democrats, and anti-war protesters."[44] In the end, McGovern edged past Humphrey during the primaries and won a first-ballot victory at the Democratic convention in July, which, like the GOP convention, was also held in Miami Beach.

McGovern's victory was helped by new rules that incentivized states to select delegates through primaries and caucuses. These changes were adopted in the aftermath of 1968, as a peace offering to activists who were agitated over the fact that Humphrey had won that year's nomination without entering a single primary. The new system diminished the power of the state and city bosses who might otherwise have pushed Humphrey over the top again in 1972. McGovern had chaired the commission that updated these rules.

Party leaders, however, were dismayed by McGovern's win because they believed he was too liberal to win a national election, with an agenda that included ending the Vietnam War, reducing the defense budget, and using the savings to increase spending on social programs.[45] He also proposed to decriminalize marijuana, leave the question of abortion rights to each state, and provide amnesty for young men who evaded the draft. These positions hardly seem extreme in the light of history, but at the time they led to a famous attack against McGovern as the candidate of "acid, amnesty, and abortion."[46] McGovern, in fact, was the son of a minister, was a former teacher with a PhD in American history, and was a decorated veteran of World War II, having piloted thirty-five bombing missions. "Ordinarily, we don't send wild-eyed radicals to the United States Senate from South Dakota," he remarked.[47] Nevertheless he couldn't shake the perception that he was a fanatic leftist.

His best chance to shape a new image for himself was in his acceptance address at the Democratic convention, where he gave a crowd-pleasing speech: "Come home, America. . . . Come home to the conviction that we can move our country forward; come home to the belief that we can seek a newer world." The delegates were energized; said one reporter, "It seemed just barely possible . . . that this George McGovern, the prophet, was indeed a serious candidate for the Presidency."[48]

Alas, the speech aired at almost 3:00 a.m., when few voters were watching. And even this high point was quickly washed away by controversy over his running mate, Senator Thomas Eagleton of Missouri. After the convention, news reports surfaced that Eagleton had previously undergone electroshock therapy for depression.[49] Eagleton said his depression had been treated earlier in

UPHEAVAL IN AMERICAN POLITICS

the 1960s and he believed it was "like a broken leg that healed."[50] McGovern, who had a daughter who also suffered from depression, thought the issue would blow over and said he was "1,000 percent" behind Eagleton.[51]

The issue didn't blow over, however. Major newspapers called for Eagleton to leave the ticket, McGovern's fundraising went dry, and Republicans gleefully added to the frenzy by suggesting that voters didn't want "a mental patient in charge of the nuclear trigger button."[52] So McGovern finally asked Eagleton to resign. But this produced its own backlash among McGovern supporters, with one newspaper criticizing him for being "a blatant opportunist, who would dump his own choice for running mate in the interest of bald expediency."[53] McGovern was thus cast as *both* a "cold-blooded opportunist and hapless bungler."[54]

After this, numerous leading Democrats turned down the opportunity to run with McGovern. He finally selected Sargent Shriver, former ambassador to France, director of the Peace Corps, and a Kennedy brother-in-law. But McGovern's campaign never recovered from this debacle. His own pollster reported as late as October that even though "no one really loved Nixon," they intended to vote for the president because McGovern was seen as "less competent."[55]

So Nixon barely needed to lift a finger to win the election. He didn't even hit the campaign trail until late fall. In November he won the popular vote by 61 to 38 percent and the electoral vote 520–17. McGovern prevailed in just one state, Massachusetts.

Although Nixon was perhaps destined to win in 1972, the McGovern camp believed it would have been a closer election had it not been for fiascos like the Eagleton affair. And a respectable defeat might have made McGovern the favorite for the 1976 Democratic nomination in the aftermath of Watergate.[56]

Ah, yes, Watergate.[57] The scandal that took down a president also began in 1972, with a June 17 break-in at Democratic National Committee headquarters in Washington's Watergate complex. The Nixon administration dismissed it as a "third-rate burglary," but it soon emerged that the thieves had ties to the White House. This was widely reported prior to November, along with the fact that Watergate was just one part of "a massive Republican spying and sabotage campaign."[58] Few voters were paying enough attention, however, for the news to affect the fall election.

As more information came to light the following year, it became obvious that White House aides had covered up their knowledge of the break-in. This prompted the Senate to investigate. Watergate would soon develop into the biggest political scandal in U.S. history. Several high-level officials went to prison, including Attorney General John Mitchell and White House Chief of Staff H. R. Haldeman, for conspiracy and obstruction of justice.

In the midst of this unfolding scandal, Vice President Spiro Agnew resigned on October 10, 1973, because of unrelated charges of bribery and tax evasion while he was a state official in Maryland. Nixon named Congressman Gerald Ford of Michigan to replace Agnew. Few people expected Ford to ever become president because it was still unfathomable that Nixon might be removed from office. As late as June 1974, Americans remained divided over impeachment, favoring it by just 44 to 41 percent.[59]

Nixon's standing weakened as the controversies grew, however, particularly with the disclosure of a secret White House recording system and the release of the Watergate tapes. On August 5 the "Smoking Gun Tape" revealed that while Nixon may not have known about the initial burglary, he did know about the cover-up. Moreover, he'd personally approved using the CIA to block the FBI from investigating Watergate on the pretext of national security. All at once Nixon's political support collapsed. Republican leaders told the president he could no longer avoid conviction during an impeachment trial.

So, on August 9, 1974, Richard Nixon became the first president to resign from office, making Gerald Ford the country's thirty-eighth president.

1976

When President Ford moved into the White House in 1974, he began with a reservoir of good will from voters, who saw him as refreshingly genuine and honest after the Nixon presidency. "Washington seemed absolutely buoyant with the normalcy of Jerry Ford," said one writer.[60]

Ford's honeymoon lasted all of one month. On September 8, driven by what he said was a determination to "do the right thing" for the country, Ford pardoned Nixon, saying the country would be further torn apart by putting a former president on trial.[61] The decision was deeply controversial, and Ford's approval rating plummeted by 21 percent.[62]

Ford also faced several other historically unique events during his time in office. For one, he was the only president who was nearly killed by a female assassin—twice in the same month, although there was no connection between the incidents. On September 5, 1975, Lynette Fromme raised a pistol at Ford as he walked past a crowd in Sacramento, California, but she was disarmed before firing. Then, on September 22 in San Francisco, Sara Jane Moore shot at the president as he left a hotel, but missed her target.

Additionally, when Ford nominated former New York governor Nelson Rockefeller as vice president, it marked the first time that neither the president nor the vice president had been elected to their offices. The choice of the liberal Rockefeller infuriated conservatives and spurred them to support a challenge to Ford's reelection bid in 1976.[63] The challenger was Ronald Reagan, the two-term former governor of California.

When the primary season got underway, Ford won the first five contests and seemed on his way to running Reagan out of the race. Some of Reagan's staff even planned for his withdrawal, prompting the Ford team to ease up before the North Carolina primary because "the feeling was Reagan was beaten and there was no sense mauling him."[64] Big mistake, as it turned out, because instead of abandoning his campaign, Reagan doubled down. He attacked Ford for pork barrel spending, for being weak against communism, and for negotiating to give the Panama Canal back to Panama.

Since Ford himself was a conservative who'd vetoed dozens

of bills in an effort to reduce federal spending, he was said to be "bewildered" at being criticized in this way.[65] But the attacks resonated with the GOP right wing, and Reagan pulled a surprise upset in North Carolina. A few weeks later he won in Texas, helped by widespread and mocking coverage of Ford in San Antonio trying to eat a tamale while it was still wrapped in its husk. Suddenly the Republicans had a nomination battle on their hands.

After this, Ford and Reagan battled to the end of primary season, with neither candidate winning a majority of delegates. Ford was ahead in the count but was 170 votes shy of victory, while Reagan was 270 votes short. The nomination would thus be decided by a few hundred uncommitted delegates. Reagan made a bold move before the convention by introducing the liberal senator Richard Schweiker of Pennsylvania as his running mate in a bid to gain support from northeastern and moderate delegates. The move backfired when Pennsylvanians stuck with Ford and conservatives howled in protest.[66] "We don't need liberal Republicans," said one Reagan supporter.[67]

Ford defeated Reagan on the first ballot at the convention, by a mere 117 votes. There was then a clamor for a Ford-Reagan ticket, but Reagan wasn't interested. So Ford chose the conservative senator Bob Dole of Kansas as his running mate, after Rockefeller took himself out of the running.

On the Democratic side, the party opened the 1976 campaign season with high hopes but without a clear favorite. The early frontrunners were Congressman Mo Udall of Arizona and Senators Henry Jackson of Washington and Birch Bayh of Indiana. Governor Wallace lurked in the background. One of the longest of long shots was a folksy Georgia governor, peanut farmer, and navy veteran named Jimmy Carter, who believed his fresh face and outsider status would benefit him in the wake of Watergate. Carter portrayed himself as "a farmer, an engineer, a businessman, a planner, a scientist, a governor, and a Christian."[68] He devised a plan to surprise the field in the Iowa caucuses, which were still relatively ignored by most candidates, as a way to gain momentum for later contests.

UPHEAVAL IN AMERICAN POLITICS

While his rivals focused on New Hampshire and other states with upcoming primaries, Carter spent months getting to know Iowans. When he defeated his nearest rival, Senator Bayh, by 28 to 13 percent in Iowa, a blast of positive media coverage propelled Carter to a 6-point win in New Hampshire over Congressman Udall.

During the next two months, although he didn't win every state, Carter managed to eliminate his biggest opponents one at a time, with wins over Wallace in Florida and North Carolina, over Jackson in Pennsylvania, and over Udall in Wisconsin. Few of his victories were overwhelming, and he was helped by the fact that Udall and other candidates split the liberal vote. Carter, who favored both civil rights and a balanced budget, straddled the middle with a blend of social liberalism and economic conservatism.[69]

Despite his success at the polls, Carter never entirely won the affection of party leaders. James Reston of the *New York Times* remarked wryly, "Democrats don't know quite what to do with him because nobody but the people seem to be for him."[70] As such, some Democrats got behind an "Anybody but Carter" movement. Carter even lost primaries in May and June to two late entrants: Jerry Brown, the thirty-eight-year-old governor of California, and Idaho senator Frank Church. But by then it was too late to stop Carter, who won the nomination and selected Senator Walter Mondale of Minnesota as his running mate.

"My name is Jimmy Carter, and I'm running for president," he declared at the start of his convention acceptance speech, reprising the line he'd often used on the campaign trail. "Our country has lived through a time of torment. It is now a time of healing. We want to have faith again. We want to be proud again. We just want the truth again."[71]

That summer Carter led Ford by 50 to 37 percent in the polls.[72] He proclaimed himself a reformer and an outsider whose administration would be "as good and honest and decent and compassionate and filled with love as are the American people."[73] Ford, meanwhile, campaigned as a tested and experienced leader. He stayed close to the White House until September, with a "Rose Garden" strategy meant to make him look presidential.[74]

After the tension of the nomination battles, the general election was rather mundane. The *New York Times* said the contest left voters "with many questions and a yawn."[75] Neither candidate was an ideologue, and even Ford's press secretary acknowledged there was "no really big issue moving people to vote one way or another. It's which man the voters feel more comfortable with."[76] Perhaps because of this, the most memorable episodes that fall were moments when each candidate had a slip of the tongue.

In Carter's case, it came during an interview with *Playboy* magazine. The piece was a thoughtful conversation about the candidate's religious beliefs and political views. But in an effort to show he wasn't self-righteous about his faith, he told the interviewer, "I've looked on a lot of women with lust. I've committed adultery in my heart many times. . . . Christ says don't consider yourself better than someone else because one guy screws a whole bunch of women while the other guy is loyal to his wife."[77]

That was all it took. Few people paid attention to the larger interview, but Carter's comments on sex and adultery—and the fact that he used the word "screw"—made headlines for days. Religious leaders claimed to be offended by the sentiments and by Carter's language. A bumper sticker proclaimed "In his heart, he knows your wife."[78]

Ford had his moment, as well, after a gaffe in the second presidential debate. The first debates since 1960 were largely unremarkable except for when the president insisted, "There is no Soviet domination of Eastern Europe, and there never will be under a Ford administration."[79] Ford later confessed that he meant to say the Eastern Europeans saw themselves as independent people even if their governments were under Soviet control. Still, it took him five days to admit his mistake, and in the meantime he was battered in the media and by Democrats.

In the end, with the candidates so evenly matched, Ford closed the polling gap and the contest went down to the wire. In the final Gallup poll, the two candidates were in "a statistical dead heat."[80] The late-night comedian Johnny Carson joked that the choice was between "fear of the unknown versus fear of the known."[81]

On Election Day, Carter won the popular vote 50 to 48 percent, but the electoral tally was so close the race wasn't called until 3:30 a.m., when Carter prevailed 297–240. If fewer than 9,300 votes in Ohio and Hawaii had shifted from Carter to Ford, then Ford would have won reelection despite losing the popular vote.[82]

Revolution in the Presidential Nominating Process

For all the drama of the 1968, 1972, and 1976 elections, one of the most consequential developments of these years was the reform of the presidential nominating system, which took power away from party leaders and turned it over to voters through primaries and caucuses. This was the fourth significant change since 1789 to the way presidential candidates were nominated.[83]

When George Washington was elected, of course, there were no political parties and so the Electoral College doubled as the nominating process. Then the King Caucus system emerged, with members of Congress choosing their party's candidates. By the Jacksonian era, this process was seen as undemocratic, so in 1832 the Democrats and Whigs held the first national conventions, with delegates from each state.

The practice of selecting nominees at conventions remained in place through 1968, although in 1912 some states also began holding primaries as a way for voters to have a say. During the next half century, a hybrid system existed, with candidates sometimes running in primaries to prove their vote-getting ability but still requiring the support of party leaders to prevail on the convention floor.

The process changed again after 1968, this time to favor voters over the party establishment, and the effect of these reforms has been monumental. The 2016 election of Donald Trump, for instance, would never have happened under the old system because the candidate lacked party support. It's likely that other contests since 1968 would also have turned out differently, most obviously the Carter and McGovern nominations and perhaps a few others.

But history happened as it did. As one writer remarked, political parties beginning in 1972 "gave up their responsibility for nominating candidates and turned it over to whatever subset of the population chose to vote in a party primary."[84] Today, as a result, it's no longer possible to win a nomination without going through the gauntlet of primaries and caucuses. This has made the process more purely democratic, as it forces contenders to amass popular support. At the same time, for better and for worse, campaigns have grown longer, fundraising has become more important, and the voices of the loudest activists have been amplified.

Additionally, because party leaders lost influence over the filtering of candidates, the job of gatekeeper fell to the media. The press always held *some* power over campaigns, but its influence grew exponentially during this era, particularly with the growing clout of television. The media determines which candidates to cover, which sound bites to air, and which memes or gaffes to turn into a symbol for an entire campaign, such as "George Romney was brainwashed" or "Ed Muskie cried in the snow."

As early as 1972, the author Timothy Crouse noted that the press "was no longer simply guessing who might run and who might win; the press was in some way determining these things."[85] And in 1976 Mo Udall complained that the Democratic nomination battle turned largely on the media's interpretation of just the Iowa and New Hampshire results. He said it was unfair for the press to decide "after one or two percent of the electorate speaks that the following person is the overwhelming choice."[86]

Little changed, however, in the intervening decades. Iowa, New Hampshire, and the media remained crucial to the nominating process, and voters retained the final say over their party's nominees. There were pros and there were cons to this system, but it remained the reality of presidential politics.

1980, 1984, and 1988: The Reagan Revolution

1980

Jimmy Carter's presidency began with high aspirations. He came into office in 1977 hoping to heal the scars of the previous decade by reinvigorating the connection between Americans and their president, starting with his inaugural parade, when he thrilled spectators by being the first president to walk down Pennsylvania Avenue to the White House. During his first months on the job he was praised for having "changed the tone" in Washington and for "making the presidency relate to the people again."[87] But by the end of his four-year term the symbolism had turned against him, and he was largely perceived as a weak and ineffectual leader.

This was not entirely for lack of accomplishments. Among other things, Carter negotiated a landmark peace treaty between Israel and Egypt, established diplomatic relations with China, developed a national energy strategy to reduce dependence on foreign oil, and created the Departments of Energy and Education. The problem was, well, everything else. Unfortunately for Carter, he was also president during a time of high inflation and unemployment, the Three Mile Island nuclear accident, the Soviet invasion of Afghanistan, and the Iranian Revolution. Not to mention a 1979 oil shock that created widespread panic, forced many gas stations to close, and left motorists waiting in hours-long lines to refill their tanks.

Carter's biggest challenge was that he seemed unable to project an aura of strength during these crises. And once a narrative of weakness develops, it feeds on itself. Thus when he gave an address about the nation's "crisis of confidence" and called for "a rebirth of the American spirit," it was dubbed the "malaise speech."[88] And when a wild rabbit swam menacingly toward his canoe in the Georgia backwoods, the story was presented as a metaphor "for a wimpy presidential leadership style" even though it had nothing to do with government.[89]

On top of these obstacles, Carter had difficulty managing relations with Congress and getting along with liberals in his own party, who complained he was too conservative in trying to reduce budget deficits while refusing to push for national health insurance.[90] By the fall of 1979, Carter's approval rating was at 29 percent and calls arose for another Democrat to challenge him for the nomination. California governor Jerry Brown made plans to enter the race, while others clamored for Ted Kennedy to make a run. Eventually Kennedy did just that, announcing his candidacy on November 7 in Boston to great fanfare.

But almost as soon as Kennedy entered the contest, his candidacy began to fall apart. Three days before his announcement, on November 4, 1979, CBS News broadcast a documentary about Kennedy, who stumbled badly in an interview with Roger Mudd while describing why he wanted to be president. He seemed more tentative than the dynamic figure of everyone's expectations, and his aura of invincibility faded.[91]

He likely could have survived this one terrible interview, but it was more difficult to overcome another event that also took place on November 4. That was the day a mob of Iranian students stormed the U.S. embassy in Tehran and took sixty-six Americans hostage. The instinct of Americans was to rally behind the president, so Carter's approval rating doubled to 61 percent in one month, much to Kennedy's detriment. Whereas Kennedy had led Carter by 54 to 32 percent when he announced his candidacy, his lead melted away entirely in just a few weeks.[92]

This proved so damaging to his campaign that it's reasonable to wonder whether Kennedy would have forgone the race altogether had the Iran crisis happened earlier. That winter Carter adopted a Rose Garden strategy, declaring that he would stay off the campaign trail and remain in the White House to manage foreign affairs. In January, bolstered by his renewed popularity, Carter won the Iowa caucuses by 59 to 31 percent. A month later he won the New Hampshire primary, 47 to 37 percent, with Brown at 10 percent.[93] The Kennedy people were stunned. "One day it's sunny and people are pissed at Carter and they want a real liberal, and the next it's raining and people are going, 'Why are you against the president?'" said one advisor.[94]

The back-to-back defeats might have ended Kennedy's candidacy. Instead he amped up his campaign, criticizing Carter's foreign policy and introducing proposals for national health insurance, a farm bailout, and a wage and price freeze.[95] It took until March, but he made a comeback. Kennedy first won primaries in New York and Connecticut, then Pennsylvania. He ended on

June 3 by winning five of eight contests, including California and New Jersey. But his winning streak had begun too late. On the last primary day President Carter won the necessary delegates to ensure his nomination.

Kennedy still fought on to the August convention in New York City, by which point Carter's national polls had dipped again because of a worsening economy and the ongoing hostage crisis. That year mortgage interest rates went as high as 16 percent, inflation was running at 14 percent, and the unemployment rate hit 8 percent.[96] And frustration was growing over Iran, especially after a hostage rescue effort ended disastrously when sandstorms caused two aircraft to collide over the Iranian desert, killing eight servicemen. So the very events in Iran that may have saved Carter's nomination earlier in the year were now weakening him in advance of the fall election.

Kennedy asserted that this new reality, combined with his own late primary wins, made him a stronger candidate than Carter. He pushed for an open convention that would empower all delegates to vote for the candidate of their choice. But when the proposal was defeated, Kennedy withdrew from the race. A decade earlier Democrats might well have abandoned Carter, but the new rules adopted in 1972 made this nearly inconceivable. "The process was opened to the people, and the people have spoken," declared a *Boston Globe* columnist.[97]

Kennedy did make one last splash with his convention address, which ended with these memorable lines: "For all those whose cares have been our concern, the work goes on. The cause endures. The hopes still lives. And the dream shall never die."[98] His speech caused the hall to erupt in a half-hour-long demonstration, "the only moment of genuine passion" during the entire convention, according to one writer.[99]

Two days later Carter was nominated and, in his acceptance speech, said the election would be a contest "between two sharply different pictures" of the country.[100] After his address, though, all he could do was smile feebly when the balloon drop inexplicably failed and when he was unable to lure Kennedy into raising his arms in a gesture of unity.[101] It symbolized the challenges of his presidency, as Carter often looked weak in the face of events that were just beyond his control.

On the Republican side, there was also a nomination battle among several contenders, but the outcome was settled well before the GOP convention.

Reagan began the campaign as a heavy favorite, following his near win over Ford in 1976. Reagan faced a challenge from George H. W. Bush, who pitched himself to voters on his wide experience as a former Texas congressman, director of the CIA, envoy to China, and ambassador to the United Nations. His campaign slogan was "A President We Won't Have to Train."[102] Bush, whose politics were said to be "somewhat to the center of center," and who famously called Reagan's economic proposals "voodoo economics," attracted support from moderates who were wary of the conservative Reagan.[103] He earned a surprise win in the Iowa caucuses, 32 to 30 percent over Reagan. No other candidate was within 15 points of the top two.

Bush's challenge, however, was that while he'd built a strong organization, he wasn't a dynamic campaigner. In a 1981 book about the election, he was described as "one of those candidates who was like a sheet of glass, undeniably there, but not always visible to the naked eye."[104] This would prove to be his undoing under the spotlight of a New Hampshire debate stage.

Since the nomination contest was now being portrayed as a two-person fight, Bush and Reagan agreed to a head-to-head debate sponsored by New Hampshire's *Nashua Telegraph*. But the Federal Election Commission ruled it would violate campaign laws for a newspaper to sponsor an event that excluded other candidates. So Reagan agreed to pay for the debate, only to then invite the other contenders after all. Campaign aides said this was to limit the chance Reagan would make a gaffe, since he'd have less time to speak, but was also meant to make Bush look weak if he refused to go along.[105] And so, on February 23, 1980, a spectacle ensued that helped settle the nomination battle.

Bush indeed refused to debate the other contenders, believing he'd earned his chance to go one-on-one with Reagan. The four other candidates showed up anyway, following Reagan's lead: Senators Bob Dole of Kansas and Howard Baker of Tennessee and Congressmen John Anderson and Phil Crane of Illinois. They stood on stage as Reagan and the audience made the case for their inclusion. Bush stared straight ahead and didn't say a word, looking like he "had the backbone of a jellyfish," said one writer.[106] The debate moderator tried to end the discussion by directing the sound technician to turn off Reagan's microphone. Reagan responded, angrily and unforgettably, "I'm paying for this microphone!"[107] The crowd erupted in applause.

In that moment Reagan defined himself as a leader who could take control of a situation, in contrast to Bush. The other four candidates were still excluded from the debate, but Reagan's moment became the story of the day and was broadcast repeatedly on the news. Reagan had already been gaining on Bush in the New Hampshire polls, but this event helped propel him to a decisive victory of 50 to 23 percent. Bush never recovered. He remained in the race to the end and prevailed in a handful of states, but Reagan won the nomination going away.

That debate almost cost Bush a chance to be vice president. At the GOP convention in Detroit, as Reagan was making his decision about a running mate, he told aides he was haunted by Bush's uncertainty under pressure in Nashua.[108] Ultimately Reagan decided Bush had shown toughness by defeating the other contenders and battling to the end. So, after flirting with the possibility of a dream ticket with former president Ford, Reagan asked Bush to be his running mate.

Reagan and Bush weren't the only Republicans who ran in the general election, however, as John Anderson mounted an independent campaign under the banner of the National Unity Party. Anderson was popular with voters who were dissatisfied with the choice of Reagan or Carter, which encouraged him to launch a third-party campaign as a moderate alternative. He hadn't won any primary contests, but he'd developed an enthusiastic national following because of his honest approach to issues and a distinctive ideology. He was a fiscal conservative who supported a balanced budget but who also wanted to invest in mass transportation and who favored civil rights and gun control legislation. His signature idea was a proposal to raise the gas tax to reduce energy consumption and to offset this with a reduction in other taxes.[109]

The Anderson phenomenon was very real, and in June he was at 24 percent in the Gallup poll.[110] A *Washington Post* article suggested that he could win the election because of discontent with the major party nominees. "Any one of the three could win it clearly," predicted pollster Louis Harris.[111] But in the end Anderson suffered the same fate as most other independent candidates, as he couldn't convince enough people to vote for a third party. In late summer and early fall his polls slid into the single digits.

Ironically, one of Anderson's best moments also proved to be his undoing, when he and Reagan engaged in a televised debate on September 21. The Carter camp refused to participate for fear of giving Anderson an equal platform, so the debate went on without the president. Anderson and Reagan both performed well, with most polls showing Anderson as a slight winner. Yet it was Reagan who gained ground in the race. The conclusion most observers drew was that, since Reagan was widely perceived as a risky choice, both for his age and his right-wing conservatism, voters needed to decide whether the Republican was "a realistic alternative" to Carter. And when they saw that Reagan was "good-humored, articulate, and apparently knowledgeable enough," this convinced some undecided or Anderson-leaning voters to shift to Reagan.[112]

The general election, then, came down to Reagan and Carter. Reagan campaigned on a pledge to reduce the size of government, cut taxes, and strengthen the military. In referring to the nation's economic challenges, he remarked, "A recession is when your neighbor loses his job and a depression is when you lose your job. Recovery is when Jimmy Carter loses his!"[113] Reagan also worked to soften his image. He joked that his opponents wanted voters to see him as "a combination of Ebenezer Scrooge and the Mad Bomber," so he presented himself as "a problem solver" rather than an ideologue.[114]

Carter indeed painted Reagan as an extremist and a warmonger, hoping to make him seem as unacceptable as Barry Goldwater had been in 1964. He also suggested Reagan wasn't up to the job of president by focusing on his various gaffes, such as when Reagan didn't seem to know who the president of France was, expressed doubts about evolution, or blamed trees for air pollution. Carter's campaign ads asserted that "a president can never escape the responsibility of truly understanding the issue himself."[115]

Carter held his own in the polls until late in the game, largely due to voter reluctance to oust an incumbent and uncertainty about turning the White House over to the conservative Reagan. But the tide turned after an October 28 debate, the only head-to-head faceoff between the two candidates. While Carter came across as well-prepared, Reagan appeared gentle and reassuring, nothing like an extremist. He brushed off Carter's attacks, including when the president criticized him for having opposed the 1965 creation of Medicare. Reagan chuckled, shook his head, and said, "There you go again!"[116] Reagan's one-liner became famous, while the facts about the health care argument were forgotten.

Even more crucial to Reagan's success was when he devastated Carter during the closing remarks with a simple question: "Are you better off now than you were four years ago?"[117] Almost overnight the complexion of the race changed. Voters decided that perhaps they could live with Reagan after all.

President Carter was also damaged considerably by the hostage crisis, especially since Election Day happened to be the one-year anniversary of the storming of the Iranian embassy. The media blanketed the airwaves with coverage of the milestone, while Republicans aired an ad warning that Iran might deliberately free the hostages to ensure Reagan's defeat because they "prefer a weak and manageable U.S. president."[118] As it turned out, negotiations were ongoing, but there was no breakthrough before the election.

The Iran issue and the debate were the two pivots that swung the election sharply toward Reagan at the end. In a matter of days he went from having a modest lead of about 3 percent in the Gallup poll to winning in a landslide.[119] Reagan took the popular vote by 51 to 41 percent, with Anderson at 7 percent. Many of Anderson's votes were from college-educated professionals and young voters who might otherwise have supported Carter. This was a factor in Reagan's crushing win in the Electoral College of 489–49, the largest win for a nonincumbent candidate in history.

After the election, Carter continued to work obsessively to free the hostages. A deal for their freedom was finally reached on January 19, 1981, the day before the next inauguration. On the morning of January 20 Carter waited in the Oval Office for a phone call informing him that the hostages were on a plane out of Iran. The call never came. Iran spited Carter by purposely delaying their release until just minutes after Reagan took the oath of office, depriving Carter of the satisfaction of announcing that the hostages, after 444 days, were finally free.[120]

1984

President Reagan took office promising a conservative transformation of government. "In this present crisis," he said in his 1981 inaugural address, "government is not the solution to our problem; government is the problem."[121] In his first months on the job, he proposed significant reductions in income tax rates, cuts to domestic spending, and an increase in the military budget.

Then, two months into his term, on March 30, a would-be assassin shot Reagan as he was leaving the Washington Hilton after a speech.[122] It wasn't a political attack but an attempt by a mentally disturbed man, John Hinckley Jr., to impress the actress Jodie Foster. Emergency surgery saved Reagan's life. He spent two weeks in the hospital, during which time his popularity soared— not only because he'd survived an assassination attempt but also because of his grace and good humor throughout, such as when he told his wife, Nancy, "Honey, I forgot to duck," or when he joked with the doctors who were about to operate on him, "I hope you're all Republicans." Reagan thus broke what seemed to be a curse of presidents who were elected every twenty years dying in office, beginning with Harrison in 1840 and continuing through Lincoln, Garfield, McKinley, Harding, Roosevelt, and Kennedy.

After he returned to the White House, Reagan's increased popularity helped him in Congress. "The President has become a hero," Speaker of the House Tip O'Neill told his Democratic caucus. "We can't argue with a man as popular as he is."[123] Soon thereafter Reagan's budget and tax proposals passed overwhelmingly.

During the next two years the president's popularity slipped again, along with the economy, which fell into a recession. In 1982 unemployment was at more than 10 percent, and the balanced budget that Reagan promised never materialized. In fact the deficit exploded during these years, as the reduction in tax revenue and increases in military spending far outpaced reductions in domestic spending. By early 1983 the president's approval rating had plummeted to 35 percent and his bid for reelection seemed at risk.[124]

When the Democratic nomination battle kicked off in 1984, the leading contenders were former vice president Walter Mondale of Minnesota and Senator John Glenn of Ohio, who was famous for having been the first American astronaut to orbit the Earth in 1962. But Glenn proved to be a weak campaigner, and he was out of the race by March. Instead the candidate who did give Mondale a run for his money was Senator Gary Hart of Colorado.

The forty-seven-year-old Hart had managed McGovern's 1972 presidential campaign before winning election to the Senate in 1974. He was known at the time as an "Atari Democrat," one who saw emerging high-tech industries as the wave of the future as the country moved beyond an industrial economy. In the presidential race, he presented himself as a "forward-thinking alternative to his party's aging liberal establishment."[125] Hart finished a surprising second in the Iowa caucuses, ahead of Glenn, McGovern, and civil rights leader Jesse Jackson, among others.

While Mondale had appeared to be a formidable frontrunner, enthusiasm for his candidacy was weaker with voters than with party officials, a reality that became clear when Hart charged into New Hampshire and stunned Mondale by winning that state's primary 39 to 27 percent. His run continued on Super Tuesday in March, when he won six out of eight primaries and caucuses.

Mondale's candidacy was on the verge of collapse, but his two Super Tuesday wins gave him just enough life to continue the fight.

Meanwhile the media began delving more closely into Hart's story, as the Coloradan had seemingly burst out of nowhere to become a national candidate. They dug up the fact that his name used to be Hartpence before it was changed to Hart, that his campaign biography had a one-year discrepancy in his age, and that his signature had changed over the years. These were not earth-shattering disclosures, but they were enough for the media to ask "Who is Gary Hart, anyway?"[126]

These questions overlapped with a new line of attack from Mondale. In one debate, playing off a famous fast-food commercial of the time, Mondale turned to Hart and said, "You know, when I hear your ideas, I'm reminded of that ad, 'Where's the beef?'"[127] It was a classic one-liner; the audience understood it immediately, and it received lots of airtime.

It was also an absurd accusation, as Hart had written a book about his policy ideas, and a 1983 magazine profile noted that he was "famous for his issue papers . . . on everything from reindustrializing America to reforming the military."[128] Hart, according to one rival political consultant, was "nothing but beef."[129] Still, Mondale's line stuck. "Where's the beef?" defined Hart's candidacy for many voters. After this, Mondale won primaries in the large states of New York, Pennsylvania, and Illinois, with support from labor unions, to take the delegate lead. Hart came back with wins in the West, including in California, but Mondale accumulated just enough delegates to take the nomination.

Despite his victory, Mondale still badly trailed Reagan in national polls. The economy had recovered from its earlier recession, and the president's approval rating rose along with the economic numbers. Mondale knew he needed to be bold to win in November, so he settled on two tactics. One was to be excessively candid with the voters, particularly about the fast-rising deficit. This led him, in his acceptance speech at the Democratic convention in San Francisco, to declare, "We are living on borrowed money and borrowed time. . . . By the end of my first term, I will cut the deficit by two-thirds. Let's tell the truth. Mr. Reagan will raise taxes, and so will I. He won't tell you. I just did."[130]

Mondale believed he would receive credit for telling the truth, but Reagan's team was ecstatic when they heard the speech. "This guy is either breaking new ground," one Republican said, "or he's the dumbest bastard I've ever seen."[131] That fall Republicans hammered Mondale as an old-fashioned, tax-and-spend liberal. Reagan ignored questions about the deficit and instead focused on Mondale's tax proposals. In one remark, for instance, Reagan made his point with humor, as he often did: "I was about to say to him very sternly, 'Mr. Mondale, you are taxing my patience.' And then I caught myself. Why should I give him another idea? That's the only tax he hasn't thought about."[132]

Aside from trying to be honest about the budget, Mondale's other move was both bold *and* historic, in selecting Congresswoman Geraldine Ferraro of New York to be the first female vice-presidential candidate of a major party. The announcement electrified Democrats. Women cheered the groundbreaking selection, and many in the party were pleased to know that Mondale was "swinging for the fences."[133] Ferraro attracted enthusiastic crowds, but her campaign was distracted by a media furor over questions about her husband's tax returns.

The dominant factor in the election was simply the economy. Reagan's strategists devised an optimistic advertising campaign, with syrupy-sweet images of people moving into new homes, getting married, or raising flags. "It's morning again in America," said the narrator. "And under the leadership of President Reagan, our country is stronger, and prouder, and better. Why would we ever want to return to where we were less than four short years ago?"[134] Because Mondale was vice president under Carter, Reagan was able to make the election "a referendum on the 'Carter-Mondale' past."[135]

Reagan led in the polls from start to finish, although there was one moment after the first presidential debate when it appeared Mondale might break through. Mondale was sharp in the debate, and he adopted a strategy of praising Reagan and thanking him for restoring patriotism, while suggesting it was time for new leadership.[136] Reagan, on the other hand, seemed disoriented and confused. Given that Reagan, at seventy-three, was already the oldest president in history, it raised questions about his fitness for office. Even the conservative *Wall Street Journal* asked, "Is oldest U.S. president now showing his age?"[137] The issue dominated media coverage, and tape surfaced of Nancy Reagan whispering an answer to her husband in front of the press.[138] Reagan's polling lead fell, raising the stakes for the second debate on October 21.

On that date Reagan rebounded. Mondale again appeared to be a stronger debater, but all Reagan needed was one moment to defuse the age issue. In response to a question about whether he was up to the stress of an extended crisis, Reagan responded, with a smile, "I will not make age an issue of this campaign. I am not going to exploit, for political purposes, my opponent's youth and inexperience."[139] Everyone laughed, even Mondale.

At that moment the election was over. The fact that Reagan looked less perplexed in the second debate and was able to get off a one-liner about his age seemed to be the only justification most voters needed to relieve their doubts. Just as Mondale had wounded Hart with his "Where's the beef?" line, so Reagan helped clinch his reelection with this remark. On Election Day, Reagan routed Mondale by 59 to 41 percent. He won the Electoral College 525–13 and prevailed in forty-nine of fifty states. Mondale won only his home state of Minnesota.

1988

By 1988 President Reagan was still exceptionally popular. In large part this was because "he came along at a time when the nation needed to believe in itself again," said one writer, "and, like FDR, he knew how to use his charismatic personality and the symbols of his office to restore America's confidence."[140] So when Reagan neared retirement in 1988, the first president to complete two full terms since Eisenhower, there was much speculation over who would fill his shoes.

For Republicans, George H. W. Bush was the obvious heir apparent after eight years as vice president, but he had never been a favorite of GOP conservatives. Additionally, some party members were concerned that he didn't have a reputation for projecting leadership. *Newsweek* summed up Bush's position by noting that he had high poll numbers "for experience and competence," even as he also suffered from "a perception that he isn't . . . tough enough for the challenges of the Oval Office. That he is, in a single word, a wimp." The magazine then put Bush on the cover with the headline "Fighting the Wimp Factor."[141]

It was baffling that Bush could be considered a wimp, given a résumé that included being a wartime fighter pilot and director of the CIA, but perception is everything in politics. "Bush had a far more macho and heroic resume than Reagan," wrote John Dickerson in his book *Whistlestop*, "but Reagan's rugged Western looks and his actor's sense of command made Bush seem slight by comparison."[142]

As the nomination contest kicked off, the vice president's team knew they had to overcome the view that their candidate was a political weakling, so they picked a fight with the media, specifically with Dan Rather of CBS, who was doing a profile of Bush in January 1988. They knew Rather would question Bush's involvement in the Iran-Contra affair, a political scandal in which the Reagan administration had illegally sold arms to Iran in exchange for freedom for seven hostages in Lebanon, and then used money from the sale to secretly fund the right-wing Contra insurgency in Nicaragua. Several high-level officials, including the secretary of defense, were indicted for withholding evidence or obstruction of justice. Bush always claimed he was out of the loop with Iran-Contra and refused to answer questions on the topic.

After insisting on a live interview with CBS rather than a taped one that could be edited, Bush's staff counseled him to "go toe-to-toe with Rather," which he did. Bush professed to be appalled at the Iran-Contra questions and accused the anchor of having "impugned [his] integrity." The interview turned into a quarrel on live TV, with the two men talking over each other. When the media declared that Bush was strong in standing his ground (ironically, it turned out, since later evidence showed he'd been more aware of Iran-Contra than he claimed), his campaign manager Lee Atwater was thrilled, declaring it a "defining event" in eliminating the idea that Bush was weak.[143]

Bush did lose the first contest of primary season when he placed third in the Iowa caucuses to Senator Bob Dole and televangelist Pat Robertson, but the vice president then routed his opponents in New Hampshire, and in sixteen of seventeen contests on Super Tuesday, effectively ending the GOP nomination battle in early March. Bush later chose Indiana senator Dan Quayle as his running mate.

Despite winning over Republicans, Bush's national poll numbers remained low early in the year. He emerged as a stronger figure at the Republican convention in New Orleans that summer, when he talked in his acceptance address about his dream of a "kinder, gentler nation" and when he made a famous antitax pledge: "Read my lips. No new taxes."[144]

Whatever drama the Republicans enacted during the spring and summer of 1988, however, was nothing compared to what descended on the Democrats.

The nomination contest initially seemed on track to be resolved quickly, as Gary Hart, the runner-up in 1984, was an overwhelming favorite. In a March 1987 Iowa poll, he was supported by 65 percent of Democrats.[145] Hart argued for a new political paradigm, one that rejected "both the liberal vision of limitless public spending and the conservative vision of limited government."[146] His politics appealed to young urban professionals who weren't comfortable with traditional New Deal Democrats.

Hart's candidacy, however, ended before a single vote was cast. As it happened, he was beset by rumors of marital infidelity at a time when the media had become hyperalert to questions of character in presidential candidates. So the *Miami Herald*, acting on an anonymous tip that Hart was having an affair, controversially staked out the candidate's Washington townhome and reported seeing him enter and leave with a twenty-nine-year-old woman named Donna Rice. Hart was quickly engulfed by a media frenzy

UPHEAVAL IN AMERICAN POLITICS

the likes of which had never before descended on a presidential candidate. A celebrity-style crush of photographers trailed him and his family, while newspapers threatened to reveal the names of other women Hart had dated during separations from his wife. He and Rice denied they were involved romantically, but the furor was so all-consuming that Hart withdrew from the race in May 1987, the country's first victim of a political sex scandal.[147]

Suddenly the Democrats lacked an obvious frontrunner. After Hart, one of the more promising candidates was a forty-four-year-old senator from Delaware, Joe Biden, who had a reputation as a rousing speaker. But Biden's campaign was also felled by an early scandal, in this case over plagiarism allegations. The candidate frequently quoted passages from a speech by the British politician Neil Kinnock, and nearly always credited Kinnock for the words. But in an August address in Iowa he didn't acknowledge his source, and a video of him seeming to plagiarize Kinnock made its way onto the news. This was followed by reports that Biden had also been accused of plagiarism in law school. (It was deemed an inadvertent mistake by a first-year law student and he was allowed to retake the course.) As with Hart, the ensuing media frenzy led Biden too to withdraw from the race.[148]

The end of Biden's campaign, however, may have been fortuitous in the long run. A few months later, in February 1988, Biden needed emergency surgery for an aneurysm. He was told he had a 50–50 chance of surviving the operation, and a priest gave him last rites. The aneurysm burst on the operating table, but the surgeon was able to clip the artery and save Biden's life. If he'd been on the campaign trail, he may not have gotten to a hospital in time. "The doctors have no doubt," Biden said later that year, "that had I remained in the race, I'd be dead." He took it to be a sign of fate. "Now I know," he told a friend, "why the campaign ended like it did."[149] Thirty-two years later, a much older Biden became the country's forty-sixth president.

With Hart and Biden out, the top remaining Democratic contenders were Massachusetts governor Michael Dukakis, Tennessee senator Al Gore, Missouri congressman Dick Gephardt, and civil rights leader Jesse Jackson. Gephardt won the Iowa caucuses, then Dukakis prevailed in the New Hampshire primary and soon took control of the contest. He not only built the best organization but also benefited from the reality that voters are often attracted to candidates who exhibit the opposite traits of the incumbent. Dukakis had a reputation for being an executive who enjoyed the nuts and bolts of governing, in contrast to Reagan's image as a more disengaged leader.[150] Dukakis won 1,792 delegates to 1,023 for Jackson, who was the first African American to finish in the top two in a nomination battle. Senator Lloyd Bentsen of Texas joined the ticket as the vice-presidential candidate.

At the party convention in Atlanta, Dukakis entered the hall to the sound of Neil Diamond's "Coming to America," in tribute to his roots as the son of Greek immigrants. He promised to "forge a new era of greatness for America" and declared the election was "not about ideology; it's about competence."[151]

Dukakis ended the convention with a double-digit lead in the polls over Bush but was woefully unprepared for what hit him as the fall campaign got underway. The Bush team had determined their best chance to win was to drive up Dukakis's negatives, so they unleashed a barrage of attacks that disparaged the governor for vetoing a bill that required students to recite the Pledge of Allegiance, for being a "card-carrying" member of the American Civil Liberties Union, for the polluted waters of Boston Harbor, for opposing the death penalty, and, most famously, for a prison furlough program that allowed a convicted murderer named Willie Horton to go free for a weekend, during which time he traveled to Maryland and raped a woman.

It mattered little that the Pledge bill had been considered unconstitutional, that Dukakis had begun a cleanup of Boston Harbor, or that the furlough program was started by his Republican predecessor and that dozens of other states had similar programs.[152] The Bush campaign skillfully defined Dukakis as a candidate who didn't represent "mainstream America."[153] As Bush media strategist (and future chairman of Fox News) Roger Ailes noted, "It was all a matter of who hit first, and who made it stick."[154] The

Bush team also did a good job of placing their candidate at flag factories, with police unions, and even on a boat tour of Boston Harbor, providing made-for-TV images to complement the negative attacks.

Dukakis was damaged as well by a phony story when a rumor spread that he'd been treated for depression.[155] There was no evidence for this, but when a reporter asked Dukakis about it, the media had license to report, as one story did, "Dukakis psychiatric rumor denied." When a journalist then asked Reagan whether Dukakis should release his medical records, the president replied, "I'm not going to pick on an invalid." All of which gave the rumors more play, forcing Dukakis's physician to step in and refute the reports. Dukakis's poll numbers dropped 8 points in the wake of these stories.

The end result was that Dukakis, in the course of only a few months, was turned into a radical leftist "who furloughed murderers, befouled harbors, spurned the American flag and might just be mentally unstable."[156] This onslaught might have been attenuated had Dukakis successfully fought back, but he didn't even try at first to counter the negative ads because he naïvely believed they'd be dismissed by voters. The problem, one strategist remarked, was that "there's only one thing the American people dislike more than someone who fights dirty. That's someone who climbs into the ring and won't fight."[157] So, as summer gave way to fall, Dukakis's poll numbers cratered.

The Dukakis campaign did eventually return fire, but with only occasional success. When Dukakis released a plan for health insurance coverage, he announced it while visiting hospitals on the same day Bush was at another flag factory. "Don't you think it's about time you came out from behind the flag," asked Dukakis, "and told us what you intend to do to provide basic health insurance for thirty-seven million Americans?"[158] It was a rare day when Dukakis won the messaging war.

On other occasions, though, he dug himself a deeper hole, such as when he delivered a major foreign policy speech that was overshadowed by a widely derided photo of the helmeted governor riding in a tank, a visual that was mockingly used to suggest he wasn't commander-in-chief material. Or when, during the second presidential debate, he stumbled in replying to a question about whether he would oppose the death penalty if his wife were raped and murdered. Dukakis answered in a dispassionate tone, as if he were "the defense attorney for the murderer and rapist of his wife, as opposed to the outraged husband."[159] These moments too were played repeatedly on the evening news.

Dukakis surged near the end, when he adopted a forceful and straightforward message: "George Bush cares about the people on Easy Street. I care about the people on Main Street. I'm on your side." But it was too little, too late, as Dukakis had long since been defined for the American people and was almost impossibly behind in the polls. And Bush may well have won the election in any case, since the economy was doing well and his candidacy was widely seen as a third Reagan term.

Bush cruised to victory. He won the popular vote by 53 to 46 percent and the Electoral College 426–111, winning forty states to ten for Dukakis. It was the third consecutive presidential victory for Republicans. And Bush made history as the first incumbent vice president since Van Buren in 1836 to win the presidency.

Social Issues and the Southern Strategy

The Reagan Revolution that arrived with the 1980 election is a perfect example of what was suggested in the introduction: that elections are best appreciated not as discrete events but as chapters in an evolving story. If we trace a line from the 1948 Dixiecrat revolt to the 1964 Goldwater crusade to the 1968 Nixon and Wallace campaigns and finally to the 1980 election of Reagan, the conservative counterrevolution of the late twentieth century becomes more comprehensible.

This political upheaval was the result of several forces working synergistically. The most obvious, certainly, was the conservative desire for limited government. Goldwater's nomination in 1964 tilted the party decisively toward its conservative wing and away from the Dewey-Eisenhower moderates. Reagan then picked up the limited-government torch from Goldwater and embedded these ideas into American politics.

At the same time, indications are that Reagan's 1980 election was only partly about a desire for smaller government. That year's exit polls showed 37 percent of Reagan voters supported him with reservations, as many people were simply voting against Carter.[160] These voters may have wanted to stunt government's growth, but they weren't ready to overturn the New Deal. Republican success during this era was more about bringing various movements together under one tent, including limited-government conservatives and anticommunist defense hawks.[161] But the real key to growing the GOP coalition may have been those voters who switched party allegiances over social issues and racial concerns.[162]

For nearly a century after the Civil War it was Democrats who were supported by racial conservatives in the South, but the party's mid-twentieth-century support for civil rights helped end their dominance in the region. Goldwater in 1964 and Wallace in 1968 wrested some of these voters away from their traditional home in the Democratic Party, and Nixon then worked to build a GOP coalition that appealed to these racial conservatives. A Nixon campaign memo from 1971, in fact, recommended utilizing African American support of the Democratic Party as a way to alienate white voters and peel away their support.[163] This new GOP playbook, which famously became known as the Southern Strategy, used code words such as "school busing," "crime," and "welfare" to subtly play on white anxieties.[164] So when Reagan in 1980 bemoaned "welfare queens" who drove expensive Cadillacs, or when the 1988 Bush campaign benefited from the Willie Horton crime ad, voters got the message. Even if the candidates themselves weren't racist, it was easy for campaigns to emphasize issues in a way that fostered racial angst.

The evolution of this strategy was explained in blunt terms by Lee Atwater, who worked on the Reagan and Bush campaigns and was later chairman of the Republican National Committee (RNC): "You start out in 1954 by saying 'N——, n——, n——.' By 1968 . . . you say stuff like 'forced busing,' 'states' rights,' and all that stuff." And by the late 1980s, he said, candidates could simply talk about cutting certain federal programs because the assumption for white voters was that "Blacks get hurt worse."[165]

Not every Republican employed this tactic, and in 2005 the then RNC chairman Ken Mehlman even apologized to African Americans for the decades in which the party had tried to "benefit politically from racial polarization."[166] Nevertheless over several decades the strategy became embedded in the party's DNA.

To be fair, the Southern Strategy wasn't entirely about race, as studies showed that racial influences alone couldn't fully explain the realignment of working-class whites.[167] Another key factor was the parallel rise of the so-called social issue. This covered a gamut of fears that began rocking America in the 1960s, from urban riots, antiwar protests, and higher crime rates to increased drug use and more sexual permissiveness.[168]

The GOP was able to play up the social issues by casting the party "as the defender of the working man and traditional values," a message that intersected nicely with voter "anxiety over social disorder and racial integration."[169] Republicans in the 1980s also began emphasizing issues that were important to the religious right, such as opposition to abortion. The Democrats, conversely, focused more on promoting equal rights and justice and so became the party of civil rights, gay rights, feminism, immigrant rights, and so on. In political terms, the Democrats were stamped as the party of special interests, while Republicans branded themselves as the party of Main Street and Middle America.

It was when Republicans took this theme of traditional values and paired it with their existing message of small government and strong national defense that they ignited their presidential winning streak. Media strategist Richard Viguerie explained, "We talked about the sanctity of free enterprise . . . until we were blue in the face [but] . . . we never really won until we began stressing issues like busing, abortion, school prayer and gun control."[170]

So there were considerable changes in the political landscape between the 1960s and the 1980s, as the South switched sides to the GOP, African Americans became more loyal to the Democratic

Party, and social issues were grafted onto the debate over big versus small government. It was, at the very least, a transformation of the New Deal party system, if not a full-scale realignment, and it led to a new era of Republican supremacy in presidential politics.

1992, 1996, 2000, and 2004: Emergence of
Red and Blue America

1992

The presidency of George H. W. Bush intersected with historic events on the world stage. Between 1989 and 1991 the Soviet Union collapsed, the Cold War ended, the Berlin Wall came down, democratic revolutions upended Eastern Europe, and a U.S.-led military coalition drove Iraq out of Kuwait. Nearly two decades later, in 2010, when Barack Obama awarded Bush the Presidential Medal of Freedom, he noted his predecessor's steady hand in managing these transformations, as well as his genuine "humility and decency."[171]

As the 1990s dawned, this was also the view many Americans had of the Bush presidency. His approval rate hit a staggering 91 percent in one poll in early 1991.[172] The *New York Times* suggested he was "all but unbeatable" for reelection, and *Saturday Night Live* caricatured the Democratic nomination battle as "the race to avoid being the guy who loses to Bush."[173]

By the end of that year, however, Bush's foreign policy successes had slipped off the front pages, the economy had declined, and the president was struggling to articulate a domestic vision. Republican conservatives were less than enthused, partly because Bush raised taxes while working to reduce the deficit, breaking his "Read my lips: No new taxes" pledge from 1988. Consequently Bush was challenged for the GOP nomination by the media commentator Patrick Buchanan.

Buchanan inhabited a unique slice of the Republican electorate, as his gripe with Bush was not only over taxes but also over some of the president's very successes on the world stage. "He is a globalist and we are nationalists," Buchanan said. "We put America first."[174] He disparaged foreign aid, free trade, cooperation with the United Nations, and immigration from non-European countries. Many of his positions, in fact, were a precursor to the Trump campaign of 2016. He even suggested building a "Buchanan Fence" along the Mexican border to stop illegal immigrants.[175] Buchanan won 23 percent of the GOP primary vote, a warning sign of discontent with Bush.

The Democrats dealt with different challenges in selecting a nominee. Given Bush's popularity in 1991, some of the party's biggest names, including Governor Mario Cuomo of New York, passed on the race, leaving a field that included Arkansas governor Bill Clinton, former Massachusetts senator Paul Tsongas, former California governor Jerry Brown, and Senators Bob Kerrey of Nebraska and Tom Harkin of Iowa.

Clinton, in his fifth term as governor, took early command of the race. He positioned himself as a centrist New Democrat pursuing a third way between the extremes of liberalism and conservatism. But in early 1992 Clinton's campaign experienced a meltdown along the lines of Hart's 1988 implosion, and it nearly drove him from the race. It began when the *Star*, a supermarket tabloid, published a story alleging an affair between Clinton and Gennifer Flowers, an Arkansas state employee and part-time singer. As reporters clamored for a response, Clinton and his wife, Hillary, went on *60 Minutes*. The candidate acknowledged "causing pain in [his] marriage" while denying an affair with Flowers. The next day Flowers held a press conference and claimed to be "Bill Clinton's lover." She played tapes of phone conversations in which he seemed to coach her to deny the rumors.[176] It created another media frenzy, but Clinton fought back. Some observers believe he benefited from Hart's experience because voters had now decided that an affair "was not, by itself, a disqualifying factor for a presidential candidate."[177]

Just when Clinton had seemingly stopped the bleeding, another bombshell dropped when the *Wall Street Journal* published a story alleging that he'd avoided the Vietnam-era draft by getting a slot in the ROTC program at the University of Arkansas and then withdrawing when he received a high number in the draft lottery. The debate over Vietnam was still a heated issue in 1992, and a letter surfaced that the twenty-three-year-old Clinton wrote to Col. Eugene Holmes, thanking him for "saving me from the draft."[178]

The accumulation of controversies now overshadowed any one issue on its own, and Clinton's polling numbers plunged 17 points in two days.[179] The moniker "Slick Willie," given to him in Arkansas, reappeared as opponents questioned his tendency to make statements that could be "both technically true and entirely deceptive."[180] With his candidacy reeling, Clinton released the entire letter to Colonel Holmes, presenting it as the thoughts of a young man who didn't believe government should draft citizens to "kill and die" in a war that "does not involve immediately the peace and freedom of the nation."[181]

This controversy erupted less than two weeks before the New Hampshire primary, which was the first contested vote in 1992 because Democrats had conceded Iowa to Harkin, the local favorite. So Clinton threw himself more feverishly into the campaign in the Granite State. He promised voters who supported him, "I'll never forget who gave me a second chance, and I'll be there for you till the last dog dies."[182]

He lost New Hampshire to Tsongas, 33 to 25 percent, but spun it as a victory, saying New Hampshire voters had "made Bill Clinton the comeback kid."[183] After this, Clinton dominated his home region when the race moved south. He won Georgia, then eight of eleven contests on Super Tuesday, including Texas and Florida. By mid-March he was the presumptive nominee.

In most years the Bush-Clinton battle would then have been joined. But in 1992 the campaign was enlivened by an additional twist that seemed to threaten the chances of both major party nominees. This was the independent candidacy of Ross Perot, a billionaire Texas businessman.

Perot made his fortune from the computer services company Electronic Data Systems and was famous for his moral uprightness and "can-do" attitude. A group called Throw the Rascals Out thought Perot was just the person to upend the two-party system. Perot resisted the idea, until February 20 on CNN's *Larry King Show*, when he proclaimed a willingness to run if volunteers got him on the ballot in every state. Almost overnight a political movement sprang to life, manned by voters who believed a businessman who wasn't beholden to any party might cure the dysfunction in Washington.

Perot pledged to reform the country's democracy, reduce the budget deficit, and overturn the North American Free Trade Agreement (NAFTA) being negotiated by the Bush administration. Along the way he uncorked various homespun lines, such as when he suggested NAFTA would create a "giant sucking sound" of jobs moving to Mexico.[184] Or when he compared the budget deficit to "a crazy aunt you keep down in the basement. All the neighbors know she's there, but nobody talks about her."[185]

After the June primaries in California, exit polls showed that voters in *both parties* preferred Perot to their own nominee.[186] He moved atop the national polls, with one Gallup survey showing him leading 39 to 31 to 25 percent over Bush and Clinton.[187]

Once Perot became a legitimate contender, though, he faced increased scrutiny. Reports surfaced about his affinity for conspiracy theories and for hiring private investigators, allegedly even to probe his own employees.[188] The Bush campaign attacked Perot, who now seemed to pose the biggest threat to the president's reelection. "Imagine having the IRS, the FBI, and the CIA under his control," said Vice President Quayle.[189] Perot's numbers slipped, and he discovered that he didn't much like the heat.

On July 16, in the midst of the Democratic convention, Perot surprised the country by withdrawing from the race, claiming he didn't want to be a spoiler who sent the election into the House of Representatives. The real reason, said one of his strategists, was that he didn't want to drag his family through a media circus, he wasn't enjoying the contest, and he realized the campaign was going to be "a lot tougher than he thought."[190]

Perot's withdrawal reset the contest in dramatic fashion. The Democrats were already gaining in the polls, partly because Bush and Perot muddied each other in June, allowing Clinton to reintroduce himself to voters. Most famously, Clinton appeared on the late-night *Arsenio Hall* show, donning sunglasses and playing "Heartbreak Hotel" on a saxophone. He also conducted a town hall meeting on the music channel MTV. The traditional media grumbled that these appearances were unpresidential, but it was another step in the blurring of politics and entertainment. Clinton advisor Mandy Grunwald later remarked, "It was the end of one way of communicating with voters and the beginning of another."[191]

Clinton also made a popular vice-presidential selection with the forty-four-year-old Senator Al Gore of Tennessee, who reinforced a message of generational change. At the Democratic convention in New York City, Clinton declared he was running "in the name of all those who do the work and pay the taxes, raise the kids and play by the rules."[192] He ended his address with a line that riffed off both his campaign message and the name of his Arkansas hometown: "I end tonight where it all began for me. I still believe in a place called Hope."[193]

This confluence of events—the rebranding of Clinton, the selection of Gore, the Democratic convention, and the withdrawal of Perot—was the equivalent of a political rocket launch. Clinton catapulted to the biggest postconvention bounce in history, putting him a stunning 24 points ahead of Bush in a national poll.[194]

This bounce solidified after the convention, when Clinton and Gore embarked on a five-day bus tour to Missouri. Beyond all expectations, large crowds lined roadways, and thirty thousand people were at the closing rally in St. Louis. *Newsweek* said the Clinton-Gore combo "conveyed a sense of enthusiasm, youth, passion and empathy that evoked a visceral reaction" from voters.[195]

A month later the Republican convention in Houston didn't go quite as well. Bush apologized for raising taxes and blamed it on Democrats, saying he'd "underestimated Congress's addiction" to new revenue.[196] But the lasting public image of the convention was an amplification of the battle over social issues. Buchanan caused a stir with strident words that laid bare the nation's divisions. "My friends, this election is . . . about who we are," he said, after excoriating Democrats for supporting abortion and gay rights. "There is a religious war going on in this country for the soul of America."[197] The convention raised enthusiasm among social conservatives, even as it fostered a backlash among swing voters who were dismayed by a message of cultural division. One columnist called it the "scowling face of conservatism," and another summed it up as "George Bush, Prisoner of the Crazies."[198]

That fall, Clinton persisted in presenting himself as a New Democrat and criticizing Bush for a weak economy. Campaign manager James Carville posted a whiteboard sign in Clinton headquarters that reminded staffers of the campaign's main messages, including "Change versus more of the same" and "It's the economy, stupid."[199]

Bush ran on his experience and portrayed Clinton as a liberal who would raise taxes and who was unqualified to be commander in chief because he'd avoided military service and participated in antiwar protests as a student. The strategy of trying to drive up Clinton's negatives didn't work as well for Bush as it had four years earlier against Dukakis because voters were more alert to such attacks and were more worried about the economy. Through September, Clinton maintained a healthy polling lead.

Then, on October 1, Perot reentered the race, suggesting he didn't want to disappoint supporters who'd worked to get him on the ballot. Perot had fallen to 7 percent in the polls but was included in the televised debates, where he offered a folksy contrast to Bush and Clinton. When questioned about his lack of experience, he responded, "Well, they've got a point. I don't have any experience in running up a $4 trillion debt. I don't have any experience in gridlock government."[200]

On the campaign trail Perot avoided most media interviews and appearances but aired several political infomercials, where he sat behind a desk with charts and explained economic issues. The broadcasts attracted a robust audience, and Perot's strategy was described as "the first electronic front porch campaign."[201] His polls began rising again, until he appeared on the CBS show 60 Minutes in late October and shot himself in the foot. He said he'd dropped out of the race in July because Republicans were planning to disrupt his daughter's wedding and publish fake lewd photos of her. Suddenly the earlier doubts about Perot's habit of latching onto conspiracy theories bounded back into public consciousness. His momentum stalled.[202]

In the end, neither Bush nor Perot was able to close the polling gap with Clinton. On Election Day, Clinton received 43 percent of the vote to 37 percent for Bush and 19 percent for Perot. In the Electoral College, Clinton prevailed easily, 370–168 over Bush, returning Democrats to power for the first time in twelve years.

Perot's finish was the best for an independent candidate since Teddy Roosevelt in 1912, which led Republicans to blame him for costing Bush the election.[203] But Perot voters were actually a diverse lot. He appealed to conservatives who were disappointed in Bush, liberals who were opposed to trade deals such as NAFTA, and independents who were disenchanted with the two-party system. Without Perot on the ballot, exit polls show, his supporters would have split equally between the two major candidates, in which case Clinton would have topped 52 percent of the vote.[204]

If Perot did help Clinton, that was due to the Texan's early success as a candidate. In June the Bush team took aim at Perot while virtually ignoring Clinton. George Stephanopoulos, then Clinton's communications director, said the GOP "made a fatal mistake turning their howitzers on Ross Perot," as it enabled Clinton to recalibrate his campaign.[205] Clinton took over the polling lead in July and never lost it. In a *Washington Post*/ABC News poll in late September, Clinton led Bush by 58 to 37 percent, which is hardly a sign of a candidate headed for defeat in a two-person race.[206] The reality is that voters in 1992 were agitating for change, and Clinton simply did a better job of tapping into the mood of the electorate.

1996

The 1993 presidential inauguration marked a generational shift in power, as the forty-six-year-old Bill Clinton became the third youngest president in history. In his inaugural address he pledged a "new season of American renewal."[207]

The optimism of his inauguration faded quickly, however, as Clinton wasn't afforded the typical honeymoon of a new administration. Republicans claimed he was an accidental president who would have lost without Perot in the race, and Clinton was also dragged down by some early controversies. First there was a dispute over two candidates for attorney general who had to withdraw because of their hiring of undocumented immigrants for childcare. Then the president was rebuked by military and congressional leaders over a plan to end a ban on gays in the military.[208] These were heated topics at the time and Clinton's approval rating spiraled downward.

Clinton did eventually put notable achievements on the board, including a budget bill that reduced the deficit, the Family and Medical Leave Act, the AmeriCorps service program, and final passage of NAFTA. However, the budget passed without Republican support because of tax increases on the wealthy, while NAFTA was unpopular with some Democrats. And this flurry of legislation was itself overshadowed by an even more ambitious and controversial reform: a health care bill that proposed mandating insurance coverage for all Americans through their place of employment. Notwithstanding initial positive reviews, the bill went down in flames, partly because legislation drafted by the White House was complex and difficult to explain, and because the insurance industry discredited it with a famous series of "Harry and Louise" ads.[209] Most consequential, however, was a decision by Republicans to oppose the bill unanimously, even though a number of them had earlier endorsed the need for reform.[210]

On top of all this, Bill and Hillary Clinton themselves became ensnared in various scandals. It began with the Whitewater affair, a failed real estate investment in Arkansas that led to fraud convictions for some business partners because of their involvement in bad loans. A special prosecutor was appointed to look into the matter. No evidence emerged to implicate the Clintons, but the investigation later grew to encompass unrelated allegations, which would prove important down the road.

The cumulative effect of all this cast a pall over the Clinton administration. The scandals, the political combat, the failure to pass a health care bill—the fact that the economy was doing well was lost amid the fog of controversies. By 1994 Republicans smelled blood. Led by House Minority Whip Newt Gingrich of Georgia, they drafted the "Contract with America" that promised to balance the budget, cut welfare, get tough on crime, and reform the legislative process. This helped nationalize the midterm elections and led to a landslide fifty-four-seat swing in the House, giving Republicans control for the first time in forty years. They also won the Senate.

Most people saw this as a repudiation that spelled trouble for the president's reelection hopes. But these events, paradoxically, provided the basis for a Clinton comeback. During the next two years he both battled Republicans (blaming them for trying to cut popular social programs such as Medicare) and worked with them (signing a welfare reform bill). The strategy was dubbed "triangulation," and it was disparaged on the left. Still, it gave Clinton a way to nail down some accomplishments and to again identify himself as a New Democrat who was willing to find a middle way between the extremes on either side of the aisle.

After all this conflict and commotion during Clinton's first term, by the time the 1996 presidential election rolled around it was as if the drama of the contest had already been played out ahead of time.

President Clinton was easily nominated by Democrats for a second term. He presented himself as the steward of a booming economy, as a check against Republican extremism, and as a future-oriented president who wanted to "build a bridge to the 21st century."[211]

To oppose Clinton, Republicans nominated Senator Bob Dole of Kansas, the minority leader. Dole was well-liked and respected, but he was a seventy-three-year-old who'd been in Congress for thirty-five years, so he was hardly a change candidate. During the nomination battle, the candidates who gave Dole the biggest fight were two individuals who'd never held elective office: the conservative commentator Patrick Buchanan and Steve Forbes, publisher of *Forbes* magazine.

Buchanan and Forbes each articulated a particular conservative ideology. Buchanan ran on the same platform of populist nationalism that fueled his run against Bush four years earlier, as he criticized immigration, free trade, multiculturalism, and globalism. Forbes, meanwhile, used his candidacy to promote supply-side economics and a flat tax. These ideas had support within the GOP, but Forbes had neither the experience nor the campaigning skills to make a serious run at the nomination. In the end, Buchanan finished second with 20 percent of the GOP primary vote, and Forbes was third with 11 percent. It showed that segments of the party were enthused about these ideologies, even if neither candidate posed a threat to Dole.

The general election itself was fairly uneventful. Clinton's approval rating climbed back to near 60 percent by the fall of 1996, and he maintained a healthy polling lead for most of the campaign. Dole focused on his reputation for honesty and integrity to contrast himself with Clinton, and centered his campaign on the slogan "The Better Man for a Better America."[212] But Dole struggled to break through. As *Newsweek* put it, "If Bill Clinton was a natural, Bob Dole was so ill-suited to the role of presidential candidate that it seems a wonder anyone let him try. . . . The Senate was his natural habitat; a presidential campaign was not."[213] Another writer called him "a black and white movie in a color age."[214] To gain attention, he tried to go bold. A longtime deficit hawk, he converted to supply-side economics and proposed an across-the-board 15 percent cut in income taxes.

The Clinton campaign, however, tied Dole to the albatross of Gingrich, whose favorable ratings had been underwater since a 1995 government shutdown amid a debate over Medicare cuts. Advertisements talked about the "DoleGingrich" agenda, and some observers suggested the election seemed "less about Clinton versus Dole than Clinton versus Gingrich."[215]

Ross Perot also reemerged for a second run for the White House, this time as a candidate of the new Reform Party, which he'd founded. But Perot's issues seemed less urgent this time around, and he was shut out of the presidential debates because of low poll numbers. In the end, his vote shrank by more than half from 1992.[216]

On Election Day, Clinton sailed to an easy victory by 49 to 41 to 8 percent over Dole and Perot, winning the Electoral College 379–159. He became the third president to win two elections without a popular majority, joining Woodrow Wilson and Grover Cleveland, and was the first Democrat since Franklin Roosevelt to win a second term.

2000

Clinton was simultaneously a popular and a divisive president. When Americans went to the voting booth in 2000, they seemed torn over whether to give the Clinton era their stamp of approval by electing his successor or to move in a new direction. That uncertainty led to one of the most controversial electoral outcomes in U.S. history, and the most contentious result since the Hayes-Tilden contest of 1876.

Seen from one perspective, the Clinton years were a rousing success. The stock market was booming, unemployment was low, and budget deficits had turned into surpluses. Society itself was being transformed by personal computers and the internet. The president's job approval rating was at 66 percent when he left office and never dipped below 53 percent in his second term.[217]

Clinton remarked during his 1998 State of the Union address, "We have moved into an Information Age, a global economy, a truly new world. . . . We have moved past the sterile debate of those who say government is the enemy and those who say government is the answer. My fellow Americans, we have found a Third Way. We have the smallest government in thirty-five years, but a more progressive one."[218]

Despite all this, the Clinton legacy was a mixed blessing for Democrats in 2000 because the election was just two years removed from a presidential impeachment controversy. The investigation that began in 1994 to probe Clinton's Whitewater real estate venture dragged well into the president's second term and became an umbrella for a variety of allegations. In 1998 news emerged that the president had lied under oath during a civil deposition when questioned about an affair with a White House intern named Monica Lewinsky. Soon thereafter, talk of impeachment swirled through Congress.

On December 19 the House voted mostly along party lines to impeach Clinton on charges of perjury and obstruction of justice. The GOP argument was that perjury is illegal, and no president should break the law for any reason. The opposing view was that while the president's personal conduct may have been abhorrent, lying about a sexual affair wasn't a constitutional offense worthy of removal from office. "While the president betrayed his wife," said Florida congressman Robert Wexler, "he did not betray the country."[219] After a Senate trial, all forty-five Democrats and a handful of Republicans voted not guilty, far from the two-thirds needed to convict Clinton.

The impeachment didn't dent Clinton's popularity with voters, and he left office with approval ratings similar to those of Reagan and Eisenhower after eight years. At the same time, many Americans had grown tired of the perpetual scandals that surrounded the president. This reality would cast a shadow over the next campaign.

In the race to succeed Clinton, Vice President Al Gore easily won the Democratic nomination after dispatching a challenge from New Jersey senator Bill Bradley. As his vice-presidential running mate, Gore chose Connecticut senator Joseph Lieberman, the first Jewish candidate on a major party ticket.

Among Republicans, the early favorite was Texas governor George W. Bush, son of former president George H. W. Bush. His main challenger was Arizona senator John McCain, who'd been a prisoner of war in Vietnam and who campaigned on themes of character, honor, and candor. "I will always tell you the truth," he told voters.[220] McCain took aim at Bush in New Hampshire, traipsing through the state on a bus dubbed the Straight Talk Express. He appealed to independents because of his life story and his branding as a reformer, and he walloped Bush in the state by 48 to 30 percent.

McCain at this point seemed like a threat to win the nomination, but then the race moved to South Carolina and, as one writer remarked, "the empire struck back."[221] Bush cast himself as a "Reformer with Results," and his campaign went negative in a way the McCain camp hadn't fully anticipated. At least, private groups that were officially unaffiliated with the Bush campaign went negative. They called into radio talk shows, papered the state with flyers, and conducted push polls. McCain, they said, was a traitor who'd turned against his country in Vietnam. He was a Manchurian candidate. He gave his wife venereal disease. His adopted daughter from Bangladesh was the love child of an affair with a prostitute. It was impossible to bat back all the accusations, and they raised just enough questions in voters' minds to halt McCain's momentum.[222]

Bush won South Carolina by 53 to 42 percent and went on to thump McCain on Super Tuesday to effectively sew up the nomination. He later selected Dick Cheney, a former secretary of defense and congressman, as his running mate.

The fall campaign was then a battle between two contenders who were in many respects polar opposites of one another. Gore was recognized for his experience in government and his intellect. He'd written a best-selling book, *Earth in the Balance*, about environmental threats to the planet. What Gore didn't possess was Clinton's ability to connect with voters. "I don't consider myself a natural politician," he admitted.[223] Even one of his staffers remarked that while Gore had "the potential to be a great leader, a visionary . . . he tends to make intellectual rather than emotional connections with people."[224]

Bush, on the other hand, did convey charm on the campaign trail but was seen as lacking in intellectual firepower, despite two Ivy League degrees. He fed this perception with a penchant for verbal bloopers, dubbed "Bushisms," such as, "Rarely is the question asked: Is our children learning?" and, "Will the highways on the internet become more few?"[225] Bush saw it as a nonissue. It "doesn't mean that I don't understand how to lead," he said.[226]

These personality traits tended to overshadow discussion of

actual issues during the campaign. Debate centered on muted disagreements over, say, what to do with the budget surplus. Bush wanted tax cuts and Gore preferred shoring up Social Security. Bush also characterized himself as a "compassionate conservative" who would blend "a conservative mind with a compassionate heart."[227]

Bush's most important tactic may have been to tie Gore to the political storms of the Clinton years. He pledged to be "a uniter, not a divider," and to "restore honor and dignity" to the White House, thus making the election a subtle referendum on President Clinton.[228] As *Time* magazine put it, after "losing twice to Clinton-Gore, the Republicans are confident this year they can beat Gore-Clinton."[229]

That was the essential dilemma for Gore: how to take credit for a prosperous economy and the successes of the incumbent administration while distancing himself from the Clinton controversies. The voters themselves had dueling emotions. They appreciated "the good times," as the *New York Times* wrote, but also had "lingering resentment" about the president's personal behavior.[230]

The acceptance speeches at each party's convention highlighted variations on this theme. At the Democratic convention in Los Angeles, Gore told the audience, "I stand here tonight as my own man." And Bush, at the GOP convention in Philadelphia, criticized Clinton as a president who "embodied the potential of a generation. So many talents. So much charm. Such great skill. But in the end, to what end?"[231]

These conflicting sentiments were reflected in the closeness of the election. The candidates were neck and neck in the polls going into late October. Then, on Election Day and for more than a month afterward, a drama played out that has rarely been matched in a presidential contest.

Gore won the popular vote by 48.4 to 47.9 percent, or about five hundred thousand ballots, but the Electoral College wasn't as clear cut. At the end of the day, with one state undecided, Gore had 267 electoral votes and Bush 246, so both were short of the 270 needed to win the presidency. The election would thus come down to 25 electoral votes in Florida.

On election night, the state was first called for Gore, based on early returns and exit polling. But as more results were tabulated, the networks changed course and returned it to the undecided column. Then, just after 2:00 a.m. EST, Florida was awarded to Bush. This prompted Gore to call Bush and concede the election. The Associated Press, meanwhile, which collected its votes independently, insisted the race was still too close to call. The AP, it turned out, was correct. The networks had received faulty numbers, in part because of a reporting error in Volusia County.[232] Gore was alerted to this reality only minutes before making a concession speech, so he called Bush again, this time to suggest waiting for more definitive results. "Let me make sure I understand," said an incredulous Bush. "You're calling back to *retract* that concession?"[233]

By the time the sun rose the next morning, the two candidates were separated by the thinnest of margins in Florida, a recount had been triggered, and the media withdrew its declaration of a Bush victory. "The American people have spoken," said President Clinton, "but it's going to take a while to determine exactly what they said."[234]

The astonishing closeness of the vote, moreover, wasn't the only headline of the day. There was also an uproar over alleged ballot design errors in Florida. The biggest controversy involved a butterfly ballot in Palm Beach County, which listed candidate names on two pages, with one row of punch holes in the center. Gore's name appeared second, under Bush's, but to vote for Gore one had to punch the third hole. The second hole was for Reform Party candidate Pat Buchanan, whose name was on the facing page. Throughout Election Day calls poured in from voters who feared they had mistakenly voted for Buchanan instead of Gore.

Indeed, the conservative Buchanan received 3,407 votes in Palm Beach, his best performance in the state despite its being a liberal stronghold. Buchanan contended that no more than 400 of these votes were meant for him. "The rest, I'm quite sure, were Gore votes," he said.[235] Another 4 percent of county ballots were disqualified for having two votes for president, a much higher rate than usual. The most common combination had votes for Gore and Buchanan. The *Palm Beach Post* later reviewed these ballots and concluded that ballot confusion cost Gore about 6,000 votes in Palm Beach County.[236]

On top of this, many Democrats were incensed over the third-party run of consumer advocate Ralph Nader, the Green Party nominee. Nader had insisted there was little difference between Gore and Bush, whom he called Tweedledee and Tweedledum. He attracted just under 3 percent of the national vote, with considerable support from more liberal Democrats. Crucially, though, he received 97,488 votes in Florida, so if just 1 percent of Nader voters had supported Gore, the Democrat would have won the presidency.[237]

The Nader contretemps, of course, had nothing to do with the actual vote count. People are allowed to vote for whomever they wish. And nothing could be done about the fiasco in Palm Beach, as there was no do-over for miscast ballots. But the Gore campaign did want a review of undervotes—those where no vote for president was recorded. Counties that used punch-card technology had high rates of undervotes, often because voters didn't punch a hole all the way through or because machines accidentally discarded ballots. Gore requested a manual recount in four counties, while Bush went to court to stop the proposed recount.

The ensuing thirty-six-day legal drama began with Bush holding a 327-vote lead in Florida, out of almost 6 million ballots cast. The fact that he held this lead, along with the reality that most Americans went to bed on election night believing he had won, was important in framing the narrative over the following weeks. Bush was cast as the "president-in-waiting," while Gore was dubbed by Republicans the "Sore-Loserman," unwilling to concede graciously.[238]

The Gore perspective, on the other hand, was that if the networks hadn't been misled by a faulty vote total and had held off on calling Florida for Bush on election night (as did the Associated Press), then Americans would have awoken to the story of a close election in which Gore won the popular vote, but with the Electoral College up in the air. "The dynamic would have been totally different," insisted Gore campaign chairman William Daley.[239] As it was, the two sides battled in court for two weeks, until the Florida Supreme Court ruled on November 21 that recounts could proceed.

This hardly ended the controversies, however. For one, Bush's lead grew with absentee ballots from military personnel, some of which were missing postmarks or required signatures. A later study concluded that 680 of these ballots should have been rejected as invalid.[240] Gore overruled advisors who wanted to challenge the legitimacy of these votes, declaring that an effort to disallow military ballots might help him win, but then he "couldn't govern."[241]

There were also GOP efforts to sow controversy over recounts, such as with the so-called Brooks Brothers riot in Miami on November 22. After a partial examination of undervotes in Miami-Dade County yielded a net gain for Gore of 157 votes, the recount was disrupted by demonstrators who shouted, "Stop the fraud!" They screamed, banged on doors, and chased officials through hallways. The scene was so chaotic the board of canvassers halted the recount and never restarted it. It was later revealed that many demonstrators were Republican aides from out of state, and the clash was coordinated by GOP operative Roger Stone, stationed outside with a walkie-talkie.[242]

In Palm Beach County, meanwhile, officials asked for a two-hour extension of the 5:00 p.m. deadline on November 26 for completing the manual recount. They were turned down by Secretary of State Katherine Harris, a Bush supporter. Palm Beach then turned in the numbers it had as of 5:00, but Harris rejected them as incomplete. The county said the final numbers would have shown a net gain for Gore of 176 votes.[243]

Despite these controversies, Harris on November 26 certified Bush as the winner by 537 votes. The Gore campaign promptly contested the election because of the incomplete and rejected vote counts. After more legal disputes, the Florida Supreme Court weighed in again on December 8, ordering a resumption of manual recounts, this time in all sixty-seven counties in the state.

But this recount never happened. One day later the U.S. Supreme Court ordered it suspended. Then, on December 12, the court issued a contentious decision that ended the election. The justices said the Florida recount violated the Equal Protection Clause of the Constitution because there was no statewide standard for determining a valid ballot. The ruling was decided by a 5–4 vote along partisan lines.[244]

The court's decision was controversial even aside from its partisan tinge, not only because the court intervened in an election managed by a state but also because the Fourteenth Amendment's Equal Protection Clause was enacted in 1868 to protect freed slaves and had never been used in a voting case. Liberals were outraged, and even some conservatives were uneasy. John DiIulio, who later worked for the Bush administration, wrote in the *Weekly Standard* that the opinion was "constitutionally disingenuous."[245] Others questioned why the court hadn't just required Florida to establish a uniform standard and then finish the recount by the December 18 Electoral College vote.[246]

In any event, the court decision led Gore to concede the election. On December 13 he addressed the nation. "Let there be no doubt, while I strongly disagree with the court's decision, I accept it," he said. "And tonight, for the sake of our unity as a people and the strength of our democracy, I offer my concession."[247] Bush won the presidency with 271 electoral votes, becoming the first candidate since 1888 to win the White House after losing the popular vote.

When the election was over, the independent National Opinion Research Center undertook a study of Florida ballots to try to determine who in fact received the most votes.[248] Perhaps inevitably, the result provided grist for both parties. The study established that if the recount of undervotes had gone forward, Bush would still have won Florida. It also determined that if overvotes were counted, along with undervotes, then Gore would have won. That's because ballots with two votes for president were disqualified by machines, but when examined individually there was enough evidence for many of them to be considered valid, say, if a voter marked a preference for one candidate and then wrote the same candidate's name in the write-in section.

In the end, then, Florida was essentially a tie. Either candidate could legitimately have been declared the winner, depending on how the votes were counted.

Of course, the other reality is that the greatest failure in Florida wasn't with these undervotes and overvotes, because people make these errors in every election in every state. Rather, it was with thousands of other votes that were thrown out or miscounted because of confusion over ballot designs. The most well-known breakdown was in Palm Beach County, where we've already noted the ballot design likely cost Gore about 6,000 votes. Less famous but also significant was a two-page presidential ballot in Duval County. A sample published in the newspaper instructed people to vote on every page. Thousands did just that and thereby disqualified their vote. Many recorded a preference for Gore, and then on the next page for the Libertarian Harry Browne, possibly confusing him with Congresswoman Corrine Brown. It was estimated that these errors cost Gore another 2,600 votes.[249]

After digesting the data, analysts concluded that more people in Florida went to the polls to vote for Gore, but more votes were counted for Bush due to a combination of bad ballot designs, voter error, confusing instructions, or voting machine flaws.[250] Even Buchanan remarked, "If the results had reflected the actual sentiments of the people who voted, Al Gore would have won Florida. . . . I suppose I'll get it from my conservative friends for saying that, but . . . I think there's a certain duty to try to keep the historical record straight, even if it doesn't change the fact [that Bush won the election and became president]."[251]

Gore himself remarked in a 2004 speech, "You know the old saying: you win some, you lose some. And then there's that little-known third category."[252]

2004

In 2001 George W. Bush took office as the leader of a divided nation. In his inaugural address, he praised America's history of ensuring a "peaceful transfer of authority" and pledged to "work to build a single nation of justice and opportunity."[253] But partisan divisions were difficult to overcome, and Democrats remained troubled over the controversial end to the previous election.

Then came September 11, 2001. On that day terrorists hijacked commercial airplanes and flew them into New York's World Trade Center and the Pentagon. Another plane crashed in Pennsylvania. In all, 2,977 people were killed, and two 110-story skyscrapers collapsed. Three days later President Bush stood on a pile of rubble at Ground Zero with a bullhorn and said to rescue workers, "The rest of the world hears you, and the people who knocked down these buildings will hear all of us soon."[254] A shocked nation rallied around Bush, and memories of the contentious 2000 campaign subsided. The president's approval rating hit 90 percent in late September and remained above 70 percent for much of 2002.[255]

The attack spurred the United States to unleash a "war on terrorism," starting with a 2001 invasion of Afghanistan, where the terrorist leader Osama bin Laden was sheltered.[256] More controversially, Bush embarked on a second war in 2003, this one against Iraq for alleged development of nuclear and chemical weapons. Americans removed the dictator Saddam Hussein, but no weapons of mass destruction were found, and in the aftermath U.S. troops had to battle a jihadist insurgency.

This was the backdrop to the president's reelection campaign. People seemed to like Bush personally and respected his post–September 11 leadership but were divided over Iraq. And on the domestic front, the Bush administration had passed a $1.3 trillion tax cut and an education reform bill, but the economy was stuck in neutral after a 2001 recession. Moreover, the combination of war costs and tax cuts had turned an $86 billion surplus from 2000 into a $412 billion deficit by 2004.[257] The conflicted feelings of voters were reflected in Bush's approval rating, which settled in the 46 to 54 percent range.[258]

To oppose Bush, after Gore passed on another run, Democrats flirted with nominating a little-known governor of Vermont, Howard Dean, who enthused liberals by coming out vociferously against the Iraq War and pledging to represent "the Democratic wing of the Democratic Party."[259] Dean was the first candidate to utilize the still-growing internet in creative ways, to raise money and organize meetups of supporters. He built a healthy polling lead over a field that included, among others, Senators John Kerry of Massachusetts, John Edwards of North Carolina, and Joe Lieberman of Connecticut and former House minority leader Dick Gephardt of Missouri.

But Dean faltered before voting even began, hampered by his own errors and by a damaging ad war with Gephardt in Iowa. His slump coincided with a surge by Kerry, a longtime senator and a decorated Vietnam War veteran who was seen by some as the party's strongest candidate against Bush.[260]

Kerry's rise crested just in time for the Iowa caucuses on January 19, which he won over Edwards and Dean. That night, Dean stumbled again when he inadvertently generated one of the country's first viral political moments. During his concession speech, while yelling over the cheers of supporters and vowing to continue the fight, he gave a shrill shout that became known as the Dean Scream. To the television audience, it sounded "primal and unhinged," and when the media replayed it continually over the next few days it fed a narrative that questioned Dean's temperament.[261] Eight days later Kerry rolled to another win in New Hampshire, then wrapped up the nomination in early March after winning nine of ten states on Super Tuesday.

Kerry later tried convincing his friend John McCain to be his vice-presidential running mate, believing a ticket representing both parties could bridge partisan divisions.[262] When McCain wouldn't bite, Kerry turned to Edwards, who'd received the second-most Democratic primary votes on the strength of a "Two Americas" message about inequality.

At the party convention in Boston in late July, Democrats highlighted Kerry's biography, notably his service in Vietnam, for which he'd received a Silver Star, Bronze Star, and three Purple Hearts. "The message was the man: Kerry, the war hero," *Newsweek* remarked.[263] He opened his acceptance speech with a sharp salute and announced, "I'm John Kerry, and I'm reporting for duty." He emerged from the convention with a 5-point polling lead.[264]

The week also marked the emergence of a new Democratic star in Barack Obama, an African American Senate candidate from Illinois who thrilled convention delegates with a stirring keynote speech. "There is not a liberal America and a conservative America—there is the United States of America," asserted Obama. "There is not a Black America and a white America and Latino America and Asian America—there's the United States of America."[265] This keynote was one of the most consequential convention speeches in history, up there with William Jennings Bryan's 1896 "Cross of Gold" address, as it made Obama a national figure and paved the way for his later presidential run.

The Republicans met in New York City, near Ground Zero, where they promoted Bush as a decisive president and praised him for leadership in the war on terror. In his own speech Bush said, "I will never relent in defending America."[266] The strategy paid off, as a poll taken after the conventions showed that voters who were primarily concerned with terrorism supported Bush by the overwhelming margin of 87 to 13 percent.[267]

The GOP also focused on galvanizing its base over social issues, most notably gay marriage, which became a hot-button issue after a Massachusetts court legalized same-sex marriage in 2004. Republicans organized ballot drives in eleven states to ask voters to reject the idea.[268]

During the fall campaign Republicans were successful in driving up Kerry's negatives, in part by maligning his military record. A pro-Bush group called the Swift Boat Veterans for Truth aired two ads in August, one that suggested Kerry lied to get his navy medals and a second that highlighted his antiwar activities after coming home from Vietnam. The ad about his military record was controversial; even McCain criticized it as "dishonest and dishonorable." Nevertheless Kerry's lead over Bush faded.[269] The word "swiftboating" was later spun into a verb to describe "a particularly lethal kind of smear campaign."[270]

Kerry also hurt himself at times with his own stumbles. Once, for instance, when justifying why he voted against more money for the Iraq War after first favoring a different version of the bill (which would have rescinded tax cuts for the rich), he said, "I actually did vote for the $87 billion before I voted against it."[271] The remark was devastating when stripped of context, and the Bush team turned it into a potent TV spot.

On top of this, Republicans harped on Kerry for elitism because of his patrician bearing. The charge was ironic given that Bush was the son of a president and the grandson of a senator, but it worked. The GOP even dinged Kerry for speaking and looking French. House Majority Leader Tom Delay began speeches by saying, "Good afternoon. Or, as John Kerry might say, 'Bonjour.'" And the National Rifle Association had fun with an image of a French poodle wearing a Kerry-for-President sweater.[272]

This litany of attacks nearly backfired on Republicans when Kerry appeared self-assured and knowledgeable at the fall presidential debates—nothing like the spineless flip-flopper that some voters were expecting. Bush, meanwhile, seemed unfocused and irritable in the first debate. One report said Bush looked "whiny" and Kerry "presidential." It was enough to give Kerry another boost in the polls, and the two candidates raced to the finish in a near-dead heat.[273]

When the votes were counted, President Bush prevailed by the narrowest margin ever for an incumbent, 50.7 to 48.3 percent, slightly closer than in Wilson's 1916 reelection. Bush won the Electoral College 286–252, the difference being his win in Ohio, which wasn't called until the next morning. If Ohio had flipped, Kerry would have reprised Bush's feat of winning the presidency while losing the popular vote.

In another echo of 2000, there were more claims of voting irregularities, this time in Ohio. An undersupply of machines in urban areas caused thousands of people to leave after standing in line for up to eight hours without voting; there were reports of malfunctioning touchscreens that transferred Kerry votes to Bush, and there were high numbers of undervotes and third-party votes in some districts, apparently because poll workers mistakenly directed paper ballots into machines calibrated for different precincts. These irregularities caused the House Judiciary Committee to launch an investigation, which determined that Kerry may have been shorted by tens of thousands of votes.[274]

But even though Ohio was a close result, 51 to 49 percent, Bush did win the state by 118,000 votes and Kerry saw no benefit to challenging the outcome. "I don't want the country to be divided anymore," he told his staff before conceding.[275] So Bush returned to the White House as the first son or grandson of a former president to win a second term, a feat that had previously eluded John Quincy Adams and Benjamin Harrison.

The Fracturing of American Politics

When we look back on the 1992–2004 era, one thing that stands out is that politics began fracturing in a way that went beyond ideological differences. Three decades of conflict over social issues had already raised the political temperature, but several new dynamics during this period pushed Americans further into opposing tribes.

A sign of how politics was changing could be seen in an ad produced by a conservative group during the 2004 Democratic primaries. In the spot, presidential candidate Howard Dean was advised to "take his tax-hiking, government-expanding, latte-drinking, sushi-eating, Volvo-driving, *New York Times*–reading, body-piercing, Hollywood-loving, left-wing freak show back to Vermont, where it belongs."[276] It was a humorous and effective strike against so-called liberal elitism, and the ad went viral. At the same time, it reflected the nation's rising polarization, as it wasn't standard practice prior to this for people's lifestyle and cultural choices to be seen as synonymous with their politics.

Not coincidentally this was also when the concept of blue states for Democrats and red states for Republicans first took hold among voters and pundits. The television networks had used color-coded electoral maps since the 1970s, but there wasn't a standard color associated with either party until the Bush-versus-Gore clash of 2000.[277] Talk of a red-blue divide entered the lexicon, and it resonated with Americans because of how the country's political culture had been split open in recent years.

This splintering could be traced to various factors, one of which was a deliberate attack on political traditions and civility in the 1990s by GOP congressman Gingrich. He'd made a name for himself in Washington by suggesting that politics was akin to warfare, and when Clinton took office Gingrich persuaded his party to oppose most every Democratic proposal, even those that would have had bipartisan support. He believed voters wouldn't notice GOP obstructionism and would instead blame the majority Democrats for a lack of progress.[278]

Gingrich also developed a list of recommended words for his colleagues to use when talking about Democrats, including *anti-family, anti-flag, pathetic, bizarre, radical, sick, corrupt,* and *traitors.* His goal, he explained, was for voters to see Democrats as "the enemy of normal Americans."[279] Whatever the merits of this strategy, it indeed helped Republicans regain control of Congress in 1994, and these tactics have been part of the GOP playbook ever since.

A second factor in the decline of the country's political culture was a changing media environment. CNN was founded in 1980 as the country's first twenty-four-hour news channel, and as viewership increased over the years so did the demand for tantalizing stories to attract audiences. Not surprisingly, perhaps, 1987 and 1992 are when journalistic feeding frenzies first erupted over sex scandals in the Hart and Clinton presidential campaigns.

Additionally, this is when a right-wing media ecosystem roared to life. The Fox News network was founded in 1996, not long after conservative talk radio became popular. Prior to 1987, few radio stations aired political talk shows, in part because the government required broadcasters to give equal time to different parties, a rule known as the Fairness Doctrine. But in 1987 a court of appeals overturned the rule by a 2–1 vote. One year later Rush Limbaugh launched a national talk show and transformed the format. Within eight years the percentage of talk radio stations quadrupled, as broadcasters discovered that "conservative rage drew listeners."[280]

The other formidable factor that changed politics was the internet. The proportion of U.S. households with internet access rose from just 19 percent in 1997 to 55 percent in 2003.[281] When this era began, the internet was barely a blip on the political radar, but by 2004 Howard Dean was raising money and organizing volunteers online, and bloggers were being given press credentials to party conventions. With all these changes, the way Americans consumed news underwent a dramatic shift. Fewer voters relied on the major networks and newspapers as their primary source of information, while the new partisan media helped more voters sink into information bubbles that hardened their own political leanings.[282]

Put it all together, and it's obvious that the tremors of the 1992–2004 era reshaped presidential politics and were perhaps a harbinger of bigger changes to come. Comparably disruptive events in the past, such as the Dixiecrat revolt of 1948 or the growing influence of television in the 1950s, have foreshadowed larger transformations. When seen in this context, it's probable that these years will someday be seen as an interlude between the conservative Republican dominance of the late twentieth century and whatever political landscape emerges from the 2010s and 2020s.

This doesn't mean the fractious politics of the time will fade into oblivion. In fact, the vitriol only seemed to intensify during the following decade, and the polarization that sent politics down a rabbit hole of red-versus-blue rancor continued to divide Americans. But as the twenty-first century dawned, the fault lines of politics did appear to be shifting, and a new era was peeking over the horizon.

7

★ ★ ★

2008-20

History in the Making

Coffee at Starbucks in Seattle

During this next political era, which is still ongoing, Americans have lived through a string of extraordinary events. It began with the Great Recession of 2008, the country's worst economic downturn since the 1930s. That same year Barack Obama won a momentous election and became the nation's first African American president. In 2016 the country turned to Donald Trump, a reality television star and businessman, and the first president with no experience in government or the military. Then 2020 brought the coronavirus, the worst pandemic in a century, which hit in the middle of a presidential election.

When the final draft of this history is written, these stories will all figure prominently in the narrative. Along with these events, however, it will also be said that this era was molded by numerous changes in technology and society, above all the escalating influence of the internet and the advent of social media.

If John Kennedy's 1960 victory was the first one propelled by television, then Obama's 2008 election was likewise the first one dominated by the internet. This development was aided by profound changes in the online landscape in the four years between 2004 and 2008. Facebook was launched in 2004, YouTube made its debut in 2005, Twitter came online in 2006, and the first iPhone was unveiled in 2007. These inventions revolutionized the way people interacted with each other, with the internet, and with politics. As a result, presidential campaigns were transformed in ways that would have been unimaginable to earlier generations, whether it was Obama's creation of a grassroots online community or Trump's use of Twitter to gain attention, sow controversy, and drive the media narrative. The internet upended American politics every bit as much as television had done a half century earlier.

Other technological trends also accelerated during this period, notably the rise of laptop computers, which began outselling desktops in 2005.[1] This, along with the prevalence of wi-fi, contributed to a rise in telecommuting and freelancing, which in turn fueled an explosion in the number of people who used coffee shops as a place to work—or as a place to enjoy a coffee while discussing life, books, and politics.

Which brings us to Starbucks. Coffee shops have of course been in America for quite some time, considering that Café du Monde in New Orleans, for instance, was founded in 1862. But while there are now independent coffee shops in most communities, the reality is that many Americans didn't have access to such cafés before the rise of Starbucks.[2] And the ubiquity of these coffee shops happened to coincide with the rise of the internet in the 1990s and early twenty-first century.

Moreover, the companies most responsible for these developments all have Pacific Coast roots. The original Starbucks is just a few miles from the Seattle offices of Amazon and Microsoft and eight hundred or so miles from the Silicon Valley headquarters of Apple, Google, Facebook, and Twitter. It was the convergence of these companies and events that generated such groundbreaking changes in American life and politics. That's why Starbucks, and particularly the original Starbucks at Seattle's Pike Place Market, is an ideal place in which to reflect on the next age of American politics.

With this in mind, then, let's grab a coffee and take a look at the era of presidential history that is still being written.

2008, 2012, and 2016: Obama and Trump—
Earthquake and Aftershock

2008

The 2008 presidential election was another one for the history books. There was a dramatic nomination battle in the spring, a vice-presidential nominee who stole headlines in the fall, and an election that took place in the shadow of the biggest economic crisis in seven decades. And all this was just a prelude to the biggest story of all: the first election of an African American as president of the United States. The *New York Times* dubbed it "one of the most remarkable contests in American political history."[3]

When the campaign began, there was little inkling of the drama to come. The Bush administration was winding to a close with the president's popularity plummeting. The Iraq War remained controversial, and Bush's reputation hadn't quite recovered from the government's slow response to Hurricane Katrina in 2005, which killed more than 1,800 people, destroyed three hundred thousand homes, and left much of New Orleans under water.[4]

The early GOP frontrunner to succeed Bush was Arizona senator John McCain, the runner-up in the party's 2000 nomination battle, although conservatives were lukewarm on his candidacy because he'd opposed the Bush tax cuts and was a moderate on immigration issues. It was McCain's support for a bipartisan immigration reform bill in 2007, in fact, that nearly sank his campaign amid a barrage of fire from right-wing talk radio. What kept McCain in the game was that his chief rivals, former Massachusetts governor Mitt Romney and New York mayor Rudy Giuliani, also failed to warm conservative hearts. So when Romney lost the Iowa caucuses on January 3 to Governor Mike Huckabee of Arkansas and McCain won the New Hampshire primary five days later, the Arizona senator became the default option for voters who saw him as the most electable Republican. After McCain defeated Huckabee in South Carolina and Romney in Florida, he then won nine of twenty-one contests on Super Tuesday, effectively ending the nomination battle.

While the GOP contest concluded with minimal drama in March, the Democrats engaged in a historic struggle that lasted into June. It began with eight candidates but quickly turned into a race between Senators Hillary Clinton of New York and Barack Obama of Illinois, the first woman and the first African American to emerge as serious contenders for the presidency. Clinton, a former first lady and a two-term senator, had a wealth of experience, whereas Obama had been in national office for only two years. On the other hand, Clinton remained a polarizing figure from her eight years in the White House, while Obama was still basking in the glow of his 2004 convention keynote speech. A native of Hawaii with a Kansan mother and a Kenyan father, Obama, suggested *Newsweek*, was "the perfect mirror for a country that craves to see itself as beyond race, beyond boundaries."[5]

For much of 2007 Clinton's nomination seemed inevitable. In the ABC News/*Washington Post* poll, she led Obama 37 to 20 percent in April and 49 to 26 percent in October.[6] But as fall turned to winter, Obama gained ground. In Iowa his team focused on mobilizing new voters, while the candidate thrilled audiences with a stump speech that railed at partisanship and politics-as-usual. David Broder of the *Washington Post* noted that there seemed to be "a jolt of pure electric energy" coursing through the crowd as Obama built to the closing crescendo of each address.[7] Obama's momentum carried him to a surprisingly large eight-point win in the Iowa caucuses. Because of the low population of Blacks in the state, this performance was compared by some to the Catholic Kennedy's 1960 primary victory in Protestant West Virginia.[8]

After this, Clinton rebounded to win the New Hampshire primary and the Nevada caucuses, before Obama came back with another big win in South Carolina. The two then had a split decision in the twenty-two states that voted on Super Tuesday. This is how the rest of primary season played out, as a series of peaks and valleys for both candidates. Obama gained a modest delegate lead in February, which proved difficult for Clinton to overcome, but they each had important wins the rest of the way and neither seemed able to fully vanquish the other.

Along the way, Obama also fought through two controversies that threatened his candidacy. In mid-March a story broke about the Reverend Jeremiah Wright, the pastor of his Chicago church. A reporter discovered old sermons in which Wright had thundered about "The US of KKK A" and "Not God bless America—God*damn* America!" This ignited a media inferno that threatened to consume Obama's campaign.[9] He responded by giving a speech about race on March 18 at the National Constitution Center in Philadelphia. In the address, "A More Perfect Union," Obama reflected both on America's and his own racial journey. He urged whites to appreciate the reality of "Black pain" and Blacks to recognize "white fear of economic and cultural displacement."[10] The address became one of the most viewed videos on YouTube; one newspaper called it "the most articulate and profound speech on race in America since the Rev. Martin Luther King, Jr."[11]

The following month he was quoted at a fundraiser discussing economic challenges in former factory towns. When the jobs disappear, said Obama, it's not surprising that some people "get bitter, they cling to guns or religion or . . . anti-immigrant sentiment or anti-trade sentiment as a way to explain their frustrations." In trying to make a point about economic pain, Obama came across as condescending, and Clinton seized on the comments. "Americans need a president that will stand up for them, not a president that looks down on them," she said.[12]

The storms eventually subsided, and the two candidates slugged it out until the final day of voting on June 3, when Obama clinched the nomination. He edged Clinton in the total primary vote by just 48.1 to 48 percent out of more than 35 million ballots, and the pledged delegate race by 127.[13] On June 7 Clinton conceded defeat. "Although we weren't able to shatter that highest, hardest glass ceiling this time," she told supporters, "thanks to you, it's got about 18 million cracks in it."[14] Obama later made Delaware senator Joe Biden his running mate, choosing a candidate who had foreign policy credentials and long experience in Washington. It was a significant choice, one that would even impact the 2020 election more than a decade later.

With the nomination battle over, Obama embarked on an overseas trip in July, to the Middle East, South Asia, and Europe. He proved to be as great an attraction abroad as at home, as two hundred thousand Germans turned out in Berlin for a public speech in which Obama called for collaboration to solve global challenges. "Partnership and cooperation among nations is not a choice," he said. "That is why the greatest danger of all is to allow new walls to divide us from one another."[15]

In August attention turned to the party conventions. The Democrats were up first, starting August 25 in Denver, Colorado. Obama's acceptance address was staged at the Invesco Field football stadium, mirroring Kennedy's 1960 outdoor convention address at the Los Angeles Coliseum. "I stand before you tonight because all across America something is stirring," Obama told the crowd. "For 18 long months, you have stood up, one by one, and said, 'Enough,' to the politics of the past. . . . Change happens because the American people demand it, because they rise up and insist on new ideas and new leadership, a new politics for a new time."[16]

The Republican convention opened a few days later, on September 1 in St. Paul, Minnesota. McCain took advantage of the timing to announce his vice-presidential selection the day after Obama's speech, hoping to blunt Democratic momentum. He seriously considered running with Senator Joe Lieberman of Connecticut, the former Democratic vice-presidential candidate who turned independent after splitting with his party over the Iraq War, but advisors feared it would divide the GOP.[17] So, trailing in the polls, McCain threw a Hail Mary and selected Alaska governor Sarah Palin.

The second woman ever nominated by a major party for vice president, Palin had been governor for two years but was so new to national politics that most Americans had never heard of her. She had a reputation as a reformer, and she was pro-life, a hunter, and a forty-four-year-old "hockey mom" with five children, including a son who would soon deploy to Iraq.[18] Many of these qualities endeared her to the GOP base, and Palin's acceptance speech exhilarated the convention. "You know what they say the difference between a hockey mom and a pit bull is?" she asked. "Lipstick!"[19] McCain's acceptance address, in which he exhorted the party to "stand up and fight," was almost an afterthought next to Palin, who became an instant sensation.[20] She gave McCain a boost in the polls and was a phenomenon in her own right, attracting large crowds and thrilling social conservatives and working-class voters who felt alienated from national politics. She was the harbinger, it turned out, of an emergent political force that would engulf the GOP a few years later.

But in the near term Palin was a shooting star, a streak of light that shot through the sky and then faded when the country discovered she wasn't well-versed on major issues. She drew blanks on several questions during one network television appearance, and another time defended her foreign policy experience by reminding the interviewer that "you can actually see Russia from land here in Alaska." That led to a memorable skit on *Saturday Night Live* in which the actress Tina Fey satirized Palin, exclaiming, "I can see Russia from my house!"[21] Before long, the narrative turned again, and voters questioned why the seventy-two-year-old McCain had selected a relative novice as his running mate.

As the campaign headed into its final months, Obama appeared to have one substantial advantage and one disadvantage. The advantage was his campaign's skill in using the internet to reimagine the electoral contest. While raising record-setting sums of money, his team organized an online grassroots army by developing its own social networking site, a first for a presidential race.[22] Obama was successfully branded as the embodiment of a new politics, typified by an iconic poster, with the candidate's image stenciled over the words "Hope" or "Change." *Advertising Age* later named Obama its 2008 Marketer of the Year, an unusual accolade for a politician.[23] In these ways the Obama effort was similar to pioneering campaigns of the past—Andrew Jackson's in 1828, William Henry Harrison's in 1840, William McKinley's in 1896, John Kennedy's in 1960, and others—that took advantage of new tools and tactics.

At the same time, Obama faced headwinds of racism. He seemed to touch a nerve not only because of his skin color but also because of his exotic name (Barack Hussein Obama), his unusual child-hood growing up in Hawaii and Indonesia, and baseless rumors that he was a Muslim. The Secret Service reported an increase in threats against his life, and the vitriol got so heated that McCain came to his opponent's defense, telling one audience that Obama "is a decent person and not a person you have to be scared of as president."[24]

By the end, however, most everything was overshadowed by the near meltdown of the economy that fall.[25] A housing bubble had burst earlier in the year, and in September the economy spiraled into a crisis that immobilized the banking system, ravaged the stock market, and pushed Wall Street firms, mortgage lenders, and insurance companies to the edge of bankruptcy. As President Bush described it, "all hell broke loose."[26] The most severe economic slump since the Great Depression had a surprising effect on the presidential campaign, as it was the newcomer Obama who emerged looking like the steady and experienced leader, whereas McCain came across as more erratic.

Soon after the crisis erupted, McCain blundered by asserting, "The fundamentals of our economy are strong."[27] He walked back the comment, though the gaffe haunted him until Election Day. Then he announced he was suspending his campaign, and he asked President Bush to convene a bipartisan White House meeting about the economy, wagering that he'd be seen as rising above politics to help solve a national emergency. But when the candidates and congressional leaders gathered for the meeting he'd requested, McCain remained mostly quiet. Vice President Dick Cheney, obviously not an Obama supporter, later remarked that McCain "added nothing of substance" while Obama seemed "at ease and in command of the situation."[28] Details of the meeting soon leaked, and McCain's standing took a hit. It was the final blow to his campaign. One writer commented that McCain had "hammered the point that he was the only one who had been tested in a crisis. It was working great—until he was tested in a crisis."[29]

On Election Day, Obama won decisively, 53 to 46 percent in the popular vote and 365–173 in the Electoral College. His popular vote was the best performance of a candidate who hadn't previously been president or vice president since Eisenhower in 1952.

When the election was called for Obama at 11:00 p.m. EST, the history-making event ignited waves of celebration. "There was a rush of noise, of horns honking and kids shouting and strangers hugging in the streets," reported *Time* magazine. "People danced in Harlem and wept at Ebenezer Baptist Church and lit candles at Dr. King's grave. More than a thousand people shouted 'Yes, we can!' outside the White House."[30] McCain delivered a gracious concession speech. "This is an historic election," he said, "and I recognize the special significance it has for African Americans and for the special pride that must be theirs tonight."[31]

When Obama came out to speak, it was before 125,000 people in Chicago's Grant Park. "If there is anyone out there who still doubts that America is a place where all things are possible," he said, "who still wonders if the dream of our founders is alive in our time, who still questions the power of our democracy, tonight is your answer."[32]

2012

In January 2009 a record 2 million people crowded the National Mall to witness Barack Obama's inauguration as the forty-fourth president. He alluded to the history of the moment in his inaugural address by saying, "A man whose father less than 60 years ago might not have been served at a local restaurant can now stand before you to take a most sacred oath."[33]

The excitement, however, was tempered by angst over the economic crisis that had now been raging for more than four months. The unemployment rate was rising, home values were collapsing, the credit market was frozen, and the auto industry was on the edge of bankruptcy. It was the worst economy a president had inherited since FDR in 1933, and some economists suggested there was a one-in-three chance of a second Great Depression.[34] Dan Balz of the *Washington Post* noted, "Rarely has a president come into office with the public in such a seemingly conflicted mood," balanced between hope and despair.[35]

To combat the Great Recession, the Obama administration proposed a $787 billion stimulus plan, which passed with virtually no Republican support. The GOP opposition was a deliberate tactic, echoing the Gingrich strategy of sixteen years earlier. From the GOP perspective, if legislation passed with bipartisan votes, Obama would get credit and likely win reelection. On the other hand, if Republicans professed a desire to work with the president but unanimously opposed every bill, Obama would presumably be blamed for continued partisanship and gridlock.

This is why, when Obama proposed health care reform with an individual mandate to buy insurance, Republicans declared it unconstitutional, even though the same mandate was hailed as "the ultimate conservative idea" when implemented in Massachusetts in 2006.[36] Likewise, when Obama announced support for a task force on deficit reduction, a GOP priority, it was blocked in the Senate by the same Republicans who'd introduced the bill.[37] One writer remarked that Obama was the first president "to face an opposition party that repudiated many of its own positions to make a political point."[38]

In many respects, this was a continuation of the fracturing of national politics that had been accelerating since the 1990s. But there was also, as observers pointed out, an imbalance to these divisions. The political scientists Norm Ornstein and Thomas Mann coined the term "asymmetrical polarization" in a 2012 book to assert that the GOP had become an "outlier" in comparison to political parties of the past because it was "scornful of compromise" and "dismissive of the legitimacy of its political opposition."[39]

The Democrats certainly engaged in their own norm-shattering during this era, such as by filibustering judicial nominees during the Bush administration. At the same time, several dozen Democrats voted for the Bush tax cuts, and the party helped Bush pass a 2008 financial bailout that arguably saved the financial system from collapse. In contrast, Republicans refused to work with Obama in 2009 when the economy was reeling and businesses were shedding eight hundred thousand jobs a month, and they opposed the president even when he moved toward their positions on health care and deficit reduction.[40] As Senator George Voinovich of Ohio later admitted, if Obama was for something, Republicans "had to be against it."[41] In this sense, everything was about the politics of the 2012 election.

Legislation still passed Congress, but mostly on party-line votes, including the Affordable Care Act (popularly known as Obamacare), which provided access to health insurance for millions of Americans, and legislation to reform the financial regulatory system in the wake of the 2008 crash. During his term Obama also approved a bailout of the American auto industry, wound down the Iraq War, and sent troops after the terrorist leader Osama bin Laden in a secret raid in Pakistan.

Aside from struggles with congressional Republicans, Obama had to contend with a Tea Party movement that arose within weeks of his inauguration. Hundreds of thousands of people rallied to protest federal bailouts, proposals for health care reform, and a rising national debt. But what appeared on the surface to be a conservative grassroots uprising against big government also contained threads of nativism. Studies showed that Tea Partiers approved of some federal spending, such as for Social Security and Medicare, but resisted other programs that were perceived as handouts for "undeserving" immigrants and people of color.[42] Many of these voters also feared that "America was in danger of losing its culture," a point driven home by the prevalence of "Take Our Country Back" signs at rallies.[43] So the nativism and the hostility to federal spending were, in a sense, interwoven strands of one movement.

Another right-wing cause that erupted during this period was a birther crusade alleging that Obama was born in Kenya, not Hawaii, and therefore was ineligible to serve as president. This unfounded rumor, which had kicked around for a few years, gained momentum when the real estate developer and television star Donald Trump talked it up while contemplating a 2012 presidential run. It was part of a larger drive to cast the president as somehow anti-American. Gingrich literally called him the "first anti-American president," and Giuliani said, "I do not believe that the president loves America."[44]

All of this—the defiance of Obama, the Tea Party, and the birther movement—represented elements of a budding uprising in GOP politics. Palin started tapping into it in 2008; it was partly responsible for the Democratic loss of sixty-three House seats in the 2010 midterms; and it would erupt more forcefully in 2016. But in 2012, when the presidential campaign kicked off, these energies simmered just below the surface, still in search of a candidate.

The most prominent GOP contender was former Massachusetts governor Mitt Romney, a man with an impressive résumé in government and business but not someone who excited the conservative base. Social conservatives remained suspicious of him, and Tea Partiers were wary because his health care initiative in Massachusetts was a model for Obamacare.[45] These voters thus embarked on an almost desperate search for another candidate, casting their eyes first on Texas governor Rick Perry and then on Herman Cain, a Black businessman and former chairman of the Federal Reserve of Kansas City. When those campaigns faltered, there were late surges for former Pennsylvania senator Rick Santorum, a staunch social conservative, and former Speaker of the House Gingrich.

When voting began, Santorum fought his way to a virtual tie with Romney in the Iowa caucuses on January 3. Romney lapped the field in the New Hampshire primary a week later, but Gingrich took aim at the frontrunner when the contest moved south. After depicting Romney as a "greedy, job-killing corporate raider" for his past leadership of Bain Capital, Gingrich won South Carolina by 12 points.[46] Romney rebounded to win Florida and Nevada, while Santorum countered with victories in Colorado, Missouri, and Minnesota. But just when it seemed the GOP might ride this political rollercoaster for months, Romney recovered to win Arizona and Michigan, and then six of ten contests on Super Tuesday. By early April the race was over. Romney made history as the first Mormon presidential candidate and selected Congressman Paul Ryan of Wisconsin as his running mate.

Heading into the general election, Romney touted his business background and his comfort with economic issues in a year when voters were frustrated by a slow recovery from the Great Recession. If the country was looking for a Mr. Fix-It for the economy, Romney was an obvious choice, and this was the message he took to voters. "What America needs is jobs—lots of jobs," he said in his acceptance speech at the GOP convention in Tampa, Florida.

However, Romney battled the perception that he couldn't relate to the lives of average Americans. This was exacerbated by some inelegant remarks he made during the primaries, such as saying that he liked "being able to fire people," casually mentioning that his wife had a "couple of Cadillacs," and making fun of inexpensive raincoats worn by NASCAR fans.[47] And his tax returns showed that he'd parked money in various tax havens, including Switzerland and the Cayman Islands—all entirely legal, but not a great look for someone with presidential ambitions.[48]

Obama's challenge, meanwhile, was to convince voters to reelect him despite a slow-moving recovery and a job approval rating that remained stuck between 45 and 48 percent for most of 2012.[49] The "hope and change" mantra of 2008 was by now a distant memory. In Obama's favor was the fact that the economy was improving, with steady growth in the jobs number and the stock market. Obama also polled better than Romney for personal likeability and for caring about people's needs.[50]

Obama previewed his reelection message with a December 2011 speech in Osawatomie, Kansas. This was where Teddy Roosevelt gave his 1910 "New Nationalism" address, laying out a progressive platform for combating inequality. Obama described what he saw as philosophical differences between the parties. Republicans, he asserted, believe the country is "better off when everybody is left to fend for themselves and play by their own rules. I am here to say they are wrong. . . . I believe this country succeeds when everyone gets a fair shot."[51]

He emphasized this theme throughout 2012, including in his convention address in Charlotte, North Carolina. At the same convention, former president Bill Clinton said the GOP case against Obama "went something like this: 'We left him a total mess. He hasn't cleaned it up fast enough, so fire him and put us back in.'"[52]

That summer and fall the Obama camp hammered Romney over his business career, much as Gingrich had during the primaries, by airing ads that disparaged his record of cutting and outsourcing jobs while in the private sector. Romney, meanwhile, provided extra ammunition for the claim that he didn't understand struggling Americans when a recording surfaced in September of his remarks at a GOP fundraiser. "There are 47 percent of the people . . . who believe that they are entitled to health care, to food, to housing, to you name it," Romney asserted. "My job is not to worry about those people. I'll never convince them that they should take personal responsibility and care for their lives."[53] The video triggered a firestorm, and Romney's polling numbers took a hit.

Obama was then besieged by his own troubles when he turned in a lackluster performance in the first presidential debate on October 3. He was criticized for giving overly detailed answers and for seeming distracted, whereas Romney came across as sharp and decisive. As one headline put it, "Obama Snoozes and Loses."[54] The polls tightened again, with some showing the candidates in a dead heat.[55]

Then, on October 29, the back-and-forth campaign was jolted one last time when Hurricane Sandy battered the Mid-Atlantic coast, killing more than seventy people, causing billions of dollars in damage, and devastating the New Jersey shore. This prompted a pause in campaigning and gave Obama a chance to appear presidential. While he had already bounced back with stronger performances in the final two debates, the news coverage and bipartisan praise Obama received for his handling of the disaster gave him one more boost before voters went to the polls on November 6.

On Election Day, Obama won the popular vote by 51 to 47 percent and the Electoral College 332–206. While he received a smaller percentage of the vote than he had in 2008, his reelection guaranteed his place in history, not only as the first African American president but also as just the seventh president since 1828 to top 50 percent of the popular vote in consecutive elections, joining Andrew Jackson, Ulysses S. Grant, William McKinley, Franklin Roosevelt, Dwight Eisenhower, and Ronald Reagan.

President Obama's second inaugural was held on Martin Luther King Day in 2013. In his address he spoke about the polarization that continued to plague American politics: "Progress does not compel us to settle centuries-long debates about the role of government for all time, but it does require us to act in our time. We cannot mistake absolutism for principle, or substitute spectacle for politics, or treat name-calling as reasoned debate."[56]

The grip of partisanship, however, never loosened. Consequently the president's second-term agenda was focused more on foreign policy. His administration helped orchestrate the Paris Climate Agreement, coordinated a multination agreement with Iran to restrict its nuclear program, normalized relations with Cuba, and negotiated the twelve-nation Trans-Pacific Partnership trade deal. Nevertheless most domestic legislation was blocked, and government remained stalemated. In Obama's last year in office, Senate Republicans even made the unprecedented decision to refuse to hold hearings for a Democratic Supreme Court nominee.

In 2016 voter exasperation boiled over. That year's election, wrote Ronald Brownstein in *The Atlantic*, was "almost physically vibrating with the accumulated frustration of political life under a divided government."[57] Both parties faced populist insurgencies in their nomination battles, and the campaign ended with the stunning election of an outsider who reveled in shattering political norms.

When the campaign kicked off, the overwhelming Democratic favorite was former secretary of state Hillary Clinton, the 2008 runner-up. Clinton excited those who yearned to elect the first female president, although she was weighed down by negative baggage after a quarter-century on the national scene. She also stumbled into trouble when news surfaced about her use of a private email server while secretary of state. The action, while not illegal, violated federal guidelines for preserving government records. Much was made of reports that some emails contained classified information and that Clinton's legal team deleted thirty thousand personal emails while organizing her records. There was no evidence of criminal mischief, and Clinton was cleared of wrongdoing after an FBI investigation, but her actions were deemed "careless."[58] The issue tormented her for the entire campaign.[59]

In the Democratic primaries, Clinton faced a spirited challenge from Senator Bernie Sanders of Vermont. Sanders was an unlikely presidential contender, given that he was seventy-four and wasn't even officially a Democrat but an independent democratic socialist. Yet Sanders tapped into simmering voter discontent and energized liberals by vowing to pass universal health care, make college tuition-free, and renegotiate trade deals. Whereas Clinton labeled herself "a progressive who likes to get things done," Sanders called for "a political revolution to transform our country."[60]

In the Iowa caucuses on February 1, Sanders came within a whisker of upsetting Clinton, losing 49.8 to 49.6 percent. One week later he won the New Hampshire primary by 60 to 38 percent. Sanders's dream of a monumental upset faded, though, when the race moved south. Clinton trounced him in South Carolina by 47 points, then took eight of twelve matches on Super Tuesday. Sanders battled to the end, winning 43 percent of the vote and acquiring a legion of devoted followers, but Clinton won the nomination. She chose Senator Tim Kaine of Virginia as her vice-presidential candidate.

The Republicans began with seventeen presidential hopefuls, including former Florida governor Jeb Bush, the brother and son of presidents; Senators Marco Rubio of Florida and Ted Cruz of Texas; and Governors Chris Christie of New Jersey and John Kasich of Ohio. But the candidate who surprised everyone by darting up early polls was Donald Trump, the New York real estate developer and star of the reality television show *The Apprentice*. Trump had never run for any office, and many Republicans didn't take his candidacy seriously, believing it was a vehicle for gaining publicity. But Trump tapped into something visceral in the GOP base from the moment he launched his campaign by pledging to build a wall along the southern border to keep out Mexican immigrants, whom he called criminals and rapists.[61]

From then on Trump ran one of the most atypical and astonishing campaigns in the annals of presidential politics. In the months ahead he would suggest that Pope Francis was "disgraceful," mock a disabled reporter, claim a federal judge couldn't be impartial because of his Mexican heritage, denigrate the Muslim parents of a U.S. soldier who died in Iraq, and complain that Fox News anchor Megyn Kelly had "blood coming out of her wherever" after she questioned him aggressively at a debate.[62] He also derided Senator John McCain, the party's 2008 nominee, saying the former POW was "not a war hero" and adding, "I like people who weren't captured."[63] These statements would have sunk almost any other candidate, but nothing dented Trump's support. "I could stand in the middle of Fifth Avenue and shoot somebody, and I wouldn't lose any voters," he declared.[64]

Trump's popularity wasn't due to his allegiance to Republican ideology, as he resisted GOP positions in favor of small government, free trade, and entitlement reform. "This is called the Republican Party. It's not called the Conservative Party," he said.[65] His fans were more enticed by his message of putting "America first" by tearing up trade deals and keeping out illegal immigrants. They also reveled in his "Make America Great Again" slogan, imprinted on red hats, which were pervasive at Trump gatherings.

Many voters were attracted as well to Trump's style and swagger. "When you vote for Trump," said one supporter, "it's almost giving a middle finger to the establishment or the status quo."[66] At rallies, shouts and fistfights sometimes broke out between Trump enthusiasts and anti-Trump protestors, and the candidate even seemed to condone violence against demonstrators. "Knock the crap out of 'em, would you," he told one Iowa crowd. "I promise you, I will pay the legal fees."[67] The discord bore a striking similarity to the furies that erupted during the 1968 George Wallace campaign.

But as Trump was turning the Republican Party upside down, none of his opponents seemed able or willing to take him on. Many believed his candidacy would crumple under the weight of accumulated controversies and saw no reason to brawl with him.

And despite his seeming popularity, Trump's early poll numbers rarely topped 30 percent. Thus every other candidate harbored dreams of becoming the non-Trump alternative who could defeat the frontrunner in a head-to-head matchup.

When the Iowa caucuses kicked off the voting, Cruz's popularity with social conservatives helped vault him to victory over Trump and Rubio by 28 to 24 to 23 percent. But in the New Hampshire primary eight days later, Trump topped the field by 20 points. After that, Trump won Nevada, South Carolina, and seven of eleven states on Super Tuesday. Republicans were stunned by how the contest was playing out. Romney, the party's most recent nominee, came forward to denounce Trump as a candidate who had "neither the temperament nor the judgment to be president."[68] Still, Trump kept winning. One strategist compared his candidacy to "Godzilla walking into a power plant. Everybody thought he'd blow up, and he just got stronger every time."[69]

Cruz, Rubio, and Kasich were the last three candidates left standing against Trump. But none of them were able to build a coalition big enough to topple Trump, who wrapped up the nomination in May and became the most surprising and controversial nominee since voters took over the process in 1972. Trump chose Indiana governor Mike Pence, a favorite of conservative and evangelical voters, as his running mate.

As stunning as Trump's victory was, his campaign actually overlapped in various ways with the Bernie Sanders movement, which tells us a lot about politics in 2016. The candidates were polar opposites, but both were political outsiders who railed against the globalized economy. And while Trump supporters were riled up about government and immigrants, and Sanders's followers were indignant with the financial elite, both factions wanted to upend politics and were united in anger over an economic system they felt was rigged against them.[70]

Both campaigns were also the product of a nominating process that was being transformed yet again. As we've seen, when voters were given power over nominations the parties could no longer act as filters against unorthodox candidacies. By the 2010s the door had opened wider to unconventional campaigns because candidates were able to build independent followings through social media or cable television, while raising millions of dollars via small online donations. Neither Trump nor Sanders had strong establishment ties, but they were able to take over (or nearly take over) a major political party with the support of an intensely loyal band of followers.

These churning political waters were manifest at both party conventions that summer. At the GOP meeting in Cleveland, numerous big-name Republicans stayed away, including Romney, McCain, and both President Bushes. But delegates didn't seem bothered that the establishment was spurning Trump. "They can stay home. . . . This is not their Republican Party anymore," said one person.[71]

In his acceptance speech Trump assailed Democrats for weakness and painted a dystopian picture of a country threatened by waves of crime, terrorism, and illegal immigration. "Our convention occurs at a moment of crisis for our nation," he said. "I alone can fix it."[72]

At the Democratic gathering in Philadelphia in late July, Clinton labored to calm the Sanders wing of the party, especially after the whistleblowing organization WikiLeaks released twenty thousand hacked emails from the Democratic National Committee (DNC), some of which showed party officials expressing anti-Sanders sentiment during the primaries. There was no evidence anyone had undermined the process, but the news inflamed party divisions and triggered protests from some Sanders delegates.[73]

Amid these challenges, Clinton made history as the first female presidential nominee of a major party. For her acceptance speech, she dressed in white, the color of the woman's suffrage movement, and emphasized a theme of community. "Powerful forces are threatening to pull as apart," she said. "We have to decide whether we all will work together so we can all rise together."

With that, the race to Election Day began. In early August, Clinton led by eight points in a *Washington Post*/ABC News poll, but it was a battle between two candidates with the highest unfavorable ratings of any presidential candidates ever.[74] Clinton then added to her unfavorables when she remarked at a private fundraiser, "You could put half of Trump's supporters into what I call the basket of deplorables." While her remarks were meant as a criticism of alt-right Trump voters, whom she described as "racist, sexist, homophobic, xenophobic," it seemed as if she were rebuking a wide swath of Americans.[75] From then on, "basket of deplorables" became shorthand for condemning Clinton as an elitist, and the gaffe plagued her in the same way that Romney's "47 percent" comment stuck to him in 2012.

Republicans were also persistent in pushing the story of Clinton's email controversy. Trump labeled her "Crooked Hillary," while his crowds chanted, "Lock her up!" and wore T-shirts that read "Hillary for Prison." Beyond this there was a campaign to discredit Clinton specifically with African Americans, young women, and Sanders supporters, with a goal of depressing Democratic turnout on Election Day.[76] As Trump campaign manager Steve Bannon put it, "My goal is that by November eighth, when you hear her name, you're gonna throw up."[77]

It didn't hurt matters that Trump was a master at steering the campaign narrative. Studies show he received at least $5 billion of earned media coverage during the contest, about $2 billion more than Clinton.[78] He used the media's penchant for reporting on controversy to his advantage and often drove the news with just a blast from his Twitter account. Ironically, he berated journalists, claiming, "If the disgusting and corrupt media covered me honestly . . . I would be beating Hillary by 20%."[79] The reality was that he and the press had a symbiotic relationship, because each Trump controversy generated higher interest in the news. Leslie Moonves, then president of CBS, remarked, "It may not be good for America, but it's damn good for CBS."[80]

In spite of Trump's mastery of the airwaves, Clinton maintained a steady polling lead into the fall. Then, on October 7, the race was shaken up by three momentous events on the same afternoon. At about 2:30 p.m., the U.S. intelligence community announced that Russia was unquestionably involved with the earlier theft of DNC

emails and was attempting "to interfere with the U.S. election process."[81] At 4:00 p.m., news broke of an eleven-year-old videotape
that showed Trump on the television show *Access Hollywood* making crude comments off camera about his approach to women.
And at 4:32 p.m., WikiLeaks released more hacked emails, these
stolen from John Podesta, chairman of the Clinton campaign.

The story that had the greatest immediate impact was that of
Trump's videotape. "I just start kissing them . . . I don't even wait,"
he said of his approach to women. "And when you're a star, they
let you do it. . . . Grab 'em by the pussy. You can do anything."[82] It
was one of the more stunning statements ever attributed to a presidential candidate, and during the following week nine women
came forward to say Trump had indeed kissed or touched them
against their will or forced himself on them. Afterward more than
thirty Republicans called on Trump to withdraw from the race.[83]

Trump, however, wasn't one to back down. He apologized but
also dismissed the remarks as "locker room banter."[84] More bra-
zenly he endeavored to change the narrative before the second
presidential debate on October 9 by holding a press conference
with several women who years earlier had accused former president Bill Clinton of sexual assault. At that night's debate, the candidates skipped the traditional predebate handshake, and Clinton
questioned Trump's "fitness to serve" as president. She brought
up his refusal to release his tax returns, questioning whether he'd
avoided paying income taxes or had conflicts of interest with foreign governments. Trump, for his part, accused Clinton of having
"tremendous hate in her heart," insinuated that she belonged "in
jail," and promised to have her investigated if he won.[85]

Clinton was judged by viewers as the debate winner, but the
advantage she gained was fleeting because her campaign still had
to deal with a steady drumbeat of news about Podesta's emails, as
WikiLeaks staggered their release to keep the story alive.[86] There
was nothing unusually damaging in the messages, except that it
put the word "email" back in the headlines. The news merged in
the public mind with the earlier controversy over Clinton's use
of private emails, although the stories were unrelated.

The news that Russia was trying to influence the election was perhaps the most significant of the three October 7 developments, but it received the least attention, unable to compete with Trump's words or Clinton's emails. Significantly, it was later revealed that Roger Stone, a GOP political operative and Trump confidant, knew about the WikiLeaks documents and advised the organization to "drop the Podesta emails immediately" after the Trump videotape story to divert the media's attention.[87]

This series of events left the nation flabbergasted. And there was more turbulence yet to come, including when Trump—who had long claimed the election was being "rigged" against him—suggested he might not accept the election results if he lost. "I will keep you in suspense," he said, surely the first instance of a presidential candidate making such a statement before an election.[88]

Finally, on October 28, just eleven days before the finish, another storm erupted when FBI director James Comey notified Congress that thousands of additional Clinton emails had been discovered and would be investigated. They were on a laptop used by Anthony Weiner, a former congressman who'd sent sexually explicit text messages to a teenage girl and who was the husband of a Clinton aide. The media universe exploded with more stories about the email controversy, now tied to a sex scandal. Trump dubbed the news "the biggest political scandal since Watergate" and suggested Clinton would be "under investigation for years."[89]

Comey was criticized for breaking Justice Department policy against announcing investigations prior to an election, but he was said to be concerned the FBI would otherwise be accused of protecting Clinton, who nearly everyone believed would be the next president.[90] The story dominated headlines for a week, during which time Clinton's polling lead was cut in half, from 6 to 3 points.[91] The FBI soon concluded the emails contained nothing new, leading Comey to close the investigation again on November 6.

The Comey news clearly altered the race's trajectory, though most analysts still expected Clinton to prevail on Election Day.[92] And Clinton did win the popular vote by nearly 2.9 million ballots, or 48.2 to 46.1 percent. But when Trump won Pennsylvania, Michigan, and Wisconsin by fewer than seventy-eight thousand votes combined, it propelled him to a stunning victory in the Electoral College, 306–232, marking the second time in sixteen years that the popular vote winner lost the electoral tally.[93] NBC News called it "an upset for the ages" after "one of the most bitter and wildly unpredictable campaigns in the nation's history."[94]

In the aftermath, observers scrambled to understand how a candidate who consistently trailed in national polls had prevailed. The polls, in fact, were fairly accurate, as Clinton won the popular vote by 2.1 percent when the final numbers had her leading by 3.2 percent, a difference in line with historical averages.[95] Clinton was defeated, simply, because she lost by less than 1 percent in three key battleground states in the industrial Midwest. This was due to several factors: Trump gained votes from working-class whites in the region; African American turnout declined from 2012; some liberals voted for a third-party candidate instead of the Democrat; and late-deciding voters broke heavily for Trump, driven by a drop in support for Clinton after the Comey letter.[96]

Another factor was the country's tumble into "negative partisanship," an early twenty-first-century phenomenon that saw voters become more driven by dislike for the opposition than by support for their own party.[97] One of the more remarkable statistics to come out of the 2016 contest was that Trump won the election even though more than 60 percent of voters found him *unqualified* to be president.[98] This, needless to say, is not a normal occurrence in presidential history. The country's extreme polarization meant that even Republicans who weren't thrilled with Trump as their nominee felt an obligation to support him. So for many voters it was a binary choice in which their dislike of Clinton overruled their discomfort with Trump.

In a fitting coda to the long, strange trip of the 2016 election, there was one last set of bombshell headlines in December and January, prior to the inauguration. That's when it was reported that U.S. intelligence agencies had "high confidence" that Russia, on the orders of President Vladimir Putin, actively interfered in the presidential campaign with the goals of undermining confidence in American democracy and of electing Trump.[99]

It was a staggering assessment, but evidence showed that Russia was behind the stolen emails passed to WikiLeaks, as well as a sophisticated effort to manipulate public opinion through social media campaigns and the planting of phony stories. Russian agents also worked to suppress the vote by urging Blacks and liberals to stay home rather than vote for "the lesser of two devils."[100] While there is no clear-cut proof that this changed the final vote, Russia was able to exploit the country's partisan divisions with strategies that at the very least harmonized with Trump campaign goals. It was a story that would continue unfolding for years to come.

Two Nations within a Nation

The country's shift from the Obama to the Trump presidencies between 2008 and 2016 appeared to be a severe case of electoral whiplash, one that defied easy explanation. In fact the two events were closely linked—"an earthquake and its aftershock," as the *New York Times* described it.[101]

Obama's election in 2008 was heralded as a sign that the country was growing more comfortable in its multicultural skin. The Obama coalition, which produced the biggest presidential victory in two decades, included large majorities of Blacks, Hispanics, and Asians, along with progressives, college-educated whites, and young voters, many of whom lived in cities. A cultural symbol of this new America even materialized during Obama's presidency, with the 2015 debut of the Broadway musical *Hamilton*. The show retold the story of America's founding, and did so by fusing hip-hop music with show tunes and using a multiracial, multiethnic cast to represent the Founding Fathers. It was, in the words of the show's creator, Lin-Manuel Miranda, "a story about America then, told by America now."[102]

But the Obama era, it turned out, wasn't quite the catalyst for racial harmony that some had imagined. It also kindled a backlash among those who weren't quite as gung-ho over the idea of a pluralistic society. It's not a coincidence that the birther movement erupted during these years to challenge Obama's American-ness. "It's as if my very presence in the White House had triggered a deep-seated panic, a sense that the natural order had been dis-rupted," Obama later wrote.[103]

Amid these cultural tensions, Trump burst onto the scene and turbocharged the racial polarization of the parties. After gaining attention in 2011 as a self-appointed spokesman for the birther movement, he rode to victory in 2016 on a wave of ethnonation-alist populism. Numerous studies have shown that the strongest predictor of support for his candidacy was neither economic anxi-ety nor explicit racism but a more nebulous perception that whites were being "treated unfairly relative to minorities."[104] Trump insin-uated that a "silent majority" of Americans was under attack by illegal immigrants, by Muslim terrorists, by people of color in crime-infested cities, and even by elites in their own country. Only an outsider like himself, he asserted, could take back the country and restore American greatness.[105]

None of these sentiments were new. They had surfaced all the way back in 1856 with the Know Nothings, and threads of Trump-ism were evident in the more recent Wallace, Buchanan, Perot, and Palin campaigns. Listen, for instance, to Buchanan in 1992: "When we take America back, we are going to make America great again, because there is nothing wrong with putting Amer-ica first."[106] While the attitudes may be familiar, however, no one had ever before won the presidency on Trump's platform. He did win, though, and he did so with a coalition that was whiter, more rural, more religious, less educated, and more culturally homoge-neous than the voters who'd propelled Obama to victory in 2008.

Once Trump was entrenched in office, he doubled down on ethnonationalism and effectively staged a takeover of the GOP. He became so popular with the base that he, in essence, became the Republican Party. When he ran for reelection four years later the GOP didn't even bother to write a new platform, instead promising to "continue to enthusiastically support the president's America-first agenda."[107] It mattered little that the president's agenda was vague and, aside from tax cuts and conservative judges, paid little heed to long-standing Republican issues, such as small government and free trade. That's because Trumpism was defined, in large part, by opposition. Opposition to Democrats, to elites, to cities, to political correctness, to globalization, and to any program that was perceived as being for undeserving recipients. Trump, in effect, merged the Southern strategy of Nixon, which pitted Americans of different races against each other, with the Gingrich tactic of persuading voters that Democrats were anti-American.

Trumpism, like Obamaism, was also driven by the changes that were transforming American life. People were contending with a dramatic rise in inequality and with labor market disruptions caused by technology and globalization. Because of an upsurge in immigration from non-European nations, American communities had more diverse populations than ever before in the country's history. And the culture was experiencing a wave of changes in gender roles, sexual identities, and family structures. Like tectonic plates, these forces all pushed against each other below the surface, until eventually the landscape cracked and new political energies were unleashed.

Obama and Trump were the political figures who first tapped into these energies and emerged as the most prominent symbols of two divergent movements. One side represented the values of a more diverse, secular, cosmopolitan, urban America. They tended to be more well-educated and open to the transformations being wrought by globalization, immigration, and shifting societal values. The other half was representative of a white, Christian, rural America. These voters saw themselves as upholding traditional values and were less enthused by the upheavals that had reshaped American culture. They were "two nations-within-a-nation" that became locked in a cold civil war.[108]

The danger for the country was that elections were becoming a battle over cultural identities rather than governing philosophies. As the political analyst William Schneider noted, "Both the right and the left draw support from people who feel certain about their own values and resentful that the rest of society does not embrace them."[109]

A realignment of the political landscape was plainly underway, although the road ahead was unclear. Gingrich, for one, suggested that one of these coalitions would "simply defeat the other. There is no room for compromise."[110] Or these partisan tribes could instead settle into a long struggle for political supremacy, with each side winning battles here and there, until new issues and coalitions form some years or decades down the road. But this is where American politics stood as 2020 dawned.

2020: A Divided Nation Navigates a Tumultuous Election

When Trump became the country's forty-fifth president on January 20, 2017, he delivered an inaugural address in line with the style and rhetoric of his campaign. "From this day forward, it's going to be only America first," he declared, offering a nationalist philosophy of government. The new president painted a gloomy picture of the current state of the nation, describing a landscape engulfed by crime, drugs, poverty, abandoned factories, and broken schools. "This American carnage stops right here and stops right now," he said.[111]

With that began one of the most boisterous presidencies ever, culminating in what was surely one of the more unusual presidential campaigns in the nation's history.

President Trump did notch several achievements during his term, including a $1.5 trillion tax cut, criminal justice reform to reduce mass incarceration, the establishment of the Space Force, and the reshaping of the federal judiciary with a near record number of appointments. The economy continued to grow, as the expansion that began in Obama's first term became the longest recovery on record in July 2019.[112]

But Trump's tenure was marked as well by a near constant stream of controversy. Among other things, he signed a travel ban barring visitors from seven predominantly Muslim nations, shut down the government over a dispute about funding for a border wall, and maintained there were "fine people on both sides" after white supremacists and counterprotesters clashed at a rally in Charlottesville, Virginia.[113] He also mounted a historically unprecedented drive to tear down his predecessor's legacy.[114] He pulled the United States out of the Paris Climate Agreement, the Trans-Pacific Partnership, and the Iran nuclear deal; rolled back efforts to rebuild relations with Cuba; overturned scores of environmental regulations; and came within one Senate vote of repealing Obamacare. This pile-up of provocations was one factor that helped Democrats win back the House of Representatives in the 2018 midterms with a net gain of forty seats.

Not one of these events, however, touched on the biggest controversies of all during the Trump years: those related to foreign influence in American elections.

First was the continuing story of Russian intervention in the 2016 campaign. The Justice Department in 2017 appointed a special counsel, Robert Mueller, to examine Russian election interference. During the next two years, Mueller uncovered evidence that Russia had indeed hacked Democratic emails and had promoted a social media campaign designed to sow discord, disparage Clinton, and boost Trump.[115] He indicted twenty-five Russian nationals on charges related to these activities and obtained convictions or guilty pleas from various Trump campaign officials, some for lying to investigators or for unrelated financial crimes. Trump himself was scrutinized, but not charged, for obstruction of justice for trying to hinder the investigation. Notably, though, the special counsel did not find any compelling evidence of cooperation between Russian agents and the Trump campaign.

Almost as soon as this story receded from the headlines, news emerged of a second tale of electoral meddling involving a different government. This controversy erupted in August 2019 when a whistleblower from the intelligence community expressed concern that Trump was enlisting foreign assistance for the 2020 election. Trump had asked the Ukrainian president to launch an investigation of former vice president Joe Biden, then a leading contender for the Democratic nomination. The premise was that Biden had pressured Ukraine in 2015 to fire its top prosecutor, allegedly to stop an investigation of a company that employed his son. Numerous investigations failed to turn up evidence to support the claim, but Trump held up $391 million in military aid in hopes that the announcement of a Ukrainian inquiry would tar Biden with the taint of corruption.[116]

When the House of Representatives looked into the charges, the Trump administration blocked witnesses from testifying and refused to turn over subpoenaed documents. Some officials testified anyway and supported the allegation that the president tried to leverage help from Ukraine. In December the House voted to impeach Trump for abuse of power in soliciting foreign assistance against a political rival and for obstruction of Congress. The vote was almost entirely along party lines, and Trump reacted by calling it a "witch hunt" and a "hoax," as he had with Mueller's investigation.[117]

After the Senate trial that followed, Trump was acquitted, 52–48 and 53–47 on the two charges, with Republicans arguing that his actions were perhaps inappropriate but not serious enough to warrant conviction. The one Republican who did vote to convict the president, Senator Mitt Romney, asserted that Trump was "guilty of an appalling abuse of public trust."[118]

Trump thus became the third president to survive impeachment, following Andrew Johnson and Bill Clinton, but he would be the first one to run for reelection after his trial. Coincidentally Trump was acquitted on February 5, 2020, just two days after the Iowa caucuses that kicked off the next presidential race.

The Democrats in 2020 had a record-setting field of twenty-six presidential candidates, including six women and six representatives of the Black, Hispanic, Asian, and Pacific Islander communities. In the end, however, the main contenders were Biden, Senators Bernie Sanders of Vermont, Elizabeth Warren of Massachusetts, and Amy Klobuchar of Minnesota, and former mayors Michael Bloomberg of New York and Pete Buttigieg of South Bend, Indiana.

The nomination contest played out as a battle between the party's liberal and moderate wings, with candidates differing over whether American politics and institutions needed to be radically transformed or merely renovated.[119] Sanders and Warren came down on the side of radical transformation, with Sanders campaigning as a democratic socialist who wanted to provide universal health care and free college tuition. Biden and others took what they saw as a more pragmatic approach to the same issues, such as by allowing more people to buy into Medicare rather than replacing the existing system of private insurance.

Sanders emerged as the favored candidate of liberals over Warren, building on the following he'd gained in 2016. Among moderates, Biden was the early favorite, though Klobuchar and Buttigieg gained support as centrist alternatives. Each candidate had weaknesses, however. Some considered Sanders too left-wing to win a national election; Biden seemed to represent the party's past more than its future; Buttigieg was just thirty-eight, and his only elected experience was as mayor of a medium-size city; and quite a few voters resisted Klobuchar and Warren because of post-2016 fears that a woman couldn't defeat Trump.[120] This smorgasbord of options caused some Democrats to become almost "paralyzed by fear of making the wrong choice."[121] Even the *New York Times* made the unprecedented move of endorsing two candidates—Klobuchar and Warren—because, the editors wrote, "both the radical and the realist models warrant serious consideration."[122]

The early voting reflected this bewilderment. In the Iowa caucuses on February 3, Sanders and Buttigieg finished in a virtual tie for first, at about 26 percent each. Sanders won the New Hampshire primary eight days later, but again with only 25.6 percent of the vote, edging Buttigieg and Klobuchar. Biden placed fourth and fifth in the two contests, causing observers to all but write off his candidacy. This convinced the moderate Bloomberg to make a late entry into the race, further muddling the field. Even after another Sanders win in the Nevada caucuses, many observers believed no Democrat would emerge with a majority of delegates. "I just don't see any of the candidates coming in and winning the first ballot [at the convention]," said one Democratic insider at the time.[123]

It was at that moment that the contest shifted suddenly and dramatically in a new direction when Biden made his last stand on February 29 in South Carolina. A coalition of Blacks and moderate Democrats helped him thump the field by 28 percentage points. It was Biden's first win in four contests, but it opened the floodgates. Coming off weak finishes in South Carolina, Klobuchar and Buttigieg suspended their campaigns to unite moderates and give Biden a clearer lane from which to run against Sanders. In the Super Tuesday contests on March 3, Biden swept past Sanders, Warren, and Bloomberg, winning ten of fourteen states. Many voters broke for Biden based on the tactical calculation that he was the remaining candidate best positioned to defeat Trump in the general election.

One month later Biden became the presumptive nominee when Sanders was the last major contender to withdraw from the race, on April 8. By then, however, the news caused barely a ripple. That's because, just as Biden was taking control of the nomination battle, the nation and the world were besieged by an extraordinary turn of events that drowned out almost all other national news.

A novel coronavirus, named COVID-19, had emerged in China in January, and during the next two months it tore across the globe. The World Health Organization declared a pandemic on March 11, eight days after Super Tuesday. With stunning quickness, by April 1 more than two hundred thousand Americans had been infected, school districts were shut down, most of the nation was under a stay-at-home order, and millions of people had been thrown out of work. It was the worst infectious disease outbreak in a century, since the 1918 flu.[124]

Another national crisis then erupted in late spring. On May 25 a Black man named George Floyd, who was arrested for allegedly using a counterfeit bill, died when a white Minneapolis police officer knelt on his neck on a public street for almost nine minutes. A video taken by a bystander showed a helpless Floyd gasping "I can't breathe" shortly before he died. The intensity of the video shocked Americans. For many, it was the last straw after a string of violent incidents between police and the Black community, and it triggered a nationwide uprising, with tens of thousands of people of all races turning out to protest in at least 140 cities. Most demonstrations were nonviolent, but some were marked by violence, arson, looting, and clashes with police, a scenario that triggered yet more controversy in the midst of the election.

By the end of May more than one hundred thousand people had died from COVID-19, and 40 million Americans had lost their job, the biggest surge in unemployment since the Great Depression.[125] In the span of just a few months, the nation had cartwheeled from a presidential impeachment to a deadly pandemic, a grim economic crisis, and widespread racial protests. It was a peculiar case of history seeming to replicate itself, as the convergence of traumas evoked memories of the two-year period between 1918 and 1920, when a flu pandemic, racial riots, a recession, labor strife, and anarchist bombings all combined to batter and exhaust the nation just before a presidential election.

On that note, the contest staggered into summer and into uncharted waters. There was no playbook for running a campaign during a pandemic—when Americans were being encouraged to wear masks in public, practice social distancing, and avoid large gatherings—not to mention doing so while also dealing with ongoing racial protests. These demonstrations were upending the national conversation in real time, and even influenced the choice of Biden's running mate. He had already promised to put a female on the ticket; during the summer pressure grew for this nominee to be a woman of color to better reflect the national moment and the demographics of the Democratic Party. This helped solidify Biden's choice of California senator Kamala Harris, who had herself run for the presidential nomination. As the daughter of Jamaican and Indian immigrants, Harris made history as both the first Black woman and the first Asian American on a major party ticket.

As summer unfurled across a beleaguered nation, the two presidential campaigns took divergent approaches to the 2020 election. Biden opted to follow public health recommendations for wearing masks and avoiding meetings with large groups, so he turned the basement of his Delaware home into a television studio. He ran the equivalent of an old-style front-porch campaign, this one aimed at voters' computer screens and televisions, as politics became a series of broadcast interviews, social media posts, podcasts, and virtual town halls.

Trump, on the other hand, downplayed the threat from COVID-19, telling Americans that, "like a miracle, it will disappear."[126] He returned to staging full-scale rallies and mocked others for wearing masks. The result was that a culture war broke out over mask wearing, some of his supporters claiming that state and local mandates were a violation of their rights.

The party conventions that summer reflected the opposing styles and messages embraced by Biden and Trump, as the candidates presented dueling dystopian visions of a country governed by their opponent.

Democrats gave American politics its first-ever virtual convention beginning on August 17. Gone was the four-day show of live speeches in front of cheering, sign-waving delegates, which had endured in some form since 1832. In its place was a made-for-television production of shorter talks and virtual gatherings, taped in various locales around the country. "The current president has cloaked America in darkness for much too long—too much anger, too much fear, too much division," Biden said in his acceptance speech. "Here and now, I give you my word: If you entrust me with the presidency, I will draw on the best of us, not the worst. . . . It is time for us, for we the people, to come together."[127]

This was the message Biden carried into the fall campaign. He framed the election as a "battle for the soul of the nation," with the future of democracy at risk in a second Trump term.[128] While Biden introduced proposals to combat the coronavirus, expand health care access, and invest in infrastructure projects and clean energy, he also presented himself as a calming influence who would strive to rebuild trust and bipartisanship. "I campaigned as a Democrat, but I will govern as an American president," he promised.[129]

One week later the GOP convention was a spectacle of an entirely different nature. The Republicans permitted live crowds for some speeches, and staged events at the White House, which had traditionally been off limits for political activity. In his own address, Trump framed the election as a vote between two wildly distinct alternatives: "At no time before have voters faced a clearer choice between two parties. . . . Your vote will decide whether we protect law-abiding Americans or whether we give free rein to violent anarchists and agitators and criminals who threaten our citizens."[130]

Trump's law-and-order pitch was aimed at voters he believed were reeling from the ongoing racial protests, particularly since more demonstrations broke out on the eve of the GOP convention after another police shooting of an unarmed Black man, this time in Kenosha, Wisconsin. It was a replay of the law-and-order message that Republicans had used against Democrats in other campaigns going back to 1968, and it was a variation on the theme Trump himself had employed four years earlier. In 2016 he railed against Hispanic immigrants and Muslim terrorists, whereas in 2020 it was left-wing protesters who presumably threatened the nation. It was another iteration of the time-honored tactic of fostering an us-versus-them dynamic and convincing people to vote based on fear of the other.

By fall the country had ridden a rollercoaster of drama for nearly a year, but 2020 wasn't finished with its surprises. On September 18 Supreme Court Justice Ruth Bader Ginsburg died, less than seven weeks before Election Day. The GOP rushed to fill the vacancy, despite having refused to consider an Obama nomination in 2016 for a seat that opened nine months before that year's election.

Eleven days later, on September 29, the country witnessed the most jarring presidential debate ever held. President Trump attacked, bullied, and interrupted his way through the event, with the result that little of substance was discussed. He interrupted so many times that, at one point, Biden sighed "Will you shut up, man?" Biden called Trump a racist, a liar, and a clown, which in other years would have been considered lamentable breaches of decorum. But all the rules had been broken during the Trump era. The debate was described as an "epic moment

HISTORY IN THE MAKING

of national shame" and "a sad example of the state of American democracy."[131] Biden's performance wasn't extraordinary, but he was steady and conventional next to a president who appeared to be blowing a fuse, and that was enough for voters in every major poll to award Biden a victory.[132]

Then, on October 2, President Trump announced that he and First Lady Melania Trump had tested positive for the coronavirus. After experiencing a high fever and low oxygen levels, the president was hospitalized for three days. This was the bookend to a wild two-week news cycle in the closing month of a crisis-filled election year.

Trump did recover his health and went back to holding live rallies. He also continued to hurl charges at Biden and the Democrats at a staggering pace. He accused them of being Marxists and "anti-American radicals." He contended that various political opponents, including former president Obama, should be arrested. He suggested Biden wasn't mentally competent and would "prolong the pandemic," "take away [Americans'] guns," "defund the police," and "abolish the suburbs." He even accused Biden, a practicing Catholic who often carried rosary beads in his pocket, of being "against God" and of wanting to "wipe away every trace of religion from national life."[133] This bluster was part of the long-established Trumpian style, but set against the sweep of American history it was an unparalleled barrage of invective from a sitting president.

Just as startling was Trump's insistence that the election would be fraudulent. He claimed it would be the "most corrupt election in our nation's history" and refused to say whether he'd accept the results or cooperate in a peaceful transfer of power.[134] "The only way we're going to lose this election is if the election is rigged," he told supporters.[135]

Biden, meanwhile, maintained a more cautious and restrained campaign. He focused on making the election a referendum on Trump's leadership, while suggesting he could tamp down the vitriol and lead the country out of crisis. In his closing argument, he told voters, "This is our opportunity to leave the dark, angry politics of the past four years behind us. . . . I run to unite this nation. And to heal this nation."[136] He entered the final week with a comfortable lead in the polls, in a race that had remained remarkably stable amid all the drama, even as Trump retained hopes of a second consecutive Electoral College victory.

In another quirk of this contest, owing to the pandemic about 100 million people cast ballots before Election Day, many of them by mail. And whether it was the ease of voting from home or the emotions that swelled during a divisive election, voter turnout in 2020 smashed all modern records. More than 66 percent of eligible voters cast a ballot, the highest percentage in more than a century, since the election of 1900.[137]

However, since not every state counted its mail-in ballots ahead of time, Election Day turned into Election Week. Biden took a decisive lead in the popular vote, but key states remained undecided while election workers counted ballots. This led to the unusual situation of the incumbent president essentially declaring victory on election night, in a 2:30 a.m. speech from the White House, even though the electoral vote was undecided. Trump said the early lead he took in certain swing states that day should be the legitimate result and that any mail-in ballots not yet counted were somehow fraudulent. Two days later he insisted, "If you count the legal votes, I easily win."[138]

In the days ahead, crowds of Trump supporters protested what they claimed was an illegitimate election. In states where the president led the early vote count, the demonstrators shouted, "Stop the count!" and in states where he was behind they chanted, "Count the votes!"[139] Despite the protests, Michigan and Wisconsin were soon called for Biden, and on Saturday, November 7, Pennsylvania's electoral votes clinched his victory. Arizona and Georgia were later added to Biden's total, giving him a 306–232 win in the Electoral College to go with a 51 to 47 percent victory in the popular vote. At seventy-eight, Biden became the oldest president ever, while Harris made history as the country's first female vice president.

Although Trump lost the election, he saw a considerable jump in his popular vote total from 2016, notably by attracting support-ers who hadn't voted in that election. But while Trump received 11 million more votes than he had four years earlier, Biden received 15 million more votes than did Hillary Clinton. The story of the campaign was that white, rural, and working-class voters doubled down on support for Trump, while suburban, college-educated vot-ers went with Biden. This made the country's urban-rural divide more pronounced, as Trump won 2,547 of the nation's counties to 509 for Biden, while Biden prevailed in more densely popu-lated regions that represented 71 percent of the country's eco-nomic activity.[140]

Another example of this divide could be seen in the variance between the popular and electoral votes. Biden won the national vote by just over 7 million ballots. His 51.3 percent was the sec-ond best performance of any presidential candidate in thirty-two years, behind only Obama's 2008 victory.

And yet Biden was just forty-three thousand votes away from losing the election.

It doesn't seem possible, but it's true. It's because Biden won close races in Arizona, Georgia, and Wisconsin by fewer than forty-three thousand combined votes.[141] If those three states had instead gone to Trump, the Electoral College would have finished in a historic 269–269 tie. The election would then have been forced into the House of Representatives for the first time since 1824, where each state would have had one vote. And even though Democrats held a majority of House seats, Republicans controlled a majority of state delegations, which would have enabled them to reelect Trump. Such a vote would have ignited an inferno of controversy, but Trump would nevertheless have gone on to a sec-ond term despite being crushed in the popular vote.

Fortunately the country was spared this drama. Still, the end of the balloting didn't mean the controversies were over, because for the first time ever an American president declined to accept the legitimacy of the vote. Trump did what he had long telegraphed he might do, and refused to concede defeat. His campaign filed more than fifty lawsuits alleging improprieties in the vote across a handful of swing states. His advisors also unleashed a torrent of allegations, including that computer software with a connection to Venezuelan socialists was responsible for flipping millions of Trump votes to Biden and that truckloads of fraudulent ballots were delivered to voting sites in the middle of the night.[142]

The courts found no evidence of fraud or misconduct and rejected nearly every case. One Trump-appointed judge even wrote, "Charges of unfairness are serious. But calling an election unfair does not make it so. Charges require specific allegations and then proof. We have neither here."[143]

Still, the Trump team continued to cast doubt on the vote. The president tried to convince officials to hold off on certifying the results, on the theory that state legislatures would then be able to appoint electors who supported him, irrespective of the popular vote. And eighteen states, led by Texas and joined by 126 members of Congress, asked the Supreme Court to invalidate the vote in Pennsylvania, Michigan, Wisconsin, and Georgia. The court rejected the request without a hearing. It was nevertheless a striking effort to overturn the electoral result, which led to this disquieting headline in *The Atlantic*: "The GOP Abandons Democracy."[144]

The chairman of the Joint Chiefs of Staff, Gen. Mark Milley, expressed alarm at the time over threats to the stability of the government. He was concerned the president might fuel further unrest and try to use the military to maintain power, but Milley insisted the armed forces would remain out of politics. "We're going to have a peaceful transfer of power. We're going to land this plane safely," he said.[145]

There is no way to overstate how unprecedented this was in comparison to more than two centuries of presidential history. Not one of Trump's defeated predecessors, stretching back to John Adams in 1800, had ever tried to overturn the results of an election. In the end, the institutions of democracy held in 2020, but only because individual state officials insisted on following their own election laws, sometimes even in the face of death threats from Trump loyalists.[146] Even if the tactics ultimately failed, however, the scheme was harmful to the country's democracy, and it delegitimized Biden's presidency for millions of voters. A month after the election, 222 of 249 Republicans in Congress still hadn't acknowledged Biden's victory, while a poll showed that 70 percent of Republicans didn't believe the president-elect had won a "free and fair" election.[147]

Biden's election was finally confirmed when the Electoral College voted on December 14, although the movement to deny the election results persisted. January 6, 2021, when Congress met to confirm the Electoral College vote, was one of the more shocking days in the history of American democracy. After a speech by President Trump in which he claimed the election was "rigged" and vowed he would "never concede," thousands of his supporters marched on the Capitol, hoping to prevent Congress from counting the electoral votes.[148] Protesters forced their way past police barricades and into the Capitol, where they ransacked congressional offices and occupied the Senate and House chambers. Vice President Mike Pence and Speaker of the House Nancy Pelosi were evacuated by the Secret Service; senators, representatives, and staff members sheltered in safe rooms or locked themselves in offices, while police and the National Guard worked to regain control of the building. By the time it was over, five people were dead, including one police officer. It was the first time the Capitol had been breached since the War of 1812, when British forces burned the building while invading Washington in 1814.

The next day, newspaper front pages across the country blared headlines such as "Pro-Trump Mobs Storm US Capitol" (*USA Today*), "Insurrection" (*Baltimore Sun*), and "Democracy Attacked" (*Hartford Courant*).[149] Despite the dramatic events, Congress reconvened later the same night to continue counting the electoral votes. Eight Republican senators and 139 representatives objected to the results from at least one state, but Biden's victory was affirmed.[150]

One week later, still reeling from the attack on the Capitol, the House of Representatives on January 13 impeached President Trump for "incitement of insurrection," with ten Republicans joining Democrats to support the charges. This made Trump the first president to be impeached twice and the first to be charged with inciting insurrection. But he was out of office by the time the trial was held in February, and the Senate couldn't muster the two-thirds vote necessary to convict him. Many Republicans suggested the vote was irrelevant or unconstitutional because Trump was no longer president, although a conviction could have barred him from running for office again. The vote was 57–43 to convict Trump, as seven Republican senators voted with all the Democrats. It was the largest bipartisan vote ever for an impeachment conviction but still ten votes shy of two-thirds.

The election of 2020 thus joined the elections of 1800, 1860, 1876, and 2000 on the list of those contests that have generated the most postelection controversy and drama. This one, however, stood alone in marking the first time that a sitting president actively worked to deny the result of the vote. In the end, the transfer of power did take place peacefully on January 20, 2021. Washington was lined with National Guard troops for security, the National Mall was mostly empty because of the coronavirus pandemic still raging in the country, and Trump was the first president since Andrew Johnson in 1869 to skip the inauguration of his successor, but the transfer was peaceful nonetheless.

"Through a crucible for the ages, America has been tested anew and America has risen to the challenge," said President Biden, in his inaugural address. "We've learned again that democracy is precious. Democracy is fragile. And at this hour, my friends, democracy has prevailed."[151]

Epilogue

The Past, Present, and Future of Politics in America

There have been fifty-nine presidential elections in U.S. history, from the 1789 vote for George Washington to the 2020 contest that sent Joe Biden to the White House. Some of these were momentous, history-rattling elections, while others were more mundane, but each one was captivating in its own time and its own way. One of the reasons I was attracted to this subject was for the opportunity to tell the story of these contests, which have fascinated me for as long as I can remember. I wanted to gather in a single volume some of the tales, strategies, and anecdotes behind every presidential campaign in U.S. history.

But my other goal, as I've noted, was to present these elections as chapters in the ongoing narrative of American democracy. Because while each contest may stand on its own as a story, it is simultaneously linked to all the electoral battles that preceded it, and my aim was to explore what past elections can tell us about contemporary politics.

The most obvious manifestation of these connections are in certain themes that resurface throughout presidential history—for instance, the immigration battles that intermittently overwhelm national politics, as in the 1850s, 1920s, and 2010s, when some Americans believed their culture was slipping away in the face of a rising tide of immigrants from Ireland or Italy or Mexico. However, in an effort to consider more far-reaching implications of what the past can tell us about the present and future of presidential elections, I'd like to wrap up by discussing two other notable features of contemporary politics that deserve attention.

First is the realignment of American politics that is taking place before our eyes. Realignments can seem to happen all at once, as in 1860 or 1932, or more slowly, as with the conservative ascendance that crested in 1980, but every major shift is preceded by years of changes to the political landscape. Lincoln's election came twelve years after the United States acquired new territory from Mexico, exacerbating the debate over slavery in the West, and forty years after the Missouri Compromise. Reagan's presidency was sixteen years after Goldwater conservatism upended the GOP and thirty-two years after the Dixiecrats first tilted Southern states away from the Democratic Party. Political realignments, it seems, happen "gradually and then suddenly," to borrow a phrase from Hemingway.[1]

Signs of a realignment today are pervasive. Evidence includes recent shifts in the electoral map, President Trump's upending of the traditional GOP agenda, and a range of new issues that are eclipsing the big- versus small-government debates that animated much of the twentieth century. Americans now are dealing with changes wrought by globalization; by technological advances with computers, the internet, and artificial intelligence; by climate change; by the advent of new forms of employment and career options; and by the country's transformation into a multiracial and multiethnic democracy. All of this will inevitably lead to a new politics.

In many ways, today's landscape resembles that of the early twentieth century, when the second industrial revolution and various social changes caused tremendous upheaval in American society. People were leaving farms for factory jobs in cities, inequality was on the rise, the nature of work was changing, immigrants from southern and eastern Europe were pouring into the country, and new technologies were transforming old ways of life. This is when the progressive-versus-conservative debate arose and new political coalitions were forged. The Democrats of 1892 were a conservative, antigovernment party, but by 1932 they'd morphed into a liberal, progovernment movement. Why? Because the ground shifted. The issues changed, and so did the agendas of the major parties. Something similar is afoot today. And while we don't know where this new road is leading, it seems probable that the Obama and Trump elections were the first shots of a coming transformation of the political landscape.

There are various ways in which the major parties could be reshaped in the coming years. The Democrats might form a governing majority with an agenda that caters both to suburban moderates and left-wing populists. The Republicans might construct a coalition of the conservative working class. A populist party could bring together the extremes of both left and right as an anti-elitist, pro-nationalist movement. The Democrats could morph into more of a liberal, social justice party. The GOP could double down on Trumpian ethnonationalism. One of these factions could form a third party.[2] Or none of the above. All we know is that change is coming. It isn't the first time this has happened in American politics, and it won't be the last. We're just fortunate (or unfortunate) enough to be living through the cataclysm.

The second topic to address is a good one on which to end this book: the current state of American democracy. The United States has weathered numerous crises in its history, including a Civil War that nearly ripped the country apart and a Great Depression that gave rise to autocratic movements of both the right and left. The country withstood these tempests by respecting traditions that stretched back to the founding era and by insisting on the need to preserve democracy for future Americans. "Freedom is a fragile thing," said Reagan, "and is never more than one generation away from extinction. It is not ours by inheritance; it must be fought for and defended constantly by each generation."[3]

But now, in the first decades of the twenty-first century, the United States finds itself at an almost unfathomable crossroads. The past few decades have seen a dramatic decline of faith in government, the overturning of time-honored political traditions, and the rise of a polarized electorate in which opponents are frequently seen as the enemy. Studies show the country stumbling toward autocracy, regressing on so many benchmarks that it's on a path from which just one in five democracies has ever recovered.[4] It's encouraging that America's democratic institutions prevailed in 2020 despite efforts to overturn the vote, but alarm bells are still wailing. The reality is that most democracies today don't perish dramatically after a coup; they die a slow death at the hands of elected leaders who erode democratic norms.[5]

This all brings to mind the oft-told story about Benjamin Franklin, who, during the Constitutional Convention, was asked what sort of government the delegates were creating. "A republic, if you can keep it," he replied.[6] That answer hangs in the air still. *If you can keep it.* The Founders were well aware of conditions that led to the fall of the Roman Republic many centuries earlier, which in some cases were strikingly similar to our own challenges today. Mike Duncan, in *The Storm Before the Storm*, notes that the declining years of Rome were characterized by such factors as "rising economic inequality, dislocation of traditional ways of life, increasing political polarization, [and] the breakdown of unspoken rules of political conduct."[7]

What is poignant about this decline in the democratic vitality of the United States is that it appears linked to racial discord. The country is suffering through its most extreme divisions since the Civil War era, and this latest bout of polarization began with the convulsions of the 1960s, after which the electorate became more divided over racial anxieties and cultural issues. During the years when the country was governed primarily by whites, note Steven Levitsky and Daniel Ziblatt in their book, *How Democracies Die*, neither party "was likely to view the other as an existential threat."[8] But once Blacks were fully welcomed into American democracy, polarization grew and the parties became more firmly differentiated by race. This is what makes the current moment so perilous. The most treacherous path forward is for people of color to gather in one party while an opposing faction stands for white nationalism. A better course would be for both parties to forge identities that attract multiracial coalitions so that elections can focus more on ideology and less on fear of the other.

In the late eighteenth century, the United States launched a great experiment in democracy that inspired people around the world. America in the twenty-first century has the opportunity to perfect the first truly multiracial democracy. If it fails, the future is ominous. If it succeeds, America can again serve as an inspiration for small-d democrats everywhere. Let's hope it's the latter, because it's my hope—and I'm sure yours, as well—that America's presidential history continues to be written for centuries yet to come.

Notes

Introduction

1. Tocqueville, *Democracy in America*, 152.
2. Abraham Lincoln to Joshua Speed, August, 24, 1855, Lincoln, Selected Speeches and Writings.

1. The Founding Generation

1. John Adams to Abigail Adams, January 14, 1797, Adams Family Papers.
2. Ferling, *Adams vs. Jefferson*, 57.
3. McCullough, *John Adams*, 405.
4. Larson, *The Return of George Washington*, 283–86; Ellis, *His Excellency*, 184–85.
5. Bowen, *Miracle at Philadelphia*, 55.
6. Unger, *Mr. President*, 38.
7. Bowen, *Miracle at Philadelphia*, 62; Jones, *The American Presidency*, 10.
8. Ellis, *The Quartet*, 196–97; Larson, *The Return of George Washington*, 245.
9. Unger, *Mr. President*, 18.
10. Wood, *Revolutionary Characters*, 32.
11. Ellis, *The Quartet*, 196.
12. Ellis, *His Excellency*, 183–84.
13. Larson, *The Return of George Washington*, 254.
14. *Presidential Elections, 1789–2004*, 18.
15. Coe, *You Never Forget Your First*, 149.
16. Wood, *The Idea of America*, 244; Amar, *America's Constitution*, 135–36; Coe, *You Never Forget Your First*, 122.
17. Lorant, *The Glorious Burden*, 37.
18. Breen, *George Washington's Journey*, 2.
19. Ellis, *His Excellency*, 238–39.

20. Brands, *Andrew Jackson*, 74–75.

21. Wood, *Friends Divided*, 220.

22. Lorant, *The Glorious Burden*, 48.

23. Ferling, *Adams vs. Jefferson*, 90.

24. Wood, *Friends Divided*, 284.

25. Lorant, *The Glorious Burden*, 50; *Presidential Elections, 1789–2004*, 19.

26. Wood, *Friends Divided*, 286–87.

27. Weisberger, *America Afire*, 228; Wood, *The Idea of America*, 262.

28. Ferling, *Adams vs. Jefferson*, 76.

29. McCullough, *John Adams*, 505.

30. Wood, *Friends Divided*, 305.

31. Ferling, *Adams vs. Jefferson*, 106.

32. Wood, *Friends Divided*, 304–5.

33. Larson, *A Magnificent Catastrophe*, 35; Ferling, *Jefferson and Hamilton*, 299–300.

34. Raphael, *Mr. President*, 221.

35. *Presidential Elections, 1789–2004*, 20.

36. Weston, *The Runner-Up Presidency*, 67.

37. Larson, *A Magnificent Catastrophe*, 100–104; Ferling, *Adams vs. Jefferson*, 127–31.

38. Ferling, *Adams vs. Jefferson*, 188–89.

39. Larson, *A Magnificent Catastrophe*, 252.

40. Ferling, *Adams vs. Jefferson*, 190–95.

41. Raphael, *Mr. President*, 237.

42. Brookhiser, *Founding Father*, 103.

43. Weisberger, *America Afire*, 26.

44. Michener, *Presidential Lottery*, 46.

45. Raphael, *Mr. President*, 49.

46. Weston, *The Runner-Up Presidency*, 118; Amar, *America's Constitution*, 155.

47. James Madison to George Hay, August 23, 1823, Madison Papers, 1723 to 1859.

48. Michener, *Presidential Lottery*, 23.

49. Johnson, *A History of the American People*, 248–49; Ferling, *Jefferson and Hamilton*, 349.

50. Ellis, *American Sphinx*, 242.

51. Johnson, *A History of the American People*, 252.

52. Lorant, *The Glorious Burden*, 76.

53. Lorant, *The Glorious Burden*, 77.

54. Cunningham, *In Pursuit of Reason*, 319.

55. Borneman, *1812*, 40.

56. Stewart, *Madison's Gift*, 303.

57. Wilentz, *The Rise of American Democracy*, 132.

58. Lorant, *The Glorious Burden*, 87.

59. Stewart, *Madison's Gift*, 241.

60. Brookhiser, *James Madison*, 197.

61. Stewart, *Madison's Gift*, 244.

62. Brookhiser, *James Madison*, 197–98.

63. Wilentz, *The Rise of American Democracy*, 159.

64. Borneman, *1812*, 88.

65. Borneman, *1812*, 231.

66. Johnson, *A History of the American People*, 266.

67. Borneman, *1812*, 244–48.

68. Johnson, *A History of the American People*, 278.

69. Stewart, *Madison's Gift*, 268.

70. Wilentz, *The Rise of American Democracy*, 165–66; Borneman, *1812*, 253–56.

71. Borneman, *1812*, 257–59, 296.

72. Johnson, *A History of the American People*, 312.

73. Lorant, *The Glorious Burden*, 101.

74. Reynolds, *Waking Giant*, 21–22.

75. Wilentz, *The Rise of American Democracy*, 203.

76. Parsons, *The Birth of Modern Politics*, 64.

77. Johnson, *A History of the American People*, 312; Reynolds, *Waking Giant*, 33.

78. Reichley, *The Life of the Parties*, 30.

79. Cole, *Vindicating Andrew Jackson*, 197.

80. James Madison, *Federalist No. 10*, in Hamilton, Madison, and Jay, *The Federalist Papers*, 78–79.

81. Reichley, *The Life of the Parties*, 29.

82. Brookhiser, *James Madison*, 188.

2. The Rise of the Parties

1. Wilentz, *The Rise of American Democracy*, 339.

2. Brands, *Andrew Jackson*, 408.

3. Brands, *Andrew Jackson*, 411.

4. Borneman, *1812*, 299.

5. Parsons, *The Birth of Modern Politics*, xiii.

6. Wilentz, *The Rise of American Democracy*.

7. Ratcliffe, *The One-Party Presidential Contest*, 40.

8. Brands, *Andrew Jackson*, 313.

9. Ratcliffe, *The One-Party Presidential Contest*, 150–54.

10. Wilentz, *The Rise of American Democracy*, 245.

11. Ratcliffe, *The One-Party Presidential Contest*, 233–34.

12. Ratcliffe, *The One-Party Presidential Contest*, 213–16; Kirwan, "Congress Elects a President."

13. Brands, *Andrew Jackson*, 384; Ratcliffe, *The One-Party Presidential Contest*, 9.

14. Cheathem, *The Coming of Democracy*, 26.

15. Brands, *Andrew Jackson*, 387.

16. Ratcliffe, *The One-Party Presidential Contest*, 254.

17. Kaplan, *John Quincy Adams*, 64.

18. Wilentz, *The Rise of American Democracy*, 301.

19. Kaplan, *John Quincy Adams*, 428.

20. Wilentz, *The Rise of American Democracy*, 308.

21. Cole, *Vindicating Andrew Jackson*, 40–41.

22. Cole, *Vindicating Andrew Jackson*, 26–27.

23. Parsons, *The Birth of Modern Politics*, 73.

24. Parsons, *The Birth of Modern Politics*, 133–34.

25. Reynolds, *Waking Giant*, 72–73; Lorant, *The Glorious Burden*, 124.

26. Reynolds, *Waking Giant*, 76.

27. Parsons, *The Birth of Modern Politics*, 152.

28. Brands, *Andrew Jackson*, 389.

29. Cole, *Vindicating Andrew Jackson*, 149–50.

30. Johnson, *A History of the American People*, 335; Cole, *Vindicating Andrew Jackson*, 151.

31. Lorant, *The Glorious Burden*, 124.

32. Johnson, *A History of the American People*, 334.

33. Farris, *Almost President*, 30.

34. A comprehensive and accessible history of the Bank of the United States is provided by the Federal Reserve Bank of Philadelphia. An article, "The Second Bank of the United States: A Chapter in the History of Central Banking," can be accessed at https://www.philadelphiafed.org/-/media/frbp/assets/institutional/education/publications/second-bank-of-the-united-states.pdf.

35. Boller, *Presidential Campaigns*, 55.

36. Meacham, *American Lion*, 201.

37. Brands, *Andrew Jackson*, 470–71.

38. Meacham, *American Lion*, 227–28.

39. Cole, *Vindicating Andrew Jackson*, 91.

40. Reynolds, *Waking Giant*, 113.

41. Boller, *Presidential Campaigns*, 62.

42. *Presidential Elections, 1789–2004*, 27.

43. Cheathem, *The Coming of Democracy*, 103.

44. Crockett and Clayton, *The Life of Martin Van Buren*, 80–81.

45. Lorant, *The Glorious Burden*, 149.

46. Boller, *Presidential Campaigns*, 64.

47. There are descriptions of Johnson's personal life with these slaves in Widmer, *Martin Van Buren*, 119–20; and Cheathem, *The Coming of Democracy*, 95–96.

48. Lichtman, *The Embattled Vote in America*, 14.

49. Cole, *Vindicating Andrew Jackson*, 9.

50. Parsons, *The Birth of Modern Politics*, 45.

51. Hofstadter, *The American Political Tradition*, 66.

52. Meacham, *American Lion*, xviii.

53. Brands, *Andrew Jackson*, 432.

54. Ratcliffe, *The One-Party Presidential Contest*, 4.

55. Good overviews of Van Buren's contributions to the development of political parties can be found in Widmer, *Martin Van Buren*, 56–58; and *Presidential Elections, 1789–2004*, 28.

56. Reichley, *The Life of the Parties*, 99–100; Howe, *The Political Culture of the American Whigs*, 18–20.

57. Howe, *The Political Culture of the American Whigs*, 136–37.

58. Lorant, *The Glorious Burden*, 160.

59. Norton, *The Great Revolution of 1840*, 7.

60. Borneman, *Polk*, 45.

61. Wilentz, *The Rise of American Democracy*, 497–98; Lorant, *The Glorious Burden*, 157.

62. Shafer, *The Carnival Campaign*, 25–39.

63. More detailed descriptions of the Whig parades and rallies can be found in Shafer, *The Carnival Campaign*, 75–80; Cheatham, *The Coming of Democracy*, 137–38; Boller, *Presidential Campaigns*, 66–67.

64. Boller, *Presidential Campaigns*, 67.

65. Lorant, *The Glorious Burden*, 160; Shafer, *The Carnival Campaign*, 115–16.

66. Boller, *Presidential Campaigns*, 65.

67. Cheathem, *The Coming of Democracy*, 147; Shafer, *The Carnival Campaign*, 132–48.

68. Shafer, *The Carnival Campaign*, 103.

69. Wilentz, *The Rise of American Democracy*, 501; Shafer, *The Carnival Campaign*, 55–60.

70. Shafer, *The Carnival Campaign*, 60; Lorant. *The Glorious Burden*, 167.

71. Widmer, *Martin Van Buren*, 138.

72. Shafer, *The Carnival Campaign*, 125.

73. Barbara Coles, "The Immortal Daniel Webster," *New Hampshire Magazine*, October 18, 2018; Paul Waldman, "The Real Stakes in the Veepstakes," *American Prospect*, April 28, 2016.

74. Borneman, *Polk*, 79.

75. For more on the Princeton explosion, see May, *John Tyler*, 106–9.

76. Merry, *A Country of Vast Designs*, 73–74.

77. Bicknell, *America 1844*, 55–63.

78. Borneman, *Polk*, 108.

79. Lorant, *The Glorious Burden*, 180.

80. May, *John Tyler*, 113–14.

81. Bicknell, *America 1844*, 187.

82. Boller, *Presidential Campaigns*, 79–80.

83. Borneman, *Polk*, 128.

84. Lorant, *The Glorious Burden*, 183.

85. Johnson, *A History of the American People*, 371.

86. Borneman, *Polk*, 254.

87. Bicknell, *America 1844*, 251.

88. Bicknell, *America 1844*, 251–52.

89. Rayback, *Millard Fillmore*, 147.

90. Silbey, *Party over Section*, 62–65.

91. Silbey, *Party over Section*, 56.

92. Cohen, *Accidental Presidents*, 52.

93. Lorant, *The Glorious Burden*, 191–92.

94. Boller, *Presidential Campaigns*, 85.

95. For a more extensive description of the Free Soil Party movement, see Wilentz, *The Rise of American Democracy*, 617–27; Silbey, *Party over Section*, 72–79.

96. Lorant, *The Glorious Burden*, 192.

97. Boller, *Presidential Campaigns*, 85–86.

98. Carlson, *Dead Presidents*, 67–71.

99. Eisenhower, *Zachary Taylor*, xix, 137–40.

100. Walther, *The Shattering of the Union*, 1–3; Rayback, *Millard Fillmore*, 289–93.

101. *Presidential Elections, 1789–2004*, 30.

102. Boller, *Presidential Campaigns*, 89.

103. Lorant, *The Glorious Burden*, 201–11.

104. Boller, *Presidential Campaigns*, 88–90.

105. Johnson, *A History of the American People*, 428.

106. Walther, *The Shattering of the Union*, 40.

107. Walther, *The Shattering of the Union*, 99.

108. Rayback, *Millard Fillmore*, 316–17.

109. Reichley, *The Life of the Parties*, 109.

110. Baker, *James Buchanan*, 70; Bicknell, *Lincoln's Pathfinder*, 224.

111. Boller, *Presidential Campaigns*, 92.

112. Bicknell, *Lincoln's Pathfinder*, 183.

113. Wilentz, *The Rise of American Democracy*, 701.

114. Baker, *James Buchanan*, 71.

115. See, for instance, Thomas Balcerski, "The 175-Year History of Speculating about President James Buchanan's Bachelorhood," *Smithsonian Magazine*, August 27, 2019; Ezekiel Emanuel, "American Has Already Had a Gay President," *Washington Post*, March 26, 2019.

116. Carlson, *Dead Presidents*, 223.

117. Bicknell, *Lincoln's Pathfinder*, 222; Rayback, *Millard Fillmore*, 328–29.

118. Wilentz, *The Rise of American Democracy*, 700.

119. Bicknell, *Lincoln's Pathfinder*, 278.

120. For a more in-depth look at the literary explosion of the 1850s, see Johnson, *A History of the American People*, 415–19.

121. Wilentz, *The Rise of American Democracy*, 622.

122. Reichley, *The Life of the Parties*, 125–28.

3. The Civil War and Its Aftermath

1. Jon Grinspan, "How Coffee Fueled the Civil War," *New York Times*, July 9, 2014.

2. Merry, *President McKinley*, 25; Rove, *The Triumph of William McKinley*, 8–9.

3. James Buchanan, inaugural address, March 4, 1857, Famous Presidential Speeches, https://millercenter.org/the-presidency/presidential-speeches/march-4-1857-inaugural-address.

4. Walther, *The Shattering of the Union*, 135.

5. Holt, *The Election of 1860*, 128–29.

6. Chadwick, *Lincoln for President*, 87–88.

7. Jason Steinhauer, "Electability Has a Vital Role in Presidential Primaries," *Washington Post*, July 31, 2019.

8. Goodwin, *Team of Rivals*, 257.

9. For more on the Constitutional Union Party, see Egerton, *Year of Meteors*, 88–93; Holt, *The Election of 1860*, 69–87.

10. Holt, *The Election of 1860*, 171.

11. Egerton, *Year of Meteors*, 187.

12. Chadwick, *Lincoln for President*, 120.

13. Chadwick, *Lincoln for President*, 160.

14. Lorant, *The Glorious Burden*, 236–37.

15. More on the Wide Awakes can be found in Grinspan, *The Virgin Vote*, 117–19; Holt, *The Election of 1860*, 138–41; Boller, *Presidential Campaigns*, 111–12.

16. Holzer, *Lincoln at Cooper Union*, 96–100.

17. More on the secession crisis and Buchanan's response can be found in Wilentz, *The Rise of American Democracy*, 779–81; Baker, *James Buchanan*, 121–30.

18. Abraham Lincoln, "First Inaugural Address," Inaugural Addresses of the Presidents, http://avalon.law.yale.edu/19th_century/lincoln1.asp.

19. Goodwin, *Team of Rivals*, 497–501.

20. For more on the Gettysburg Address, see Oates, *With Malice toward None*, 366–67; Goodwin, *Team of Rivals*, 585–87.

21. Daniel Farber, "Lincoln, FDR, and the Growth of Federal Power," in Weber, *Lincoln*, 91–96.

22. Oates, *With Malice toward None*, 381.

23. Waugh, *Reelecting Lincoln*, 270.

24. Waugh, *Reelecting Lincoln*, 89.

25. Waugh, *Reelecting Lincoln*, 89.

26. Information on the Democratic campaign attacks is in Brookhiser, *Founder's Son*, 254; Lorant, *The Glorious Burden*, 268; Boller, *Presidential Campaigns*, 117.

27. Boller, *Presidential Campaigns*, 121–22.

28. For more on the Democrats in 1864, see Waugh, *Reelecting Lincoln*, 12–13, 89–91.

29. Lorant, *The Glorious Burden*, 265.

30. Waugh, *Reelecting Lincoln*, 62.

31. "Congratulating the President; A Serenade by the Clubs, and a Speech by Mr. Lincoln," *New York Times*, November 11, 1864.

32. Oates, *With Malice toward None*, 395.

33. More on Lincoln's Second Inaugural is in Oates, *With Malice toward None*, 278–81; Goodwin, *Team of Rivals*, 698–700.

34. Egerton, *Year of Meteors*, 281–82; Wilentz, *The Rise of American Democracy*, 774–75.

35. Goodwin, *Team of Rivals*, 78.

36. Holzer, *Lincoln at Cooper Union*, 31.

37. Wilentz, *The Rise of American Democracy*, 790.

38. The quote and the sentiment in this paragraph, as well as a more in-depth description of the political and sectional divisions between North and South, can be found in Sundquist, *Dynamics of the Party System*, 98–105.

39. DeRose, *The President's War*, 311.

40. Johnson, *A History of the American People*, 498.

41. Cohen, *Accidental Presidents*, 125; Reichley, *The Life of the Parties*, 134–35.

42. Jon Meacham, "Andrew Johnson," in Engel et al., *Impeachment*, 78.

43. Brands, *The Man Who Saved the Union*, 418.

44. For more on Grant's transitions between civilian and military life, see Calhoun, *From Bloody Shirt to Full Dinner Pail*, 11–12.

45. Lorant, *The Glorious Burden*, 304.

46. Brands, *The Man Who Saved the Union*, 422.

47. Boller, *Presidential Campaigns*, 124.

48. Bunting, *Ulysses S. Grant*, 83.

49. "Equal Rights Party Platform and Declaration of Principles," *New York Herald*, May 11, 1872, https://www.newspapers.com/clip/7032380/equal_rights_party _platform_1872/.

50. For much more on Victoria Woodhull, see Underhill, *The Woman Who Ran for President*.

51. Howe, *The Political Culture of the American Whigs*, 197.

52. Shafer, *The Carnival Campaign*, 234; Boller, *Presidential Campaigns*, 129.

53. Morris, *Fraud of the Century*, 3.

54. Trefousse, *Rutherford B. Hayes*, 67.

55. Boller, *Presidential Campaigns*, 134.

56. Lorant, *The Glorious Burden*, 333.

57. Boller, *Presidential Campaigns*, 134.

58. Morris, *Fraud of the Century*, 120.

59. Holt, *By One Vote*, 146; Boller, *Presidential Campaigns*, 134.

60. Lorant, *The Glorious Burden*, 334.

61. Holt, *By One Vote*, 173.

62. Boller, *Presidential Campaigns*, 135; Holt, *By One Vote*, 181.

63. Holt, *By One Vote*, 205.

64. Morris, *Fraud of the Century*, 173.

65. Brands, *The Man Who Saved the Union*, 576.

66. Weston, *The Runner-Up Presidency*, 43.

67. Reichley, *The Life of the Parties*, 150.

68. Weston, *The Runner-Up Presidency*, 43.

69. Morris, *Fraud of the Century*, 241.

70. Madden, *Thomas Wolfe's Civil War*, 1–2.

71. Bunting, *Ulysses S. Grant*, 107.

72. For more on the almost incomprehensible Reconstruction-era violence against Blacks and President Johnson's response, see Anderson, *White Rage*, especially 16–19, 30–31; Langguth, *After Lincoln*, especially 108–11, 143–49, 222–32.

73. More information on some of these mass murders can be found in Gordon-Reed, *Andrew Johnson*, 117–18; Langguth, *After Lincoln*, 143–49; Anderson, *White Rage*, 30.

74. Brands, *The Man Who Saved the Union*, 474.

75. Lichtman, *The Embattled Vote in America*, 88–89; Holt, *By One Vote*, 20–21, 46–47, 164.

76. Summers, *Rum, Romanism and Rebellion*, 252.

77. Holt, *By One Vote*, 22.

78. Amar, *America's Constitution*, 399.

79. More on these court decisions is in Lichtman, *The Embattled Vote in America*, 92–95; Anderson, *White Rage*, 32–35.

80. Morris, *Fraud of the Century*, 241.

81. For more on the spoils system, see Karabell, *Chester Alan Arthur*, 6–8; Hofstadter, *The American Political Tradition*, 219–25.

82. Lorant, *The Glorious Burden*, 345; Summers, *Rum, Romanism and Rebellion*, 64.

83. Summers, *Rum, Romanism and Rebellion*, 65.

84. Karabell, *Chester Alan Arthur*, 19.

85. Millard, *Destiny of the Republic*, 49; Ackerman, *Dark Horse*, 92.

86. Millard, *Destiny of the Republic*, 50.

87. Ackerman, *Dark Horse*, 97.

88. For a longer and fascinating look into how Arthur came to be the vice-presidential nominee, see Ackerman, *Dark Horse*, 106–13.

89. Boller, *Presidential Campaigns*, 143; Ackerman, *Dark Horse*, 165.

90. Calhoun, *From Bloody Shirt to Full Dinner Pail*, 75.

91. Ackerman, *Dark Horse*, 335.

92. Millard, *Destiny of the Republic*, 105; Ackerman, *Dark Horse*, 349.

93. For an excellent source of information on Garfield's medical condition from the time of the shooting to his death, see Millard, *Destiny of the Republic*, which devotes several chapters to the topic.

94. Cohen, *Accidental Presidents*, 170.

95. Ackerman, *Dark Horse*, 341.

96. For more on the Pendleton Civil Service Act, both its passage and its consequences, see Karabell, *Chester Alan Arthur*, 104–10.

97. Ackerman, *Dark Horse*, 386–87.

98. One can find several variations of this quote by Sherman, but this appears to be the most frequently reported version.

99. Calhoun, *From Bloody Shirt to Full Dinner Pail*, 97.

100. Boller, *Presidential Campaigns*, 151–52.

101. Graff, *Grover Cleveland*, 55.

102. Hofstadter, *The American Political Tradition*, 229–30.

103. Boller, *Presidential Campaigns*, 146.

104. Dickerson, *Whistlestop*, 288–90.

105. For a good overview of the Cleveland scandal, see Summers, *Rum, Romanism and Rebellion*, 179–93.

106. Graff, *Grover Cleveland*, 64.

107. Dickerson, *Whistlestop*, 297.

108. Summers, *Rum, Romanism and Rebellion*, 185–88.

109. Graff, *Grover Cleveland*, 64; Boller, *Presidential Campaigns*, 148; Lorant, *The Glorious Burden*, 383.

110. Boller, *Presidential Campaigns*, 153.

111. Boller, *Presidential Campaigns*, 148.

112. Summers, *Rum, Romanism and Rebellion*, 279–85.

113. See a reproduction of the cartoon in Lorant, *The Glorious Burden*, 386; Boller, *Presidential Campaigns*, 150.

114. Summers, *Rum, Romanism and Rebellion*, 296.

115. Boller, *Presidential Campaigns*, 149.

116. Gerhardt, *The Forgotten Presidents*, 132; Graff, *Grover Cleveland*, 85.

117. For more on Cleveland and Frances Folsom, see Algeo, *The President Is a Sick Man*, 46–48; Graff, *Grover Cleveland*, 78–81.

118. Calhoun, *Minority Victory*, 172.

119. For more on tariffs and their role in the partisan debate, see Merry, *President McKinley*, 75–80; Calhoun, *Minority Victory*, 15–18; Rove, *The Triumph of William McKinley*, 12–15.

120. Calhoun, *Minority Victory*, 133.

121. Boller, *Presidential Campaigns*, 158.

122. Shafer, *The Carnival Campaign*, 236.

123. Calhoun, *Minority Victory*, 161; Summers, *Rum, Romanism and Rebellion*, 309.

124. Peter Baker, "'I'll See You in Four Years': Trump and the Ghost of Grover Cleveland," *New York Times*, December 3, 2020.

125. *Presidential Elections, 1789–2004*, 44.

126. Lorant, *The Glorious Burden*, 415.

127. Boller, *Presidential Campaigns*, 164; Calhoun, *From Bloody Shirt to Full Dinner Pail*, 140.

128. Lorant, *The Glorious Burden*, 423.

129. Wolfe, "The Four Lost Men," 127–29.

130. Grinspan, *The Virgin Vote*, 124.

131. Calhoun, *Minority Victory*, 1; Rove, *The Triumph of William McKinley*, 11.

132. Karabell, *Chester Alan Arthur*, 38, 98–99.

133. Underhill, *The Woman Who Ran for President*, 292–94.

4. A New Politics for a New Century

1. For more on Coolidge's ascension to the presidency and his middle-of-the-night oath of office, see Greenberg, *Calvin Coolidge*, 43–46; Dan Karlinsky, "In Plymouth Notch Time Stands Still," *New York Times*, June 6, 1976.

2. Greenberg, *Calvin Coolidge*, 131.

3. Donald, *Lion in the White House*, 241.

4. Williams, *Realigning America*, 24.

5. For an entertaining, book-length version of events surrounding Cleveland's surgery, see Algeo, *The President Is a Sick Man*.

6. For more on the Pullman strike and the Coxey march, see Graff, *Grover Cleveland*, 117–20; Algeo, *The President Is a Sick Man*, 186–89.

7. Williams, *Realigning America*, 29.

8. Stirewalt, *Every Man a King*, 51.

9. Comparisons between the populist movement and the *Wizard of Oz* are from several sources, including Algeo, *The President Is a Sick Man*, 121–22; Peter Liebhold, "Populism and the World of Oz," National Museum of American History blog, November 2, 2016, https://americanhistory.si.edu/blog/populism-oz; Taylor, "Money and Politics in the World of Oz."

10. For more details on McKinley's campaign against the bosses, see Merry, *President McKinley*, 98–100.

11. Rove, *The Triumph of William McKinley*, 236.

12. Graff, *Grover Cleveland*, 127.

13. The descriptions of Bryan's "Cross of Gold" speech derive from longer overviews in Williams, *Realigning America*, 84–86; Rove, *The Triumph of William McKinley*, 272–76. A transcript and studio recording of Bryan's speech is available from the American Social History Project at George Mason University, http://historymatters.gmu.edu/d/5354/.

14. Hofstadter, *The Age of Reform*, 60–61.

15. Stone, *They Also Ran*, 76.

16. Farris, *Almost President*, 82.

17. Algeo, *The President Is a Sick Man*, 192.

18. Williams, *Realigning America*, 94. For a longer description of Bryan's speaking tour, see 94–106.

19. Merry, *President McKinley*, 139.

20. Rove, *The Triumph of William McKinley*, 310–12; Williams, *Realigning America*, 134.

21. Lorant, *The Glorious Burden*, 445.

22. Boller, *Presidential Campaigns*, 171.

23. Miller, *The President and the Assassin*, 28–29; Williams, *Realigning America*, 150.

24. Barone, *How America's Political Parties Change*, 13.

25. Lorant, *The Glorious Burden*, 447; Miller, *The President and the Assassin*, 266.

26. Miller, *The President and the Assassin*, 118–27.

27. Miller, *The President and the Assassin*, 349–50.

28. Donald, *Lion in the White House*, 125.

29. Lorant, *The Glorious Burden*, 456.

30. Lorant, *The Glorious Burden*, 459.

31. Miller, *The President and the Assassin*, 269.

32. Lorant, *The Glorious Burden*, 467.

33. Calhoun, *From Bloody Shirt to Full Dinner Pail*, 179.

34. Dalton, *Theodore Roosevelt*, 194; Boller, *Presidential Campaigns*, 180.

35. Miller, *The President and the Assassin*, 304.

36. For more background on the shooting and the cause of death, see Miller, *The President and the Assassin*, 300–330.

37. Vowell, *Assassination Vacation*, 230.

38. Hofstadter, *The American Political Tradition*, 289–93.

39. Lorant, *The Glorious Burden*, 486.

40. Stone, *They Also Ran*, 110.

41. Stirewalt, *Every Man a King*, 76.

42. Dalton, *Theodore Roosevelt*, 271; Boller, *Presidential Campaigns*, 185.

43. For more on these bills, see Donald, *Lion in the White House*, 184–89.

44. Lorant, *The Glorious Burden*, 488.

45. Dalton, *Theodore Roosevelt*, 339; Boller, *Presidential Campaigns*, 187.

46. Rosen, *William Howard Taft*, 42.

47. Rosen, *William Howard Taft*, 46; David Rabin, "The Presidential Debates of '08 — 1908, That Is," National Public Radio, November 1, 2008.

48. Lorant, *The Glorious Burden*, 502.

49. Boller, *Presidential Campaigns*, 187.

50. Miller, *The President and the Assassin*, 341.

51. Boller, *Presidential Campaigns*, 189.

52. Chace, *1912*, 57; Donald, *Lion in the White House*, 240–42; Dalton, *Theodore Roosevelt*, 365–66.

53. Milkis, *Theodore Roosevelt*, 60.

54. Milkis, *Theodore Roosevelt*, 30.

55. Donald, *Lion in the White House*, 239.

56. Boller, *Presidential Campaigns*, 192.

57. Milkis, *Theodore Roosevelt*, 57.

58. Milkis, *Theodore Roosevelt*, 55.

59. Boller, *Presidential Campaigns*, 197.

60. Gould, *Four Hats in the Ring*, 63.

61. Cowan, *Let the People Rule*, 195.

62. Chace, *1912*, 116.

63. Chace, *1912*, 161.

64. Reichley, *The Life of the Parties*, 200.

65. O'Mara, *Pivotal Tuesdays*, 47.

66. Chace, *1912*, 167.

67. Gould, *Four Hats in the Ring*, 88.

68. Sundquist, *Dynamics of the Party System*, 179.

69. Cooper, *Woodrow Wilson*, 155.

70. Milkis, *Theodore Roosevelt*, 255.

71. Hofstadter, *The American Political Tradition*, 332.

72. Brands, *Woodrow Wilson*, 20–21; Cooper, *Woodrow Wilson*, 176–77; Chace, *1912*, 196.

73. Cooper, *Woodrow Wilson*, 172.

74. Gould, *Four Hats in the Ring*, 158–59.

75. O'Mara, *Pivotal Tuesdays*, 51.

76. Boller, *Presidential Campaigns*, 194.

77. Gould, *Four Hats in the Ring*, 126.

78. Chace, *1912*, 221.

79. For more on the assassination attempt on Roosevelt, see Helferich, *Theodore Roosevelt and the Assassin*, 173–87; Chace, *1912*, 230–33.

80. For more on the fusion between the Populists and Progressives, see Dionne, *Our Divided Political Heart*, 23–24; Sundquist, *Dynamics of the Party System*, 171; Hofstadter, *The Age of Reform*, 131–34.

81. Gould, *Four Hats in the Ring*, 181–82; Williams, *Realigning America*, 168–71; O'Mara, *Pivotal Tuesdays*, 36.

82. O'Mara, *Pivotal Tuesdays*, 125.

83. Johnson, *A History of the American People*, 635–38.

84. Gould, *The First Modern Clash over Federal Power*, 75.

85. Chace, *1912*, 253.

86. Gould, *The First Modern Clash over Federal Power*, xi.

87. Cooper, *Woodrow Wilson*, 351.

88. Lorant, *The Glorious Burden*, 543.

89. Boller, *Presidential Campaigns*, 203.

90. Boller, *Presidential Campaigns*, 205.

91. Cooper, *Woodrow Wilson*, 360; Gould, *The First Modern Clash over Federal Power*, 129.

92. Gould, *The First Modern Clash over Federal Power*, 126.

93. Chace, *1912*, 269.

94. Brands, *Woodrow Wilson*, 126–27; Algeo, *The President Is a Sick Man*, 56–57; Chace, *1912*, 270–71.

95. Centers for Disease Control and Prevention, "1918 Pandemic (H1N1 Virus)," https://www.cdc.gov/flu/pandemic-resources/1918-pandemic-h1n1.html.

96. Erik Ortiz, "Racial Violence and a Pandemic: How the Red Summer of 1919 Relates to 2020," NBC News, June 21, 2020; Jesse J. Holland, "Hundreds of Black Deaths during 1919's Red Summer Are Being Remembered," Associated Press, July 23, 2019.

97. For more on this turmoil and unrest, see Meacham, *The Soul of America*, 111–13; Pietrusza, *1920*, 140–54, 266–71; Kevin Jennings, "What the 1920 Wall Street Bombing Tells Us about Modern Immigration Scare Tactics," *Washington Post*, January 29, 2018; Olivia B. Waxman, "A Century before Trump's ICE Raids, the U.S. Government Rounded Up Thousands of Immigrants: Here's What Happened," *Time*, July 18, 2019.

98. Stone, *They Also Ran*, 33.

99. Dean, *Warren G. Harding*, 57.

100. Dean, *Warren G. Harding*, 67.

101. Pietrusza, *1920*, 225.

102. Tucker, *The High Tide of American Conservatism*, 19.

103. Peter Baker, "DNA Is Said to Solve a Mystery of Warren Harding's Love Life," *New York Times*, August 12, 2015; Ronald G. Shafer, "Sex, Hush Money and an Alleged Poisoning: Before Trump and Stormy Daniels, a Wild Presidency," *Washington Post*, October 2, 2018.

104. Boller, *Presidential Campaigns*, 218.

105. Boller, *Presidential Campaigns*, 219.

106. Murray, *The 103rd Ballot*, 9.

107. Murray, *The 103rd Ballot*, 109.

108. Murray, *The 103rd Ballot*, 197–99.

109. Burner, *The Politics of Provincialism*, 121; Tucker, *The High Tide of American Conservatism*, 94; Prude, "William Gibbs McAdoo and the Democratic National Convention of 1924," 623.

110. Meacham, *The Soul of America*, 120.

111. Murray, *The 103rd Ballot*, 255.

112. Stone, *They Also Ran*, 377.

113. Stone, *They Also Ran*, 378.

114. Overview of the La Follette campaign from Shideler, "The La Follette Progressive Party Campaign of 1924."

115. Murray, *The 103rd Ballot*, 298.

116. Stone, *They Also Ran*, 380.

117. Shideler, "The La Follette Progressive Party Campaign of 1924"; Greenberg, *Calvin Coolidge*, 105.

118. Tucker, *The High Tide of American Conservatism*, 182, 209–10.

119. Karlinsky, "In Plymouth Notch Time Stands Still."

120. Tucker, *The High Tide of American Conservatism*, 231.

121. Greenberg, *Calvin Coolidge*, 6.

122. Greenberg, *Calvin Coolidge*, 136–37.

123. Lorant, *The Glorious Burden*, 575.

124. Ritchie, *Electing FDR*, 21–22; Hofstadter, *The American Political Tradition*, 377; Johnson, *A History of the American People*, 737.

125. Ritchie, *Electing FDR*, 26.

126. Farris, *Almost President*, 104.

127. Boller, *Presidential Campaigns*, 225.

128. Murray, *The 103rd Ballot*, 344.

129. For more on the anti-Catholic campaign against Smith, see Boller, *Presidential Campaigns*, 225; Lorant, *The Glorious Burden*, 579; Stone, *They Also Ran*, 341.

130. Murray, *The 103rd Ballot*, 346.

131. Lorant, *The Glorious Burden*, 581.

132. Farris, *Almost President*, 96, 111–13.

133. Boller, *Presidential Campaigns*, 226–27.

134. Lorant, *The Glorious Burden*, 583.

135. Boller, *Presidential Campaigns*, 227.

136. Greenberg, *Calvin Coolidge*, 5.

137. Greenberg, *Calvin Coolidge*, 5.

138. Greenberg, *Calvin Coolidge*, 81; Ritchie, *Electing FDR*, 11.

139. Ritchie, *Electing FDR*, 14.

5. The New Deal to the Great Society

1. Michael Beschloss, "Eisenhower, an Unlikely Pioneer of TV Ads," *New York Times*, October 30, 2015; Hollitz, "Eisenhower and the Admen."

2. Karabell, *Chester Alan Arthur*, 91.

3. Greenberg, *Calvin Coolidge*, 145.

4. Ritchie, *Electing FDR*, 52.

5. Leuchtenburg, *Herbert Hoover*, 111; Hofstadter, *The American Political Tradition*, 382.

6. Sundquist, *Dynamics of the Party System*, 202.

7. Leuchtenburg, *Herbert Hoover*, 132.

8. Ritchie, *Electing FDR*, 38.

9. There are intriguing narratives of some of these behind-the-scenes machinations in Neal, *Happy Days Are Here Again*, especially 270–94; Ritchie, *Electing FDR*, 102–9.

10. Neal, *Happy Days Are Here Again*, 297.

11. A longer narrative about Roosevelt's flight is in Neal, *Happy Days Are Here Again*, 295–308. A description of the flight can also be found in Kathryn Smith, "Missy LeHand: FDR's Influential but Largely Forgotten Assistant," *American Heritage*, Summer 2017.

12. Neal, *Happy Days Are Here Again*, 307.

13. Boller, *Presidential Campaigns*, 233; Neal, *Happy Days Are Here Again*, 311–13.

14. For more on Roosevelt's battle with polio than is described in these few paragraphs, see Neal, *Happy Days Are Here Again*, 166–70; Ritchie, *Electing FDR*, 71–72.

15. Alter, *The Defining Moment*, 327.

16. Leuchtenburg, *Herbert Hoover*, 138.

17. O'Mara, *Pivotal Tuesdays*, 100.

18. Ritchie, *Electing FDR*, 87.

19. Boller, *Presidential Campaigns*, 235.

20. Ritchie, *Electing FDR*, 142–47.

21. Ritchie, *Electing FDR*, 164.

22. Boller, *Presidential Campaigns*, 239.

23. Hofstadter, *The American Political Tradition*, 431.

24. Meacham, *The Soul of America*, 139–41.

25. Hofstadter, *The American Political Tradition*, 437.

26. Lorant, *The Glorious Burden*, 620.

27. Stone, *They Also Ran*, 350–52; Boller, *Presidential Campaigns*, 240.

28. Lorant, *The Glorious Burden*, 620; Stone, *They Also Ran*, 346.

29. Stone, *They Also Ran*, 346.

30. Lorant, *The Glorious Burden*, 623; Boller, *Presidential Campaigns*, 243.

31. *Presidential Elections, 1789–2004*, 58.

32. Farris, *Almost President*, 309.

33. Jeffries, *A Third Term for FDR*, 99.

34. Indeed, Eleanor Roosevelt famously told delegates at the 1940 Democratic convention that it was "no ordinary time," a phrase that later become the title of the Pulitzer Prize–winning book by Doris Kearns Goodwin.

35. For more on the debates over isolationism and fascism, see Dunn, *1940*, 46–48, 241–43; Moe, *Roosevelt's Second Act*, 11–14, 52–55.

36. Dunn, *1940*, 58.

37. Moe, *Roosevelt's Second Act*, 11; Dunn, *1940*, 46.

38. Moe, *Roosevelt's Second Act*, 172.

39. Hofstadter, *The American Political Tradition*, 447.

40. Moe, *Roosevelt's Second Act*, 150.

41. Moe, *Roosevelt's Second Act*, 84–88.

42. Moe, *Roosevelt's Second Act*, 105–8, 172–75.

43. Jeffries, *A Third Term for FDR*, 58.

44. Dunn, *1940*, 89.

45. Dunn, *1940*, 78.

46. Jeffries, *A Third Term for FDR*, 66.

47. Jeffries, *A Third Term for FDR*.

48. Stone, *They Also Ran*, 400; Jeffries, *A Third Term for FDR*, 71.

49. Lorant, *The Glorious Burden*, 638.

50. Jeffries, *A Third Term for FDR*, 65.

51. Moe, *Roosevelt's Second Act*, 212.

52. Moe, *Roosevelt's Second Act*, 223.

53. Moe, *Roosevelt's Second Act*, 223–24.

54. Jeffries, *A Third Term for FDR*, 112.

55. Lorant, *The Glorious Burden*, 645.

56. Jeffries, *A Third Term for FDR*, 138.

57. More on the nationwide tour and on Willkie's speeches is in Jeffries, *A Third Term for FDR*, 137–38; Dunn, *1940*, 156–57; Stone, *They Also Ran*, 402–3; Boller, *Presidential Campaigns*, 252–53.

58. Dunn, *1940*, 256.

59. Moe, *Roosevelt's Second Act*, 277.

60. Dunn, *1940*, 257.

61. Meacham, *The Soul of America*, 158–59; Moe, *Roosevelt's Second Act*, 316–27.

62. Jordan, *FDR, Dewey and the Election of 1944*, 139.

63. McCullough, *Truman*, 295–96; Jordan, *FDR, Dewey and the Election of 1944*, 130–35.

64. For longer narratives on the selection of Truman as the 1944 vice-presidential candidate, see Ferrell, *Choosing Truman*; Baime, *The Accidental President*, 94–106; McCullough, *Truman*, 294–323.

65. Ferrell, *Choosing Truman*, 52.

66. McCullough, *Truman*, 314.

67. Ferrell, *Choosing Truman*, 62.

68. Jordan, *FDR, Dewey and the Election of 1944*, 168–69.

69. McCullough, *Truman*, 320.

70. Jordan, *FDR, Dewey and the Election of 1944*, 203.

71. Farris, *Almost President*, 131.

72. Jordan, *FDR, Dewey and the Election of 1944*, 27–28.

73. Stone, *They Also Ran*, 436; Jordan, *FDR, Dewey and the Election of 1944*, 28.

74. Lorant, *The Glorious Burden*, 655.

75. Stone, *They Also Ran*, 448.

76. Lorant, *The Glorious Burden*, 663–64; Boller, *Presidential Campaigns*, 262–63.

77. Jordan, *FDR, Dewey and the Election of 1944*, 272–74.

78. Meacham, *The Soul of America*, 148.

79. Baime, *The Accidental President*, ix.

80. Lorant, *The Glorious Burden*, 683; Baime, *The Accidental President*, 3.

81. For descriptions of when Truman learned about Roosevelt's death, see McCullough, *Truman*, 341–42; Baime, *The Accidental President*, 24–26.

82. For more on these political coalitions, see Reichley, *The Life of the Parties*, 247–49; Sundquist, *Dynamics of the Party System*, 217–27; Jeffries, *A Third Term for FDR*, 21–23.

83. Jordan, *FDR, Dewey and the Election of 1944*, 258.

84. For more depth on the emergence of New Deal liberalism, see Reichley, *The Life of the Parties*, 251–54; Alter, *The Defining Moment*, 91–98, 129–30; DiStefano, *The Next Realignment*, 111–18.

85. Stone, *They Also Ran*, 358.

86. Ritchie, *Electing FDR*, 185.

87. Reichley, *The Life of the Parties*, 252.

88. McCullough, *Truman*, 698.

89. Boller, *Presidential Campaigns*, 269; Lorant, *The Glorious Burden*, 697.

90. Dickerson, *Whistlestop*, 227.

91. Dickerson, *Whistlestop*, 44.

92. Lorant, *The Glorious Burden*, 701.

93. For more on Truman and civil rights, see Karabell, *The Last Campaign*, 41–43; McCullough, *Truman*, 586–89.

94. Busch, *Truman's Triumphs*, 107; McCullough, *Truman*, 639.

95. Reichley, *The Life of the Parties*, 292–97; Busch, *Truman's Triumphs*, 39–40, 118–19; Karabell, *The Last Campaign*, 30.

96. Dickerson, *Whistlestop*, 45; Lorant, *The Glorious Burden*, 705–8.

97. Karabell, *The Last Campaign*, 199.

98. Dickerson, *Whistlestop*, 46.

99. McCullough, *Truman*, 653–57.

100. Boller, *Presidential Campaigns*, 271; Johnson, *A History of the American People*, 816.

101. Johnson, *A History of the American People*, 816.

102. McCullough, *Truman*, 664.

103. McCullough, *Truman*, 672.

104. Dickerson, *Whistlestop*, 50.

105. See examples of these cartoons in Lorant, *The Glorious Burden*, 722–23.

106. Dickerson, *Whistlestop*, 50.

107. Boller, *Presidential Campaigns*, 268–72; Lorant, *The Glorious Burden*, 721–28; Dickerson, *Whistlestop*, 52.

108. Boller, *Presidential Campaigns*, 273; Lorant, *The Glorious Burden*, 728; Dickerson, *Whistlestop*, 52.

109. McCullough, *Truman*, 711.

110. Miller, *Two Americans*, 215; *Presidential Elections, 1789–2004*, 63.

111. Boller, *Presidential Campaigns*, 273; Lorant, *The Glorious Burden*, 731.

112. Boller, *Presidential Campaigns*, 274.

113. For more on these various challenges and events, see Greene, *I Like Ike*, 6–15; Miller, *Two Americans*, 279–80; Busch, *Truman's Triumphs*, 187–88.

114. Cohen, *Accidental Presidents*, 325.

115. Greene, *I Like Ike*, 67–68.

116. Greene, *I Like Ike*, 119.

117. Lorant, *The Glorious Burden*, 752.

118. Greene, *I Like Ike*, 122.

119. Lorant, *The Glorious Burden*, 752–53.

120. Hitchcock, *The Age of Eisenhower*, 47.

121. Greene, *I Like Ike*, 34.

122. Farris, *Almost President*, 144.

123. Greene, *I Like Ike*, 102.

124. More in-depth overviews of the machinations that took place at the Republican convention can be found in Dickerson, *Whistlestop*, 220–37; Hitchcock, *The Age of Eisenhower*, 69–71.

125. Farris, *Almost President*, 155.

126. Boller, *Presidential Campaigns*, 284–85.

127. Farris, *Almost President*, 152; Boller, *Presidential Campaigns*, 287.

128. Greene, *I Like Ike*, 141.

129. Hitchcock, *The Age of Eisenhower*, 76–77.

130. Greene, *I Like Ike*, 91, 145–47.

131. Boller, *Presidential Campaigns*, 282.

132. Hollitz, "Eisenhower and the Admen."

133. Boller, *Presidential Campaigns*, 280.

134. Boller, *Presidential Campaigns*, 283.

135. For more details on the Nixon crisis and the Checkers speech, see Malsberger, *The General and the Politician*, 6–23; Greene, *I Like Ike*, 151–57; Boller, *Presidential Campaigns*, 283–84, 287–88.

136. Malsberger, *The General and the Politician*, 18.

137. Lorant, *The Glorious Burden*, 765.

138. Hitchcock, *The Age of Eisenhower*, 303–4.

139. Donaldson, *The First Modern Campaign*, 30; Lorant, *The Glorious Burden*, 792; Hitchcock, *The Age of Eisenhower*, 294–96.

140. Lorant, *The Glorious Burden*, 793.

141. Boller, *Presidential Campaigns*, 292; Lorant, *The Glorious Burden*, 793–95.

142. Boller, *Presidential Campaigns*, 295.

143. For more on events in Egypt and Hungary, see Hitchcock, *The Age of Eisenhower*, 310–30; Greene, *I Like Ike*, 183–85; Lorant, *The Glorious Burden*, 798–802.

144. Donaldson, *The First Modern Campaign*, vii.

145. White, *The Making of the President 1960*, 279.

146. Busch, *Truman's Triumphs*, 213.

147. Greene, *I Like Ike*, 177.

148. To further explore the ideological tensions within both parties during this era, see Sundquist, *Dynamics of the Party System*, 269–84.

149. Norman Mailer, "Superman Comes to the Supermarket," *Esquire*, November 1960.

150. Donaldson, *The First Modern Campaign*, 90.

151. An entire book was written about Kennedy's multiyear pursuit of the presidency: Oliphant and Wilkie, *The Road to Camelot*.

152. The "political philosopher" quote is from Craig Fehrman, "'I Would Rather Win a Pulitzer Prize Than Be President,'" *Politico*, February 11, 2020.

153. For more on Kennedy's appearance on the *Tonight Show* and his use of television in 1960, see Ron Simon, "See How JFK Created a Presidency for the Television Age," *Time*, May 29, 2017; and Frank Rich, "Paar to Leno, J.F.K. to J.F.K.," *New York Times*, February 8, 2004.

154. For more extensive descriptions of the primary battles between Kennedy and Humphrey, see Donaldson, *The First Modern Campaign*, 49–59; Oliphant and Wilkie, *The Road to Camelot*, 195–213.

155. Donaldson, *The First Modern Campaign*, 50.

156. Donaldson, *The First Modern Campaign*, 58–59; Oliphant and Wilkie, *The Road to Camelot*, 201.

157. White, *The Making of the President 1960*, 158–59; Donaldson, *The First Modern Campaign*, 72–77.

158. For examples of the Kennedy convention organization, see Rorabaugh, *The Real Making of the President*, 78–82.

159. Oliphant and Wilkie, *The Road to Camelot*, 265.

160. John Kennedy, "Acceptance of Democratic Nomination for President," Kennedy, Historic Speeches, https://www.jfklibrary.org/learn/about-jfk/historic-speeches /acceptance-of-democratic-nomination-for-president.

161. Mathews, *Jack Kennedy*, 108–9.

162. Alan Peppard, "As Friend, Foe of Kennedy, Nixon Was Near—Even at End," *Dallas Morning News*, November 19, 2018.

163. Hitchcock, *The Age of Eisenhower*, 479–80; Rorabaugh, *The Real Making of the President*, 122; Boller, *Presidential Campaigns*, 297.

164. Rorabaugh, *The Real Making of the President*, 144.

165. Oliphant and Wilkie, *The Road to Camelot*, 291. This quote is from a Kennedy appearance the same day at the Alamo, though video of his speech that night shows that he made the same assertion to the ministers.

166. Boller, *Presidential Campaigns*, 298; Oliphant and Wilkie, *The Road to Camelot*, 293.

167. For a more detailed overview of this whole episode, see Oliphant and Wilkie, *The Road to Camelot*, 340–45; Donaldson, *The First Modern Campaign*, 131–33.

168. Mathews, *Jack Kennedy*, 310; Donaldson, *The First Modern Campaign*, 132.

169. White, *The Making of the President 1960*, 323; Donaldson, *The First Modern Campaign*, 132.

170. There are many excellent descriptions of the Kennedy-Nixon debates, but for these next paragraphs I relied on White, *The Making of the President 1960*, 279–94; Rorabaugh, *The Real Making of the President*, 149–55; Donaldson, *The First Modern Campaign*, 109–23.

171. Donaldson, *The First Modern Campaign*, 110.

172. White, *The Making of the President 1960*, 292–93.

173. Donaldson, *The First Modern Campaign*, 118.

174. Mathews, *Jack Kennedy*, 115.

175. Rorabaugh, *The Real Making of the President*, 149.

176. White, *The Making of the President 1960*, 294.

177. Lorant, *The Glorious Burden*, 840.

178. Thomas, *Being Nixon*, 123; Donaldson, *The First Modern Campaign*, 143–44.

179. Michael Beschloss, "No Concession, No Sleep: Election Night 1960," *New York Times*, October 30, 2016.

180. Oliphant and Wilkie, *The Road to Camelot*, 356–58.

181. Thomas, *Being Nixon*, 128–29.

182. Lyndon B. Johnson, "Remarks at the University of Michigan, May 22, 1964," Johnson, Selected Speeches and Messages, http://www.lbjlibrary.net/collections/selected -speeches/november-1963-1964/05-22-1964.html.

183. *Presidential Elections, 1789–2004*, 69.

184. Goldwater, *The Conscience of a Conservative*, 14.

185. Young, *Two Suns of the Southwest*, 52.

186. Lorant, *The Glorious Burden*, 877.

187. Lorant, *The Glorious Burden*, 875–77.

188. Lorant, *The Glorious Burden*, 879.

189. Donaldson, *Liberalism's Last Hurrah*, 62–64.

190. For more on the GOP California primary, see Young, *Two Suns of the Southwest*, 90–91; Donaldson, *Liberalism's Last Hurrah*, 150–53.

191. Dickerson, *Whistlestop*, 148.

192. Donaldson, *Liberalism's Last Hurrah*, 90; Lorant, *The Glorious Burden*, 883.

193. Farris, *Almost President*, 192.

194. Dickerson, *Whistlestop*, 158.

195. Young, *Two Suns of the Southwest*, 94.

196. Lorant, *The Glorious Burden*, 888.

197. Lorant, *The Glorious Burden*, 888.

198. Young, *Two Suns of the Southwest*, 7.

199. Donaldson, *Liberalism's Last Hurrah*, 246.

200. Young, *Two Suns of the Southwest*, 166.

201. For more on these TV commercials, see Donaldson, *Liberalism's Last Hurrah*, 247–51; Young, *Two Suns of the Southwest*, 174–77. For an interesting piece on some of the Madison Avenue thinking behind the ads, see David Greenberg, "How a Little Girl Beat Barry Goldwater," *Daily Beast*, February 19, 2016.

202. Lorant, *The Glorious Burden*, 897.

203. These quotes are taken from Darman, *Landslide*, 222; Donaldson, *Liberalism's Last Hurrah*, 293.

204. Donaldson, *Liberalism's Last Hurrah*, ix.

205. Sundquist, *Dynamics of the Party System*, 269.

206. Lowndes, *From the New Deal to the New Right*, 25.

207. Donaldson, *Liberalism's Last Hurrah*, 124.

208. Darman, *Landslide*, 219. For more on Reagan's speech, also see Donaldson, *Liberalism's Last Hurrah*, 286–88.

209. Young, *Two Suns of the Southwest*, 194.

6. Upheaval in American Politics

1. Julian E. Zelizer, "How Jimmy Carter Revolutionized the Iowa Caucuses," *Atlantic*, January 25, 2016.

2. O'Donnell, *Playing with Fire*, 104.

3. O'Donnell, *Playing with Fire*, 128.

4. Cohen, *American Maelstrom*, 99.

5. O'Donnell, *Playing with Fire*, 228; Cohen, *American Maelstrom*, 112.

6. O'Donnell, *Playing with Fire*, 270.

7. Cohen, *American Maelstrom*, 150.

8. Cohen, *American Maelstrom*, 146–49.

9. O'Mara, *Pivotal Tuesdays*, 126.

10. For more on some convention scenarios, including a movement to draft Ted Kennedy for the nomination, see White, *The Making of the President 1968*, 328–32; Reichley, *The Life of the Parties*, 341; O'Donnell, *Playing with Fire*, 351–56.

11. Clarke, *The Last Campaign*, 222.

12. Cohen, *American Maelstrom*, 270–72.

13. White, *The Making of the President 1968*, 348.

14. Mailer, *Miami and the Siege of Chicago*, 178.

15. For more descriptions of the scenes at the Chicago convention, see White, *The Making of the President 1968*, 339–54; Cohen, *American Maelstrom*, 270–82; O'Donnell, *Playing with Fire*, 360–68.

16. O'Donnell, *Playing with Fire*, 360.

17. O'Donnell, *Playing with Fire*, 154.

18. O'Donnell, *Playing with Fire*, 201.

19. Stirewalt, *Every Man a King*, 135–36.

20. Weston, *The Runner-Up Presidency*, 97; Dickerson, *Whistlestop*, 378–79.

21. Cohen, *American Maelstrom*, 220.

22. White, *The Making of the President 1968*, 408; Cohen, *American Maelstrom*, 219–20; Dickerson, *Whistlestop*, 378–79.

23. White, *The Making of the President 1968*, 405.

24. Michener, *Presidential Lottery*, 10–11.

25. Richard Nixon, "Acceptance Speech to the G.O.P. Convention," transcript, *New York Times*, August 9, 1968. Also see Nelson, *Resilient America*, 155; Cohen, *American Maelstrom*, 258.

26. O'Mara, *Pivotal Tuesdays*, 147.

27. White, *The Making of the President 1968*, 412; Cohen, *American Maelstrom*, 292.

28. Cohen, *American Maelstrom*, 293.

29. Boller, *Presidential Campaigns*, 325.

30. Boller, *Presidential Campaigns*, 326.

31. White, *The Making of the President 1968*, 418; Cohen, *American Maelstrom*, 297; Boller, *Presidential Campaigns*, 326.

32. Cohen, *American Maelstrom*, 300.

33. O'Donnell, *Playing with Fire*, 382–84; Cohen, *American Maelstrom*, 300–301.

34. Background on the Vietnam talks and the Chennault affair are taken from Farrell, *Richard Nixon*, 342–45; Cohen, *American Maelstrom*, 319–26; O'Donnell, *Playing with Fire*, 392–404; White, *The Making of the President 1968*, 440–45; Thomas, *Being Nixon*, 174–81.

35. Farrell, *Richard Nixon*, 342; O'Donnell, *Playing with Fire*, 404. Also see Peter Baker, "Nixon Tried to Spoil Johnson's Vietnam Peace Talks in '68, Notes Show," *New York Times*, January 2, 2017.

36. O'Donnell, *Playing with Fire*, 405.

37. For overviews of this electoral movement, see Wegman, *Let the People Pick the President*, 148–56; and Gillian Brockell, "Of the 700 Attempts to Fix or Abolish the Electoral College, This One Nearly Succeeded," *Washington Post*, December 5, 2020.

38. Wegman, *Let the People Pick the President*, 155–56; Brockell, "Of the 700 Attempts."

39. Carroll Kilpatrick and Don Oberdorfer, "Richard M. Nixon Becomes President with 'Sacred Commitment' to Peace," *Washington Post*, January 21, 1969.

40. White, *The Making of the President 1972*, 59.

41. For a longer examination of some of Nixon's domestic policies and proposals, see Drew, *Richard M. Nixon*, 46–59.

42. A more extensive look at Muskie's situation in New Hampshire, including the quotes in this paragraph, can be found in Dickerson, *Whistlestop*, 89–105.

43. This quote and the previous one from David Broder are from Dickerson, *Whistlestop*, 98.

44. Reichley, *The Life of the Parties*, 348.

45. For more detail on these policy positions, see White, *The Making of the President 1972*, 116–19.

46. Dickerson, *Whistlestop*, 110–11; Timothy Noah, "Acid, Amnesty, and Abortion: The Unlikely Source of a Legendary Smear," *New Republic*, October 21, 2012.

47. Farris, *Almost President*, 213–14.

48. White, *The Making of the President 1972*, 187.

49. For more in-depth looks at the Eagleton affair, see White, *The Making of the President 1972*, 193–209; Dickerson, *Whistlestop*, 108–24.

50. White, *The Making of the President 1972*, 199.

51. White, *The Making of the President 1972*, 203.

52. Dickerson, *Whistlestop*, 119.

53. Boller, *Presidential Campaigns*, 336.

54. Dickerson, *Whistlestop*, 123.

55. White, *The Making of the President 1972*, 335–36.

56. Noah, "Acid, Amnesty, and Abortion."

57. There are many good sources for information on the Watergate saga, but sources for these next paragraphs include Drew, *Richard M. Nixon*, 98–132; Farrell, *Richard Nixon*, 465–84, 503–33; White, *The Making of the President 1972*, 269–98.

58. Crouse, *The Boys on the Bus*, 311.

59. Andrew Kohut, "How the Watergate Crisis Eroded Public Support for Richard Nixon," *Pew Research FactTank*, reprinted September 25, 2019, https://www.pewresearch.org/fact-tank/2019/09/25/how-the-watergate-crisis-eroded-public-support-for-richard-nixon/.

60. Witcover, *Marathon*, 47.

61. Witcover, *Marathon*, 47–48.

62. Jeffrey M. Jones, "Gerald Ford Retrospective," Gallup News Service, December 29, 2006, https://news.gallup.com/poll/23995/gerald-ford-retrospective.aspx.

63. Dickerson, *Whistlestop*, 196–97.

64. Witcover, *Marathon*, 438.

65. Witcover, *Marathon*, 447–48.

66. Witcover, *Marathon*, 486–93.

67. Lorant, *The Glorious Burden*, 1049.

68. Jibran Khan, "Government Cannot Solve Our Problems," *National Review*, May 10, 2018.

69. Witcover, *Marathon*, 239, 254.

70. James Reston, "Does It Really Matter?" *New York Times*, May 28, 1976.

71. Jimmy Carter, "Acceptance Speech at Democratic National Convention," July 15, 1976, Carter, Selected Speeches, https://www.jimmycarterlibrary.gov/assets/documents/speeches/acceptance_speech.pdf.

72. Jones, "Gerald Ford Retrospective."

73. Boller, *Presidential Campaigns*, 343.

74. Witcover, *Marathon*, 590–91; Boller, *Presidential Campaigns*, 347.

75. Lorant, *The Glorious Burden*, 1051.

76. Boller, *Presidential Campaigns*, 348.

77. Witcover, *Marathon*, 602–3.

78. Boller, *Presidential Campaigns*, 351.

79. For a full exploration of the presidential debates and of Ford's gaffe, see Witcover, *Marathon*, 616–48.

80. Jones, "Gerald Ford Retrospective."

81. Boller, *Presidential Campaigns*, 352.

82. Lorant, *The Glorious Burden*, 1054; T. R. Reid, "Direct Presidential Election Again Sought by Sen. Bayh," *Washington Post*, January 28, 1977.

83. For a more in-depth look at this history, see *Presidential Elections, 1789–2004*, 101–11. For a book-length examination of the topic, one good source is Kamarck, *Primary Politics*.

84. Kamarck, *Primary Politics*, ix.

85. Crouse, *The Boys on the Bus*, 39.

86. Kamarck, *Primary Politics*, 59.

87. Zelizer, *Jimmy Carter*, 2.

88. White, *America in Search of Itself*, 268.

89. Busch, *Reagan's Victory*, 56; Isenberg, *White Trash*, 284–85.

90. Busch, *Reagan's Victory*, 32–35. Also see Mary Russell and Spencer Rich, "Carter's Fiscal Conservatism Irks Party Leaders," *Washington Post*, May 8, 1977.

91. Germond and Witcover, *Blue Smoke and Mirrors*, 77; Tom Shales, "The TV Campaign: 'Teddy,' Set, Go!" *Washington Post*, November 3, 1979.

92. Busch, *Reagan's Victory*, 59.

93. For an in-depth description of the primary battle between Carter and Kennedy, see Dickerson, *Whistlestop*, 348–65.

94. Ward, *Camelot's End*, 179.

95. Ward, *Camelot's End*, 203.

96. Weisberg, *Ronald Reagan*, 64.

97. Ward, *Camelot's End*, 234.

98. Dickerson, *Whistlestop*, 363.

99. Busch, *Reagan's Victory*, 90.

100. Busch, *Reagan's Victory*, 91.

101. Busch, *Reagan's Victory*, 92.

102. Meacham, *Destiny and Power*, 211.

103. Boller, *Presidential Campaigns*, 358; Busch, *Reagan's Victory*, 46.

104. Germond and Witcover, *Blue Smoke and Mirrors*, 118–19.

105. Dickerson, *Whistlestop*, 6–7; Germond and Witcover, *Blue Smoke and Mirrors*, 125–26.

106. Dickerson, *Whistlestop*, 10.

107. For longer descriptions of the scene at the Nashua debate, see White, *America in Search of Itself*, 30–32; Dickerson, *Whistlestop*, 3–13; Germond and Witcover, *Blue Smoke and Mirrors*, 125–39.

108. Germond and Witcover, *Blue Smoke and Mirrors*, 170.

109. Germond and Witcover, *Blue Smoke and Mirrors*, 228–39.

110. Gallup News, "Gallup Presidential Trial-Heat Trends, 1936–2008," accessed June 16, 2021, https://news.gallup.com/poll/110548/gallup-presidential-election-trial -heat-trends.aspx.

111. Robert G. Kaiser, "Anderson Could Win, Pollsters Agree," *Washington Post*, June 18, 1980.

112. Germond and Witcover, *Blue Smoke and Mirrors*, 227.

113. Boller, *Presidential Campaigns*, 359.

114. Meacham, *Destiny and Power*, 253.

115. Zelizer, *Jimmy Carter*, 115.

116. Germond and Witcover, *Blue Smoke and Mirrors*, 280; Zelizer, *Jimmy Carter*, 122.

117. Busch, *Reagan's Victory*, 199; Germond and Witcover, *Blue Smoke and Mirrors*, 281.

118. Zelizer, *Jimmy Carter*, 120.

119. Germond and Witcover, *Blue Smoke and Mirrors*, 320.

120. Ward, *Camelot's End*, 293–94; Germond and Witcover, *Blue Smoke and Mirrors*, 307–10.

121. Ronald Reagan, "First Inaugural Address," January 21, 1981, transcript, Ronald Reagan Presidential Foundation, https://www.reaganfoundation.org/ronald-reagan/reagan-quotes-speeches/inaugural-address-1/.

122. For more details on the assassination attempt, see Brands, *Reagan*, 286–94.

123. Weisberg, *Ronald Reagan*, 73.

124. Weisberg, *Ronald Reagan*, 76–77.

125. Bai, *All the Truth Is Out*, 44.

126. Germond and Witcover, *Wake Us When It's Over*, 191–93.

127. Germond and Witcover, *Wake Us When It's Over*, 188.

128. Garry Clifford and Peter Carlson, "Gary Hart," *People*, August 22, 1983.

129. Germond and Witcover, *Wake Us When It's Over*, 189.

130. Germond and Witcover, *Wake Us When It's Over*, 409.

131. Germond and Witcover, *Wake Us When It's Over*, 414.

132. Boller, *Presidential Campaigns*, 372.

133. Germond and Witcover, *Wake Us When It's Over*, 380. For more background on Mondale's entire selection process, see 353–67.

134. Germond and Witcover, *Wake Us When It's Over*, 478.

135. Germond and Witcover, *Wake Us When It's Over*, 545.

136. *Presidential Elections, 1789–2004*, 77.

137. Brands, *Reagan*, 455.

138. Boller, *Presidential Campaigns*, 370.

139. Brands, *Reagan*, 456; Germond and Witcover, *Wake Us When It's Over*, 533.

140. Eleanor Clift, "You're Going to Miss Me," *Newsweek*, November 21, 1988.

141. Meacham, *Destiny and Power*, 312.

142. Dickerson, *Whistlestop*, 75.

143. Quotes from this paragraph, and the overall description of the Bush-Rather incident, are drawn from Germond and Witcover, *Whose Broad Stripes and Bright Stars?*, 125–26; Dickerson, *Whistlestop*, 76–78; Meacham, *Destiny and Power*, 318–20.

144. Meacham, *Destiny and Power*, 339.

145. Polling data from James R. Dickenson and Paul Taylor, "Newspaper Stakeout Infuriates Hart," *Washington Post*, May 4, 1987.

146. Bai, *All the Truth Is Out*, 138.

147. For an extensive look at the circumstances of Hart's scandal and withdrawal from the race, see Germond and Witcover, *Whose Broad Stripes and Bright Stars?*, 169–215. For an excellent book-length treatment of the topic, see Bai, *All the Truth Is Out*.

148. For more on the Biden controversy, see Germond and Witcover, *Whose Broad Stripes and Bright Stars?*, 231–41.

149. Cramer, *What It Takes*, 910.

150. Meacham, *Destiny and Power*, 330.

151. Edward Walsh, "Dukakis Accepts Nomination, Promises New Era of Greatness," *Washington Post*, July 22, 1988; Boller, *Presidential Campaigns*, 378.

152. Staff, "How Bush Won: The Inside Story of Campaign '88," *Newsweek*, November 21, 1988, 69–73; Dickerson, *Whistlestop*, 83–85.

153. Germond and Witcover, *Whose Broad Stripes and Bright Stars?*, 400.

154. Germond and Witcover, *Whose Broad Stripes and Bright Stars?*, 9.

155. For more on the Dukakis mental health rumors, including the quotes in this paragraph, see Germond and Witcover, *Whose Broad Stripes and Bright Stars?*, 360–61. Also see Carter, *From George Wallace to Newt Gingrich*, 75–76.

156. Staff, "How Bush Won," 69.

157. Germond and Witcover, *Whose Broad Stripes and Bright Stars?*, 410.

158. Germond and Witcover, *Whose Broad Stripes and Bright Stars?*, 407–8.

159. Germond and Witcover, *Whose Broad Stripes and Bright Stars?*, 7.

160. Sundquist, *Dynamics of the Party System*, 434; Adam Clymer, "Displeasure with Carter Turned Many to Reagan," *New York Times*, November 9, 1980.

161. For more on elements of this coalition, see Sundquist, *Dynamics of the Party System*, 414–21; Busch, *Reagan's Victory*, 20–23.

162. For more on these shifting coalitions, see the book-length examinations of the topic in Scammon and Wattenberg, *The Real Majority*; and Phillips, *The Emerging Republican Majority*.

163. Stevens, *It Was All a Lie*, 25–27.

164. Cohen, *American Maelstrom*, 347; Dickerson, *Whistlestop*, 374–75.

165. McVeigh and Estep, *The Politics of Losing*, 85.

166. Stevens, *It Was All a Lie*, 174.

167. Thomas B. Edsall and Mary D. Edsall, "Race," *Atlantic*, May 1991.

168. Scammon and Wattenberg, *The Real Majority*, 20–22, 39–43.

169. Cohen, *American Maelstrom*, 339.

170. Cohen, *American Maelstrom*, 339.

171. Meacham, *Destiny and Power*, 598–99.

172. Germond and Witcover, *Mad as Hell*, 50; Meacham, *Destiny and Power*, 466.

173. Kornacki, *The Red and the Blue*, 80–83; Dickerson, *Whistlestop*, 58. You can also see a clip of this SNL satire at https://www.nbc.com/saturday-night-live/video/campaign-92-the-race-to-avoid-being-the-guy-who-loses-to-bush/2859836.

174. Germond and Witcover, *Mad as Hell*, 134.

175. Staff, "How He Won: The Untold Story of Bill Clinton's Triumph," *Newsweek* special election issue, November/December 1992, 63.

176. A more in-depth description of the Gennifer Flowers situation can be found in Germond and Witcover, *Mad as Hell*, 168–89; and Dickerson, *Whistlestop*, 60–63.

177. Bai, *All the Truth Is Out*, 191.

178. Germond and Witcover, *Mad as Hell*, 196.

179. Joe Klein, "Clinton's Challenge," *Newsweek* special issue, "The Age of Clinton," Winter/Spring 1993, 28.

180. Kornacki, *The Red and the Blue*, 137.

181. Germond and Witcover, *Mad as Hell*, 196–97.

182. Dickerson, *Whistlestop*, 67.

183. Dickerson, *Whistlestop*, 68.

184. Eduardo Porter, "Ross Perot's Warning of 'Giant Sucking Sound' on Nafta Echoes Today," *New York Times*, July 9, 2019.

185. Farris, *Almost President*, 246.

186. Dan Balz and E. J. Dionne Jr., "Clinton Secures Party Nomination," *Washington Post*, June 3, 1992.

187. Kornacki, *The Red and the Blue*, 167.

188. Howard Kurtz, "Perot's Late Entry into Race Greatly Compresses Media Scrutiny," *Washington Post*, June 25, 1992.

189. Kornacki, *The Red and the Blue*, 187.

190. Germond and Witcover, *Mad as Hell*, 372.

191. Danny Spiegel, "Today in TV History: Bill Clinton and His Sax Visit Arsenio," *TV Insider*, June 3, 2015, https://www.tvinsider.com/2979/rerun-bill-clinton-on-arsenio-hall/.

192. Germond and Witcover, *Mad as Hell*, 346.

193. Staff, "How He Won," 56.

194. Germond and Witcover, *Mad as Hell*, 382.

195. For more on the Clinton-Gore bus tour, see Germond and Witcover, *Mad as Hell*, 373–85. For the *Newsweek* quote, see Klein, "Clinton's Challenge," 31.

196. Kornacki, *The Red and the Blue*, 196–97.

197. Germond and Witcover, *Mad as Hell*, 410.

198. Kornacki, *The Red and the Blue*, 196; O'Mara, *Pivotal Tuesdays*, 192.

199. O'Mara, *Pivotal Tuesdays*, 197.

200. Germond and Witcover, *Mad as Hell*, 476.

201. Staff, "How He Won," 72.

202. Farris, *Almost President*, 253–54.

203. Former vice president Dan Quayle, for instance, wrote in a 2010 op-ed that "Perot cost the Republican Party the White House" because a majority of his supporters would have otherwise backed Bush. Dan Quayle, "Don't Let the Tea Party Go Perot," *Washington Post*, April 4, 2010.

204. Meacham, *Destiny and Power*, 521. Also see E. J. Dionne Jr., "Perot Seen Not Affecting Vote Outcome," *Washington Post*, November 8, 1992.

205. Germond and Witcover, *Mad as Hell*, 354.

206. Dan Balz and Ann Devroy, "Clinton's Lead Appears Solid, May Be Growing," *Washington Post*, September 22, 1992.

207. Ann Devroy and Ruth Marcus, "Clinton Takes Oath as 42nd President Asking Sacrifice, Promising Renewal," *Washington Post*, January 21, 1993.

208. For more context on the issues surrounding "Don't Ask, Don't Tell," about gays in the military, see Kornacki, *The Red and the Blue*, 220–29; and Sam Stein, "Barney Frank: Don't Blame Bill Clinton for 'Don't Ask, Don't Tell,'" *Huffington Post*, August 9, 2017.

209. Some of this background on the health care bill comes from Kornacki, *The Red and the Blue*, 267–73; and Klein, *The Natural*, 119–26.

210. James Fallows, "A Triumph of Misinformation," *Atlantic*, January 1995.

211. Bill Clinton, "Speech Accepting the Democratic Nomination for President," transcript, *New York Times*, August 30, 1996.

212. Schneider, *Standoff*, 228.

213. Staff, "Victory March," *Newsweek*, November 18, 1996, 31–32.

214. Boller, *Presidential Campaigns*, 401.

215. Kornacki, *The Red and the Blue*, 339; Staff, "Victory March," 31.

216. Farris, *Almost President*, 256–57.

217. Gallup Poll, "Presidential Approval Ratings—Bill Clinton," accessed June 16, 2021, https://news.gallup.com/poll/116584/presidential-approval-ratings-bill-clinton.aspx.

218. Quoted in Klein, *The Natural*, 17.

219. Kornacki, *The Red and the Blue*, 378.

220. Dickerson, *Whistlestop*, 172.

221. Dickerson, *Whistlestop*, 184.

222. For more on the GOP South Carolina primary, see Simon, *Divided We Stand*, 96–111.

223. Boller, *Presidential Campaigns*, 408.

224. Simon, *Divided We Stand*, 152.

225. Simon, *Divided We Stand*, 55.

226. Simon, *Divided We Stand*, 54.

227. Simon, *Divided We Stand*, 65.

228. Frank Bruni, "Bush Calls on Gore to Denounce Clinton Affair," *New York Times*, August 12, 2000; Rich Lowry, "I'm a Uniter, Not a Divider," *Washington Post*, October 29, 2000.

229. Boller, *Presidential Campaigns*, 407.

230. Simon, *Divided We Stand*, 196.

231. R. W. Apple Jr., "Gore, in Debut as Presidential Nominee," *New York Times*, August 17, 2000; R. W. Apple Jr., "Bush, Accepting GOP Nomination," *New York Times*, August 4, 2000.

232. Toobin, *Too Close to Call*, 19–22; Nichols, *Jews for Buchanan*, 19–21; Freeman and Bleifuss, *Was the 2004 Presidential Election Stolen?*, 50–51.

233. Reports of election night details are drawn from several sources, including Toobin, *Too Close to Call*, 18–25; and Simon, *Divided We Stand*, 30–43.

234. Nancy Gibbs, "Reversal of Fortune," *Time*, November 20, 2000.

235. Nichols, *Jews for Buchanan*, 87.

236. Tom Fiedler, "The Encore of Key Largo," in Sabato, *Overtime!*, 9; Nichols, *Jews for Buchanan*, 96; Weston, *The Runner-Up Presidency*, 23.

237. Toobin, *Too Close to Call*, 275–76; Steve Lopez, "No Apologies," *Time*, November 20, 2000.

238. Simon, *Divided We Stand*, 261–62; Nichols, *Jews for Buchanan*, 25; Freeman and Bleifuss, *Was the 2004 Presidential Election Stolen?*, 51.

239. Simon, *Divided We Stand*, 261–62.

240. Toobin, *Too Close to Call*, 176; Nichols, *Jews for Buchanan*, 75.

241. Toobin, *Too Close to Call*, 174–76, 201.

242. For more in-depth narratives of this scene, see Toobin, *Too Close to Call*, 153–59; Simon, *Divided We Stand*, 277–82; Nichols, *Jews for Buchanan*, 150–59.

243. Toobin, *Too Close to Call*, 188.

244. For more of a blow-by-blow account of the court proceedings and its decision, see Toobin, *Too Close to Call*, 248–69.

245. Boller, *Presidential Campaigns*, 410.

246. Weston, *The Runner-Up Presidency*, 25; Toobin, *Too Close to Call*, 264.

247. "Text of Gore's Concession Speech," *New York Times*, December 13, 2000.

248. The postelection analysis of the vote in the next paragraphs is drawn from the following sources: Toobin, *Too Close to Call*, 278–82; Nichols, *Jews for Buchanan*, 64–71; Wade Payson-Denney, "So, Who Really Won? What the Bush v. Gore Studies Showed," CNN Politics, October 31, 2015; Dan Keating and Dan Balz, "Florida Recounts Would Have Favored Bush," *Washington Post*, November 12, 2001.

249. Sabato, *Overtime!*, 9; Toobin, *Too Close to Call*, 173.

250. Toobin, *Too Close to Call*, 282; Payson-Denney, "So, Who Really Won?"

251. Nichols, *Jews for Buchanan*, 90.

252. "Remarks of Former Vice President Al Gore to the Democratic National Convention," *New York Times*, July 26, 2004.

253. "The Inauguration; President: 'I Ask You to Be Citizens,'" transcript of Bush's inaugural address, *New York Times*, January 21, 2001.

254. Ceaser and Busch, *Red over Blue*, 41.

255. Gallup Poll, "Presidential Approval Ratings—George W. Bush," accessed June 16, 2021, https://news.gallup.com/poll/116500/presidential-approval-ratings-george -bush.aspx.

256. Todd S. Purdum, "After the Attacks: The White House; Bush Warns of a Wrathful, Shadowy and Inventive War," *New York Times*, September 17, 2001.

257. *Presidential Elections, 1789–2004*, 93.

258. Gallup Poll, "Presidential Approval Ratings—George W. Bush."

259. Ceaser and Busch, *Red over Blue*, 73.

260. For more on the Democratic nomination battle, see Ceaser and Busch, *Red over Blue*, 69–103; and Staff, "The Democrats: Fits and Starts," *Newsweek*, November 15, 2004, 42–53.

261. Dickerson, *Whistlestop*, 140–42; Mark Murray, "As Howard Dean's 'Scream' Turns 15, Its Impact on American Politics Lives On," *Meet the Press*, January 18, 2019, https://www.nbcnews.com/politics/meet-the-press/howard-dean-s-scream-turns-15-its-impact-american-politics-n959916.

262. Staff, "Teaming Up," *Newsweek*, November 15, 2004, 77–78.

263. Staff, "Teaming Up."

264. Ceaser and Busch, *Red over Blue*, 116–18; James Carney, "Measure of a Tight Race," *Time*, September 6, 2004.

265. "Barack Obama's Remarks to the Democratic National Convention," *New York Times*, July 27, 2004.

266. Ceaser and Busch, *Red over Blue*, 120; Adam Nagourney and Richard W. Stevenson, "Bush Outlines Plan for a 2nd Term and Attacks Kerry's Record," *New York Times*, September 3, 2004.

267. Schneider, *Standoff*, 233.

268. Ceaser and Busch, *Red over Blue*, 14–16, 133–34.

269. Quotes and information from this paragraph are from Ceaser and Busch, *Red over Blue*, 118–20; Farris, *Almost President*, 270; Staff, "The Vets Attack," *Newsweek*, November 15, 2004, 90–96; Carney, "Measure of a Tight Race."

270. Karen Tumulty, "What Biden Can Learn from John Kerry's Mistakes," *Washington Post*, October 15, 2019.

271. Staff, "Trench Warfare," *Newsweek*, November 15, 2004, 62–71.

272. Frank, *What's the Matter with Kansas*, 258; Roger Cohen, "The Republicans' Barb: John Kerry Looks French," *New York Times*, April 3, 2004.

273. Staff, "Face to Face," *Newsweek*, November 15, 2004, 107–16; Ceaser and Busch, *Red over Blue*, 128–29.

274. For much more detail on these allegations and investigations, see Miller, *What Went Wrong in Ohio*; Michael Powell and Peter Slevin, "Several Factors Contributed to 'Lost' Voters in Ohio," *Washington Post*, December 15, 2004; Christopher Hitchens, "Ohio's Odd Numbers," *Vanity Fair*, March 2005.

275. Howard Fineman, "A Sweet Victory . . . and a Tough Loss," *Newsweek*, November 15, 2004.

276. Frank, *What's the Matter with Kansas*, 16.

277. Kornacki, *The Red and the Blue*, 422; Ceaser and Busch, *Red over Blue*, 1–2; Jodi Enda, "When Republicans Were Blue and Democrats Were Red," *Smithsonian*, October 31, 2012.

278. Mann and Ornstein, *It's Even Worse Than It Looks*, 33.

279. For more on the Gingrich strategies, see Mann and Ornstein, *It's Even Worse Than It Looks*, 32–39; Carter, *From George Wallace to Newt Gingrich*, 118–19; McKay Coppins, "The Man Who Broke Politics," *Atlantic*, November 2018.

280. Tomasky, *Bill Clinton*, 31–32; Tomasky, *If We Can Keep It*, 167.

281. Camille Ryan and Jamie M. Lewis, "Computer and Internet Use in the United States," U.S. Census Bureau, September 2017, https://www.census.gov/content/dam/Census/library/publications/2017/acs/acs-37.pdf.

282. Tomasky, *If We Can Keep It*, 164–69; Ceaser and Busch, *Red over Blue*, 29.

7. History in the Making

1. Charles Arthur, "How Laptops Took Over the World," *Guardian*, October 28, 2009.

2. For more on the history of Starbucks, see "Starbucks Company Timeline," www .starbucks.com; or Colin Marshall, "The First Starbucks Coffee Shop, Seattle," *Guardian*, May 14, 2015.

3. Adam Nagourney, "Obama Elected President as Racial Barrier Falls," *New York Times*, November 4, 208.

4. Mann, *George W. Bush*, 100; National Weather Service, "Hurricane Katrina— August 2005," accessed June 17, 2021, https://www.weather.gov/mob/katrina.

5. Ellis Cose, "Walking the World Stage," *Newsweek*, September 11, 2006, 27.

6. Real Clear Politics, "Polling Data—2008 Democratic Presidential Nomination," accessed June 17, 2021, https://www.realclearpolitics.com/epolls/2008/president/us /democratic_presidential_nomination-191.html.

7. David S. Broder, "Obama Finds His Address," *Washington Post*, December 23, 2007.

8. Cowan, *Let the People Rule*, 294.

9. Heilemann and Halperin, *Game Change*, 234–37; Wolfe, *Renegade*, 176–78; Axelrod, *Believer*, 269–71.

10. Dionne and Reid, *We Are the Change We Seek*, 51.

11. Plouffe, *The Audacity to Win*, 214.

12. Heilemann and Halperin, *Game Change*, 240–41.

13. Real Clear Politics, "Polling Data—2008 Democratic Presidential Nomination."

14. Balz and Johnson, *The Battle for America*, 219.

15. Axelrod, *Believer*, 293–94.

16. Plouffe, *The Audacity to Win*, 305–6; Dionne and Reid, *We Are the Change We Seek*, 85.

17. Staff, "How He Did It: The Inside Story of Campaign 2008," *Newsweek*, November 17, 2008, 92.

18. For more on Palin's selection, see Heilemann and Halperin, *Game Change*, 353–64; Balz and Johnson, *The Battle for America*, 327–39; Axelrod, *Believer*, 304–7; Plouffe, *The Audacity to Win*, 307–15.

19. Wolfe, *Renegade*, 226; Balz and Johnson, *The Battle for America*, 342.

20. Balz and Johnson, *The Battle for America*, 342.

21. For more on Palin's interview sessions and the SNL skit, see Heilemann and Halperin, *Game Change*, 396–403; and Balz and Johnson, *The Battle for America*, 343–55.

22. For more on the Obama campaign's innovative use of the internet and social media, see David Talbot, "How Obama Really Did It," *MIT Technology Review*, August 19, 2008; and Sara Lai Stirland, "Propelled by Internet, Barack Obama Wins Presidency," *Wired*, November 4, 2008.

23. Matthew Creamer, "Obama Wins! . . . Ad Age's Marketer of the Year," *Ad Age*, October 17, 2008.

24. Staff, "How He Did It," 110; Balz and Johnson, *The Battle for America*, 363.

25. For a more in-depth account of the economic crisis, see Mann, *George W. Bush*, 124–37; Balz and Johnson, *The Battle for America*, 345–51; Heilemann and Halperin, *Game Change*, 377–89.

26. Mann, *George W. Bush*, 132.

27. Plouffe, *The Audacity to Win*, 332; Balz and Johnson, *The Battle for America*, 347.

28. Mann, *George W. Bush*, 135.

29. Nancy Gibbs, "'This Is Our Time,'" *Time*, November 17, 2008, 37.

30. Gibbs, "'This Is Our Time,'" 35.

31. Balz and Johnson, *The Battle for America*, 373.

32. Balz and Johnson, *The Battle for America*, 373–74.

33. "Barack Obama's Inaugural Address," *New York Times*, January 20, 2009; Wolfe, *Renegade*, 306–8.

34. Alter, *The Center Holds*, 6; Axelrod, *Believer*, 333.

35. Dan Balz, "Obama Signals Sharp Break with Past to an Uncertain but Optimistic Nation," *Washington Post*, January 21, 2009.

36. Klein, *Why We're Polarized*, 81–85; Brian C. Mooney, "Romney and Health Care: In the Thick of History," *Boston Globe*, May 30, 2011.

37. Mann and Ornstein, *It's Even Worse Than It Looks*, xix–xx.

38. Alter, *The Center Holds*, 181.

39. Mann and Ornstein, *It's Even Worse Than It Looks*, 102–3.

40. Michael Grunwald, "The Victory of 'No,'" *Politico*, December 4, 2016.

41. Grunwald, "The Victory of 'No'"; Greg Sargent, "Biden: McConnell Decided to Deny Us Cooperation before We Took Office," *Washington Post*, August 10, 2012.

42. An excellent overview of the Tea Party movement can be found in Williamson, Skocpol, and Coggin, "The Tea Party and the Remaking of Republican Conservatism."

43. Sides, Tesler, and Vavreck, *Identity Crisis*, 176–77; Alter, *The Center Holds*, 20; Williamson, Skocpol, and Coggin, "The Tea Party and the Remaking of Republican Conservatism," 35; Eugene Scott, "In New Memoir, Obama Confronts the 'Racial Anxiety' of Trump Supporters," *Washington Post*, November 16, 2020.

44. Levitsky and Ziblatt, *How Democracies Die*, 159.

45. For more on Romney's balancing act regarding Obamacare, see Balz, *Collision 2012*, 93–97; and Heilemann and Halperin, *Double Down*, 106–8.

46. Heilemann and Halperin, *Double Down*, 245.

47. Alter, *The Center Holds*, 207; David Von Drehle, "For Obama, Survival Is the New Winning," *Time*, November 19, 2012, 50.

48. Alter, *The Center Holds*, 212–13.

49. Gallup Poll, "Presidential Approval Ratings—Barack Obama," accessed June 17, 2021, https://news.gallup.com/poll/116479/barack-obama-presidential-job-approval.aspx.

50. Jeffrey M. Jones, Frank Newport, and Lydia Saad, "Obama's Challenge: Higher Likability Than Approval," Gallup Poll, September 6, 2012, https://news.gallup.com/poll/157292/obama-challenge-higher-likability-approval.aspx.

51. Dionne and Reid, *We Are the Change We Seek*, 176.

52. Heilemann and Halperin, *Double Down*, 387.

53. Alberta, *American Carnage*, 131–32.

54. Roger Simon, "Obama Snoozes and Loses," *Politico*, October 4, 2012.

55. Real Clear Politics, "2012 Presidential Polls," accessed June 17, 2021, https://www
.realclearpolitics.com/epolls/2012/president/us/general_election_romney_vs_obama
-1171.html#polls.

56. Dionne and Reid, *We Are the Change We Seek*, 202–7; Tom Cohen, "Obama's
Speech Ties Current Issues to Founding Principles," CNN, January 21, 2013.

57. Ronald Brownstein, "Party Gridlock Haunts the Races in Iowa," *Atlantic*, January 29, 2016.

58. Mark Landler and Eric Lichtblau, "F.B.I. Director James Comey Recommends
No Charges for Hillary Clinton on Email," *New York Times*, July 5, 2016.

59. For more on the email scandal, see Allen and Parnes, *Shattered*, 60–69, 92–
93; Michael S. Schmidt, "Hillary Clinton Used Personal Email Account at State
Dept., Possibly Breaking Rules," *New York Times*, March 2, 2015; Mike Levine, "Why
Hillary Clinton Deleted 33,000 Emails on Her Private Server," ABC News, September 27, 2016.

60. Eliza Collins, "12 Quotable Moments from Hillary Clinton's Primary Campaign,"
USA Today, June 6, 2016; "10 Quotable Moments in Bernie Sanders' Campaign," *USA
Today*, July 12, 2016.

61. Green, *Devil's Bargain*, 161–62; Alexander Burns, "Donald Trump, Pushing Someone Rich, Offers Himself," *New York Times*, June 26, 2015.

62. For more on these controversies, see Jeff Stein, "Here Are 11 Times Donald
Trump's Campaign Should Have Imploded," *Vox*, February 9, 2016; Ben Jacobs, "Donald Trump Calls Pope Francis 'Disgraceful' for Questioning His Faith," *Guardian*, February 18, 2016; David A. Graham, "Trump: Mexican American Judge Has an 'Absolute
Conflict,'" *Atlantic*, June 2, 2016; Maggie Haberman and Richard A. Oppel Jr., "Donald
Trump Criticizes Muslim Family of Slain U.S. Soldier, Drawing Ire," *New York Times*,
July 30, 2016; Philip Rucker, "Trump Says Fox's Megyn Kelly Had 'Blood Coming Out
of Her Wherever,'" *Washington Post*, August 8, 2015.

63. Alberta, *American Carnage*, 236.

64. Jenna Johnson, "Donald Trump: They Say I Could 'Shoot Somebody' and Still
Have Support," *Washington Post*, January 23, 2016.

65. Ceaser, Busch, and Pitney, *Defying the Odds*, 13.

66. MJ Lee, "How Donald Trump Blasted George W. Bush in S.C.—and Still Won,"
CNN Politics, February 21, 2016.

67. Tur, *Unbelievable*, 174–76; Dara Lind, "What the Hell Is Going on with Violence
at Trump Rallies, Explained," *Vox*, March 21, 2016.

68. Ceaser, Busch, and Pitney, *Defying the Odds*, 85; Alberta, *American Carnage*, 295.

69. Ceaser, Busch, and Pitney, *Defying the Odds*, 94.

70. Allen and Parnes, *Shattered*, 38–39.

71. Alberta, *American Carnage*, 354.

72. Alex Altman, "Midnight in America: Donald Trump's Gloomy Convention
Speech," *Time*, July 22, 2016.

73. For more on the situation surrounding the DNC emails, see Allen and Parnes, *Shattered*, 263–64, 278–80; and Timothy B. Lee, "DNC Email Leaks, Explained," *Vox*, July 25, 2016.

74. Dan Balz and Scott Clement, "Poll Finds Clinton Has Widened Lead Ahead of Trump to 8 Points," *Washington Post*, August 7, 2016; Sides, Tesler, and Vavreck, *Identity Crisis*, 131.

75. Allen and Parnes, *Shattered*, 315–16.

76. Joshua Green and Sasha Issenberg, "Inside the Trump Bunker, with Days to Go," *Bloomberg News*, October 27, 2016.

77. Green, *Devil's Bargain*, 8.

78. Estimates are that Trump received $5 billion to $5.6 billion in media coverage, compared to $3.2 billion to $3.5 billion for Clinton. See Philip Bump, "Assessing a Clinton Argument That the Media Helped to Elect Trump," *Washington Post*, September 12, 2017; Roger Yu, "How Do You Use the Media to Win? Just Ask Donald Trump," *USA Today*, November 11, 2016.

79. Madeline Berg, "Donald Trump May Hate the Media, but They Are Both Winners This Election," *Forbes*, November 10, 2016.

80. Sides, Tesler, and Vavreck, *Identity Crisis*, 55.

81. Rice, *Tough Love*, 443; Lichtman, *The Embattled Vote in America*, 221.

82. Alberta, *American Carnage*, 367.

83. For more on the response to Trump, see Green, *Devil's Bargain*, 214–15; Alberta, *American Carnage*, 368–69; Tur, *Unbelievable*, 248–49; Ceaser, Busch, and Pitney, *Defying the Odds*, 110.

84. Alberta, *American Carnage*, 369.

85. Robert Costa and Philip Rucker, "Second Presidential Debate Takes the Low Road as Attacks and Slurs Dominate," *Washington Post*, October 9, 2016; Alberta, *American Carnage*, 376.

86. For more details on the Podesta emails, see Sam Frizell, "What Leaked Emails Reveal about Hillary Clinton's Campaign," *Time*, October 7, 2016; Jeff Stein, "What 20,000 Pages of Hacked Wikileaks Emails Teach Us about Hillary Clinton," *Vox*, October 20, 2016; Allen and Parnes, *Shattered*, 340–48; Alberta, *American Carnage*, 369–70.

87. The connection between Roger Stone, WikiLeaks, and the *Access Hollywood* videotape was documented by a U.S. Senate investigation. See U.S. Senate, "Report of the Select Committee on Intelligence on Russian Active Measures Campaigns and Interference in the 2016 U.S. Election, Volume 5: Counterintelligence Threats and Vulnerabilities," 249–52, https://www.intelligence.senate.gov/sites/default/files/documents/report_volume5.pdf.

88. Patrick Healy and Jonathan Martin, "Donald Trump Won't Say If He'll Accept Result of Election," *New York Times*, October 19, 2016; Max Fisher, "Trump's Threat to Reject Election Outcome Alarms Scholars," *New York Times*, October 23, 2016; Lauren Carroll, "Is Trump the First-Ever Candidate Not to Say He'll Accept Election Results?" *Politifact*, October 25, 2016.

89. Green, *Devil's Bargain*, 230; Mark Murray, "12 Days That Stunned a Nation: How Hillary Clinton Lost," NBC News Politics, August 23, 2017.

90. Devlin Barrett, "Book Excerpt: An FBI Sex Crimes Investigator Helped Trigger 2016's 'October Surprise,'" *Washington Post*, September 18, 2020; Ceaser, Busch, and Pitney, *Defying the Odds*, 113.

91. Nate Silver, "The Comey Letter Probably Cost Clinton the Election," FiveThirtyEight.com, May 3, 2017; Sides, Tesler, and Vavreck, *Identity Crisis*, 148.

92. The model that was most favorable to Trump was from FiveThirtyEight.com, which gave him just under a 30 percent chance to prevail and mentioned the possibility of his winning the Electoral College while losing the popular vote. Other models gave Trump just a 2 to 15 percent chance of winning. See "FiveThirtyEight 2016 Election Forecast," FiveThirtyEight.com, https://projects.fivethirtyeight.com/2016-election -forecast/; Nate Silver, "The Odds of an Electoral College-Popular Vote Split Are Increasing," FiveThirtyEight.com, October 31, 2016; Philip Bump, "Your Critique That FiveThirtyEight Misfired on the 2016 Race Is Wrong," *Washington Post*, September 27, 2017.

93. The official electoral count was 304–227 because seven faithless electors did not cast ballots for the two main candidates (two for Trump and five for Clinton). The electoral count based on the results of the election by state was 306–232.

94. Daniel Arkin and Corky Siemaszko, "Donald Trump Wins the White House in Upset," NBC News, November 8, 2016.

95. Harry Enten, "Trump Is Just a Normal Polling Error behind Clinton," FiveThirtyEight.com, November 4, 2016; RealClear Politics, "General Election: Trump vs. Clinton," polling averages, https://www.realclearpolitics.com/epolls/2016/president /us/general_election_trump_vs_clinton-5491.html.

96. Philip Bump, "4.4 Million 2012 Obama Voters Stayed Home in 2016—More Than a Third of Them Black," *Washington Post*, March 12, 2018; Silver, "The Comey Letter Probably Cost Clinton the Election"; Sean McElwee, Matt McDermott, and Will Jordan, "4 Pieces of Evidence Showing FBI Director James Comey Cost Clinton the Election," *Vox*, January 11, 2017.

97. Abramowitz, *The Great Alignment*, 7, 164.

98. Schneider, *Standoff*, 1.

99. Reporting on the intelligence assessment comes from Mark Mazzetti and Eric Lichtblau, "C.I.A. Judgment on Russia Built on Swell of Evidence," *New York Times*, December 11, 2016; Greg Miller and Adam Entous, "Declassified Report Says Putin 'Ordered' Effort to Undermine Faith in U.S. Election and Help Trump," *Washington Post*, January 6, 2017; Zack Beauchamp, "The Key Findings from the US Intelligence Report on the Russia Hack, Decoded," *Vox*, January 6, 2017.

100. Jonathan Martin and Maggie Haberman, "Moscow's Hand Swirled in U.S., but Whether It Tipped Election Is Unclear," *New York Times*, February 19, 2018; David Ignatius, "How Russia Used the Internet to Perfect Its Dark Arts," *Washington Post*, December 18, 2018.

101. Matt Flegenheimer, "Earthquake and Aftershock," *New York Times*, November 8, 2016.

102. Edward Delman, "How Lin-Manuel Miranda Shapes History," *Atlantic*, September 29, 2015.

103. Obama, *A Promised Land*, 672.

104. Chua, *Political Tribes*, 171. For more on these studies of Trump voters, see Sides, Tesler, and Vavreck, *Identity Crisis*, 88–89, 176–77; and Abramowitz, *The Great Alignment*, 153–59.

105. For more on Trump's ethnonationalist populism, see Schertzer and Woods, "#Nationalism."

106. Kornacki, *The Red and the Blue*, 157.

107. Reid J. Epstein, "The G.O.P. Delivers Its 2020 Platform: It's from 2016," *New York Times*, August 25, 2020.

108. Zack Beauchamp, "The Midterm Elections Revealed That America Is in a Cold Civil War," *Vox*, November 7, 2018.

109. Schneider, *Standoff*, 27.

110. Coppins, "The Man Who Broke Politics."

111. Inaugural quotes from "'This Moment Is Your Moment,' Donald J. Trump's Inaugural Address," *New York Times*, January 21, 2017.

112. Yun Li, "This Is Now the Longest US Economic Expansion in History," CNBC, July 2, 2019.

113. Christal Hayes, "Here Are 10 Times President Trump's Comments Have Been Called Racist," *USA Today*, August 14, 2018; Sides, Tesler, and Vavreck, *Identity Crisis*, 202.

114. Peter Baker, "Can Trump Destroy Obama's Legacy?" *New York Times*, June 23, 2017.

115. Special Counsel Robert S. Mueller III, U.S. Justice Department, "Report on the Investigation into Russian Interference in the 2016 Presidential Election," March 2019, https://www.justice.gov/archives/sco/file/1373816/download. For additional context on the Russia story or other conclusions drawn from the Mueller Report, see Scott Shane and Mark Mazetti, "The Plot to Subvert an Election: Unraveling the Russia Story So Far," *New York Times*, special report, September 20, 2018; Andrew Prokop, "The Mueller Report, Explained," *Vox*, April 18, 2019.

116. This includes an investigation by the Republican-led Senate homeland security and finance committees, which found no evidence of wrongdoing. See Nicholas Fandos, "Republican Inquiry Finds No Evidence of Wrongdoing by Biden," *New York Times*, September 23, 2020. For additional context, see Glenn Kessler, "A Quick Guide to Trump's False Claims about Ukraine and the Bidens," *Washington Post*, September 27, 2019.

117. Nicholas Fandos and Michael D. Shear, "Trump Impeached for Abuse of Power and Obstruction of Congress," *New York Times*, December 18, 2019.

118. Kyle Cheney, Andrew Desiderio, and John Bresnahan, "Trump Acquitted on Impeachment Charges, Ending Gravest Threat to His Presidency," *Politico*, February 5, 2020.

119. Editorial Board, "Amy Klobuchar and Elizabeth Warren Are Democrats' Top Choices for President," *New York Times*, January 20, 2020.

120. For more on voter fears of women presidential candidates, see Pema Levy, "Trump's Greatest Trick Was Convincing Voters That Women Can't Win Elections," *Mother Jones*, January 29, 2020; and Ella Nilsen, "Voters Are Back to Worrying Whether a Woman Can Win," *Vox*, January 29, 2020.

121. Molly Ball, "In New Hampshire, Democratic Voters Are Paralyzed by Fear of Making the Wrong Choice," *Time*, February 11, 2020.

122. Editorial Board, "Amy Klobuchar and Elizabeth Warren Are Democrats' Top Choices for President."

123. Matt Viser, Dan Balz, and Annie Linskey, "The Democratic Race Is Now Sanders against the Field, and a Contested Convention Possibly Awaits the Party," *Washington Post*, February 20, 2020.

124. For coronavirus statistics, see CDC, "CDC COVID Data Tracker," accessed June 17, 2021, https://covid.cdc.gov/covid-data-tracker/#trends_totalandratecases. For background on comparisons to the 1918 flu, see Apoorva Mandavilli, "In N.Y.C.'s Spring Surge, a Frightening Echo of 1918 Flu," *New York Times*, August 13, 2020.

125. For coronavirus and unemployment statistics, see CDC, "CDC COVID Data Tracker"; Peter Baker, "President Needles as America Burns," *New York Times*, May 31, 2020; Lucy Bayly, "New Weekly Figures Show Almost 40 Million People Lost Their Jobs since the Pandemic," NBC News, May 21, 2020.

126. Aaron Blake and J. M. Rieger, "Timeline: The 184 Times Trump Has Downplayed the Coronavirus Threat," *Washington Post*, October 30, 2020.

127. Matt Stevens, "Joe Biden Accepts Presidential Nomination: Full Transcript," *New York Times*, August 20, 2020.

128. David Scharfenberg, "Joe Biden Told Us the Election Was a 'Battle for the Soul of the Nation': He Was Right," *Boston Globe*, September 12, 2020.

129. Burgess Everett, Alex Thompson, and Marianne Levine, "America's New Power Couple: Joe and Mitch," *Politico*, November 5, 2020.

130. Glenn Thrush, "Full Transcript: President Trump's Republican National Convention Speech," *New York Times*, August 28, 2020.

131. Debate quotes and descriptions from Dan Balz, "Trump Sets the Tone for the Worst Presidential Debate in Living Memory," *Washington Post*, September 29, 2020; and John F. Harris, "An Epic Moment of National Shame: The Debate Was an Embarrassment for the Ages," *Politico*, September 30, 2020.

132. Philip Bump, "There's No Real Question That Biden Won the First Presidential Debate," *Washington Post*, October 4, 2020.

133. For more on these Trump allegations, see Peter Baker, "Trump Uses Health to Attack Biden: Now, He's Defending His Own," *New York Times*, September 3, 2020; David Nakamura, "In Trump's New Version of American Carnage, the Threat Isn't Immigrants or Foreign Nations: It's Other Americans," *Washington Post*, July 4, 2020; Sahil Kapur, "Unable to Land Hits on Biden, Trump Paints Him as a Socialist Trojan Horse," NBC News, July 19, 2020; Jill Colvin and Brian Slodysko, "Trump Leans into Fear Tactics in Bid to Win Midwest States," Associated Press, October 17, 2020; Brett Samuels, "Trump Claims Biden Is 'Against' and Will 'Hurt the Bible,'" *Hill*, August 6,

2020; Peter Baker and Maggie Haberman, "President Lashes Out at His Aides with Calls to Indict Political Rivals," *New York Times*, October 9, 2020.

134. Katie Glueck, "At the Top of the Ticket, Little Trust in the Election," *New York Times*, July 26, 2020; Reid J. Epstein, Emily Cochrane, and Glenn Thrush, "Trump Reiterates Refusal to Honor Election Results," *New York Times*, September 25, 2020.

135. Dan Balz, "Facing Possible Defeat, Trump Threatens the Integrity of the Election," *Washington Post*, September 26, 2020.

136. Jonathan Martin and Katie Glueck, "Biden, Invoking F.D.R., Tries to Siphon Off Trump Voters in Georgia," *New York Times*, October 27, 2020.

137. Kevin Schaul, Kate Rabinowitz, and Ted Mellnik, "2020 Turnout Is the Highest in over a Century," *Washington Post*, updated December 5, 2020.

138. Peter Baker and Maggie Haberman, "In Torrent of Falsehoods, Trump Claims Election Is Being Stolen," *New York Times*, November 5, 2020.

139. Katie Shepherd and Hannah Knowles, "Driven by Unfounded 'Sharpiegate' Rumor, Pro-Trump Protesters Mass Outside Arizona Vote-Counting Center," *Washington Post*, November 5, 2020; Mike Householder and Tim Sullivan, "Trump Supporters Demand Michigan Vote Center 'Stop the Count!'" Associated Press, November 4, 2020.

140. Mark Muro, Eli Byerly Duke, Yang You, and Robert Maxim, "Biden-Voting Counties Equal 70% of America's Economy: What Does This Mean for the Nation's Political-Economic Divide?" *Avenue*, Brookings Institution blog, updated December 8, 2020.

141. The vote totals, both nationally and in individual states, are from "2020 National Popular Vote Tracker," *Cook Political Report*, https://cookpolitical.com/2020-national-popular-vote-tracker.

142. A fact check of some of these allegations can be found in Glenn Kessler, "Fact-Checking the Craziest News Conference of the Trump Presidency," *Washington Post*, November 19, 2020.

143. Philip Rucker, Ashley Parker, Josh Dawsey, and Amy Gardner, "20 Days of Fantasy and Failure: Inside Trump's Quest to Overturn the Election," *Washington Post*, November 28, 2020.

144. David A. Graham, "The GOP Abandons Democracy," *Atlantic*, December 10, 2020.

145. Leonnig and Rucker, *I Alone Can Fix It*, 366, 434–37, 487.

146. Peter Baker and Kathleen Gray, "Even as Trump Claimed Fraud, These Republicans Didn't Bend," *New York Times*, November 29, 2020.

147. Paul Kane and Scott Clement, "Just 27 Congressional Republicans Acknowledge Biden's Win, Washington Post Survey Finds," *Washington Post*, December 5, 2020; Kaelan Deese, "Poll: 70 Percent of Republicans Don't Believe Election Was Free and Fair," *Hill*, November 10, 2020.

148. Philip Rucker, "Trump's Presidency Finishes in 'American Carnage' as Rioters Storm the Capitol," *Washington Post*, January 6, 2021.

149. "Front Pages Capture Chaos of Riots at US Capitol," *USA Today*, January 7, 2021, https://www.usatoday.com/picture-gallery/news/nation/2021/01/07/front-pages-capture-chaos-riots-us-capitol/6577931002/.

150. Harry Stevens, Daniela Santamarina, Kate Rabinowitz, Kevin Uhrmacher, and John Muyskens, "How Members of Congress Voted on Counting the Electoral College Vote," *Washington Post*, January 7, 2021.

151. Peter Baker, "Biden Inaugurated as the 46th President amid a Cascade of Crises," *New York Times*, January 20, 2021.

Epilogue

1. Hemingway, *The Sun Also Rises*, 136.

2. Many pieces have been written about the parties' changing coalitions. For some of these views, see DiStefano, *The Next Realignment*, 368–74; Alberta, *American Carnage*, 610–11; Levitsky and Ziblatt, *How Democracies Die*, 222–27; David Brooks, "Where Do Republicans Go from Here?" *New York Times*, August 9, 2020; Ross Douthat, "Win or Lose, Trump's Power over the G.O.P. Will Not End," *New York Times*, August 23, 2020; Jennifer Schuessler, "Rebranding Nationalism in the Age of Trump," *New York Times*, July 20, 2019.

3. Ronald Reagan, "January 5, 1967: Inaugural Address," Reagan, Speeches, https://www.reaganlibrary.gov/archives/speech/january-5-1967-inaugural-address-public-ceremony.

4. Christopher Ingraham, "The United States Is Backsliding into Autocracy under Trump, Scholars Warn," *Washington Post*, September 18, 2020; Amanda Taub, "Warning Signs Flashing Red for Democracies," *New York Times*, November 29, 2016.

5. Levitsky and Ziblatt, *How Democracies Die*, 3–9.

6. Zara Anishanslin, "What We Get Wrong about Ben Franklin's 'A Republic, If You Can Keep It,'" *Washington Post*, October 29, 2019.

7. Duncan, *The Storm before the Storm*, xx–xxi.

8. Levitsky and Ziblatt, *How Democracies Die*, 143–44.

Bibliography

Archives and Manuscript Materials

Adams, John and Abigail. Correspondence. Adams Family Papers: An Electronic Archive. Massachusetts Historical Society. http://www.masshist.org/digitaladams/archive/.

Carter, Jimmy. Selected Speeches. Jimmy Carter Presidential Library. https://www .jimmycarterlibrary.gov/research/selected_speeches/.

Famous Presidential Speeches. Miller Center. University of Virginia. https://millercenter .org/the-presidency/presidential-speeches.

History Matters. American Social History Project/Center for Media & Learning, City University of New York, and the Center for History and New Media, George Mason University. http://historymatters.gmu.edu/.

Inaugural Addresses of the Presidents. Avalon Project: Documents in Law, History and Diplomacy. Yale Law School, Lillian Goldman Law Library. https://avalon.law.yale .edu/subject_menus/inaug.asp.

Johnson, Lyndon B. Selected Speeches and Messages. LBJ Presidential Library. http:// www.lbjlibrary.net/collections/selected-speeches/.

Kennedy, John F. Historic Speeches. John F. Kennedy Presidential Library. https://www .jfklibrary.org/learn/about-jfk/historic-speeches.

Lincoln, Abraham. Selected Speeches and Writings. Abraham Lincoln Online. http:// www.abrahamlincolnonline.org/lincoln/speeches/speechintro.htm.

Madison, James. Papers, 1723 to 1859. Library of Congress. https://www.loc.gov /collections/james-madison-papers/.

Reagan, Ronald. Speeches. Ronald Reagan Presidential Library. https://www.reaganlibrary .gov/archives.

Published Works

Abramowitz, Alan I. *The Great Alignment: Race, Party Transformation, and the Rise of Donald Trump.* New Haven CT: Yale University Press, 2018.

Ackerman, Kenneth D. *Dark Horse: The Surprise Election and Political Murder of President James A. Garfield.* Falls Church VA: Viral History Press, 2011.

Alberta, Tim. *American Carnage: On the Front Lines of the Republican Civil War and the Rise of President Trump.* New York: HarperCollins, 2019.

Algeo, Matthew. *The President Is a Sick Man: Wherein the Supposedly Virtuous Grover Cleveland Survives a Secret Surgery at Sea and Vilifies the Courageous Newspaperman Who Dared Expose the Truth.* Chicago: Chicago Review Press, 2011.

Allen, Jonathan, and Amie Parnes. *Shattered: Inside Hillary Clinton's Doomed Campaign.* New York: Broadway Books, 2017.

Alter, Jonathan. *The Center Holds: Obama and His Enemies.* New York: Simon & Schuster, 2013.

———. *The Defining Moment: FDR's Hundred Days and the Triumph of Hope.* New York: Simon & Schuster, 2006.

Amar, Akhil Reed. *America's Constitution: A Biography.* New York: Random House, 2005.

Anderson, Carol. *White Rage: The Unspoken Truth of Our Racial Divide.* New York: Bloomsbury, 2016.

Axelrod, David. *Believer: My Forty Years in Politics.* New York: Penguin Books, 2015.

Bai, Matt. *All the Truth Is Out: The Week Politics Went Tabloid.* New York: Vintage Books/Penguin Random House, 2014.

Baime, A. J. *The Accidental President: Harry S. Truman and the Four Months That Changed the World.* Boston: Houghton Mifflin Harcourt, 2017.

Baker, Jean H. *James Buchanan.* New York: Times Books, Henry Holt, 2004.

Balz, Dan. *Collision 2012: The Future of Election Politics in a Divided America.* New York: Penguin Books, 2014.

Balz, Dan, and Haynes Johnson. *The Battle for America: The Story of an Extraordinary Election.* New York: Penguin Books, 2010.

Barone, Michael. *How America's Political Parties Change (and How They Don't).* New York: Encounter Books, 2019.

Bicknell, John. *America 1844: Religious Fervor, Westward Expansion, and the Presidential Election That Transformed the Nation.* Chicago: Chicago Review Press, 2015.

———. *Lincoln's Pathfinder: John C. Fremont and the Violent Election of 1856.* Chicago: Chicago Review Press, 2017.

Boller, Paul F., Jr. *Presidential Campaigns: From George Washington to George W. Bush.* New York: Oxford University Press, 2004.

Borneman, Walter R. *1812: The War That Forged a Nation.* New York: Harper Perennial, 2004.

———. *Polk: The Man Who Transformed the Presidency and America.* New York: Random House, 2008.

Bowen, Catherine Drinker. *Miracle at Philadelphia: The Story of the Constitutional Convention May to September 1787.* Boston: Little, Brown, 1966.

Brands, H. W. *Andrew Jackson: His Life and Times*. New York: Anchor Books, 2005.

———. *The Man Who Saved the Union: Ulysses Grant in War and Peace*. New York: Anchor Books, 2012.

———. *Reagan: The Life*. New York: Anchor Books/Penguin Random House, 2015.

———. *Woodrow Wilson*. New York: Times Books, 2003.

Breen, T. H. *George Washington's Journey: The President Forges a New Nation*. New York: Simon & Schuster, 2016.

Brookhiser, Richard. *America's First Dynasty: The Adamses 1735–1918*. New York: Free Press, 2002.

———. *Founder's Son: A Life of Abraham Lincoln*. New York: Basic Books, 2014.

———. *Founding Father: Rediscovering George Washington*. New York: Free Press Paperbacks, 1996.

———. *James Madison*. New York: Basic Books, 2011.

Bunting, Josiah, III. *Ulysses S. Grant*. New York: Times Books, 2004.

Burner, David. *The Politics of Provincialism: The Democratic Party in Transition 1918–1932*. Cambridge MA: Harvard University Press, 1986.

Burstein, Andrew. *The Passions of Andrew Jackson*. New York: Vintage Books, 2003.

Busch, Andrew E. *Reagan's Victory: The Presidential Election of 1980 and the Rise of the Right*. Lawrence: University Press of Kansas, 2005.

———. *Truman's Triumphs: The 1948 Election and the Making of Postwar America*. Lawrence: University Press of Kansas, 2012.

Calhoun, Charles W. *From Bloody Shirt to Full Dinner Pail: The Transformation of Politics and Governance in the Gilded Age*. New York: Hill and Wang, 2010.

———. *Minority Victory: Gilded Age Politics and the Front Porch Campaign of 1888*. Lawrence: University Press of Kansas, 2008.

Carlson, Brady. *Dead Presidents: An American Adventure into the Strange Deaths and Surprising Afterlives of Our Nation's Leaders*. New York: Norton, 2016.

Carter, Dan T. *From George Wallace to Newt Gingrich: Race in the Conservative Counterrevolution, 1963–1994*. Baton Rouge: Louisiana State University Press, 1996.

Ceaser, James W., and Andrew E. Busch. *Red over Blue: The 2004 Elections and American Politics*. Lanham MD: Rowman & Littlefield, 2005.

Ceaser, James W., Andrew E. Busch, and John J. Pitney Jr. *Defying the Odds: The 2016 Election and American Politics*. Lanham MD: Rowman & Littlefield, 2017.

Chace, James. *1912: Wilson, Roosevelt, Taft and Debs—The Election That Changed the Country*. New York: Simon & Schuster, 2004.

Chadwick, Bruce. *Lincoln for President: An Unlikely Candidate, an Audacious Strategy, and the Victory No One Saw Coming*. Naperville IL: Sourcebooks, 2009.

Cheathem, Mark R. *The Coming of Democracy: Presidential Campaigning in the Age of Jackson*. Baltimore MD: Johns Hopkins University Press, 2018.

Chua, Amy. *Political Tribes: Group Instinct and the Fate of Nations*. New York: Penguin Books, 2018.

Clarke, Thurston. *The Last Campaign: Robert F. Kennedy and 82 Days That Inspired America*. New York: Henry Holt, 2008.

Coe, Alexis. *You Never Forget Your First: A Biography of George Washington*. New York: Viking, 2020.

Cohen, Jared. *Accidental Presidents: Eight Men Who Changed America*. New York: Simon & Schuster, 2019.

Cohen, Michael A. *American Maelstrom: The 1968 Election and the Politics of Division*. New York: Oxford University Press, 2016.

Cole, Donald B. *Vindicating Andrew Jackson: The 1828 Election and the Rise of the Two-Party System*. Lawrence: University Press of Kansas, 2009.

Cooper, John Milton, Jr. *Woodrow Wilson: A Biography*. New York: Vintage Books, 2009.

Cowan, Geoffrey. *Let the People Rule: Theodore Roosevelt and the Birth of the Presidential Primary*. New York: Norton, 2016.

Cramer, Richard Ben. *What It Takes: The Way to the White House*. 1992. New York: Vintage Books/Random House, 1993.

Crockett, Davy, and Augustin Smith Clayton. *The Life of Martin Van Buren*. 1835. R. Wright, 1837. https://books.google.com/books?id=uZZCFF0zX6kC&dq.

Crouse, Timothy. *The Boys on the Bus*. New York: Ballantine Books, 1972.

Cunningham, Noble E., Jr. *In Pursuit of Reason: The Life of Thomas Jefferson*. New York: Ballantine Books, 1987.

Dalton, Kathleen. *Theodore Roosevelt: A Strenuous Life*. New York: Random House, 2002.

Darman, Jonathan. *Landslide: LBJ and Ronald Reagan and the Dawn of a New America*. New York: Random House, 2015.

Dean, John W. *Warren G. Harding*. New York: Times Books, 2004.

DeRose, Chris. *Congressman Lincoln: The Making of America's Greatest President*. New York: Threshold Editions, 2013.

———. *The President's War: Six American Presidents and the Civil War That Divided Them*. Guilford CT: Lyons Press, 2014.

Dickerson, John. *Whistlestop: My Favorite Stories from Presidential Campaign History*. New York: Twelve Books, 2017.

Dionne, E. J., Jr. *Our Divided Political Heart: The Battle for the American Idea in an Age of Discontent*. New York: Bloomsbury, 2012.

Dionne, E. J., Jr., and Joy-Ann Reid, eds. *We Are the Change We Seek: The Speeches of Barack Obama*. New York: Bloomsbury, 2017.

DiStefano, Frank J. *The Next Realignment: Why America's Parties Are Crumbling and What Happens Next*. Amherst NY: Prometheus Books, 2019.

Donald, Aida D. *Lion in the White House: A Life of Theodore Roosevelt*. New York: Basic Books, 2007.

Donaldson, Gary A. *The First Modern Campaign: Kennedy, Nixon, and the Election of 1960*. Lanham MD: Rowman & Littlefield, 2007.

———. *Liberalism's Last Hurrah: The Presidential Campaign of 1964*. New York: Skyhorse, 2002.

Drew, Elizabeth. *Richard M. Nixon*. New York: Times Books, 2007.

Duncan, Mike. *The Storm before the Storm: The Beginning of the End of the Roman Republic*. New York: Public Affairs/Hachette, 2017.

Dunn, Susan. *1940: Roosevelt, Willkie, Lindbergh, Hitler—The Election amid the Storm.* New Haven CT: Yale University Press, 2013.

Egerton, Douglas R. *Year of Meteors: Stephen Douglas, Abraham Lincoln, and the Election That Brought on the Civil War.* New York: Bloomsbury Press, 2010.

Eisenhower, John S. D. *Zachary Taylor.* New York: Times Books, Henry Holt, 2008.

Ellis, Joseph J. *American Creation: Triumphs and Tragedies at the Founding of the Republic.* New York: Knopf, 2007.

———. *American Sphinx: The Character of Thomas Jefferson.* New York: Vintage Books, 1996.

———. *His Excellency: George Washington.* New York: Vintage Books, 2004.

———. *The Quartet: Orchestrating the Second American Revolution, 1783–1789.* New York: Vintage Books, 2015.

Engel, Jeffrey A., Jon Meacham, Timothy Naftali, and Peter Baker. *Impeachment: An American History.* New York: Random House/Modern Library, 2018.

Farrell, John A. *Richard Nixon: A Life.* New York: Vintage Books, 2017.

Farris, Scott. *Almost President: The Men Who Lost the Race but Changed the Nation.* Guilford CT: Lyons Press, 2012.

Ferling, John. *Adams vs. Jefferson: The Tumultuous Election of 1800.* New York: Oxford University Press, 2004.

———. *Jefferson and Hamilton: The Rivalry That Forged a Nation.* New York: Bloomsbury Press, 2013.

Ferrell, Robert H. *Choosing Truman: The Democratic Convention of 1944.* Columbia: University of Missouri Press, 1994.

Frank, Thomas. *What's the Matter with Kansas: How Conservatives Won the Heart of America.* New York: Picador, 2004.

Freeman, Steven F., and Joel Bleifuss. *Was the 2004 Presidential Election Stolen? Exit Polls, Election Fraud, and the Official Count.* New York: Seven Stories Press, 2006.

Gerhardt, Michael J. *The Forgotten Presidents: Their Untold Constitutional Legacy.* New York: Oxford University Press, 2013.

Germond, Jack W., and Jules Witcover. *Blue Smoke and Mirrors: How Reagan Won and Why Carter Lost the Election of 1980.* New York: Viking Press, 1981.

———. *Mad as Hell: Revolt at the Ballot Box.* New York: Warner Books, 1993.

———. *Wake Us When It's Over: Presidential Politics of 1984.* New York: Macmillan, 1985.

———. *Whose Broad Stripes and Bright Stars? The Trivial Pursuit of the Presidency 1988.* New York: Warner Books, 1989.

Goldwater, Barry. *The Conscience of a Conservative.* 1960. Kindle edition, 2009.

Goodwin, Doris Kearns. *Lyndon Johnson and the American Dream.* 1976. New York: St. Martin's Griffin, 1991.

———. *No Ordinary Time.* New York: Simon & Schuster, 1995.

———. *Team of Rivals: The Political Genius of Abraham Lincoln.* New York: Simon & Schuster, 2005.

Gordon-Reed, Annette. *Andrew Johnson.* New York: Times Books, 2011.

Gould, Lewis L. *The First Modern Clash over Federal Power: Wilson versus Hughes in the Presidential Election of 1916*. Lawrence: University Press of Kansas, 2016.

——. *Four Hats in the Ring: The 1912 Election and the Birth of Modern American Politics*. Lawrence: University Press of Kansas, 2008.

Graff, Henry F. *Grover Cleveland*. New York: Times Books, 2002.

Green, Joshua. *Devil's Bargain: Steve Bannon, Donald Trump, and the Nationalist Uprising*. New York: Penguin Books, 2018.

Greenberg, David. *Calvin Coolidge*. New York: Times Books, 2006.

Greene, John Robert. *I Like Ike: The Presidential Election of 1952*. Lawrence: University Press of Kansas, 2017.

Grinspan, Jon. *The Virgin Vote: How Young Americans Made Democracy Social, Politics Personal, and Voting Popular in the Nineteenth Century*. Chapel Hill: University of North Carolina Press, 2016.

Hamilton, Alexander, James Madison, and John Jay. *The Federalist Papers*. Edited by Clinton Rossiter. New York: Penguin Books, 1961.

Hart, Gary. *James Monroe*. New York: Times Books, 2005.

Heilemann, John, and Mark Halperin. *Double Down: Game Change 2012*. New York: Penguin Books, 2014.

——. *Game Change: Obama and the Clintons, McCain and Palin, and the Race of a Lifetime*. New York: HarperCollins, 2010.

Helferich, Gerard. *Theodore Roosevelt and the Assassin: Madness, Vengeance, and the Campaign of 1912*. Guilford CT: Lyons Press, 2013.

Hemingway, Ernest. *The Sun Also Rises*. 1926. New York: Charles Scribner's Sons, 1993.

Hitchcock, William I. *The Age of Eisenhower: America and the World in the 1950s*. New York: Simon & Schuster, 2018.

Hofstadter, Richard. *The Age of Reform: From Bryan to F.D.R.* New York: Vintage Books, 1955.

——. *The American Political Tradition and the Men Who Made It*. 1948. New York: Vintage Books, 1989.

Hollitz, John E. "Eisenhower and the Admen: The Television 'Spot' Campaign of 1952." *Wisconsin Magazine of History* 66, no. 1 (Autumn 1982): 25–39. https://www.jstor.org/stable/4635688.

Holt, Michael F. *By One Vote: The Disputed Presidential Election of 1876*. Lawrence: University Press of Kansas, 2008.

——. *The Election of 1860: "A Campaign Fraught with Consequences."* Lawrence: University Press of Kansas, 2017.

Holzer, Harold. *Lincoln at Cooper Union: The Speech That Made Abraham Lincoln President*. New York: Simon & Schuster, 2004.

Howe, Daniel Walker. *The Political Culture of the American Whigs*. Chicago: University of Chicago Press, 1979.

Isenberg, Nancy. *White Trash: The 400-Year Untold History of Class in America*. New York: Penguin Books, 2016.

Jeffries, John W. *A Third Term for FDR: The Election of 1940*. Lawrence: University Press of Kansas, 2017.

Johnson, Paul. *A History of the American People*. New York: Harper Perennial, 1997.

Jones, Charles O. *The American Presidency: A Brief Insight*. New York: Sterling, 2009.

Jordan, David M. *FDR, Dewey and the Election of 1944*. Bloomington: Indiana University Press, 2011.

Kamarck, Elaine C. *Primary Politics: Everything You Need to Know about How America Nominates Its Presidential Candidates*. Washington DC: Brookings Institution Press, 2019.

Kane, Bradford R. *Pitchfork Populism: Ten Political Forces That Shaped an Election and Continue to Change America*. Guilford CT: Prometheus Books, 2019.

Kaplan, Fred. *John Quincy Adams: American Visionary*. New York: Harper Perennial, 2014.

Karabell, Zachary. *Chester Alan Arthur*. New York: Times Books, 2004.

———. *The Last Campaign: How Harry Truman Won the 1948 Election*. New York: Vintage Books, 2000.

Kennedy, John F. *Profiles in Courage*. 1956. New York: Perennial Classics, 2000.

Kinzer, Stephen. *The True Flag: Theodore Roosevelt, Mark Twain, and the Birth of American Empire*. New York: St. Martin's Griffin, 2017.

Kirwan, Albert D. "Congress Elects a President: Henry Clay and the Campaign of 1824." *Kentucky Review* 4, no. 2 (Winter 1983). https://uknowledge.uky.edu/kentucky-review/vol4/iss2/2.

Klein, Ezra. *Why We're Polarized*. New York: Avid Reader Press, 2020.

Klein, Joe. *The Natural: The Misunderstood Presidency of Bill Clinton*. New York: Broadway Books, 2002.

Kornacki, Steve. *The Red and the Blue: The 1990s and the Birth of Political Tribalism*. New York: Ecco/HarperCollins, 2018.

Langguth, A. J. *After Lincoln: How the North Won the Civil War and Lost the Peace*. New York: Simon & Schuster, 2014.

Larson, Edward J. *A Magnificent Catastrophe: The Tumultuous Election of 1800, America's First Presidential Campaign*. New York: Free Press, 2007.

———. *The Return of George Washington: Uniting the States, 1783–89*. New York: William Morrow, 2014.

Leonnig, Carol, and Philip Rucker. *I Alone Can Fix It*. New York: Penguin Press, 2021.

Leuchtenburg, William E. *Herbert Hoover*. New York: Times Books, 2009.

Levitsky, Steven, and Daniel Ziblatt. *How Democracies Die*. New York: Broadway Books, 2018.

Lichtman, Allan J. *The Embattled Vote in America: From the Founding to the Present*. Cambridge MA: Harvard University Press, 2018.

Lorant, Stefan. *The Glorious Burden: The History of the Presidency and Presidential Elections from George Washington to James Earl Carter, Jr.* Lenox MA: Authors Edition, 1976.

Lowndes, Joseph E. *From the New Deal to the New Right: Race and the Southern Origins of Modern Conservatism*. New Haven CT: Yale University Press, 2008.

Madden, David, ed. *Thomas Wolfe's Civil War*. Tuscaloosa: University of Alabama Press, 2004.

Mailer, Norman. *Miami and the Siege of Chicago: An Informal History of the Republican and Democratic Conventions of 1968*. New York: Random House, 1968.

Malsberger, John W. *The General and the Politician: Dwight Eisenhower, Richard Nixon, and American Politics*. Lanham MD: Rowman & Littlefield, 2014.

Mann, James. *George W. Bush*. New York: Times Books, 2015.

Mann, Thomas E., and Norman J. Ornstein. *It's Even Worse Than It Looks: How the American Constitutional System Collided with the New Politics of Extremism*. New York: Basic Books, 2012.

Mathews, Chris. *Jack Kennedy: Elusive Hero*. New York: Simon & Schuster, 2011.

May, Gary. *John Tyler*. New York: Times Books, 2008.

McCullough, David. *John Adams*. New York: Simon & Schuster, 2001.

——— . *Truman*. New York: Simon & Schuster, 1992.

McVeigh, Rory, and Kevin Estep. *The Politics of Losing: Trump, the Klan, and the Mainstreaming of Resentment*. New York: Columbia University Press, 2019.

Meacham, Jon. *American Lion: Andrew Jackson in the White House*. New York: Random House, 2008.

——— . *Destiny and Power: The American Odyssey of George Herbert Walker Bush*. New York: Random House, 2015.

——— . *The Soul of America: The Battle for Our Better Angels*. New York: Random House, 2018.

Merry, Robert W. *A Country of Vast Designs: James K. Polk, the Mexican War, and the Conquest of the American Continent*. New York: Simon & Schuster, 2009.

——— . *President McKinley: Architect of the American Century*. New York: Simon & Schuster, 2017.

Michener, James A. *Presidential Lottery: The Reckless Gamble in Our Electoral System*. 1969. New York: Dial Press, 2016.

Milkis, Sidney M. *Theodore Roosevelt, the Progressive Party, and the Transformation of American Democracy*. Lawrence: University Press of Kansas, 2009.

Millard, Candice. *Destiny of the Republic: A Tale of Madness, Medicine, and the Murder of a President*. New York: Anchor Books, 2011.

Miller, Anita, ed. *What Went Wrong in Ohio: The Conyers Report on the 2004 Presidential Election*. Chicago: Academy Chicago, 2005.

Miller, Scott. *The President and the Assassin: McKinley, Terror, and Empire at the Dawn of the American Century*. New York: Random House, 2011.

Miller, William Lee. *Two Americans: Truman, Eisenhower and a Dangerous World*. New York: Vintage Books, 2012.

Moe, Richard. *Roosevelt's Second Act: The Election of 1940 and the Politics of War*. New York: Oxford University Press, 2013.

Morris, Roy, Jr. *Fraud of the Century: Rutherford B. Hayes, Samuel Tilden, and the Stolen Election of 1876*. New York: Simon & Schuster, 2003.

Murray, Robert K. *The 103rd Ballot: The Legendary 1924 Democratic Convention That Forever Changed American Politics*. 1976. New York: HarperCollins, 2016.

Neal, Steve. *Happy Days Are Here Again: The 1932 Democratic Convention, the Emergence of FDR—And How America Was Changed Forever*. New York: HarperCollins, 2004.

Nelson, Michael. *Resilient America: Electing Nixon in 1968, Channeling Dissent, and Dividing Government*. Lawrence: University Press of Kansas, 2014.

Nichols, John. *Jews for Buchanan: Did You Hear the One about the Theft of the American Presidency?* New York: New Press, 2001.

Norton, A. Banning. *The Great Revolution of 1840: Reminiscences of the Log Cabin and Hard Cider Campaign*. Mount Vernon OH: A. B. Norton, 1888. https://hdl.handle .net/2027/nyp.33433081791141.

Oates, Stephen B. *With Malice toward None: A Life of Abraham Lincoln*. New York: HarperCollins, 1977.

Obama, Barack. *A Promised Land*. New York: Crown, 2020.

O'Donnell, Lawrence. *Playing with Fire: The 1968 Election and the Transformation of American Politics*. New York: Penguin Books, 2017.

Oliphant, Thomas, and Curtis Wilkie. *The Road to Camelot: Inside JFK's Five-Year Campaign*. New York: Simon & Schuster, 2017.

O'Mara, Margaret. *Pivotal Tuesdays: Four Elections That Shaped the Twentieth Century*. Philadelphia: University of Pennsylvania Press, 2015.

Parsons, Lynn Hudson. *The Birth of Modern Politics: Andrew Jackson, John Quincy Adams, and the Election of 1828*. New York: Oxford University Press, 2009.

Pasley, Jeffrey L. *The First Presidential Contest: 1796 and the Founding of American Democracy*. Lawrence: University Press of Kansas, 2013.

Phillips, Kevin. *The Emerging Republican Majority*. 1970. Princeton NJ: Princeton University Press, 2015.

Pietrusza, David. *1920: The Year of the Six Presidents*. New York: Basic Books, 2007.

Plouffe, David. *The Audacity to Win: The Inside Story and Lessons of Barack Obama's Historic Victory*. New York: Viking Penguin, 2009.

Presidential Elections, 1789–2004. Washington DC: CQ Press, 2005.

Prude, James C. "William Gibbs McAdoo and the Democratic National Convention of 1924." *Journal of Southern History* 38, no. 4 (1972). www.jstor.org/stable/2206152.

Raphael, Ray. *Mr. President: How and Why the Founders Created a Chief Executive*. New York: Vintage Books, 2012.

Ratcliffe, Donald. *The One-Party Presidential Contest: Adams, Jackson, and 1824's Five-Horse Race*. Lawrence: University Press of Kansas, 2015.

Rayback, Robert J. *Millard Fillmore: Biography of a President*. 1959. Buffalo NY: Buffalo Historical Society and Henry Seward, 2017.

Reichley, A. James. *The Life of the Parties: A History of American Political Parties*. New York: Free Press, 1992.

Reynolds, David S. *Waking Giant: America in the Age of Jackson*. New York: Harper Perennial, 2008.

Rhodes, Ben. *The World as It Is: A Memoir of the Obama White House*. New York: Random House, 2018.

Rice, Susan. *Tough Love: My Story of the Things Worth Fighting For*. New York: Simon & Schuster, 2019.

Ritchie, Donald A. *Electing FDR: The New Deal Campaign of 1932.* Lawrence: University Press of Kansas, 2007.

Rodden, Jonathan. *Why Cities Lose: The Deep Roots of the Urban-Rural Political Divide.* New York: Basic Books, 2019.

Rorabaugh, W. J. *The Real Making of the President: Kennedy, Nixon, and the 1960 Election.* Lawrence: University Press of Kansas, 2009.

Rosen, Jeffrey. *William Howard Taft.* New York: Times Books, 2018.

Rove, Karl. *The Triumph of William McKinley: Why the Election of 1896 Still Matters.* New York: Simon & Schuster, 2015.

Sabato, Larry J., ed. *Overtime! The Election 2000 Thriller.* New York: Longman, 2002.

Scammon, Richard M., and Ben J. Wattenberg. *The Real Majority.* 1970. New York: Donald J. Fine, 1992.

Schertzer, Robert, and Eric Woods. "#Nationalism: The Ethno-Nationalist Populism of Donald Trump's Twitter Communication." *Ethnic and Racial Studies*, January 27, 2020. doi:10.1080/01419870.2020.1713390.

Schlesinger, Arthur M., Jr. *The Crisis of the Old Order: 1919–1933.* 1957. New York: Mariner Books/Houghton Mifflin, 1985.

Schneider, Bill. *Standoff: How America Became Ungovernable.* New York: Simon & Schuster, 2018.

Shafer, Ronald G. *The Carnival Campaign: How the Rollicking 1840 Campaign of "Tippecanoe and Tyler Too" Changed Presidential Elections Forever.* Chicago: Chicago Review Press, 2016.

Shideler, James H. "The La Follette Progressive Party Campaign of 1924." *Wisconsin Magazine of History* 33, no. 4 (1950): 444–57. http://www.jstor.org/stable/4632172.

Sides, John, Michael Tesler, and Lynn Vavreck. *Identity Crisis: The 2016 Presidential Campaign and the Battle for the Meaning of America.* Princeton NJ: Princeton University Press, 2018.

Silbey, Joel H. *Party over Section: The Rough and Ready Presidential Election of 1848.* Lawrence: University Press of Kansas, 2009.

Simon, Roger. *Divided We Stand: How Al Gore Beat George Bush and Lost the Presidency.* New York: Crown, 2001.

Stevens, Stuart. *It Was All a Lie: How the Republican Party Became Donald Trump.* New York: Knopf, 2020.

Stewart, David O. *Madison's Gift.* New York: Simon & Schuster, 2015.

Stirewalt, Chris. *Every Man a King: A Short, Colorful History of American Populists.* New York: Twelve Books, 2018.

Stone, Irving. *They Also Ran: The Fascinating Story of the Men Who Almost Became President.* 1943. New York: Pyramid Books, 1964.

Strauss, Robert. *Worst. President. Ever. James Buchanan, the POTUS Rating Game, and the Legacy of the Least of the Lesser Presidents.* Guildford CT: Lyons Press, 2016.

Summers, Mark Wahlgren. *Rum, Romanism and Rebellion: The Making of a President 1884.* Chapel Hill: University of North Carolina Press, 2000.

Sundquist, James L. *Dynamics of the Party System: Alignment and Realignment of Political Parties in the United States*. Washington DC: Brookings Institution, 1983.

Sykes, Charles J. *How the Right Lost Its Mind*. New York: St. Martin's Press, 2017.

Taylor, Quentin P. "Money and Politics in the World of Oz." *Independent Review: A Journal of Political Economy* 9, no. 3 (Winter 2004–5). https://www.independent.org /publications/tir/article.asp?id=504.

Thomas, Evan. *Being Nixon: A Man Divided*. New York: Random House, 2015.

Thompson, Hunter S. *Fear and Loathing on the Campaign Trail '72*. New York: Simon & Schuster, 1973.

Tocqueville, Alexis de. *Democracy in America*. Translated by Arthur Goldhammer. New York: Library of America, 2004.

Tomasky, Michael. *Bill Clinton*. New York: Times Books, 2017.

———. *If We Can Keep It: How the Republic Collapsed and How It Might Be Saved*. New York: Liveright, 2019.

Toobin, Jeffrey. *Too Close to Call: The Thirty-Six-Day Battle to Decide the 2000 Election*. New York: Random House, 2002.

Trefousse, Hans L. *Rutherford B. Hayes*. New York: Times Books, 2002.

Tucker, Garland S., III. *The High Tide of American Conservatism: Davis, Coolidge, and the 1924 Election*. Austin TX: Emerald, 2010.

Tur, Katy. *Unbelievable: My Front-Row Seat to the Craziest Campaign in American History*. New York: Dey St./HarperCollins, 2017.

Underhill, Lois Beachy. *The Woman Who Ran for President: The Many Lives of Victoria Woodhull*. New York: Penguin Books, 1995.

Unger, Harlow Giles. *Mr. President: George Washington and the Making of the Nation's Highest Office*. Boston: Da Capo Press, 2013.

Vowell, Sarah. *Assassination Vacation*. New York: Simon & Schuster, 2005.

Wallace, David Foster. *McCain's Promise: Aboard the Straight Talk Express with John McCain and a Whole Bunch of Actual Reporters, Thinking about Hope*. New York: Back Bay Books, 2006.

Walther, Eric H. *The Shattering of the Union: America in the 1850s*. Lanham MD: Scholarly Resources Books, 2004.

Ward, Jon. *Camelot's End: Kennedy vs. Carter and the Fight That Broke the Democratic Party*. New York: Twelve Books, 2019.

Waugh, John G. *Reelecting Lincoln: The Battle for the 1864 Presidency*. New York: Crown, 1997.

Weber, Karl, ed. *Lincoln: A President for the Ages*. New York: Public Affairs/Perseus Books, 2012.

Wegman, Jesse. *Let the People Pick the President: The Case for Abolishing the Electoral College*. New York: St. Martin's Press, 2020.

Weisberg, Jacob. *Ronald Reagan*. New York: Times Books, 2016.

Weisberger, Bernard A. *America Afire: Jefferson, Adams and the Revolutionary Election of 1800*. New York: William Morrow, 2000.

Weston, Mark. *The Runner-Up Presidency: The Elections That Defied America's Popular Will (and How Our Democracy Remains in Danger)*. Guilford CT: Lyons Press, 2016.

White, Theodore H. *America in Search of Itself: The Making of the President 1956–1980*. New York: Warner Books, 1982.

———. *The Making of the President 1960*. 1961. New York: HarperCollins, 2009.

———. *The Making of the President 1968*. 1969. New York: HarperCollins, 2010.

———. *The Making of the President 1972*. 1973. New York: HarperCollins, 2010.

Widmer, Ted. *Martin Van Buren*. New York: Times Books, 2005.

Wilentz, Sean. *The Rise of American Democracy: Jefferson to Lincoln*. New York: Norton, 2005.

Williams, R. Hal. *Realigning America: McKinley, Bryan and the Remarkable Election of 1896*. Lawrence: University Press of Kansas, 2010.

Williamson, Vanessa, Theda Skocpol, and John Coggin. "The Tea Party and the Remaking of Republican Conservatism." *Perspectives on Politics* 9, no. 1 (March 2011): 25–43.

Witcover, Jules. *Marathon: The Pursuit of the Presidency 1972–1976*. New York: Signet Books/Viking Penguin, 1977.

Wolfe, Richard. *Renegade: The Making of a President*. New York: Three Rivers Press, 2010.

Wolfe, Thomas. "The Four Lost Men." In *Thomas Wolfe's Civil War*, edited by David Madden. Tuscaloosa: University of Alabama Press, 2004.

Wolff, Michael. *Fire and Fury: Inside the Trump White House*. New York: Henry Holt, 2018.

Wood, Gordon S. *Friends Divided: John Adams and Thomas Jefferson*. New York: Penguin Press, 2017.

———. *The Idea of America: Reflections on the Birth of the United States*. New York: Penguin Books, 2011.

———. *Revolutionary Characters: What Made the Founders Different*. New York: Penguin Books, 2006.

Young, Nancy Beck. *Two Suns of the Southwest: Lyndon Johnson, Barry Goldwater, and the 1964 Battle between Liberalism and Conservatism*. Lawrence: University Press of Kansas, 2019.

Zelizer, Julian E. *Jimmy Carter*. New York: Times Books, 2010.

Index

Delay, Tom, 283

democracy, 21–24, 56–57, 324–26, 329–31

and 1980 election, 245; and 1988 election, 254; and 1992 election, 265–66; and 2000 election, 274; and 2004 election, 282; and 2008 election, 292–93; and 2012 election, 299; and 2016 election, 305; and 2020 election, 319–20

republicanism, 17, 46

Republican National Committee (RNC), 140, 171

Republican Party: and 1856 election, 75–77; and 1860 election, 84–87; and 1864 election, 90–91; and 1868 election, 94–97; and 1872 election, 97–98; and 1876 election, 100–103; and 1880 election, 107–8; and 1884 election, 111–12; and 1888 election, 116; and 1892 election, 118–19; and 1896 election, 127–28, 130–31; and 1900 election, 132, 133–34; and 1904 election, 136; and 1908 election, 137; and 1912 election, 139–44; and 1916 election, 147–49; and 1920 election, 152–53; and 1924 election, 157; and 1928 election, 158–60; and 1932 election, 166; and 1936 election, 171; and 1940 election, 174–75, 177; and 1944 election, 180–81; and 1948 election, 186; and 1952 election, 192–93, 194–96; and 1956 election, 196; and 1960 election, 201; and 1964 election, 209–11; and 1968 election, 223–24, 226; and 1972 election, 230; and 1976 election, 235–36; and 1980 election, 244–45; and 1984 election, 251; and 1988 election, 252–54; and 1992 election, 261–62, 265–66; and 1996 election, 269–70; and 2000 election, 272–73; and 2004 election, 282–83; and 2008 election, 289, 292–93; and 2012 election, 298–99; and 2016 election, 302–5, 306; and 2020 election, 319–20, 323, 325–26; Barack Obama on, 299; and conservative revival, 213–14; and Donald Trump, 311–12; and the Great Recession, 296–97; and impeachment of Donald Trump, 315; and Iran crisis, 247; and isolationism, 172, 174; and law-and-order message, 320; and modern politics, 146; and New Deal liberalism, 185; and North-South divide, 92–94; and partisanship, 301, 309; and political realignment,

78–79; and progressive vs. conservative debate, 328–29; and protectionism, 115–17; and Reconstruction, 104–5; and red-blue divide, 284–85; and social issues, 260–61; and transitional age, 200; and triangulation, 269; William Jennings Bryan on, 128

Reston, James, 212–13, 237

Revels, Hiram Rhodes, 104

Rhode Island, 163–64

Ribicoff, Abraham, 223

Rice, Donna, 254–55

Richmond Examiner, 91

right-wing media, 285–86

Ripon WI, 75

RNC. *See* Republican National Committee (RNC)

Roaring Twenties, 162

Robertson, Pat, 254

Rockefeller, Nelson, 210–11, 224, 235–36

Rogers, Will, 154, 160

Romanism, 114

Romney, George, 224

Romney, Mitt, 289, 298–300, 304, 315

Roosevelt, Eleanor, 182

Roosevelt, Franklin, 21, 146, 153, 159, 166–85, 176

Roosevelt, Theodore, 124–25, 133–45, 147, 149, 152, 156–57

Roosevelt Recession, 177

Roper, Elmo, 188

Roper poll, 189

Rose Garden strategy, 242

Rubio, Marco, 302–4

"Rum, Romanism and Rebellion" speech (Burchard), 114

Russell, Richard, 191

Russia, 306–10, 314

Ryan, Paul, 298

Sanders, Bernie, 302–5, 315–17

Santorum, Rick, 298

Saturday Evening Post, 156

Saturday Night Live, 261

scandals, 97, 100–101, 112–13, 154, 233–34, 253–55, 268–69, 271–72, 308

Schneider, William, 312

Schrank, John, 144